RUSSIA AND THE WEST IN IRAN, 1918-1948

Map of Iran.

RUSSIA and the WEST
IN IRAN, 1918-1948
A Study in Big-Power Rivalry

BY GEORGE LENCZOWSKI

Hamilton College

Cornell University Press

ITHACA, NEW YORK, 1949

PRINTED IN THE UNITED STATES OF AMERICA BY THE
VAIL-BALLOU PRESS, INC., BINGHAMTON, NEW YORK

TO MY WIFE

Foreword

IT would be foolish to pretend that Big-Power rivalry no longer exists in Iran. However, the major problem in Iran today, as everywhere else in the world, results from rivalry between two different ideologies, not from conflicting national interests. One of those ideologies, supported by Soviet Russia, promises the hungry peasants and workers of Iran a Utopia under Communism. The other, supported by the United States and other Western Powers, offers an opportunity for gradual improvement under democracy. While democracy offers continued respect for individual liberty, which Iranians enjoy today to a very considerable degree, the Soviet spokesmen speak of "true democracy" in a classless society without landlords.

The common man in Iran is bewildered by these conflicting appeals. Which will prove more persuasive to him is not yet certain. The principal ally of the democratic forces in Iran is the Soviets themselves, whose heavy-handed methods and threats of force to achieve purely Russian ends have deprived their propaganda of much of its effectiveness. Moreover, if the Soviets had been more successful in bringing Utopia to the U.S.S.R. during the past thirty years, their appeal to Iranians would carry more weight.

The principal ally of the Soviets in Iran is poverty, disease, and an ineffective governmental structure in Teheran. The people of Iran have suffered through several generations of Great-Power rivalry, often at the expense of the Iranians. The experience has left a deep mark on their social and political thinking. As a consequence, it is natural that many Iranians today consider the present situation in their country to be merely a continuation of Iran's experiences during the past century, with Washington vs. Moscow substituted for London vs. St. Petersburg as the chief protagonists. Many students of the Iranian scene fall into the same error.

A study such as Mr. Lenczowski's is valuable in order to permit students of present-day conditions in Iran to understand not only the background out of which these conditions have emerged, but also the difference between the present situation and what has happened in the past. His volume contains convincing evidence that the problem in Iran today is strikingly different from the problems of previous generations.

The United States has no territorial or imperialistic interests in Iran. Its only desire is to assist Iran to become strong enough to maintain its independence and integrity against anyone who might have imperialistic aims there. We desire to see Iran develop industrially and stand on its own feet. This is the very opposite of imperialism.

The contrast between American and Soviet foreign policy in Iran during the past few years has been sharp and clear. The Soviet Union has frequently, since the end of World War II, used force and threats of force in an effort to obtain commercial and other concessions in Iran. The American government has lent assistance to Iran without exacting any concessions or promises in return. We have taken no steps except at the request of the Iranian government, and have at all times made it clear that we had no desire to press American military or other advisers, or material assistance, on Iran or any other country unless the recipient showed clear desire to receive our help.

There are those who will contend that I have oversimplified the picture and that American policy in Iran has not been as altruistic as I have claimed. My reply is that my statement is based on personal experience in executing that policy and is as honest as I can make it.

Imperialism, or colonialism, is an effort by a Great Power to keep another country weak and dependent—politically, militarily, and industrially. The good neighbor is a nation that tries to help another country become strong and independent—politically, militarily, and industrially.

Let those who would understand Iran today study its background, but let them not conclude that the rivalry in Iran today is between Big Powers. The rivalry is between big ideas.

GEORGE V. ALLEN
Assistant Secretary of State,
formerly United States Ambassador to Iran

Preface

THE purpose of this book is to acquaint the reader with Big-Power rivalry in Iran between 1918 and 1948. While there are many valuable studies that deal exhaustively with the diplomatic history of Iran up to 1918, the literature dealing with the subsequent period is much less abundant. To the author's knowledge, there is no single book devoted exclusively to the study of modern political developments in Iran. Works that have appeared since 1920 are mostly of a general descriptive character and deal with such diverse aspects as Iranian geography, climate, people, culture, and economics. They seldom devote more than one or two chapters to international relations.

These thirty years between 1918 and 1948 constitute a very stormy period and are characterized by two outstanding features that make them unique in Iran's long history. One is the emergence of Reza Khan, who on becoming absolute ruler of Iran adopted radical measures to Westernize his country. The other is the clash of the Big Powers for influence. And while this rivalry is not a new phenomenon in itself, its character is new because it is colored by profound ideological differences.

In this study the author's intention has been to concentrate on political matters, with special stress on the external relations of Iran with foreign powers. Thus internal developments are treated only insofar as they have bearing upon international relations.

The conflict between Soviet Russia and the West is the essence of this study. The author has attempted to describe and analyze, on the one hand, the program and techniques of Soviet expansion, which constitute a novelty in the traditional pattern of diplomacy, and, on the other, the methods employed by the West to counteract this expansion.

The author derived his information from four main sources. These were the original documents, such as treaties, Comintern publications, and memoirs; the existing literature covering various aspects of the period here investigated; the press, both Iranian and Western; and personal observations made during the author's three-year stay in Iran in the crucial period between 1942 and 1945.

The book is addressed to the general reader, but with an eye to the specialist in the area. The author's sojourn in Iran convinced him of the necessity of supplying foreign service officers and industrial, commercial, or military representatives whose interests may link them to Iran with a body of political information that is not available elsewhere within the framework of a single volume.

The structure of the book has been adapted to the author's view of the period under description. To use literary analogy, this period resembles a drama in three acts. Act One presents the first clash between the new dynamic Communist State and the opposing forces in an Eastern country, jealous of its independence. The attempt to extend Communism to this area fails. Act Two provides a lull after the storm. Violent operations give way to undercover activity under the pretense of calm on the surface. In Act Three the storm returns with greater force than before. All the experience that the Soviet State has gained during the preceding two acts is utilized to secure success. But the resistance that the Communist offensive encounters is also stronger. At the time when this book is written it looks as if Act Three had ended with the victory of anti-Communist forces. Such a victory, however, can never be definite as long as there is a center from which Communism radiates and as long as the opposition is apt to make mistakes. That is why Act Three, though concluding this study, does not conclude the course of history, and may be followed by the flow and ebb of action and inaction.

If there is any moral in this book, it is the same as that derived from the study of international affairs in general—namely, that an understanding of the past serves as a guide to the future.

I wish to express my thanks to Mr. Thomas B. Rudd, President of Hamilton College, 1947–1949; to Mr. David T. Wilder and Miss Helen Gaffney, Librarian and Reference Librarian of Hamilton

College; to Professor Edgar B. Graves, head of the Department of History at Hamilton; to Professor C. Grove Haines, of the School of Advanced International Studies; to Mr. Kalixt Synakowski, of the Harvard Graduate School; and to Mrs. Theodore R. Bowie for their friendly helpfulness during the preparation of this book. I wish also to express my gratitude to Professor T. Cuyler Young of Princeton University for his transliteration of Iranian names as well as for the valuable information he has given me on the crisis of August, 1941, and the events in Tabriz, December 5–12, 1945. Last and not least I wish to acknowledge the tireless work of my wife in reading and translating a number of original and microfilmed documents in Russian.

GEORGE LENCZOWSKI

Hamilton College
April, 1949

Contents

[xiii]

CONTENTS

CONTENTS

CHAPTER ONE

Introduction

THE modern history of Iran is largely a history of Big-Power rivalry. Owing to this fact, Iran during the past century and a half has often appeared to be a pawn of international diplomacy. In the great struggle for influence in Iran two forces seem to have been permanent throughout the nineteenth and a good part of the twentieth century, namely, Russia and Britain. Other great Powers appeared like meteors, outshone temporarily the brightness of two constant stars, but soon faded into oblivion. Such was the case of Napoleonic France in the beginning of the nineteenth century and of Imperial Germany one hundred years later.

The ancient Empire of Iran entered modern world politics around 1800 when Napoleon undertook gigantic schemes to destroy England. Convinced that England's doom must be preceded by French domination of the East, Bonaparte launched a hazardous adventure in Egypt and planned the conquest of India. His negotiations with Tsar Paul of Russia in 1801 ended in a scheme of joint invasion of India by French and Russian forces, the former to traverse the Black and Azov seas, the Don and Volga rivers, and the Caspian Sea and to march through Iran. The plan was only partially carried out. Tsar Paul gave orders to Ataman Orlov to lead a Cossack expedition through the Turkoman steppe. The expedition, because of inadequate preparations, proved a failure, and the subsequent death of the Tsar put an end to the scheme. Napoleon's grand strategy, however, still envisaged Iran as an important factor. He tried to establish a military alliance with the Shah as an instrument of his anti-British or anti-Russian policy. The Franco-Iranian Treaty of Finkenstein in 1807 was the apogee of French influence in Iran. A mission headed

[1]

by General Gardanne was sent to train Iranian troops for action. Yet in 1807 Napoleon destroyed the edifice of friendship he had built by concluding the Treaty of Tilsit with Russia. The Shah felt offended and betrayed. In 1809 he expelled Gardanne and was ready to receive a British mission, which offered him an alliance.

With the passing of French influence, Iran remained face to face with her two neighbors, Russia and Britain (through British-controlled India), who proved to be permanent factors in Iran's foreign relations. Of these two, Russia has constantly been on the offensive. Aspiring to gain access to warm-water ports, Russia was jealous of Britain's position in India and displayed unsatiated territorial and economic ambitions. Her relationship to Iran was one of steady pressure and advance at the expense of her southern neighbor. As far back as 1724 Peter the Great raided and temporarily occupied Iran's northern province of Gilan.

Beginning with the reign of Catherine the Great, Russian pressure increased. Russia fought aggressive wars with Iran in 1796 and 1800–1813; the later one was concluded by the Treaty of Gulistan. A new war was waged in 1826–1828. These wars resulted in the gradual loss by Iran of her rich Caucasian provinces. Mingrelia, Karabagh, Shirvan, Derbent, Baku, Erivan, and Nakhichevan were one by one annexed by Russia. The Treaty of Turkomanchai of 1828 crowned this victorious advance by establishing the frontier on the Aras River south of the Caucasus range and by subjecting Iran to the political and economic supremacy of Russia. By a clever arrangement Russia assumed the role of protector of the ruling Qajar dynasty and as a result secured the obedient servility of weak and degenerate Iranian monarchs.

The Treaty of Turkomanchai triumphantly closed one chapter of Russian expansion, but it did not exhaust it. The second chapter began with the occupation of the island of Ashur-Ada in the Bay of Astarabad in 1837. It was characterized by a gradual movement on the part of Russia to dominate Central Asia, and it was executed partly at the expense of Iran. In 1869 a Russian military expedition occupied Krasnovodsk on the eastern shore of the Caspian. The city was nominally under Iranian suzerainty, but protests from Teheran were of no avail. In 1873 another Russian expedition conquered the hitherto independent khanates of Khiva and Bukhara. As a result the Turkoman steppe—an Iranian domain—was encircled on three sides by Russian forces. In 1881, after valorous defense, the Turkoman tribes were subdued by the Russians at the famous desert stronghold of Geok Tepe. The same year a Russo-Iranian agreement fixed the Atrek River as a boundary between the two countries. Russia now bordered directly on the ethnic territory of Iran and gained access to mountain passes leading to the northeastern province of Khorasan. Russian conquest of the Queen of the Cities—Merv oasis —in 1884 completed her expansion in the Transcaspian region and put her in a commanding position as regards the strategic routes to India.

In the meantime Britain was clearly on the defensive. Protection of India was the main objective of her policy. The meteorlike appearance of Napoleon and his threat to India dictated emergency measures to keep Iran out of his grasp. In 1800 Captain Malcolm arrived in Iran in the midst of a tense atmosphere caused by Bonaparte's invasion of Egypt. The agreements he concluded with Iran, were soon, however, overshadowed by a stronger French diplomacy. The eclipse of French influence in 1809 promptly brought another British mission to Teheran that in the same year concluded the Preliminary Treaty of Alliance with the Shah. This "Jones Treaty" was drafted as an anti-French instrument, but with an eye to a more formidable danger—that of Russia. It was followed by the Treaty of Teheran in 1814. The latter provided for British subsidy and military help to Iran in case of aggression and, according to an acute English observer, fulfilled the maxim that "the enemy of Russia is the natural ally of Persia." In return Iran promised to resist the passage of any foreign troops toward India. The effects of this treaty were largely nullified by a new Russo-Iranian war and the abovementioned Treaty of Turkomanchai of 1828. Britain's influence shrank, and at one time she was even obliged to have recourse to arms to protect her approaches to India. This happened in 1856 when Iran, following Russian instigation, attacked Britain's ally Afghanistan in order to seize the strategic fortress of Herat. The British considered it a *casus belli* and declared war on Iran. Their troops landed on the coast of the Persian Gulf and compelled the

[3]

Shah to sue for an armistice. Peace was concluded in 1857 in Paris. Iran renounced Herat, and thus, indirectly, Russia was deprived of an opportunity to infiltrate this buffer territory of India. Simultaneously, owing to the unsuccessful Crimean War, Russia suffered humiliation in another sector, and a semblance of balance was restored between her and Britain in Iran. The British, who could easily have annexed part of the Iranian coast on the Gulf and thus have established a naval base there, did not avail themselves of the opportunity. In contrast to Russia with her territorial advances, Britain seems to have concentrated exclusively on the search for economic advantages.

In 1872 a naturalized British subject, Baron Julius de Reuter, obtained a huge concession from Shah Nasir ed-Din. The concession gave him, among other things, the exclusive right to exploit all the minerals of Iran, except gold, silver, and precious stones, and to build railways, telegraph lines, and so forth. This grant opened a new dramatic chapter that may justly be labeled as the race for concessions in Iran. The Russians, upon learning of Reuter's concession, did not stand idly by. Their pressure on the Shah prompted him to cancel the grant. Thereafter a series of new concessions were given to the British to compensate them for the lost advantage, coupled with a series of concessions to the Russians. By the end of the nineteenth century most of the country's resources and technical projects were exploited or directed by foreign interests.

During this period Russian political and economic preponderance became more and more pronounced. Not only was Russia supreme in the five Iranian provinces adjoining her borders, she also maintained a firm hold on the Shah in Teheran by granting him large loans, which he used for his own enjoyment. Russian troops were stationed in various parts of Iran, and an Iranian Cossack Brigade was officered by the Russians. Russia benefited greatly also from the special customs tariff favoring her goods. In those circumstances it is a wonder that a British subject in 1901 managed to obtain an important oil concession.

In 1906 a new era opened in Iranian history. A bloodless revolution was carried out by a few thousand merchants who sought asylum in the summer residence of the British Embassy and presented the

[4]

Shah with an ultimatum. Reluctantly Shah Mozaffar ed-Din granted a constitution. Thus, at least formally, a door was opened for the introduction of parliamentary democracy. The British were generally identified with this progressive movement. In the ensuing few years Mozaffar's successor (backed by Russia) tried to destroy the Constitution and restore the old order, but the Democrats, aided by the powerful Bakhtiyari tribe, managed to defend it. Thus the Constitution was saved. But unfortunately for the British, their link with the progressive forces was lost. The Democrats now turned against Great Britain and allied themselves with the new power emerging in the Middle East, Imperial Germany. This shift in friendship was due to the disillusionment of Iranian liberals following the Anglo-Russian Agreement of 1907. The latter was a result of the growing menace of Germany to both Russia and Britain who, to ward it off, decided to compose their differences in Asia. The agreement provided for the division of Iran into Russian and British spheres of influence and, naturally, provoked indignation among the Iranians. From the Russians' point of view the agreement was a distinct advantage as it gave them control of a large area in Iran and brought them closer to India and the Persian Gulf. Consequently their influence in Teheran assumed more and more the proportions of a protectorate. An Iranian attempt to bring order into Iranian finances by hiring an American expert, Dr. Morgan Shuster, as adviser, failed miserably owing to ruthless Russian opposition. Shuster had to leave the country and, bitter about the failure of his mission, vividly described the prevailing conditions in his book entitled *The Strangling of Persia.*

The outbreak of war in 1914 found the British and the Russians in agreement to prevent German penetration toward the Caucasus and the Persian Gulf. Iran remained officially neutral but emotionally pro-German. This neutrality was soon violated by both warring coalitions, so that a sector of the eastern front actually ran through Iranian territory. At the time when this study begins, in the winter of 1917–1918, the Russian front south of the Caucasus was in a state of disintegration due to the Bolshevik Revolution. The new regime in Moscow, proclaiming a radical change in foreign policy, was watched with mixed feelings by Russia's oriental neighbors. To the British the Bolshevik Revolution meant, first, that there would be one less ally to fight Germany; secondly, that the new Communist doctrine would eventually affect British imperial interests in the East.

In the following pages an attempt is made to analyze Soviet and British policies toward Iran since 1918; to describe the ensuing Iranian reaction; and to present some new factors in this drama, as exemplified by the rise and fall of German influence and the emergence of active American interest.

PROLOGUE: THE MAKING OF THE COLONIAL REVOLUTION

The key Russian oil city Baku was the scene of a memorable event in the fall of 1920. Conquered by the Red Army earlier in the year, Baku became the host to the First Congress of the Peoples of the East. The Congress had been called by the newly created Communist International to rally the East around the State of the Victorious Proletariat. For a long time Lenin had taught that revolution in the East was a concomitant to revolution in Russia and a prerequisite to the success of Communism all over the world. Now, in 1920, after the ordeal of civil war, Moscow was finally in a position to convoke an imposing meeting of Orientals and to make it a signal for action in the East.

An able and eloquent team represented the capital of the world revolution. It comprised Gregory Zinoviev, President of the Comintern, who acted as Chairman of the Congress; Karl Radek, at that time shining in the sun of Lenin; and the dethroned Hungarian Communist Bela Kun. Comrade Ostrovsky of the Bolshevik Party was elected Secretary.

The East, from Morocco to Manchuria, sent 1,891 delegates, of whom 1,273 were Communists, and—an innovation in oriental politics—fifty-five were women. A sixteen-man Presidium was elected. It was composed of both Communists and non-Communists inasmuch as the East was encouraged to co-operate irrespective of its formal adherence to the party.

Defining the aim of the Congress as the "awakening of the millions of peasants" in the Orient, Chairman Zinoviev made it clear in his

[6]

keynote speech that he expected a full Communist revolution, although the East had not passed through the stage of capitalism. "From the moment when a single country managed to throw off the chains of capitalism, . . . China, India, Turkey, Persia, Armenia also can and must make a direct struggle to obtain a Soviet system." [1]

Revolutionary action, according to Zinoviev, was to be conducted on two fronts simultaneously. First, an unrelenting struggle was to be waged against foreign imperialists. Secondly, Communists were to "educate the laboring masses of the East to hatred . . . of wealthy classes, no matter whether they be Russians, Jews, Germans, or Frenchmen."

Zinoviev concluded with a dramatic appeal: "Comrades, you have heard much during the last few years of a Holy War. . . . But you who have met for the first time in a Congress of the Peoples of the East must here and now declare a true Holy War against the English and French robber-capitalist."

On the second day the Chairman gave the floor to Radek. In a speech that was a mixture of academic erudition and revolutionary dynamism, Radek underlined the social character of the expected oriental revolution as well as the role Russian aid was to play in it. He first attacked the native exploiters: "Sultan's clique, all sorts of Shahs, Emirs, and Khans." Then he defined the role of Russia as a nerve center and arsenal of the revolution. Said he:

No enemy will be dreadful to you, nobody will stop the stream of workers and peasants of Persia, Turkey, and India, if they unite with Soviet Russia. Soviet Russia was encircled by enemies, but now she can produce weapons with which she will arm the Indians, the Persian and Anatolian peasants, all oppressed, and will lead them to common struggle and to common victory.

Radek adhered strictly to the Leninist line that proclaimed the inevitable clash of the Communist and capitalist systems. "There can be no permanent peace," he said, "between the countries of labor and

[1] This and the subsequent quotations in this section are taken from the stenographic record of the First Congress of the Peoples of the East. In Russian: *Kommunisticheskiy Internatsional i Osvobozhdenie Vostoka-Piervyi Zyezd Narodov Vostoka 1920. Baku 1–8 Sept. 1920. Stenograficheskiye Otchety*. (Zdatielstvo Kommunisticheskovo Internatsionala, Petrograd, Smolnyi, 63. 1920.)

the countries of exploitation." Hence, he argued, "The oriental policy of the Soviet government is not an opportunistic maneuver but a sincere endeavor to help the downtrodden masses of the East in their struggle against the oppressors."

As the third principal speaker Bela Kun presented the "Theses on Soviet Authority in the East." The Theses laid stress on the agrarian revolution and hailed the institution of the Soviet as a form of government to be promoted in the colonies and semicolonies. Native bourgeoisie, together with foreign exploiters, was attacked with particular vigor.

Following these principal declarations many other delegates held the floor. Through their mouths the Orient manifested its hostility to Western imperialism. There was, however, little genuine discussion inasmuch as declarations had been prepared in advance by the Communists heading various national groups. This Moscow-patterned unanimity was disrupted only once during the nominations to the newly created Council of Action and Propaganda in the East. When Zinoviev presented the list of candidates for acceptance, one among the audience shouted: *"Ot Persii niepravilno"* ("In the case of Persia it is irregular"). This was the only dissenting voice. The chairman hushed the resulting commotion and declared that the candidates had been unanimously elected by those present.

In the perspective of nearly thirty years since the Baku Congress, one may evaluate it with more detachment than did the Western statesmen at the time. The Congress was important more as a symbol than as a practical action. The oriental delegates were not yet ready to understand and accept everything that was said to them by the fiery Marxist trio from Moscow. They were not a homogeneous group. Linguistic barriers separated them, despite the efforts of a group of interpreters to translate the speeches. The Communism outwardly professed by some of them was but a thin layer superimposed on a deep oriental base. Others were simply non-Communists. Their loyalties were still deeply rooted in the traditional structure of their societies. The delegates resented Zinoviev's attack on Islam and Bela Kun's denunciation of monarchy. The only thing they understood well was the Communist hostility toward the British. The Congress as a signal for a general oriental revolution failed. Yet it would be a mistake to underrate its significance. Moscow, by summoning this meeting, revealed its far-reaching ambitions in Asia and indicated the tactics which it was determined to employ.

IRAN IN COMMUNIST STRATEGY AND TACTICS

The incident of the lonely voice from the Iranian group during the closing stage of the Congress was in its own way symbolical. Iran had had sufficient experience with Russian imperialism in the past not to be too easily reconciled to her northern neighbor upon the change of government in Moscow. At the very time of the Congress Iran experienced a new manifestation of the Russian drive to the south. Soviet troops were stationed in Iran's Caspian provinces and were lending active support there to the revolutionary movement. Even the Iranian delegation at the Congress was not entirely voluntary. Under the combined pressure of the Iranian Communist party and the Red Army, some intellectuals from the north of Iran were compulsorily recruited to go to Baku. On the other hand, one should not ignore the fact that the Iranian delegation was the second largest at the Congress (192 delegates) and even larger than the notoriously pro-Communist Armenian group (157 delegates). It was surpassed in number only by the Turkish delegation (235).

During the Congress two Iranian Communist representatives were particularly active: Haidar Khan (Gaydarkhanov), who was elected to the Presidium, and Sultan-zadeh. Both were elected to the Council of Action and Propaganda on behalf of the Communist faction.

The large number of Iranians at the Congress, the election of their representatives to the leading bodies, and the frequent references to Iran in the speeches of Zinoviev, Kun, and Radek were not a mere accident. Iran had an important place in the strategy of oriental revolution elaborated in Moscow. As early as 1918 the Bolshevik writer K. Troyanovsky assigned a precise role to Iran in his *Vostok i Revolutsia:*

The importance of Persia for the creation of the Oriental International is considerable. If, however, the primary task of Persia is to constitute the natural "basin" for the movement of political emancipation of Central Asia, it is necessary that this basin be freed of the sediment and waste which ac-

[9]

cumulate in its reservoirs and likewise in its canals. Then only will Persia be in a position to fulfill the mission which history and nature assigned to her. The best friend of the Persian people is proletarian Russia, the Russia of bolshevism. . . . Revolutionary Russia is the sincere and disinterested inspiration of Persia, a precious counselor, a guide worthy of confidence to orient her toward democracy.

Our policy with regard to Persia must be simply a revolutionary democratic policy. Hence, our interests coincide perfectly with those of the Persian people. The purification of the natural basin of Asia is as important to the Persians as to the Russians. If Persia is the door through which one has to go in order to invade the citadel of the Revolution of the Orient, that is to say India, we must foment the Persian revolution. . . . The Persian uprising will be the signal for a series of revolutions that will spread through all of Asia and part of Africa.

A political situation favorable to democracy in Persia has an extraordinary importance for the emancipation of the entire Orient. A propitious terrain for the outbreak of the revolution has long been prepared. The imperialists of England, Russia, France, and Germany have labored there. *All that is needed is an impulse from the outside, an external aid, an initiative, and a resolute decision. This impulse, this initiative, this resoluteness, can come from our Russian revolutionaries through the intermediary of the Russian Moslems.*

India is our principal objective. Persia is the only path open to India. The Persian revolution is the key to the revolution of all of the Orient, just as Egypt and the Suez Canal are the key to the British domination of the Orient. Persia is the Suez Canal of the revolution. If we shift the political center of gravity of the revolutionary movement to Persia, the Suez Canal loses its strategic value and importance. . . . *For the success of the oriental revolution Persia is the first nation that must be conquered by the Soviets.* This precious key to the uprising of the Orient must be in the hands of Bolshevism, cost what it may. . . . Persia must be ours; Persia must belong to the revolution.[2]

Conquest of Iran was thus the key to the Communist success in the Orient. There was no gap in the logic of Troyanovsky's argument. In its own strange way it reminds one of the alleged testament of Peter the Great, which was reported to read as follows:

[2] Italics mine. Quoted by Aurelio Palmieri, *La politica asiatica dei Bolscevichi* (Bologna, 1924), pp. 173 ff.

Approach as near as possible to Constantinople and India. Whoever governs there will be the true sovereign of the world. Consequently, excite continual wars not only in Turkey but in Persia. Establish dockyards on the Black Sea; seize upon little pieces near this sea as well as on the Baltic which is doubly necessary for the attainment of our project. And in the decadence of Persia penetrate as far as the Persian Gulf; re-establish if it be possible, the ancient commerce with the Levant; advance as far as India, which is the depot of the world. Arrived at this point, we shall have no longer need of England's gold.[3]

The fact that Iran was considered the "Suez Canal of the revolution" did not in itself solve the strategic problems of the Communist advance. The Bolshevik revolution began in the north and center of the Russian Empire. It had first to assert itself in the Empire's outlying and non-Russian districts before reaching Iran's frontiers. Between revolutionary Russia and Iran was a belt of territory inhabited by Moslems, which had to be conquered first. It is in these areas, comprising the Caucasian region, Transcaspia, and Turkestan, that the Soviet concepts of national self-determination and revolutionary emancipation had to meet their first test. It is here also that the Bolshevik and the British interests clashed for the first time in the Middle East. The drama of Russia's border regions was instructive to the Moslem world and especially to the Moslem peoples adjacent to Russia. This drama is strictly linked to the further events in Iran. It will be useful, therefore, to recapitulate briefly its salient features before embarking upon the study of Iran herself.

[3] The entire will of Peter the Great is reproduced by P. M. Sykes, *History of Persia* (2d ed.; London, 1921), II, 244.

CHAPTER TWO

Communism, Nationalism,

and Imperialism

in Caucasia and Central Asia

W HEN, in March of 1917, the democratic government of Lvov and
Kerensky succeeded the autocratic monarchy in Russia, echoes
of this event were heard in the non-Russian border regions of the
Empire. The momentary weakness of Russia presented to the subject
nations of the Empire a unique opportunity for emancipation. The
new government could not expect the border regions to be willing
to continue as oppressed vassals. Yet it was not at all certain that the
March Revolution in Russia would necessarily result in the complete
severance of links between the center and the border regions. The
new regime, pledged to democracy and honest parliamentarism,
might introduce such liberal conditions in the Empire and grant such
generous representation of border regions in the parliament and administration that separation would not be necessary. Indeed, with
some kind of broad autonomy based on equality, the advantages of belonging to a larger political structure might eventually outweigh the
gains of self-determination and complete sovereignty.

Thus the border regions were faced with two alternatives: either
self-determination pushed to the extreme or the maintenance of links
with Russia on an autonomous basis. As long as Russia had democratic government, the border regions preferred autonomy to separation. Nevertheless, the first news about the revolution in Petrograd
acted like strong wine on the imagination of border-region patriots.

Their primary thought was to get rid of the Russian administration, police, and army—the hated instruments of oppression. Local committees of native nationalists, ambitious to assume authority, were created without much delay in the Caucasus and Transcaucasia. Similar developments took place in Transcaspia and Turkestan. The emirs of Bukhara and Khiva also manifested their determination to free themselves from the Russian yoke. An atmosphere of hopeful expectation and optimism developed everywhere.[1] Grand Duke Nicolas, Viceroy of the Caucasus, was expelled from Tiflis two days after the revolution, on the nineteenth of March. The Russian Governor-General of Turkestan had to leave Tashkent hurriedly during the same week. The old tsarist bureaucracy was quickly replaced by executive committees in which such diverse elements as native nationalists, Social Democrats, Russian Socialist Revolutionaries, and nonparty Russian colonists and Cossacks were represented.

THE EMANCIPATION OF TRANSCAUCASIA

In the areas north and south of the Caucasus Range the dominant elements in these executive committees were native Social Democrats motivated as much by a desire for progressive social change as by purely nationalistic feelings. They belonged mostly to the Menshevik wing of the Social Democratic Party and were opposed to the extreme Communist doctrines of the Bolshevik wing. These Caucasian nationalists decided in most cases to remain faithful to Russia, provided Russia were to liberalize her minorities policy. They knew that the attitude of the Provisional Government was to delay the solution until the meeting of the first Constituent Assembly. Besides, the Provisional Government had made a gesture of good will toward the Caucasus by appointing the Duma deputy, Akaky Chenkeli, a Georgian Social Democrat and patriot, as High Commissioner for Transcaucasia (including Georgia, Azerbaijan, and Armenia) in the place of the expelled Viceroy. Another evidence of good will was the inclusion of the Georgian Iraklii Tseretelli, formerly Chairman of the Social Democrats in the Second Duma, as Minister of

[1] For a more detailed description of events in Tiflis immediately after the March Revolution, see M. Philips Price, *War and Revolution in Asiatic Russia* (New York, 1918), pp. 270 ff.

Interior in the Provisional Government at Petrograd. On the other hand, the leader of the Social Democratic Party (Mensheviks) in the Duma, Nicolai Semenovich Chkheidze, also a Georgian, was elected President of the Petrograd Soviet of Workers' and Soldiers' Deputies.

This situation lasted till November, 1917, when the Bolsheviks forcibly overthrew the Provisional Government and assumed power in Russia. Complete chaos followed in Transcaucasia: the remnants of the Russian administration of the region fled and joined the counterrevolutionary forces led by tsarist generals in southern Russia. The responsibility for the preservation of law and order fell to the local politically conscious elements. The Georgian Menshevik leaders Chkheidze and Tseretelli, eliminated from power in Petrograd, arrived in Transcaucasia. They and other native Social Democrats, opposed to Bolshevism, immediately set to work to separate Georgia and other Caucasian areas from Russia. On November 15, Georgians, Armenians, and Tatars of Azerbaijan formed the Transcaucasian Committee.

From now on the organization of independent Transcaucasia proceeded at a quick pace. First the Transcaucasian regions formed a common Assembly (*Seim*) in February, 1918. Then after a formal declaration of independence on April 22, 1918, they created the Transcaucasian Federation. It was not destined, however, to last long. The impact of the Brest-Litovsk Treaty, concluded in March, 1918, between the Central Powers and Soviet Russia, caused the division of the Federation into three separate states. On May 26, Georgia declared her independence. This act was followed by similar declarations, on May 28, by Azerbaijan and Armenia.

Another result of the Brest-Litovsk Treaty was the gradual penetration of Turkish and German forces into the newly established Transcaucasian republics. According to the treaty Turkey was authorized to occupy three formerly Russian districts, Kars, Ardahan, and Batum. These districts constituted, however, part of the newly proclaimed Republic of Georgia. Despite Georgia's protests the Turks promptly moved into Kars and Ardahan and were about to enter Batum when they were suddenly preceded by their own ally, Germany. Under the guise of military co-operation a German division was landed in Batum, thus depriving the Turks of an important

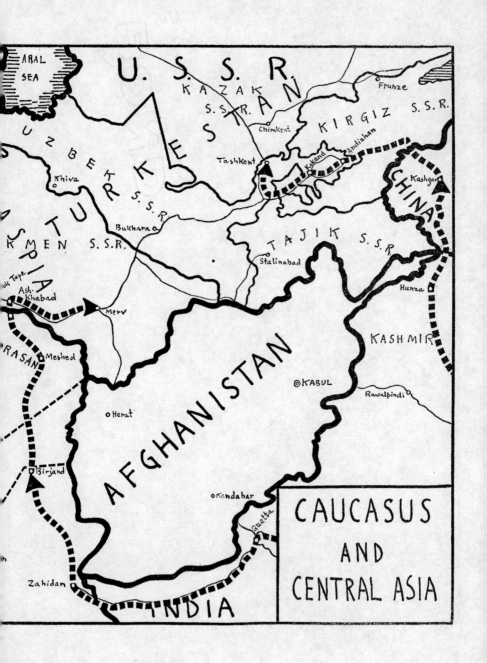

CAUCASUS
AND
CENTRAL ASIA

LEGEND

Railways in 1948 ———

British Expe-
ditions in 1918 ▰▰▰

Russo-Turkish
Front in 1917 • • •

British and
Russian Spheres
of Influence, 1907 – – –

Frontiers of
Soviet Republics ∿∿∿

spoil of war. This bold German move was greeted with relief by the people of the Republic of Georgia, who were in deadly fear of Turkish advance. German troops went further, occupied the Republic's capital, Tiflis, and extended diplomatic recognition and protection to the new Georgian state. This protection was accepted by the government of Georgia as a safeguard against both the Turkish and the Bolshevik menace.

In this behavior the Germans were not motivated by any altruistic sympathy toward Georgia. Their entry into the Caucasus was dictated by the desire to seize the rich Baku oil fields in the neighboring Republic of Azerbaijan before the Turks could lay their hands upon them.

Thus the separation of the Transcaucasian republics from Russia not only created three new states, it also provoked changes of tremendous strategic significance for both camps fighting the World War. In order to grasp the military implications of these events, we must realize that prior to the Bolshevik Revolution Russia maintained a front running from the vicinity of Trebizond in the north, through Lake Van and Kurdistan, to the southern parts of Iranian Azerbaijan. This was a mobile front, with the Russians penetrating deep into Turkish territory as far as the city of Erzerum, and the Turks getting hold of the Lake Urumia region in Iran. Owing to the Bolshevik Revolution the Russian armies gradually melted away. Soldiers deposed their officers, formed soviets and organized the evacuation of troops from Turkey and Iran, or spontaneously deserted their units. This Russian withdrawal produced a vacuum. To be sure, the new republics replaced Russian political authority with their own. But militarily they were too weak to serve as a substitute for the seasoned Russian divisions. Besides, the new states were not uniformly opposed to the advance of the Central Powers. Their sympathies were divided. While Georgia, as mentioned previously, did not mind permitting Germany to enter her territory, Azerbaijan as a Moslem state was willing to collaborate with the Turks. Hence there was no question of any unified Transcaucasian resistance to the invasion of Turko-German armies. The Germans and their Turkish allies were resolved to penetrate into this vacuum and reach, if possible, the Caspian Sea coast through Azerbaijan. If this plan succeeded, the Central Powers could project an offensive across the Caspian into Turkestan and Afghanistan and eventually kindle a flame of anti-British revolt in India.

THE BRITISH EXPEDITION TO BAKU

To the British the situation created by the defection of Russia seemed alarming. At the beginning of the war the responsibility of containing the eastern Turkish front had been divided between the British and the Russians. The northern sector, Armenia and Kurdistan, had been the Russian responsibility; the southern, involving the invasion of Mesopotamia from the Persian Gulf, had been the British assignment. As long as tsardom existed, this plan was honestly fulfilled by both allies. The Russian gains in Turkey have already been mentioned. On the British side, General Maude's expeditionary force had landed in Basra and, after a prolonged campaign, had driven the Turks out of Bagdad in 1917. Thereafter it continued its march northwards toward Mosul. Thus the gap between Russian and British forces had been gradually narrowed, and a solid barrier against any further penetration by the Turkish forces toward the east had almost been completed. Then the collapse of the Russian front, as a result of the Bolshevik Revolution, presented an entirely new problem to the British. The task before the British Headquarters in Bagdad was to prevent the Turks and the Germans from penetrating the Caucasus and establishing a stronghold on the Caspian Sea. The difficulty of the British task becomes evident if we recall that the former Russian sector had been held by several excellent divisions. It was clear that Britain, faced with German concentrations on the French front in Europe as a result of the Soviet-German Armistice, could spare few troops for the Middle Eastern campaign. Yet the situation demanded urgent measures. It was met with courage and determination. In January, 1918, an expeditionary force was organized in Mesopotamia under Major-General L. C. Dunsterville. Comprising fourteen officers and forty-one trucks, whose drivers were the only reserve manpower, Dunsterville's motorized cavalcade was ordered to proceed via Khanaqin on the Mesopotamian-Iranian border, Kermanshah, Hamadan, Qazvin, and the province of Gilan to the Iranian port of Enzeli (now Pahlavi) on the Caspian; thence it was to move to Tiflis and there organize a native Transcaucasian force for resistance to the Turkish-German troops.

To fulfill these orders, the "Dunsterforce" obviously had to pass through the neutral territory of Iran and to be received in a friendly way in Tiflis. The British command had no compunction about transgressing on Iranian soil since that country's neutrality had previously been violated both by the Turks and the Russians. As Iran had been powerless to thwart the free roaming of Turkish and Russian troops in the territory of Tabriz and Urumia, she could reasonably be expected not to resist the passage of the "Dunsterforce."

The prospect of a friendly reception in Tiflis, however, was clouded by many uncertainties. In January, 1918, the political situation in Transcaucasia was in a state of flux. Neither the Transcaucasian Federation, nor its three member states had as yet declared their formal independence. Two things were, however, certain: first, Transcaucasia did not want to belong to Soviet Russia, second, it did not want to be overrun by Turkish armies. The Christian elements of Transcaucasia—especially the Armenians and to some degree the Georgians—were afraid of the Turkish advance, in view of the notoriously hostile Turkish attitude toward the Armenians in particular. Of the two dangers, Bolshevik and Turkish, the latter seemed more immediate as the Bolsheviks were at that time busy with their own affairs in Russia proper. Hence the enterprising Armenian politicians, both from Tiflis and Baku, decided to get in touch with the British and investigate the possibility of aid from them. With such encouragement the British sent a staff officer, General Offley, to Tiflis to act as a liaison between them and the Transcaucasian nationalists.

When the "Dunsterforce," in pursuance of its instructions, arrived in Hamadan, in Iran, General Dunsterville met General Offley, who had just come back from Tiflis. His report did not augur well for the British expedition: according to Offley the Tiflis politicians were hesitant and rather pro-German. They considered a deal with the Germans as possibly a better safeguard against the Turks than reliance on British assistance. They seemed to be motivated by realistic

reasons: the Germans had, as Turkish allies, influence at Constantinople and could probably prevent the Turks from encroaching too
much on the freedom of Transcaucasia. In any case the Germans were
unwilling to surrender to the Turks the rich oil fields of this region. And, furthermore, secret German agents were at that time making far-reaching promises to Tiflis.

Thus the situation in Tiflis itself caused Dunsterville uneasiness
concerning his welcome there. Moreover at that moment the approaches to Tiflis bristled with encumbrances. First the road from
Hamadan to the Caspian was barred, in its Gilan sector, by the insurgent bands of Kuchik Khan. Kuchik Khan, who organized an insurrection of the Jangali tribes in Gilan against the central government of Iran, was hostile to the British. The second difficulty
was in the possible port of embarkation on the Caspian coast—
Enzeli (Pahlavi), which had come under the control of a Communist
soviet, run by the local Russian elements and demobilized soldiers.
The third obstacle was in Baku, where the expedition would have to
disembark to reach Tiflis. Chaos reigned there owing to the Bolshevik agitation, and eventually Baku found itself under the control
of a soviet, dominated by the Russian Bolsheviks.

All these obstacles prevented Dunsterville from reaching Tiflis
immediately. Instead he had to stay in Iran till the middle of August,
1918, waiting for more favorable developments in Transcaucasia.
His trucks were patrolling the whole length of the road between
Khanaqin and Qazvin, watching for a possible Turkish break-
through via Kurdistan into Iran and the Caspian coast. Oriental
imagination is vivid, and the rumor went around that the "Dunsterforce" had four hundred instead of forty trucks. These exaggerated
reports must have reached the Turkish Headquarters and formed
one of the reasons why the Turks did not launch a bold offensive toward the east at that time. The "Hush-Hush Army,"
as the "Dunsterforce" was called, thus played a most important
role in containing the Turkish-German advance toward Central
Asia.

While Dunsterville was waiting in Iran, the major disturbance in
Transcaucasia was concentrated in the port of Baku. This oil city of
Azerbaijan, subjected to a Bolshevik coup on March 22, 1918, had
submitted to a soviet headed by Lenin's Armenian friend, Stepan

Shaumian. The Soviet of Baku challenged the authority of the free Republic of Azerbaijan, for whose prosperity the control of Baku was of vital importance.

Meanwhile the Germans occupied Georgia and, according to a deal with Lenin, were supposed to penetrate further east and take military and economic control of Baku.[2] The Turks, on the other hand, having occupied some Georgian border districts, wistfully viewed Baku as their goal.[3] In order to fulfill their plan, the Turks prepared the ground by propaganda among the Mohammedan elements of Transcaucasia. Their agitation among the Tatars of Azerbaijan was one of the reasons why the Transcaucasian Federation could not maintain itself and had to be divided along ethnic and religious lines. Eventually the Turks organized, with the help of the Azerbaijan Republic, an auxiliary All-Islam Army. This army, together with regular Turkish troops, had the objective of conquer-

[2] On August 27, 1918, a supplementary treaty to the Brest-Litovsk Treaty was signed at Berlin between the Imperial German Government and the Government of the Russian Soviet Federated Socialist Republic. Part VI entitled "The Caucasus" was composed of the following two articles:

"Art. 13—Russia agrees to Germany's recognizing Georgia as an independent State.

"Art. 14—Germany will give no assistance to any third Power in any military operations in the Caucasus outside Georgia or the districts mentioned in Article 4, Paragraph 3, of the Peace Treaty [these were Kars, Ardahan, and Batum]. She will also take measures to prevent the military forces of any third Power in the Caucasus over-stepping the following lines: The Kuban, from its mouth to Petropavlovskaje; from there onwards, the boundaries of the district Shemakha to Agrioba; thence a straight line to the point where the boundaries of the districts of Baku, Shemakha, and Kuban meet; thence along the northern boundary of the district of Baku to the sea.

"Russia will do her utmost to further the production of crude oil and crude oil products in the Baku district, and will supply to Germany a quarter of the amount produced, or at least a number of tons, to be agreed upon later, per month. In so far as the quantities produced in the Baku district are not sufficient to supply this number of tons, or must be used for other purposes, they will be supplemented by quantities produced elsewhere. The price will be reckoned by the price of the coal Russia is allowed to have in accordance with Article 12, Paragraph 3, and, moreover, by the amount of goods to be supplied by Russia to Germany, in accordance with Article 3, Para. 2, of the Russo-German Financial Agreement of this date" (quoted from J. W. Wheeler-Bennett, *The Forgotten Peace* [New York, 1939], p. 433).

[3] The differences that arose between the Germans and the Turks concerning military operations in the Caucasus are described by General Liman von Sanders in his book *Five Years in Turkey* (Annapolis, 1927), pp. 196, 241–246, 268–269.

ing Baku. The government of the free Republic of Azerbaijan, residing in Elizabethpol (Gandja), was friendly to the Turks; this co-operation promised to reconquer Baku from the Bolsheviks. The Bolshevik Committee in Baku was unwilling to relinquish its authority in favor of the All-Islam Army, but it was not prepared to ask the British for assistance. Besides this official committee there existed an unofficial Armenian council in the city. To the Armenians the prospect of being conquered by the fanatical Moslem army was frightening, and so the council, through its secret emissaries, urged Dunsterville to change his plans and to come to Baku instead of to Tiflis in order to put up resistance to the approaching Turko-Tatar army. For a while these urgings did not seem to be very realistic, because before defending Baku against the Turks, Dunsterville would have to conquer it from the Bolshevik Committee.

But on July 26 an event occurred in Baku that changed the whole situation and opened promising vistas to the British. The Socialist Revolutionary Party, an old enemy of the Communists, made a successful *coup d'état,* overthrew the existing regime, and put under arrest the members of the Bolshevik Committee, including two chief leaders, Shaumian and Petrov. The victorious party set up a new regime under the official name of the Centro-Caspian Dictatorship, directed by five dictators. The new government was not identical with the Armenian council, but it was eager to obtain British help and, consequently, without delay addressed an appeal to Dunsterville for assistance.

Dunsterville, who, during the summer, had received reinforcements from Mesopotamia of about a thousand men and some field guns and armored cars, was ready to go to Baku. He successfully crossed the dangerous Gilan territory infested by Kuchik Khan's guerrillas, made a deal with the Enzeli Bolshevik Committee, which permitted him to embark on ships supplied by the Baku dictators, and, on August 16, 1918, sailed for Baku. Arrived there the next day, Dunsterville found in the city two strange groups of prisoners held by the Socialist Revolutionary dictators: one group was composed of the recently dethroned Bolshevik commissars and their followers; the other was Germans. The Bolsheviks had planned an escape from Baku to Communist-held Astrakhan and intended to take away with them all the contents of the Baku arsenal on thirteen ships. The dictators, some of whom were former Russian navy men, managed, however, to prevent the escape of the ships and of the Bolsheviks.[4] As a matter of fact, their main strength lay in the backing that they had among the navy and merchant marine personnel.

The Germans found themselves in Baku through a strange set of circumstances. As mentioned earlier, the German government had concluded an agreement with Soviet Russia concerning the control of Baku and the exploitation of oil resources there. Accordingly, a German military mission was dispatched via Astrakhan to Baku. No complications were expected by Moscow or Berlin, because both Astrakhan and Baku were, in July, 1918, Communist-dominated. The Germans thus planned to take control of Baku before their Turkish allies could conquer the city. The mission embarked on a boat in Astrakhan toward the end of July. Neither the Germans nor the Astrakhan Bolshevik Committee were informed that on July 26 the Social Revolutionaries had overthrown the Bolshevik government in Baku. On August 4 the German mission arrived in Baku and stepped down confidently from the boat to the pier. To their amazement the Germans found that the city was no longer in the hands of their friends, and they were promptly put under lock and key.

Dunsterville proceeded without delay to organize the defense of the city against the approaching Turko-Tatar forces. The dictators had a few regiments of local inhabitants at their disposal, and these had to co-operate with the British. Yet, instead of co-operation, Dunsterville found apathy, suspicion, or outright hostility on the part of the dicators. The Turks approached and gradually encircled the city. After a few engagements with the enemy Dunsterville came to the conclusion that, in view of the non-co-operative attitude of the

[4] To prevent any further attempts to escape, the twenty-six arrested commissars were later sent across the Caspian and handed over to the counterrevolutionary government of Ashkhabad. There, on orders of the government, all were shot on September 20, 1918. The execution took place along the railway line between Pereval and Akhtcha-Kouym (V. Chaikin, *History of the Russian Revolution* [Moscow, 1922], vol. I, as quoted by Joseph Castagné, "Les Organizations soviétiques de la Russie musulmane," *Revue du monde musulman*, LI [1922], 109).

dictators, it would be impossible to hold the city against a determined assault of the Turks. He reluctantly decided to evacuate his forces. Having presented an ultimatum to the dictators, in which he demanded concrete proofs of co-operation, and having met with a hostile reception, Dunsterville embarked his troops on a few available ships and sailed back to Enzeli. His leaving of Baku was not without difficulties, as—strangely enough—the dictators insisted, despite everything, that he should stay and defend them. His ships were ultimately fired upon by the Baku naval artillery, to no avail however. Shortly afterwards the Turks conquered the city.[5] Together with them, the government of the free Republic of Azerbaijan moved in and established itself in Baku.

The Turkish occupation of Baku did not last long. On October 30, 1918, the Ottoman government signed the armistice of Mudros with the Allies and hostilities ceased. Germany followed suit on November 11. Both the Turkish and the German forces were withdrawn from the Caucasus and in their stead came the British forces and some French contingents. The British forces, commanded this time by General Thompson, again occupied Baku and were stationed in various parts of Transcaucasia, including Tiflis and the terminus of the oil pipes, Batum. Dunsterville continued to command the British troops in northern Iran, safeguarding the lines of communication. A detachment of the British navy was brought to the Caspian and, under Commodore Norris, assumed control of this landlocked sea.

THE FREEDOM AND DOOM OF THREE REPUBLICS

To the three independent republics of Transcaucasia a new era of freedom and hope began. Liberated from the Turks and from dubious German protection, Georgia and the two other states strove to build democratic foundations for their national life. The presence of British troops constituted a guarantee against possible expansion of the Soviet State southwards. Georgia, Azerbaijan, and Armenia all adopted constitutions that followed Western patterns, and, al-

[5] A fascinating and detailed account of the British expedition to Baku is given by Major-General L. C. Dunsterville in his book *The Adventures of Dunsterforce* (London, 1920).

though quick transplantation of Western systems into those semi-Asiatic regions might be doubted, yet genuine effort was made to make democracy a success. All these republics established parliaments, based on universal suffrage for men and women without national or religious discrimination. Thus, for example, the parliament of Azerbaijan, composed of 120 members, had not only the Azerbaijan-Tatar deputies, but also a strong national minorities' representation including 20 Armenians, 10 Russians, and a few Poles and Jews. All three republics had governments emanating from respective parliamentary majorities, which, in turn, were composed of Social Democrats. In the Georgian Assembly Social Democrats (Mensheviks) controlled 109 seats of a total of 130.[6] In Armenia the controlling party was that of the Dashnaks (*Dashnaksutiun*), also of a socialist character. In Azerbaijan the government was in the hands of Mussavatists, of a similar political tendency. While in Russia proper the Bolshevik, internationalist wing of the Social Democrats was gaining ground and was swept into power by the November Revolution, the Transcaucasian states, long oppressed by tsarist Russia, could hardly be expected to adopt a political philosophy that would ignore nationalism. In their desire to establish sound democracy in Transcaucasia, the three governments carried out several reforms in order to break the undue influence and privileges of certain groups. In Georgia the National Church separated itself not only from the Russian Orthodox Church, but also from the state; and a Layman's Committee was put in charge of the church's funds and properties. Steps were also taken to curb the economic predominance of big landowners. In Tiflis a university was created.

The independence of the Transcaucasian republics was precarious. The presence of Allied troops was essential to their security. Yet the republics made no serious attempt to unite again into some form of federation for the purpose of defense against external aggressors. Instead, petty quarrels broke out between Azerbaijan and Armenia with respect to contested territories. The nationalistic feelings of all three states were gratified when, on January 13, 1920, the independence of Georgia and Azerbaijan was recognized *de facto* by the Supreme Allied Council, followed, on April 23 of the same year, by

6 V. D. Dumbadze, *The Caucasian Republics* (New York, 1925), p. 14.

similar recognition for Armenia. The delay in Armenia's case was caused by the still unsettled delimitation of her boundaries. When the Sèvres Treaty was dictated to the Ottoman government, on August 10, 1920, it provided for the creation of Greater Armenia, which would comprise, in addition to the original Russian area, the former Turkish vilayets of Trebizond, Erzerum, Van, and Bitlis.

Armenia was not destined, however, to enjoy these Turkish fruits of international diplomacy; nor were the other two Transcaucasian states to enjoy the blessings of peace in independence. The execution of the Sèvres provisions concerning Armenia was frustrated by the expansion of militant Turkish nationalism under Mustafa Kemal. By October, 1920, Kemal's armies had reconquered all districts of Turkish Armenia and were ready to invade even Transcaucasia. The external help expected by the Armenians was not forthcoming: the American Senate had just rejected the proposal to accept Armenia as a United States mandate, and the last of the British forces had been evacuated from Transcaucasia in July of 1920.

The evacuation of British troops had begun early in 1920. It was caused by the British cabinet's decision to cease active intervention in behalf of counterrevolutionary forces in Russia. British contingents had been withdrawn from Russia proper late in 1919, and the evacuation of troops from Transcaucasia was the next logical step. This, in turn, presented an opportunity to Soviet Russia, who in the meantime had made clear her disapproval of the separation of Transcaucasia. In the eyes of the Soviet leaders the Transcaucasian nationalists were guilty on two counts: first, they were Mensheviks, and hence "petty bourgeois," reactionary and counterrevolutionary; secondly, they had taken advantage of the help proffered them by the British (or formerly German) imperialists. The hostile attitude of the Soviet government toward the republics did not prevent it from formally recognizing the independence of Georgia and concluding a treaty with that state on May 8, 1920. The consequent establishment of the Soviet Embassy in Tiflis was, however, a maneuver to infiltrate Georgia with Bolshevik agents to foster revolutionary movements. Similar processes of infiltration took place in Azerbaijan and Armenia.

[24]

Azerbaijan was to become the first victim of Soviet expansion. On April 28, 1920, the Mussavatist cabinet was overthrown by the Communists and was replaced by the "Extraordinary Commission," composed mainly of Moslem Bolsheviks. Two days later Russian forces landed in Baku, ostensibly for the purpose of capturing the remnants of General Denikin's White army, which, routed from southern Russia, had retreated to the Caucasus. The landing had two effects: one was the embarkation and escape of Russian Whites to the Iranian port of Enzeli, to seek British protection. Together with them went the last British units stationed in Baku. The second effect was the creation on April 30, 1920, of a Soviet Republic of Azerbaijan. The new government promptly arrested all foreign missions residing in the city, sent a telegram to Moscow proclaiming its desire "to enter into fraternal alliance" with Soviet Russia "for the purpose of a joint struggle against world-imperialism," [7] and, on September 30, 1920, entered into "contractual relations" with Russia by concluding a series of treaties. Thus, according to the Stalinist terminology, a new state was made to benefit from "the highest form of Soviet autonomy."

During the following year the other two republics were to share the fate of Azerbaijan. Having ended her war with Poland, Russia could now concentrate on the "settlement" of the Transcaucasian problem. Her troops released from the west were transferred in large numbers to the Caucasus, ready for action. On the other hand, the Treaty of March 16, 1921, concluded with Turkey gave Moscow a free hand in Transcaucasia and assured her of noninterference on the part of the Kemalist government.

Following this treaty the Eleventh Red Army Corps invaded Georgia and in a swift move occupied Tiflis. Simultaneously the Georgian Communist minority, aided by the Soviet Embassy in Tiflis, staged a coup and overthrew the existing democratic government. On March 21 the Soviet Socialist Republic of Georgia was proclaimed. The last phase was the invasion by the Red Army of the Armenian Republic, already weakened by steady Turkish pressure from the west. In April, 1921, Soviet forces entered Erivan, the Re-

[7] Quoted from Alfred L. P. Dennis, *The Foreign Policies of Soviet Russia* (New York, 1924), p. 209.

public's capital, and three weeks later, on April 21, the Armenian Soviet Republic was established. Thus ended a brief chapter of independence for Transcaucasia.

Political terror followed Soviet occupation of the republics. Those among their leaders who fell into Soviet hands were either destroyed or compelled to collaborate with new regimes. Others escaped abroad and conducted lively political activity to restore independence to their respective countries. Large colonies of Transcaucasian refugees were formed in Turkey and Iran. Moscow, on the other hand, insisted that the republics were free and disclaimed any desire for annexation. To stress this point the Russian government concluded treaties with all three republics, obviously to maintain the fiction of their independence. The new regimes were even encouraged to send diplomatic missions to neighboring countries. Furthermore they were instructed to conclude, on October 13, 1921, the Treaty of Kars with Kemalist Turkey to settle the boundary problems. And, as if by the irony of fate, Soviet Azerbaijan, Georgia, and Armenia were told to unite themselves in August, 1922, into the Socialist Transcaucasian Federation, which survived until 1924 when the Constitution of the U.S.S.R. provided for a new administrative redivision of the area.

REVOLUTION AND NATIONALISM IN CENTRAL ASIA

Russian Turkestan was divided before the Revolution into two political areas: an area administered directly by Russia and another area comprising two semiautonomous emirates of Khiva and Bukhara, administered indirectly. The democratic revolution of March, 1917, gave a chance to the liberal elements, both Russian and Moslem, to gain control of the area directly administered by Russia, while the emirs of Khiva and Bukhara reasserted their independence from the central government.

The parts of Turkestan under direct Russian administration comprised most of the territory known today as the Kazak, Kirghiz, Turkmen, and Tajik Soviet Socialist Republics, and the khanates roughly corresponded to the area now known as the Uzbek Soviet Socialist Republic. The capital of Russian-administered Turkestan was Tashkent. Among other larger cities of that area were Kokand, Ferghana, Chimkent, and Alma Ata in the eastern part, and Krasnovodsk,

Ashkhabad, and Merv in its western part, known as Transcaspia. The collapse of tsarist power in the spring of 1917 and the expulsion of the Russian Governor-General did not give rise to the creation of any unified administration for this large area, despite the appointment by the Provisional Government of N. N. Shchepkin, one of the leaders of the Cadet party, as Chairman of the Government Committee in Turkestan. Instead, various local committees, based either on ideology or on the revived spirit of nationalism, arose and exercised their authority in limited areas. The Kazaks of eastern Turkestan, stirred by their educated compatriots who had seen service in the Russian army during the war and who had come into contact with western ideas, called three Pan-Kirghiz congresses in April, June, and December of 1917 and organized the autonomous Kirghiz government of Alash Orda.

Aside from that movement, the Moslems of Kokand called a Congress in November, 1917, which resulted in the establishment in December of the Provisional Government of the Autonomous Peoples of Turkestan.

In Tashkent itself Russian socialist elements came to the fore, the two Social Democratic factions of Mensheviks and Bolsheviks competing with each other. Simultaneously with the November Revolution in the center of Russia, the Bolsheviks gained control in Tashkent also. As a result the Executive Committee there, which was composed of nine members, had seven Russian Communists and two Moslems.

Owing to these developments, Russian Turkestan found itself divided at the time of the Bolshevik Revolution into three political centers: two of them nationalist, with democratic tendencies, and thus automatically anti-Russian and anti-Communist (Alash Orda and the autonomous Turkestan government in Kokand), and one Russian-Communist in Tashkent. The Tashkent Bolsheviks claimed authority over the whole area; and this claim necessarily demanded the clarification, on one hand, of their relationship with the two nationalist movements and, on the other, with the vast expanse of Transcaspia, including the strategically located railway and maritime center of Krasnovodsk.

Since Kokand is situated in geographical proximity to Tashkent, it was embarrassing for the Tashkent Bolsheviks to face there a nationalist center. Consequently they turned their attention to Kokand first. An expeditionary force was dispatched from Tashkent to subdue Kokand in February, 1918. The Kokand nationalists put up resistance but were unprepared to meet an armed invasion at such an early stage of their political organization. Besides, the Bolsheviks used troops who in military experience possessed an uncontested superiority over the loosely knit nationalist Moslem forces: they were composed mainly of former prisoners of war, taken by tsarist armies and interned in Turkestan—Germans, Czechs, Magyars, and Austrians. These prisoners were being released by the Bolsheviks as a result of the truce between the Soviet government and the Central Powers; a Communist agitation among them gained a number of adherents for the Bolshevik cause; and even those who were not converted to Communism were willing to fight for the Russian Communists, because, as was suggested to them, they expected to fight their way out of Russia toward their native countries. Kokand was conquered and, according to a British observer,

was laid waste with a ruthlessness that would have surprised a Mongol conqueror of the middle ages, and more than fourteen thousand of the people were massacred. The mosques and shrines were desecrated and defamed, the fine library of Mohammedan literature was burnt, and a blockade was instituted by which the remaining inhabitants were debarred from receiving grain from adjacent provinces, their own supplies having already been commandeered. Over nine hundred thousand people are said to have perished from this famine.[8]

Thus a victory was won, a nationalist "bourgeois" center was smashed; but politically this reckless step was an error, because the news about the Kokand massacre spread widely over the whole of the Mohammedan Orient and caused not a little embarrassment to Moscow in its dealings with Moslems.[9] Soviet sources tried to mini-

---

[8] Quoted from Lt.-Colonel P. T. Etherton, *In the Heart of Asia* (Boston and New York, 1926), pp. 153 ff. The description of the Kokand massacre is also contained in Sir George Macartney, "Bolshevism as I Saw It at Tashkent in 1918," *Journal of the Central Asian Society*, VII (1920), II and III, 42–58.

[9] According to A. L. P. Dennis (*op. cit.*, p. 247), "This was later sorely to embarrass Soviet leaders at the Baku Conference of Eastern peoples."

mize the whole episode, yet even they did not pass over it completely in silence. The following reference was made to the Kokand massacre in a semiofficial Soviet publication:

> There were comparatively few Bolsheviks in Turkestan, and what is more, many of the local Bolsheviks distorted the policy of the Bolshevik Party on the national question and committed gross mistakes in their dealings with the native population. The nationalist parties—the Kazak "Alash Orda" and the Uzbek "Uleme"—therefore found it easy to gain a large following among the population.[10]

While proceeding to destroy the Alash Orda organization in the eastern part of Russian Turkestan, the Tashkent authorities also incurred the anger of the population, both Russian and non-Russian, in the Transcaspian region. The upshot was that the personnel, mostly Russian, of the Transcaspian Railway rose in revolt early in 1918 against the Tashkent Communists. The Teke-Turkoman tribes supported them, and a provisional government was set up at Ashkhabad, near the Iranian border, to resist Communist domination of the region. This government established liaison with the British in Iran and requested their aid.

THE END OF KHIVA AND BUKHARA

Events in those parts of Turkestan that were not under direct Russian administration, namely, in Khiva and Bukhara, took a somewhat different path, although the general trend was the same: the Tashkent Bolsheviks sought to destroy, if necessary by force, the native nationalist centers and to impose upon these regions Communist rule. A factor that favored the Bolshevik schemes was that in both Khanates there had existed, for some time, a ferment due to the antiquated and autocratic form of government. Both emirs continued to live in a manner common to most oriental princes in the nineteenth century, trying to ignore the changes that were being produced in the outside world in the social, economic, and political fields. Yet even in those remote regions of Central Asia a new, although small, intelligentsia had formed, eager to introduce Western

[10] *The History of the Civil War in the U.S.S.R.*, ed. by M. Gorky, V. Molotov, K. Voroshilov, S. Kirov, A. Zhdanov, and J. Stalin (a translation of the Russian edition of 1936; New York, 1938), I, 217.

innovations into the traditional way of life. This ferment produced the Young Bukhara party in Bukhara, whose members were imbued with liberal ideas, yet were not politically educated enough to distinguish between such brands of socialism as Bolshevism and Menshevism. The Tashkent Bolsheviks seemed to these Bukharan liberals to represent the radical force liberating them from the fetters of feudalism. Accordingly, when the Kokand opposition was crushed and the Communist army turned toward Bukhara, the Young Bukharans attempted, in the spring of 1918, a revolt against their emir. The revolt was, however, abortive. The Emir's forces destroyed the opposition, killed a number of its leaders, and massacred most of the Russian inhabitants of the Khanate. The Communist army, unable to penetrate into the capital, made peace with the Emir, on March 25, 1918, and retired from the Khanate.

It seemed that, for a while at least, Bukhara was free to seek her salvation without interference in her internal affairs. Yet the Bolsheviks were unrelenting. They turned now to propaganda; and by various manifestoes, emanating both from Moscow and from Tashkent, encouraged the people to support "the Workmen's and Peasants' Government of Red Turkestan" and to oppose the authority of emirs as well as the threat of British imperialism. The Young Bukharans, having recouped their strength after the first unsuccessful rising, actively aided the Bolsheviks in their efforts. When the ground was well prepared, a new Bolshevik force was sent against the Khanate which captured Bukhara on September 2, 1920. The Emir fled to Afghanistan, and a Soviet Republic of Bukhara was established.

In the meantime Khiva was also converted into a Communist state. The internal ferment there, arising from circumstances similar to those in Bukhara, caused the Emir to grant a constitution in 1917. Although the majority in the parliament was composed of liberals, the constitution remained largely a paper reform. After the November Revolution in Russia, Russian Communists infiltrating into Khiva aided the Khivan liberals in their struggle against the Emir and his conservative party. In January, 1919, the Emir fled to Afghanistan, and by June of the same year revolutionary Khivans and Russian Bolsheviks established a Soviet Republic of Khorezm.

[30]

Khiva and Bukhara, once sovietized, entered into treaties with the Russian Soviet Federated Socialist Republic on September 13, 1920, and March 4, 1921, respectively. These treaties confirmed the complete domination of the republics by Soviet Russia. Thus the more important industries in both republics were nationalized. Military policy was conducted in common with Russia. The republics had to supply Russia with raw materials in exchange for manufactured goods and bound themselves not to grant any concessions to foreigners. Russia undertook to provide expert help in the fields of trade and education. Irrigation had to be conducted under joint auspices with Russia. Mutually hostile organizations were prohibited on the contracting parties' territories. At the same time Soviet Russia renounced the old colonial policy of the tsarist government and declared null and void treaties previously concluded by the Imperial Government with the Khanates.[11] As a result of these treaties Soviet embassies were established in both republics, staffed with numerous personnel, and the Cheka (secret police) was installed under Russian advisers. The Red Army was garrisoned in both territories and was soon to find itself busy fighting armed opposition.

BRITISH INTERVENTION IN TURKESTAN

Opposition to Soviet expansionism was so widespread in the whole territory of Turkestan that, from 1918 on, developments in this area may be considered as just another chapter of counterrevolution and foreign intervention. We have mentioned previously the revolt of the Transcaspian Railway workers against the Tashkent Soviet and the call for aid that they addressed to the British. The British responded favorably to this request, and soon what seemed to be an internal Russian affair was transformed into an international conflict. The British, in their readiness to help the anti-Communist insurgents in Tashkent in 1918, were motivated by the same reasons that had prompted them, in the same year, to undertake a hazardous intervention in Transcaucasia. In the words of Colonel Etherton, a British officer who was sent on a mission to Turkestan:

The conclusion of the Brest-Litovsk Treaty with the Bolsheviks, in March 1918, placed the Germans in a favorable position for activities in Asia, since

11 For more details about these treaties see Dennis, *op. cit.*, pp. 249–252.

the treaty struck at the Russian fabric as a whole, jeopardized the welfare of Russia in Asia, and threatened to extend the war to the heart of the Asiatic continent. . . . There was . . . every possibility that Germany would, by taking advantage of the antipathy between Georgia and Armenia, open the road through the Caucasus to Central Asia. It was also considered not improbable that a Turko-German army might materialize for a campaign against India through Afghanistan. . . . German and Turkish agents were busy throughout the country lying between the Black Sea and the Indian frontier of Afghanistan. . . .

Such in brief were the dangers confronting us in the Asiatic theatre, and it was therefore essential that we should gain and maintain touch with the situation between the Caspian Sea and Chinese Turkestan. . . . There was a complete absence of all regular government in Central Asia. . . . It was known, too, that a movement was afoot for the creation of a Mohammedan state to include Russian Turkestan and the Caucasus, a scheme that had already formed the subject of overtures to Afghanistan. . . . In Central Asia there was a considerable body of opinion well disposed towards the Allied cause. . . . Although it was not contemplated to afford effective military support to pro-Allied elements, a small British military organization was essential from which the antennae could radiate for the acquisition of information, and to exploit whatever appeared favorable.[12]

Another British officer, also a participant in intervention in Central Asia, gave an even more dramatic description of the danger facing the British Empire:

In early 1918 a German Army Corps, ill spared from the West, was on its way to Baku, there to be backed by good Turkish infantry; in northern Afghanistan, Osmanli drill-sergeants and Magyar gun-layers of the "Kaiserliche and Koenigliche Ost-Indische Abteilung" laboured to drill the Afghan army and to cajole His Majesty of Kabul to wage war against the British. In Turkistan, in the remote prison camps of Kazalinsk, Perovsk, and Skobelef, emissaries worked to organize scores of thousands of Magyars, Austrians, and Germans, taken at Przemysl and in Galicia, into battalions and brigades, and to fit them out in good new boots and uniforms under the complacent sway of the treason-bacteria that incubated in Frankfort's hellbroth, had rotted Russia. . . . So news and information was essential, and since there were tens of thousands of tons of cotton of Ferghana ready baled in the warehouses and on the wharves of Turkistan, it behoved us to take some energetic step to prevent this priceless raw material from reaching the nitrating shops

[12] *Op. cit.,* pp. 1 ff.

of Germany, whether by way of Moscow or through Krasnovodsk and the Caucasus.[13]

These two quotations testify eloquently enough to the alarm with which the British viewed the consequences of the Bolshevik Revolution and the Brest-Litovsk Treaty in Central Asia. The German-Austrian prisoners in the area added about 200,000 armed men to the Red Army units and the Communist nuclei directed by the Tashkent Soviet. Together they constituted a force that the British, even with their proverbial self-control, could hardly underestimate. To cope with this difficult situation the British government dispatched two military missions to Turkestan. The first and larger expedition under Major-General Sir Wilfred Malleson, was sent to Transcaspia, in reply to the call for aid from the anti-Communist government at Ashkhabad. It was soon enlarged by regular Indian army units, which co-operated with the Ashkhabad troops against the Tashkent Red Army and their German-Austrian allies. To secure liaison with their Indian base a separate command was established in Iran, under the official name of the East Persian Line of Communications but unofficially known as the East Persian Cordon. This cordon had been in existence before the Russian Revolution, and had been divided into the northern (Russian) and southern (British) sectors. The dividing point between the tsarist armies and the British-Indian troops had been the town of Birjand, relatively deep within Iran from the Russian border. The aim of the original cordon had been to constitute a second line of defense against any Turko-German military thrust or infiltration through northern Iran toward Afghanistan, Russian Central Asia, or India. After the Bolshevik Revolution the Russian troops "melted away" and the responsibility of guarding the whole length of the line became British. Now, however, that an anti-Communist and, therefore, anti-German center of resistance was set up in Ashkhabad, the Cordon had to serve also as a link between the British troops in Transcaspia and India.[14]

[13] L. V. S. Blacker, *On Secret Patrol in High Asia* (John Murray, London, 1922), pp. 5–6. Reprinted by permission of the author.

[14] A detailed description of the work of the East Persian Cordon Command may be found in *East Persia, a Backwater of the Great War*, by Brigadier-General W. E. R. Dickson (London, 1924).

The second British mission to Turkestan was smaller and experienced hazardous, though romantic, adventures comparable to the Wassmuss' exploits in southern Iran [15] or—to a lesser degree—to T. E. Lawrence's activities in Arabia. It was led by three officers: Lt.-Colonel F. M. Bailey, Lt.-Colonel P. T. Etherton, and Major L. V. S. Blacker, all of whom had expert knowledge of Central Asia and its languages. Its destination was Tashkent, the hotbed of Bolshevism. "We were to investigate the situation on the spot," writes Colonel Etherton, "and examine questions affecting the safety and welfare of the British Empire. . . . We were also to initiate and put into effective operation a system of propaganda. . . ." [16] A staff of sixteen noncommissioned officers, mostly linguists and telegraph operators, accompanied the officers. Organized in India, the mission had to reach Tashkent by a difficult route through the Hunza principality on the border of the Pamir Plateau, Chinese Turkestan, and Kirghizia. Upon their arrival in Sin-Kiang Colonel Etherton parted with the mission owing to his appointment as Consul-General in Kashgar. His place as leader of the mission was taken by Sir George Macartney, who had been occupying the position to which Colonel Etherton was being transferred.

Arriving by rail via Andijan in Tashkent, the mission was at pains to explain to the surprised Soviet commissars that its intentions were peaceful and friendly. This explanation did not seem convincing to the Bolsheviks, who hesitated between putting the British party before a firing squad and holding them as hostages. The greatest source of embarrassment to the mission was, of course, the military operations simultaneously undertaken in Transcaspia by General Malleson against the Soviet troops. The Macartney mission therefore felt it necessary to pretend that the Indian troops in Transcaspia "were not His Majesty's troops at all, but pensioners and discharged Hazaras, Afghan subjects," [17] for whose behavior the British authorities could not be held responsible. It is really puzzling that the Bolsheviks permitted the mission to sojourn in Tashkent for three months, especially since after Ambassador Mirbach's mur-

[15] See Chapter Six.
[16] *Op. cit.,* pp. 1 ff.
[17] Blacker, *op. cit.,* p. 24.

der in Moscow Lenin had ordered the arrest of all Allied subjects in Russia. The mission could do little more than gather information, which it managed to convey despite Soviet vigilance, to Consul Etherton back in Kashgar. Finally, when the ground became too hot for them, the British left Tashkent and, again via Sin-Kiang, reached India.

In the meantime operations in Transcaspia were being undertaken on a larger scale. The Russian forces of the provisional Ashkhbad government were reinforced by Turkoman regiments and Indian troops, the latter having passed through eastern Iran. This heterogeneous group possessed only one common link—hatred of the Bolsheviks. The Russian troops themselves represented diverse elements, including some Cossack units and a large percentage of personnel skilled in military engineering and the manning of railroads and artillery. The British-Indian troops comprised the 19th Punjab Infantry Regiment and some elements of the 28th Light Cavalry. The most interesting contingent from the political angle was, however, the Teke-Turkoman units. Their participation introduced a factor of nationalist ambitions into the counterrevolutionary struggle.

This combined Russo-Indian-Turkoman force took the initiative and pushed toward the northeast, capturing Annenkov and the famous oasis of Merv. For some time the front was stabilized around Merv, as neither party was able to carry on further offensives. General Malleson's forces could not risk extending their lines of communication too far. Furthermore, they were greatly outnumbered by the combined Red and Austro-German prisoner forces. The latter also faced problems that precluded an offensive. They had to wage war on at least three fronts, including the central-southern sector of Khiva-Bukhara and the eastern sector, where the Orenburg Cossacks molested them along the Tashkent-Orenburg railway line. Moreover, owing to the aggressive spirit displayed by the Bolsheviks in their dealings with Khiva and Bukhara, many irregular bands, composed of devout Moslems, came into being and waged a fierce guerrilla warfare against the pro-Bolshevik troops. These bands, known as Basmatchi, combined ordinary banditry with patriotism and proved to be a source of constant irritation to Tashkent. Their organization was, to be sure, very feeble; yet in that very fact lay also

[35]

their strength, since it had no single nerve center on which the Bolsheviks could lay their hands.

Unless, however, the British government resolved upon sending troops in greater numbers to Central Asia, which action was in turn linked with the general policy of intervention in Russia, the Malleson-Ashkhabad contingents stood little chance of making headway or even of maintaining themselves in the conquered positions. The British in 1918 really had two objectives in mind when they decided to intervene in Turkestan: one was the immediate objective of preventing Turkestan and its raw materials from becoming the prey of the Central Powers; the other—a long-range one—was to protect India against any anti-British penetration, whether German or Communist. The first objective was fulfilled when insurrection in various parts of Turkestan paralyzed the German and Bolshevik efforts to make immediate use of this rich area for economic or strategic purposes. And this chapter may be considered as closed at the moment of Germany's surrender to the Allies in November of 1918. Any continuation of intervention after that date bore clearly an anti-Bolshevik character.

Therefore it was necessary for the British government to decide at what line a strategic belt of defense for India should be established. Should it be Afghanistan, Iran, and "preventive" British influence in Chinese Turkestan? Or should the vast expanses of Russian Central Asia be included in it? Circumstances favored the most daring plans, because of the tactless or even ruthless Bolshevik policy toward the native populations of that region. Such organizations and movements as Alash Orda, the Kokand Turkestan government, the Teke-Turkoman forces, or the Basmatchi bands bore eloquent testimony that the local peoples, irrespective of their nationality, were opposed to the Communist rule. "With more vigour and thoroughness than ever characterized the Czarist regime the Bolsheviks have carried on a policy of complete Russification," wrote Colonel Etherton.

The railways, public services and all that pertains to the execution, are entirely run by the Russians, whilst large numbers of peasants have been imported and settled on land forcibly taken from the Kirghiz. The result has been to create a feeling of bitter hostility and racial hatred quite unknown in the old Czarist days, when I travelled through Turkestan and found a general air of peace and contentment.[18]

Apart from this feeling of hostility toward the Russians, another element might have helped the British and that was the collapse of German prestige in Asia as a result of the lost war. Those Turkic elements of the Caucasus and Central Asia, who might have dreamed about a Pan-Turanian empire based on German support, were now ready to change their orientation. Having to choose between the Bolsheviks and the British, they usually preferred the latter.

The story of Enver Pasha is a case in point. Enver, former Turkish Minister of War, known for his pro-German sympathies, fled to Germany after the Armistice of Mudros, which on October 30, 1918, put an end to the war between Turkey and the Allied Powers. Anxious to regain his former glory, he was bent upon waging a struggle aginst British imperialism and against his rival Mustafa Kemal Pasha in Turkey proper. Disappointed with the impotence of Germany, herself defeated, he left Berlin and appeared in Moscow, offering his services to the Communists. Despite his upper-class status Moscow appeared to favor enlisting his support because of the prestige he enjoyed in the Mohammedan world. He was first given an assignment to organize some Turkish elements in the Caucasus, which would serve as a spearhead of Soviet influence in Turkey. The Soviet decision, however, to extend far-reaching support to Mustafa Kemal caused a change of plans; and so Enver, having momentarily appeared at the Baku Oriental Congress in 1920, was sent to Turkestan on a mission to reconcile the Khivans and Bukharans to the Soviet rule. There, however, instead of serving the Communist cause, he deserted, and some time later he reappeared as one of the leaders of the Basmatchi guerrillas. This sudden change of front exemplifies the disappointment of an astute politician such as Enver with the prospects of free development of Turanian peoples under the Soviet protection. Although fiercely anti-British at the Congress of Baku, Enver, by assuming the direction of the Basmatchi, necessarily ranged himself on the British side. He is known to have maintained liaison with the deposed emirs of Khiva and Bukhara in Afghanistan, and they, in turn, were supported by the British.

[18] *Op. cit.*, p. 153.

Referring to the situation as it existed in the course of the year 1919, Colonel Etherton, who, as mentioned earlier, was then British Consul in Kashgar, wrote: "The Bolshevik Government in Tashkent was then in no position to assume hostilities against Bukhara, for they were confronted by the British in north-east Persia, and were meeting with strong opposition from insurgent bands in Semirechia and Ferghana, *with all of whom I was in touch.*" [19]

Among the elements disappointed with the Bolshevik policy were even a number of leaders of the Young Bukhara party, who after the conquest of the Khanate by the Tashkent Communists, preferred to escape to Afghanistan or to join the Basmatchi than to be tools of the new masters of their country.

Thus the British, facing a turn of opinion in Central Asia in their favor, might have been in a position to prepare an ambitious scheme for the creation of some sort of Pan-Turanian state, which in alliance with Great Britain, would constitute an additional barrier protecting India. There are good reasons to think that, as usually in such cases, local British elements, well acquainted with the situation and aware of the potentialities, did cherish such ambitions. This attitude would have been only a normal outgrowth of the New Delhi school of political thought, which, to take an example from the Arabian Peninsula, dictated to the government of India an alliance with Ibn Saud in Nejd in preference to Sherif Husein of Mecca. Yet the statesmen in London were unwilling to go so far; they decided in September, 1919, to end intervention in Russia. An oversimplified interpretation of that decision identified both the Caucasus and Turkestan with Russia, despite the fact that these regions were, in reality, merely a colonial extension of the Russian Empire, with occasional islands of Russian settlers. On such a premise, then, the British in 1919 shrank from sending reinforcements to Transcaspia and adopted the attitude of "wait and see." The British troops already on the spot remained, but without reinforcements they were inadequate to settle the Turkestan question. Their continued presence irked the Bolshevik authorities.

In August, 1919, the Malleson-Ashkhabad coalition suffered its first major defeat at the hands of the Bolsheviks, who had been able

[19] *Op. cit.,* p. 151. Italics mine.

to concentrate their forces after the successful conquest of Khiva in June. Annenkov and Merv were evacuated; the treacherous conduct of the Armenians in the allied army was not without effect on the outcome of this battle.[20] In October the Bolsheviks occupied Ashkhabad itself and then made a move in the direction of the Iranian province of Khorasan. In February, 1920, Bolshevik forces appeared in Krasnovodsk; by spring the whole of Transcaspia had fallen into their hands. The September invasion of Bukhara, previously referred to, completed their conquest of Turkestan. The only remaining opposition to the Bolsheviks centered in the Basmatchi bands, which under Enver's leadership grew in strength for a while. Enver was killed in battle in 1922, but the Basmatchi managed to molest the Soviet authorities as late as 1925–1926, when they were finally wiped out.

The British-Indian troops were evacuated to Iran, where for some time some of their detachments guarded the Iranian Turkestan border against possible Bolshevik inroads. The Tashkent Soviet, which became an important propaganda center for the Orient, combined with the Pan-Hindu Revolutionary Committee in Tashkent in ambitious efforts to set the flame of revolution in Iran, Afghanistan, and India. A torrent of propaganda leaflets poured into those countries, accompanied by the smuggling of arms. According to a British officer, Major Blacker, who at that time was stationed at the frontier post of Bajgiran:

During April, May, June they [the Bolsheviks] smuggled no small quantities of modern weapons, of which they had no lack. . . . But we were not allowed to stop these smugglings by force of arms, since higher authority laid down that it was an internal affair of Persia. . . . Seldom did a week pass without one of my trusty henchmen bringing in a neat packet of, say, five hundred scarlet leaflets, or a couple of dozen Marxian pamphlets, with the information of the "Politicheski Oddiel" of the Ashkhabad Soviet. Accompanying these would be a beaky Armenian or astrakhan-capped Tabrizi Turk in many-pleated frock coat, as greasy and unwashed as they make them, with an N.C.O.'s heel rope around his neck. As matters developed the propaganda took a pronounced anti-British turn, appealing to the oppressed multitudes of India to shake off their "capitalistic imperialistic" oppressors.

[20] Blacker, *op. cit.*, p. 215.

One of the most interesting things that Comrades Paskutski and Baranoff, the leading Transcaspian commissars, pushed into Persia was a 5-foot lithographed poster, depicting in several colours three naked, emaciated Dravidians harnessed into a plough at the tail of which stood a ginger-whiskered John Bull, in white drill jacket and a sun helmet, complete with projecting incisors and bulldog pipe. In one hand he brandished an automatic pistol, in the other a *nagaika,* and the legend, in Russian, Persian and Turkish, told that "this is how the English plough in India." [21]

In the autumn of 1920 British forces were finally withdrawn from Khorasan; at the same time the East Persia Cordon was also liquidated.

A few words may be added concerning the fate of Central Asia after the conquest of the country by the Bolsheviks. The provisional Ashkhabad government was replaced by a soviet, which promptly embarked upon a witch hunt of "counterrevolutionary" elements. The first week of soviet rule in that city brought the execution of forty ex-officers and their friends. Similar developments took place in Krasnovodsk. The Red Terror was directed from Tashkent by Comrades Iliava and Broido, the latter responsible for the organization of the Tashkent propaganda center.[22] In Tashkent itself, in the meantime, a reorganization took place: the old Executive Committee gave way to the Turkestan Commission (*Turkkommissya*), which, instead of pretending to be a local emanation, was sent directly from Moscow. Two men headed this commission: Tomsky, president of the Central Council of Trade Unions (he was purged and committed suicide in 1937), and Rudzutak, later to be appointed Foreign Trade Commissar (also a victim of the Great Purge in the 1930's). The Turkestan Commission had instructions to pursue a more conciliatory policy toward the local population. As a result a sort of New Economic Policy experiment was tried in Turkestan: the Moslems, but not the local Russians, were permitted some measure of free trade.[23]

In the conquered Khanates, the pretense of formal independence and "contractual relationship" with Soviet Russia was gradually

[21] Blacker, *op. cit.,* pp. 232, 267. Reprinted by permission of the author.

[22] *Ibid.,* p. 236.

[23] See Elizabeth Bacon, "Soviet Policy in Turkestan," *Middle East Journal,* October, 1947, p. 392.

abandoned. Although for some time the Russian Soviet Republic maintained reciprocal diplomatic representations with Bukhara and Khorezm, it was clear from the beginning that the Soviet embassies there were considered more as administrative and revolutionary agencies than as diplomatic missions.[24] In Bukhara itself the Young Bukhara and later the Bukharan Communist party were headed by two men, Faizulla Khodjayev and Mukhedinov. Both belonged to well-known Bukharan merchant-class families and competed for power. Mukhedinov was made the first President of the Republic, yet he was of more conservative tendencies than Khodjayev and even displayed some Pan-Islamic orientation. Khodjayev took Marxism more seriously and by his unrelenting struggle to sovietize Bukhara gained the nickname of "Lenin of the Uzbeks." The rift between these two men led eventually to the desertion of Mukhedinov, together with his War Commissar Arifov, to the Basmatchi bands. Khodjayev remained as an uncontested authority in Bukhara and became instrumental in the reorganization of the two Khanates and some former Russian Turkestan territory into a new unit, Uzbekistan, which by 1924 joined the U.S.S.R. as one of the Union republics. Khodjayev became President of the Uzbek S.S.R. and enjoyed this position until 1938, when, together with Rykov, Bukharin, and other right-wing oppositionists, he was condemned as a "fascist spy" and executed.

IRAN'S PLACE IN BRITISH POLITICAL DOCTRINES: BRITISH WITHDRAWAL

The events described in the preceding section make it clear that British intervention in Transcaucasia and Central Asia was possible only because the British could use Iranian territory as a transit stage or as a base for operations. Thus political relations between Iran and Great Britain influenced the happenings in the cis- and trans-Caspian provinces, and, vice versa, events in these provinces could not fail to affect the British position in Iran. Since the presence of British troops in the neutral state of Iran during and immediately after the first World War was an obvious violation of neutrality and of the principle of self-determination, it may be useful to analyze

[24] Alexander Barmine, *One Who Survived* (4th ed.; New York, 1945), p. 97.

what prompted Great Britain to commit these violations. Such an analysis is not intended either to blacken or to purify British reputation. Its aim is to ascertain whether, in principle and in practice, Great Britain considered Iran as a territory for political expansion and eventual colonization or whether British military operations there were due to causes independent of British will and planning.

We have noted earlier [25] that Russia's traditional policy with regard to Iran was one of southward expansion at the expense of Iranian independence. It was largely due to Britain's resistance that this southward movement on the part of Russia was never completed. Yet, paradoxically enough, it was also due to Great Britain that, in the last tsarist decade, Russia approached considerably closer to her goal. In 1907 Russia and Great Britain entered into an agreement dividing Iran into British and Russian zones of influence. With British approval Russia secured exclusive political and economic penetration in the whole of northern and central Iran, including the city of Isfahan far toward the south. Teheran, the capital, was deep within the Russian zone. Great Britain satisfied herself with a relatively insignificant and economically poor area in the southeast, adjacent to Indian Baluchistan, while the southwestern region, rich in oil, remained a neutral zone in which neither power had an exclusive claim. This agreement conceded so much to Russia that it could not have been concluded without some special justification. This justification was to be found in the concern of the British government over the rise to power and intense militarization of Imperial Germany, which by that time presented an open challenge to British interests in the Middle East. Looking for allies, Great Britain entered into the Entente Cordiale with France, settling outstanding colonial claims with her in Africa. Next she turned to Russia. Intense Anglo-Russian rivalry in Central Asia, existing over many decades, had to be adjusted to the new demands of co-operation in the European theater, and so the 1907 agreement concerning Iran, Afghanistan, and Tibet came about.

The agreement may be regarded as a victory for British diplomacy in Europe, but it was clearly an expensive concession in Asia. That it was regarded as such both by Russian and British statesmen is

[25] See pp. 2 ff.

[42]

amply attested in the available historical sources. Russian Foreign Minister Sazonov wrote in this connection to the Russian Minister in Teheran, in 1911: "The English, pursuing as they do, vital aims in Europe, will if necessary sacrifice certain interests in Asia in order to maintain the convention with us. These circumstances we can naturally turn to our own advantage, for instance in our Persian policy." [26] In British circles, on the contrary, there was uneasiness lest this concession prove fatal to imperial interests in the East. Statesmen of the Indian school were particularly alarmed by the agreement. Lord Curzon, former Viceroy of India and later Foreign Secretary, gave vent to his anxiety when he wrote soon after the conclusion of the agreement: "The Russian Convention is in my view deplorable. It gives up all that we have been fighting for for years, and gives up with a wholesale abandon that is truly cynical in its recklessness. Ah, me, it makes one despair of public life. The efforts of a century sacrificed and nothing or next to nothing in return." [27]

This pessimism is intelligible in the light of the traditional British doctrine that India constituted the heart of the Empire, which had to be protected at almost any cost. The safest way to protect India was to establish on her frontiers a chain of territories that would be either under British ascendancy or free from the influence of another Big Power. Exclusive British ascendancy in the chain of territories consisting of Iran, Afghanistan, Sin-Kiang, and Tibet was barred by Imperial Russia. Accordingly two alternatives remained: (a) a shared ascendancy through agreement on Russian and British spheres of influence or (b) a preservation of the independence of the territories as a political no man's land between Russian and British imperial organisms. Of the two alternatives, the British preferred the latter. This preference was based on two facts: first, any division of territory would serve as a precedent to sanction further Russian penetration toward India or the Persian Gulf; hence any British gain would be offset by an increased Russian military threat to India; secondly, the pacification of the occupied and naturally discontented

[26] Quoted in "Anglo-Russian Rivalry in Persia," by Mary M. McCarthy, *University of Buffalo Studies,* vol. VI (1925), no. 2, p. 61.

[27] Quoted in *The Life of Lord Curzon* by the Earl of Ronaldshay (London, 1928), III, 38,

regions would entail effort and expense that might better be avoided. As the British viewed it, then, an independent Iran, free from all foreign influences, was to be preferred to an Iran under the shared domination of Britain and Russia. This view, for reasons of European policy, had to be temporarily pushed into the background in 1907, but it was never totally abandoned.

An illustration of the British worry over undue southward extension of Russian influence in Iran may be found in the attitude adopted by Great Britain in 1915 during the negotiations concerning Constantinople. These negotiations, resulting in the so-called "Constantinople Agreement," made it clear that the British desire to keep Russia from India and the Persian Gulf was even stronger than the desire to prevent Russia from controlling the Turkish straits. Russia, as an ally in the war, demanded formal recognition of her claims to the control of the Straits and Constantinople. Since the Ottoman Empire was the enemy, the British government was ready to concede this Russian demand on condition that the hitherto neutral zone in Iran should be assigned to Britain. Russia agreed.[28] For the British this agreement meant an additional safeguard against the advanced Russian positions in Iran.

The problem of the violation of Iranian neutrality during the first World War can be dealt with briefly. Certainly if the German and Ottoman General Staffs intended to make a thrust toward Central Asia and India through Iranian territory, tsarist Russia and Great Britain can scarcely be blamed for taking precautions against such an action. The situation is described by Harold Nicolson:

> It is sufficient to state that in the north the Turks were the first to cross the Persian border and were at once countered by Russian troops. Our own [British] intervention in the south was provoked by the disturbances and outrages organized by German residents and agents. The enterprise of such men as Wassmuss, Zugmayer, and Niedermayer; the slow stages by which they suborned the Persian gendarmerie (at that time commanded by Swedish officers) and finally created in Fars and Arabistan a state of civil war; the feats of energy, ingenuity and daring which these men performed; constitute some of the most fascinating pages in the history of the minor operations of

[28] Harold Nicolson, *Curzon: The Last Phase, a Study in Post-War Diplomacy* (London, 1934), p. 83.

[44]

the war. . . . Their propaganda was so efficient that it induced Mustaufi al-Mamalek, the Persian Prime Minister, to sign a treaty promising Germany the full support of the Persian administration. It was so dangerous that it obliged the British government to intervene in Persian affairs, to recruit the "South Persia Rifles" and to send armed forces to occupy Bushire and other points of strategical necessity.[29]

Thus, seemingly, the presence of British troops in Iran during the war could be justified. Great Britain must not necessarily be considered hypocritical if, at the same time, she professed to recognize the independence of Iran.

The close of the war and its immediate aftermath coincided with the revolution in Russia. Again a division of responsibility between the tsarist and British armies on the Mesopotamian and Caucasian front necessarily involved the British in what, at the beginning, seemed to be an action against the Turko-German offensive in this sector. Later, the co-operation between the Germans and the Bolsheviks in Baku and Turkestan once more made British intervention logical. Finally, after the collapse of Germany, Communist propaganda emanating from Moscow and Tashkent was so obviously and aggressively directed against the British Empire that the continuance of operations in Transcaspia, and thus in Iran, seemed to be both logical and necessary. The real test of British intentions in Iran came when the movement for the emancipation of Transcaucasia and Central Asia from Soviet rule collapsed and the British forces were withdrawn from those regions. Would the British insist on staying in Iran and subjecting her to a colonial regime similar to that in India? The reply was in the negative. As early as December, 1918, the British cabinet was in favor of a speedy evacuation of troops from Iran.[30] Lord Curzon, however, as Foreign Secretary, managed to convince his colleagues that an agreement should be concluded with Iran that would assure Britain a predominant position while maintaining Iranian independence.

The result of Curzon's policy was the conclusion, on August 9, 1919, of the Anglo-Iranian Treaty, in virtue of which Great Britain

[29] Nicolson, *op. cit.*, pp. 129–130. Reprinted by permission of the publisher, Harcourt, Brace and Company, Inc.
[30] *Ibid.*, p. 132.

was to become responsible for the organization of the Iranian army and treasury, and a number of British advisers were to assist in the work of various Iranian government departments. Great Britain undertook to grant Iran a loan of two million pounds, to assist her in the construction of railways, and to support Iran's claim for compensation for war damages perpetrated on her territory by non-British belligerents. A committee of experts was to study the revision of the existing customs tariff. Although it left the fabric of Iranian government and society untouched, the treaty was in fact a thinly disguised instrument for a protectorate. For Curzon, in whose political career Iran played a prominent role, it was a personal triumph.

A month after the conclusion of the treaty, the Foreign Secretary spoke at a dinner offered in honor of Prince Firuz Mirza, Iranian Foreign Minister, who visited London. Said Curzon:

Was it not natural that Persia, seeking to establish and stabilize her future, should turn to us? Our boundaries march with hers for hundreds of miles on her southern frontier. For a century we have pacified and policed the Gulf. At Mesopotamia we shall presently be her neighbor on the West. It is an obvious interest to us to have a peaceful and prosperous Persia; and, as regards Persia herself, if it be true—and I do not think the most ardent Persian patriot will deny it—that external assistance of some sort is necessary for her,—is it not natural that it should be to this country that she should turn? [31]

This, however, proved to be wishful thinking.

The treaty constituted the climax of British influence in Iran, and subsequent developments followed the downward trend of Britain's position there. It is true that Ahmed Shah, while paying a visit to England in the fall of 1919, gave his cordial approval to the treaty. It is also true that General Dickson and Armitage Smith started to reorganize the army and the treasury in Iran, respectively, and that a group of engineers arrived from England to make surveys for railway construction. But Iranian nationalist circles were deeply dissatisfied with the treaty. The Majlis, the Iranian parliament, never ratified it, and by the spring of 1921 the new Iranian government of Seyyid Zia ed-Din and Reza Khan officially repudiated the treaty.

[31] Nicolson, *op. cit.*, pp. 139–140. Reprinted by permission of the publisher, Harcourt, Brace and Company, Inc.

The question of British troops in Iran remains. When most of the British detachments were withdrawn from Russia in 1919, British forces in Iran shrank also. In 1920 the Bolshevik landing at Enzeli, of which more will be said later, complicated the problem of evacuation, and the British troops remained in some parts of the country through 1920. After their successful *coup d'état* in February, 1921, Seyyid Zia and Reza Khan appealed to the British not to evacuate their troops for the time being.[32] Yet despite the fact that Soviet troops were by that time on Iranian territory, the last British troops were evacuated in May, 1921. The consolidation of Reza Khan's authority, although he repudiated the Anglo-Iranian Treaty of 1919, was in the British view a welcome development. It signified a step in the right direction, a step toward the assertion of Iranian independence both against British and Soviet influence. Reza Khan's firm dealings with the Russians in the north of the country as well as with various rebellious elements constituted a guarantee that Iran would not become a base for anti-British operations. And that was all that, traditionally, Britain expected from Iran. The problem now was whether Iran would be able to maintain and solidify her neutral position. Nothing short of this would, in the long run, satisfy British policy. The British were ready, after Curzon's overzealous and unsuccessful attempt to establish a protectorate, to revert to their old attitude— that of keeping politically and militarily out of Iran, while trying to secure, through normal channels, economic advantages. The big unknown was the ultimate design of Soviet Russia. Her first moves in Iran seemed to prove that the hands-off attitude adopted by the British was not shared by Moscow.

[32] J. M. Balfour, *Recent Happenings in Persia* (London, 1922), p. 244.

CHAPTER THREE

The First Soviet

Experiment in Iran

THE conquest of the Transcaucasian republics and the forcible subjection of Turkestan to Soviet rule should leave no doubt as to the Communist concept of national self-determination. Yet it might be argued that these areas formerly constituted part of the tsarist Empire and that the Soviet State simply regained what Russia had lost in a moment of weakness. The real test of the Soviet attitude toward the national independence of oriental countries had, therefore, to be sought in the areas situated historically outside of Russia's borders. In this case Iran was to become the first testing ground.

The first official steps of the Soviet State toward Iran were designed to win her friendship. On January 14, 1918, the Soviet government addressed a note to Iran by which it repudiated all tsarist privileges that were contrary to the sovereignty of Iran and promised to assist the Iranians in expelling the British and Turkish troops from their country. It stated that Russia considered the 1907 treaty as no longer binding. The future relations between Russia and Iran were to be based, the note said, "upon a free agreement and mutual respect among nations." [1] Earlier the Brest-Litovsk Armistice Agreement of December 15, 1917, although not involving Iran directly, contained an encouraging note for the Iranians, because Soviet Russia promised to evacuate the troops which had been stationed in Iran by the tsarist government during the war. The final Brest-Litovsk Treaty of March 3, 1918, confirmed this promise in general

[1] Quoted by Dennis, *op. cit.*, p. 238.

[48]

terms.[2] A more detailed definition of Soviet attitude was contained in a longer note sent on June 26, 1919, by Deputy Foreign Commissar Leon Karakhan and delivered by Kolomyitsev, unofficial representative of Moscow in Iran. The note announced that (a) the Iranian debts to tsarist Russia were annulled; (b) the Russian privileged position in the Iranian customs, post, and telegraph administration was to be ended; (c) all Russian public and private concessions in Iran were renounced; (d) the Russian Discount Bank in Iran was to become the property of the Iranian people; (e) all the railroads, harbor equipment, highways, and similar establishments constructed and owned by tsarist Russia were declared Iranian property; and (f) the capitulations were declared null and void.[3]

If the Soviet government counted on Iranian gratitude because of this widely publicized generosity, it made a mistake. The Iranians were ready to receive these gifts, but they believed that they were entitled to compensation for the damages that Iran, as a neutral territory, had incurred during the war. Besides, the reckless abandonment by the new Russia of her privileges and possessions in Iran was, in the Iranian view, not so much a sign of sincere generosity as an obvious sign of Soviet weakness. And weakness is not a factor that, in international relations, produces feelings of friendship. The Iranian government considered that the time had come to reclaim from a weak Russia those territories that Iran had lost in the past to a strong Russia. An Iranian delegation was sent, under Foreign Minister Mushavar ul-Mamalek, to Paris to present claims before the Peace Conference. It was refused admission on the ground that

[2] The respective passages of these two documents run as follows:

(a) The armistice agreement, paragraph X: "Upon the basis of the principle of the freedom, independence, and territorial inviolability of the neutral Persian State, the Turkish and the Russian Supreme Commands are prepared to withdraw their troops from Persia. They will immediately enter into communication with the Persian Government, in order to regulate the details of the evacuation and the other necessary measures for the guaranteeing of the above-mentioned principle."

(b) The treaty, Article VII: "In view of the fact that Persia and Afghanistan are free and independent States, the contracting parties obligate themselves to respect the political and economic independence and the territorial integrity of these States."

[3] Louis Fischer, *The Soviets in World Affairs* (New York, 1930), I, 289.

Iran was not a member of allied and associated nations. Nonetheless, the Iranian delegation formulated far-reaching demands, in which the salient points were the annulment of all foreign concessions; the abolition of capitulations; compensation for wartime damages perpetrated on Iranian territory; and the inclusion within the boundaries of Iran of Transcaspia, Merv, and Khiva up to the Oxus River, of several districts in the Caucasus, including Nakhichevan, and of the Kurdish area of Mesopotamia as far as Euphrates.[4] These claims were ignored, largely owing to British unwillingness to permit Iranian participation in the Peace Conference. The point to remember is that these Iranian demands were directed mainly against what could be termed "Russian territorial integrity." Iran, to be sure, was historically right when she claimed the Caucasian and Transcaspian districts. They had been, truly enough, wrested from her by Russia, mostly during the nineteenth century, and there was no valid reason why these Moslem areas should belong to Russia rather than to Mohammedan Iran. Yet the Iranian element among the native populations was insignificant, and in 1919 the claim could hardly be based on the principle of self-determination. If anything, these regions could be contemplated as independent political units, but not as Iranian appanages.

These acts of the Iranian government, which certainly could not please Russia, did not divert her from a determined policy to establish diplomatic relations with Teheran and to pose as Iran's disinterested and anti-imperialist friend. Negotiations between the two governments took place in the course of 1920 and resulted in reciprocal diplomatic recognition. On November 28, 1920, Theodore A. Rothstein was appointed Soviet Ambassador to Iran. Before he arrived in Teheran in the spring of 1921, the Iranian representative in Moscow signed with the Soviet government, on February 26, 1921, a treaty that put relations between the two countries on a normal footing. The treaty was characteristic of early Soviet diplomatic instruments. It blended in an ingenious way concrete political provisions with propaganda destined to reverberate throughout the Orient. Article II of the treaty declared:

4 For details see *Papers Relating to the Foreign Relations of the United States* (The Paris Peace Conference, 1919), I, 263; also Nicolson, *op. cit.*, p. 135.

The government of the Russian Soviet Federated Socialist Republic brands as criminal the policy of the government of tsarist Russia which, without the agreement of the peoples of Asia and under the guise of assuring the independence of these peoples, concluded with other states of Europe treaties concerning the East which had seizure as their ultimate object. The government of the R.S.F.S.R. unconditionally rejects that criminal policy not only as violating the sovereignty of the States of Asia but also as leading to organized brutal violence of European robbers on the living body of the peoples of the East.[5]

In its concrete provisions the treaty followed closely the earlier note of Karakhan, confirming in detail and by bilateral agreement the hitherto unilateral Soviet declaration. The frontier between two countries was to follow the 1881 line. Each signatory renounced any interference in the other's internal affairs. Each undertook not to tolerate the existence of organizations hostile to the other party in their respective territories. Soviet Russia obtained the right to demand the expulsion of hostile elements from the crews of Iranian vessels on the Caspian Sea. In return Iran obtained the right to maintain a naval force in the Caspian, which earlier treaties with Russia had prohibited. The renunciation of concessions and tsarist property by Soviet Russia was accompanied by the condition that these concessions and property could not be ceded by Iran to any third Power or its citizens. The most important political provision was the one that permitted Russia to send her troops to Iran should Iran become a base for a third party's war on Russia.

The treaty was an important development in Soviet-Iranian relations, but in view of earlier declarations of Moscow it did not constitute any new or sensational act. The real concern of the Iranians was not what Soviet Russia was promising but what she was actually doing in Iran. So Chicherin's statement in February that the Soviet troops would stay in Iran as long as the British remained there had to many an Iranian a more profound meaning than the treaty phraseology.

How was it that Soviet troops were in Iranian territory? We know that after the November, 1917, revolution in Russia the Russian

[5] The full text may be found in A. H. Hamzavi, *Persia and the Powers* (London, 1947).

troops that had been in northwestern Iran were evacuated during 1918. The independence or counterrevolutionary movements in Transcaucasia and Transcaspia created, for some time, a protective belt between Iran and Russia. During 1919 British but not Russian troops were in Iran. In 1920, however, Soviet troops reappeared on Iranian territory. This was due to the collapse of free Azerbaijan and to the rout of the counterrevolutionary armies of General Denikin in southern Russia. Beaten in the spring of 1920, the remnants of Denikin's forces fell back into Azerbaijan and some ships of his flotilla anchored in Baku. The Red Army, pursuing the Whites, invaded Azerbaijan in April and, as mentioned earlier, put an end to the independence of the Republic. The remaining White forces embarked on ships at Baku and escaped to the Iranian port of Enzeli (Pahlavi), with the Red fleet, commanded by Raskolnikov, on their heels. The Whites encamped at Enzeli under British protection. The Red flotilla on May 18 opened fire on the British and White Russian vessels in the port and bombarded British land installations. The British commander, General Champain, entered into a parley with Raskolnikov, who declared that the Soviets were not fighting against the British nor against the Iranians but were trying only to recapture the White fleet and troops. When the British liaison officer stated that the White troops were in a neutral territory and, being disarmed and interned, could not be extradited, Raskolnikov answered: "It is not the prisoners of war that we claim, but the rebels who have provoked internal disorders in Russia." [6] Eventually the British, too weak in numbers and equipment to offer serious resistance, withdrew to Qazvin and later, following a general policy, withdrew from Iran altogether. The Red Army units disembarked in Enzeli.

Soon a Soviet expeditionary force was in occupation of the whole province of Gilan. It was composed of regular Red Army units, of sailors from Kronstadt, of Communist Azerbaijani troops, and of armed Iranian workers formerly employed in the Baku harbor. Teheran protested against this violation of Iranian territorial in-

[6] A description of these events in greater detail and the quotation may be found in "La Politique du gouvernement des Soviets en Perse," by Georges Ducrocq, *Revue du monde musulman*, Dec., 1922, pp. 84–180.

tegrity both in Moscow and before the League of Nations but to no avail. Moscow replied and persistently maintained that the occupation of Gilan was only a security measure undertaken by the Soviet Republic of Azerbaijan on whose actions the government of Soviet Russia had no influence.[7] This claim was alleged at the time when preparations were being made for the convocation of the First Congress of the Peoples of the East in the freshly sovietized Baku.

Moscow's policy of pretending that the conquered border regions had not lost their independence but on the contrary had gained it after their capture by the Red Army was especially evident in the case of Azerbaijan. The Soviet Republic of Azerbaijan entered into separate diplomatic relations with Estonia, Afghanistan, Turkey, and Iran. On May 30, 1921, the Teheran government issued a note granting diplomatic recognition to Azerbaijan. This was followed by the dispatch of an Iranian mission to Baku to negotiate the establishment of diplomatic and commercial relations between the two countries. As a result, one Behbud Chakhahtinski was appointed Minister of Azerbaijan in Teheran.[8] The whole story was the application in practice of the Communist theory about the "highest form of Soviet autonomy" so that Soviet Azerbaijan might display its perfect right to enter into "contractual relations" with other countries. The fact that Soviet Azerbaijan possessed a diplomatic representative in Iran, a country that has a province also called Azerbaijan, was not without its ominous significance.

For the time being, however, the Iranians were more worried about the immediate issues in Gilan, where the Soviet occupation was taking a new turn. As soon as the Soviet troops disembarked at Enzeli, they established contact with the Iranian chieftain Kuchik Khan, who since 1917 had been in a state of open rebellion against the central government of Iran and whose control of the forest-rich province of Gilan had initially caused some trouble to the "Dunsterforce" in 1918. The British throughout 1919 had managed to maintain a state of armed neutrality between their own troops and the bands of Kuchik Khan and had thus avoided an open breach, which would have complicated their operations in Iran's Caspian provinces.

[7] *Ibid.*
[8] Castagné, *op. cit.*, pp. 111 ff.

Meanwhile Kuchik Khan's movement had been entirely dedicated to the overthrow of the existing Iranian government and to radical social change. It was, therefore, not only a sharp manifestation of popular discontent based on traditional Iranian social ills, but also a natural ally for the Soviet troops. A brief outline of its development may be helpful for an understanding of events that occurred after the landing of the Red Army.

KUCHIK KHAN'S REBELLION

As early as 1915 Mirza Kuchik Khan, Ekhsanulla Khan, and a number of other progressively minded middle-class Iranians elaborated a program of reform for the Iranian state at a meeting held in Teheran. The program was directed against the prevailing reactionary system in the country and against the nefarious influence of foreigners in the affairs of Iran. Taking the program very seriously, Kuchik and Ekhsanulla eventually started agitation among the peasantry of Gilan province and by 1917 found themselves heading an open rebellion of Jangalis (inhabitants of Gilan, "jungle") against both the government and the British influence in Iran. In the course of that year a revolutionary committee, called *Ittihad-i-Islam* ("Unity of Islam"), was formed by them under the slogan of freedom from foreign influence and the independence of Iran under the banner of Islam. Headed by Mirza Kuchik Khan, it was composed of Ekhsanulla Khan and a few other men, all of whom were either merchants or petty landed gentry. Their program was, above everything, nationalistic; Ekhsanulla Khan represented the most radical tendency, inclining toward socialism. The committee engaged as instructors of its armed forces a number of German and Turkish officers, among whom von Pachen acted as a close military adviser to Kuchik Khan. These Germans and Turks had come from Kermanshah. With Kuchik's forces were also some Austrians who had escaped from Russian prisoner-of-war camps at Baku and in Transcaspia. The Russian November Revolution added to the impetus of the Jangali movement, and Ekhsanulla Khan insisted that the element of class struggle should be stressed. The year 1918 was passed in strengthening Kuchik's hold on Gilan and in intensified agitation among the local population. A newspaper, *Jangal,* was printed as the organ of the committee. The movement expanded to Mazanderan, Astarā-bad, and other Caspian regions. The Jangalis managed to capture a few Britons, among them Captain Noel, an intelligence officer who was on his way back from Baku, as well as the British Consul in Resht, MacLaren, and the manager of the British bank there, Oak-shot. The latter two were captured in a reprisal for the arrest by the British of the Iranian socialist leader Suleiman Mirza, who had been sent to London. All these men were kept as hostages.

Kuchik Khan's movement was financed by extorting ransom from Gilan landowners. "We widely practiced the system of taking hostages," wrote Ekhsanulla Khan in his memoirs.[9] "Taking any wealthy squire, feudal lord or entrepreneur, we would demand the sum of five thousand to one hundred thousand tomans under the threat of putting them in jail. If the demand sum was not paid, we deported the debtor till he would pay us." The Jangalis established contact with the Enzeli Revolutionary Committee, which had been created by the soldiers and sailors of the demoralized Russian troops who throughout 1918 were being evacuated from Iran. In July, 1918, British troops under General Dunsterville passed through Gilan on their way to Enzeli and Baku, yet, except for a skirmish at the Menjil Defile northwest of Teheran, no major battle took place between them and the rebels. This passage of troops, which manifested British strength and determination to prevent the Bolsheviks from seizing Baku, brought confusion to the members of Kuchik Khan's committee. Some of them insisted that peace should be made with the British. As a result of their pressure and over the opposition of Ekhsanulla Khan, in August, 1918, an agreement was made between Kuchik Khan and the British by which the latter recognized his authority in Gilan and even his right to appoint the governor of Resht. In return, Kuchik promised to suspend hostilities against the British, to expel his German and Turkish military instructors, and to release Captain Noel. (Consul MacLaren and Mr. Oakshot had been released earlier.) This deal was very convenient for the British because it made safe their line of communications between Mesopotamia and the Caspian. Moreover, the more conservative members of

---

[9] R. Abikh, "Natsionalnoye i Revolutsionnoye Dvizhennye v Persyi (Vospominannia Ekhsan-Ully-Khana)," *Novy Vostok*, XXIX, 106.

the Kuchik committee began a lucrative trade in rice with the British. These developments produced a definite split between the left and right wings of the committee and weakened the whole movement so much that by the summer of 1919 Jangali forces were dispersed by 20,000 fresh government troops. Kuchik and Ekhsanulla escaped to the woods of Gilan. Thus ended the first act of the rebellion.

The next few months were devoted to making contact with the Bolsheviks. Both Jangali leaders came to the conclusion that the revival and further success of the Gilan revolution would depend upon the degree of assistance from Soviet Russia. Following this line, Kuchik Khan went to Lankoran, a province of Russian Azerbaijan. There he learned that Kolomyitsev, the unofficial Soviet representative in Teheran who had been obliged to flee from Iran, was trying on his own initiative to get in touch with the Jangalis. The two failed to meet, however, owing to the rout that the Bolsheviks suffered at the hands of the Mussavatists in the Mughan steppe. Eventually contact was established through secret emissaries. In the fall of 1919, at the time that the British decided to withdraw from the Caucasus and to retreat from Iran, Kuchik Khan rallied some of his dispersed forces and reorganized his committee.[10] The winter of 1919–1920 witnessed a revival of the movement.

In the early spring of 1920 the Jangalis received a letter from a Bolshevik commander in the Caucasus informing them that the Bolsheviks would soon capture Baku. Evidently the Soviet forces were seeking closer liaison with Iranian rebels in anticipation of their invasion of Iran. The letter was followed by the dispatch of a special emissary. "In the night of May 17," wrote Ekhsanulla, "a Russian comrade came to the forest and revealed that in a few days the Bolsheviks would come to Enzeli." This proved true. On the morning of May 18 the Red fleet appeared before Enzeli and opened fire on the British fortifications. Despite his earlier resolution to seek the support of the Bolsheviks, Kuchik Khan experienced at that fateful moment some doubts. On the day of the appearance of the Soviet fleet he spent a long time in meditation and prayer. (He had had, originally, an ecclesiastical rank in the Moslem hierarchy.) Ekhsa-

10 The members of this new committee were Kuchik Khan, Hasan Khan, Khalu-Qurban, Ghulam Ali-Baba, and Ekhsanulla Khan.

nulla Khan, always an extremist, who was perturbed by the religious fervor of his colleague and chief, interrupted his meditations and advised him to "forget religion" if he wanted to be on friendly terms with the Bolsheviks. Eventually Kuchik Khan met Raskolnikov, commander of the Soviet troops that disembarked at Enzeli. Forcing the British to withdraw, the Red forces promptly occupied Resht, while Soviet political agents concentrated their attention on Kuchik Khan and his movement. Without much delay a meeting took place in Resht, during which the Soviet Republic of Gilan was proclaimed. Kuchik dispatched a telegram to Lenin in which he expressed his faith in Soviet-Iranian friendship and the "ideal system of the Third International." [11]

In addition to Kuchik and Ekhsanulla, the new Soviet had as prominent leaders Khalu Qurban and Hasan Khan. Raskolnikov brought in Ja'afar Pishevari to take charge of the Gilan Commissariat of Interior. The old Tabriz revolutionary, Haidar Khan, also joined the

---

[11] The text of the telegram, as quoted by Abikh, was as follows:
"To Comrade Lenin, R.S.F.S.R.

"We greet you and all your comrades at the time of your brilliant successes achieved against the enemies of socialism. We, Persian revolutionaries, have for a long time cherished the same hope, fighting against the evil and the hated English and Persian oppressors. Now is fulfilled the long-expected and happy act of the formation of the Persian Socialist Soviet Republic, which we proclaim before all the world. We consider it to be our duty to draw your attention to the fact that there are a number of criminals on Persian territory: Persian oppressors, English traders, and diplomats supported by English troops. As long as these enemies of the Persian people are in Persia, they will prove to be an obstacle to the introduction of our just system all over our country. In the name of humanity and the equality of all nations the Persian Socialist Soviet Republic asks you and all the socialists belonging to the Third International for help in liberating us and all weak and oppressed nations from the yoke of Persian and English oppressors. Bearing in mind the establishment of brotherly union and full unanimity between us, we expect from the free Russian nation the assistance that may prove indispensable for the stabilization of the Persian Socialist Soviet Republic. Mindful that all nations liberated from the yoke of capitalism should be united into one brotherly union, we request you to include in this union the hearts of the Persian nation, liberated from a centuries-long yoke, so that our holy revolution may be fulfilled till the end.

"We have a firm faith that all the world will be governed by one ideal system of the Third International.

"Representative of the Persian Socialist Soviet Republic proclaimed in the city of Resht: Mirza Kuchik."

Soviet. Several Russians acted as advisers or as outright executives, among them Jacob Blumkin, famous for his assassination of the German Ambassador in Moscow,[12] and Commissar Abrahamov, who installed himself at Resht, ousted the Iranian governor of the city, and issued inflammatory proclamations to the population.

The new regime started a reign of terror that was directed primarily against big landowners. Their estates were confiscated and distributed among the peasants. At the same time, the work of the political organization of the masses was undertaken, a soviet of peasants being the form of local government promoted throughout the area. In this undertaking, however, the new rulers of Gilan met with disappointment: while ready to grab the land which was offered, the Iranian peasantry was apathetic to any new experimentation.[13]

The revolutionary government extended its influence to the province of Mazanderan as well. As time went on, the pro-Soviet elements asserted themselves openly in the midst of Kuchik's movement. On one occasion Ekhsanulla Khan addressed a "spontaneous" appeal to Narimanov, Chairman of the Council of Commissars of the Soviet Republic of Azerbaijan in Baku. The telegram is illustrative of the prevailing trends: "The laboring masses of Mazanderan appeal to the Soviet Republics. The population of Mazanderan awaits the help of the Third International. . . . Long Live the World's Revolution. Long Live the Third International." [14]

The Gilan Soviet was in control of the Caspian provinces for about a year and a half, from the spring of 1920 till the fall of 1921. In its later stages internal dissensions broke out within its ranks, owing to differences between Kuchik Khan, who was always something of a moderate, and the outright Communists. This schism led eventually

---

[12] Barmine, *op. cit.*, p. 110.

[13] Iransky in his "Russko-Persitskiye Otnoshenia za Piat Let" (*Novy Vostok*, IV, 218) states: "In view of the backwardness and apathy of the Persian peasantry it [the revolutionary movement in Gilan] did not find response among them. . . . Having played its historical role, this movement, left to its own devices, lost its historical sense of mission and began to disintegrate internally." By employing the phrase "its own devices" Iransky undoubtedly alludes to the withdrawal of Soviet forces from Iran in September, 1921, which removed the necessary military and ideological support from Kuchik Khan's rebellion.

[14] Quoted in Ducrocq, *op. cit.*

in October, 1921, to the arrest and execution of Haidar Khan by Kuchik Khan. The latter, while ready to distribute land evenly among the people, was unwilling to deprive former owners of their possessions completely and in the name of justice advocated the restoration of parts of confiscated estates. Yet, despite these differences, the extreme point of view triumphed wherever Soviet troops and agents were present. Besides, Kuchik Khan owed much to the Russians: their arms and instructors permitted him to continue in control of Gilan even though at the same time they limited his freedom of action. The Iranian government viewed these events with great concern, because the presence of Soviet troops in the area signified something more than a military occupation as a safeguard against possible new British intervention. The Bolsheviks were bent upon the forcible change of the economic and social structure of Iran's Caspian provinces, and the hasty proclamation of Soviet institutions did not augur well for a speedy evacuation of Soviet troops. Moreover, it was difficult even to discuss these matters with Moscow owing to its stubborn pretense that the blame, if any, should be put on "independent" Soviet Azerbaijan. The conclusion of the Soviet-Iranian Treaty in February, 1921, did not influence the Gilan situation immediately. Unfortunately for Iran, the British, who had long before resolved to quit that country, were slow in removing their few remaining troops and did not withdraw their last detachments until May, 1921. The British delay gave the Bolsheviks an excuse to continue their rule around the Caspian. Even the withdrawal of British troops did not bring any direct easing of the situation, and in June, 1921, Kuchik Khan's forces, reinforced by some Soviet elements from Georgia, began to march on Teheran. As late as July new Soviet contingents landed at Enzeli. The Iranian Cossack Division was trying to hold the rebel and Soviet forces in check. Ultimately, following repeated Iranian protests, Soviet troops were withdrawn on September 8, 1921. Then the Iranian army could proceed, unimpeded, to restore order in Gilan. The energetic leadership of Reza Khan gave the army the impetus that it had so sadly lacked in wartime; by October the rebellion of Kuchik Khan was brought to an end. Kuchik himself was captured and executed; his head was brought to Teheran. The whole Jangali episode ended ignominiously and proved once again that, with a strong central government in Teheran, autonomist or separatist movements in Iran could thrive only so long as they obtained foreign assistance.

Why was it that the Soviet government decided finally to evacuate its troops and to abandon its willing puppet, Kuchik Khan? One reply may be that it did so because it no longer needed to fear the British troops, which by that time had been withdrawn. But that reply does not explain everything, especially since British detachments had already left Iran before the renewed Soviet landings at Enzeli in July. A better explanation seems to be that the withdrawal of Soviet troops was the ultimate test of the sincerity of the Soviet-Iranian Treaty. If the treaty was conceived mainly as a propaganda instrument for the Bolsheviks—and we know that this was so, because of the wide distribution of the text all over the Orient by Soviet agents—then it was wiser not to provoke an open breach with Iran. After the withdrawal of British troops Iran was in a position to claim that she was now the victim of the new Soviet imperialism. Russia had to choose between two methods: either the cultivation of good relations with the central government and the gradual infiltration of Iran with Communist propaganda through the Soviet Embassy in Teheran or highhanded direct action aiming at the sovietization and detachment of several Iranian provinces in connivance with discontented elements of Iran. By the autumn of 1921 Moscow apparently came to the conclusion that the first method would better suit its purposes. Accordingly the Red Army left, but the Red Ambassador, Rothstein, remained. Besides, even the adoption of an outwardly correct line toward the government of Iran did not necessarily mean the complete abandonment of attempts to gain control of Iran's northern border areas. But this enterprise need not be undertaken in such a conspicuously direct way as it had been in Gilan.

AZERBAIJAN SEPARATISM AND THE KHORASAN EPISODE

Events in the Iranian province of Azerbaijan and in Khorasan were very instructive on Soviet tactics toward an Eastern country with which, on the surface, correct if not cordial relations existed. Early in

1920 a revolt against the central government broke out in Tabriz, the capital of Iranian Azerbaijan. It was organized by Sheikh Mohammed Khiaban. Khiaban, formerly a deputy to the Majlis, had emigrated to the Caucasus in 1911 and there established contacts with Russian revolutionaries. In 1914 he returned to Tabriz and started underground activity with the aim of liberating Iran from foreign influences. Various radical elements rallied around him. His work was interrupted by the Turkish invasion of Azerbaijan during the war, which resulted in his temporary arrest and confinement in Kars. Released, he returned to Tabriz; and after the end of the war before the authority of the Iranian government was adequately restored in Azerbaijan, he gathered together 800 armed partisans and struck. His political organization was called the National Democratic party. Khiaban's forces disarmed government troops, jailing most of the Iranian officers except those who came over to his side. The Iranian gendarmerie joined the rebels, and the revolt soon spread to the provincial cities of Azerbaijan. Khiaban, who had once been a *mujtahid* (a religious rank), possessed oratorical talents and displayed vigorous political activity. In addressing mass meetings, he demanded a basic transformation of the Iranian state system. Speaking about freedom, better morals, and greater educational facilities, Khiaban asked for a new regime, which in his opinion should be republican. His party's chief organ *Tajaddod* ("Renaissance") printed his speeches and echoed his demands for radical reforms. Struggling against the "reactionary" central government of Vossuq ed-Dowleh, Khiaban and his National Democrats were, in fact, fighting against the British influence in Iran, as Vossuq was the chief architect of the Anglo-Iranian treaty of 1919.[15] As a result, the province of Azerbaijan was separated from the rest of Iran and assumed the name of Azadistan ("Country of Freedom"). To Soviet Russia these developments were of great interest and importance, especially since Soviet troops simultaneously landed at Enzeli and joined hands with Kuchik Khan. There was a strong temptation to establish contact with the

---

[15] The Iranian delegation that negotiated the treaty was composed of Vossuq ed-Dowleh, Prime Minister; Akbar Mirza Sarem ed-Dowleh; Firuz Mirza; and Nosrat ed-Dowleh. Later the members of this delegation were accused of having accepted a bribe from the British.

[61]

Tabriz separatists and, by one bold stroke, secure Iran's Caspian provinces for the Soviet Republic. Consequently the Bolshevik forces operating in Gilan turned toward the town of Zanjan, ready to invade Iranian Azerbaijan. At that moment, however, to the disappointment of Soviet leaders, the Azerbaijan separatists did not prove co-operative. The National Democrats in Tabriz, instead of joining hands with the Bolsheviks, declared that they disapproved of Soviet landings at Enzeli and, in a sudden upsurge of patriotism, denounced the pact that had been concluded between the Russians and Kuchik Khan. Toward the end of July a dramatic episode almost brought the Soviet troops into the Iranian Azerbaijan: the remnants of the first Tatar Regiment of the free Republic of Azerbaijan crossed the border of Iranian Azerbaijan to find refuge from the Bolsheviks. The regiment had been stationed in the south of the Republic when Soviet rule was set up in Baku in April, 1920, and eventually accepted the change of regime. Soviet atrocities, however, perpetrated on the Tatar population of Elizabethpol caused the regiment to revolt and to wage hopeless warfare against the numerically superior Bolshevik forces sent from Baku. Eventually the regiment crossed the Aras River and found shelter in Iran. Its commander, Colonel Sofiev, became the guest of the Kurdish Khan of Maku, a chieftain wielding uncontested influence over his district. The Soviet troops did not pursue the Tatars any farther. The "Azadistan" experiment was, in any case, nearing its end, and stronger contingents of the Iranian government's forces arrived on the scene. Governor of Azerbaijan Mokhbar as-Saltaneh, freshly appointed to that post by the new cabinet of Moshir ed-Dowleh, started energetic negotiations with the rebels, soon to be followed by military action. By the middle of September the Iranian Cossack Brigade dispersed the National Democrat forces. Khiaban himself was killed on the fourteenth of that month. The restoration of order and authority by the central government prevented any further direct action by Soviet forces, unless the Soviet government was resolved to repeat the Gilan experiment in Azerbaijan. This was not, however, the case. Instead of direct action, Moscow preferred to play on the local nationalist feelings of the Turko-Tatar Azerbaijani population, exploiting any manifestation of discontent against the central government. Strangely enough these dealings with potential separatists were parallel to the activity of the German Consul in Tabriz, Wüstrow, who also conducted anti-Teheran propaganda in the provinces.

The latent separatist agitation gave rise, two years later, to a new outbreak in Azerbaijan. In February, 1922, the followers of the late Khiaban, calling themselves "partisans of freedom" and "enemies of despotism," rose in revolt. This time their leader was Lakhuti Khan, an officer of the Iranian gendarmerie. Lakhuti had a personal quarrel with the Governor of Azerbaijan and a professional distaste for the rival Iranian Cossacks. The loyalty record of the gendarmes in Azerbaijan was dubious, if one considers their attitude during the Khiaban revolt in 1920. Their social structure and material condition compared unfavorably with that of the traditionally proroyalist Cossacks; hence it was not difficult for their leader to stir them into open defiance of the government. The gendarmes quickly established themselves as military masters of Tabriz, arrested the Governor, and demanded that the government pay them their much-delayed salaries. They also asked for the dismissal of Reza Khan, the Commander-in-Chief of the Army. While these demands were being formulated, the leadership of the rebellion passed into the hands of the left-wing elements, organized into a "Democratic Committee." The slogans and program of the committee resembled those of Khiaban's National Democrats two years earlier, though they were, perhaps, more radical and more socialist in character. Mass meetings were held and demands for the "democratization" of the Iranian state system were made. Reza Khan, on whom the main responsibility of maintaining order fell, refused to grant the insurgents any concessions and resolved to finish with this, as he called it, "new Khorasan." Upon his orders reinforced Cossack forces surrounded Tabriz and conquered it in February, 1922. Lakhuti Khan and a group of his aides escaped from the city, but a number of "Democrats" were either killed or imprisoned.

Novy Vostok, a semiofficial Soviet publication, commenting on the events in Azerbaijan, analyzed rather wistfully the reasons for the rebels' lack of success. The leadership of the revolt, it said, made a mistake in not going outside Tabriz, where it could have had the support of a gendarmerie force of three thousand, who were at that

[63]

time busy with the rebellious Kurds but who would certainly have joined the rebellion if junction had been effected. But a more fundamental cause of the failure of both Tabriz revolts was to be sought in their very character: the leadership was not well organized; there was too much discussion among the leaders. The lack of clarity of aims and ideals and also of discipline brought too much confusion, while an exaggerated weight attached to one or another personality, so characteristic of oriental ways, jeopardized the chances of success. On the other hand, the independent artisan type predominated in the rebel ranks. They lacked, therefore, the political and social consciousness of the industrial proletariat and their revolutionary impetus was blunted.[16] This criticism, so typically Marxist, was not unfounded. Moscow had hoped for better results, but the result was a fiasco. One had to draw proper conclusions and avoid the same mistakes in the future.

Reference was earlier made to the "new Khorasan." It is not difficult to see why Reza Khan disliked the idea of having to deal in Azerbaijan with a situation similar to the one in Khorasan. Since 1920 the latter province had been a scene of serious disorder engineered by the Bolsheviks. The capture of Ashkhabad in the fall of 1919, and later of the whole of Transcaspia, was followed by Soviet infiltration, after March, 1920, into the Iranian province of Khorasan. No direct invasion by the Red Army took place, but the stratagem of using a local puppet chieftain was resorted to. This time the choice fell on a Kurdish chief, Khuda Verdi Sardar, whom the Russians instigated to start a revolt against the Iranians. If his insurrection succeeded, he was then to invite the Red Army to assist him. Large-scale smuggling of arms was undertaken across the frontier, encouraging Khuda Verdi Sardar to conceive grandiose plans for the establishment of his "independent" state. Without Soviet support the movement could not hope to gain a foothold in Khorasan, as the Kurds there constitute an insignificant minority; the most they can do is to molest Iranian authorities by raiding roads and villages. Such an ambitious scheme of attaining independence or even autonomy

16 See A. Vishnegradova, "The Revolutionary Movement in Persian Azerbaijan," *Novy Vostok*, II (1922), 249 ff.

for the Kurds in this area would be unthinkable in normal circumstances. By 1921 the movement collapsed, as the Ashkhabad Soviet showed less and less zeal in sponsoring it.[17]

THE ROTHSTEIN MISSION

During the Soviet-Iranian negotiations for the conclusion of a treaty Leon Karakhan, Soviet Deputy Commissar for Foreign Affairs, informed the Iranian government on November 28, 1920 of the appointment of Theodore A. Rothstein as Soviet envoy to Iran. This announcement was followed by an exchange of notes between Russia and Iran concerning the evacuation of Soviet troops, and on January 22, 1921, Karakhan made the Red Army evacuation dependent upon the evacuation of British troops. In the first quarter of that year British troops were moving out of Iran; hence when Rothstein arrived at the Iranian border in March, Soviet troops were virtually the only foreign ones stationed in large numbers on Iranian soil. Rothstein was stopped at the frontier. The Iranian government, headed by Seyyid Zia ed-Din, dispatched a telegram to Moscow, informing it that a diplomatic visa for the envoy would be issued only if Soviet troops were evacuated from Iran. Rothstein and Moscow protested, stating that the Iranian attitude violated the Soviet-Iranian Treaty of February 26, 1921. A deadlock resulted, and it was only on April 24 that Rothstein was permitted to proceed to Teheran.

Soon after his arrival Rothstein, a former editor of the *Manchester Guardian,* set up an elaborate apparatus of propaganda. Soviet films were distributed gratis to Teheran's movie theaters. A Russian school, which had previously existed in Teheran, was reopened and staffed with Communist teachers. The press, however, became the object of Rothstein's special attentions. Receiving dispatches from Moscow through the short-wave receiving set at the Legation, the envoy distributed daily news communiqués to Iranian papers. Under his influence a number of new papers and periodicals were started. Before Rothstein's arrival only two papers had been published in Teheran, *Iran* and *Ra'd* ("The Thunder"), the latter being the organ of Zia

[17] A more detailed description of this episode is contained in Blacker, *op. cit.,* pp. 265 ff.

ed-Din. Now more than a score of papers appeared, most of them conspicuous for their xenophobia and strongly anti-British attitude. In their avowed political programs they ranged through a multitude of shades, from light pink to outright red.[18] Even a few conservative papers accepted and printed Soviet communiqués, while the openly Communist *Haqiqat* ("Truth") and *Eqdam* ("Advance") incited the working masses and the youth of Iran, respectively, against the ruling classes, the aristocracy, and capitalism. The style of the articles, their themes, and the type of invectives in most of these papers betrayed a common source of inspiration. The violence of the anti-British articles caused quite a few diplomatic incidents between the government and the offended British Minister in Teheran. As a result of the latter's protests, *Setareh Iran, Tufan,* and *Haqiqat* were temporarily suspended. This, however, only gave Rothstein an excuse for further intervention and display of a "liberal" spirit. He gave asylum to the editors of these papers in the Soviet Legation and intervened with the Iranian government in favor of the freedom of the press, guaranteed by the Constitution of 1907.[19] To add weight to his words, the Communist-inspired union of typographical workers went on strike, and the Communist faction of the Majlis strongly demanded from the government the cancellation of the suspension order. After about two and a half months of struggle, the government gave up and on September 9, 1922, permitted the reissue of the suspended papers. This victory was exalted by the Soviet expert on Iran, Vladimir Ossetrov, when he wrote in *Novy Vostok:*

The victory of the journalists is decisive for Persia. The struggle linked all the dispersed forces and laid the foundations for cordial reciprocal relations between the editors, the workers, and the owners of printing presses. Another difficult victory to be attained by the Persian press is the elevation of its moral and political level, the attainment of its full freedom of opinions, founded on economic independence, and the struggle against the existing methods of political venality, from which only one part of the press, progressive, democratic, and socialist, has succeeded in emancipating itself.[20]

[18] A detailed list and description of the newspapers and periodicals that appeared in 1921–1922 may be found in Ducrocq, *op. cit.*

[19] *Novy Vostok,* II (1922), 627 ff.

[20] *Ibid.,* p. 629.

[66]

Rothstein's behavior, cunning and arrogant, and his unceasing intrigue against the existing system in Iran, provoked incidents with the Iranian government. It was with a sigh of relief that the Iranians heard of his recall, after a year and a half in Teheran, by Moscow.

His successor, Boris Shumiatsky, although of different temperament, did not discontinue Rothstein's activities. This unceasing propaganda, partly directed against Iranian institutions, but mainly against British imperialism, eventually caused Lord Curzon, British Foreign Secretary, to make a vigorous protest in Moscow. On May 2, 1923, a ten-day ultimatum was addressed by the British government to Russia. Its main theme was the anti-British activities of Soviet agents in Iran, Afghanistan, and India. Raskolnikov, who by that time had become Soviet Minister in Afghanistan, and Shumiatsky in Teheran were the particular targets of British bad temper. The ultimatum contained texts of the dispatches that these two men were sending to Moscow. Raskolnikov was accused of fomenting trouble in the Northwestern Frontier Province of India and his communication to the Soviet government asking for three thousand rubles and ten boxes of cartridges to aid the rebellious elements in Waziristan was quoted in extenso. As to Shumiatsky, the note said: "The Government of His Majesty knows exactly the sums that the Russian Government sent him from time to time and which were in great part destined to foment anti-British intrigues. . . ." Then Curzon quoted the following dispatch of Shumiatsky sent in February, 1923, to the People's Commissariat for Foreign Affairs:

Our mission, in putting into practice the instructions indicated in your telegram, has decided to follow those political directives especially in northern Persia and in Teheran. There has been organized a good group of propagandists who will be able to develop a really effective anti-British action. If the Commissariat for Foreign Affairs approve the program of the mission, it will be necessary to have for the initial expenses 300,000 tomans . . . of credit to begin the work.[21]

An impressive number of other documents proving Soviet smug-

21 *British Blue Book: A Selection of Papers Dealing with the Relations between His Majesty's Government and the Soviet Government, 1921–1927* (London, 1927), Cmd 2895.

gling of arms to India, Moscow's sponsorship of the Hindu Revolutionary Committee, and the reception by the Indian Communist party of subsidies from the Comintern were also mentioned. The ultimatum demanded a repudiation of, and an apology for, these acts by the Soviet government and the recall of guilty officials. It accused the Soviet Union of violating the nonpropaganda clause of the Soviet-British Trade Agreement of 1921 and set a ten-day time limit for Soviet compliance. The ultimatum, which reached Moscow on May 8, brought a reply within five days. The Soviet reply was generally conciliatory and satisfied British demands with regard to the compensation of some British families who had lost relatives in Russia in the postwar period, as well as on some other points. On the score of propaganda in Central Asia, however, the Soviet note was evasive. It did not deny outright the authenticity of the documents cited by the British, but it pointed out that "similar material is at the disposal of all governments, and if they use them for creating conflicts and as a foundation for protests, then friendly relations between any two governments could hardly exist." [22] It also tried to put blame on the British for similar anti-Soviet activities undertaken by Great Britain in the Caucasus and Transcaspia during the period of civil war and intervention in Russia.

The Soviet note was generally well received in England, as it proved that firm British policy, with the threat of economic boycott of the Soviets, was apt to produce changes in the Soviet attitude. But still the propaganda issue remained unsolved, and the British government, in further correspondence, pressed Moscow for a definite pledge in this respect. The exchange of notes on this subject between the two governments lasted till June 13, 1923, and eventually produced the signing of an additional agreement concerning the renunciation of hostile propaganda by both countries, an agreement which contained more precise definitions than the original nonpropaganda pledge of the Trade Agreement. As a result, Moscow recalled Raskolnikov from Afghanistan but retained Shumiatsky in Iran. Curzon congratulated himself in a letter to Lord Crewe about his success: "I think I may claim to have won a considerable victory

[22] *Ibid.*

over the Soviet government, and I expect them to behave with more circumspection for some time to come." [23]

Thus in the summer of 1923 it seemed that, with British intervention in Russia a matter of the past and with Soviet renunciation a hostile propaganda just announced, the foundations had been laid for a more durable peace in the Middle East. Yet the peace was only superficial. The causes of Anglo-Soviet hostility had not been removed and could not be as long as Great Britain was an empire-owning country and Soviet leaders believed in Marxism. Soviet ideological expansionism and the spirit of proselytism could not be suppressed by a diplomatic pledge given to solve an immediate difficulty. Several factors came into play that caused the period between 1923 and 1941 in the Middle East, and in Iran in particular, to be an armed truce rather than genuine peace.

[23] Quoted in Fischer, *op. cit.*, I, 448.

CHAPTER FOUR

A Period of Armed Truce

Fᴵⱽᴱ days before the conclusion of the Soviet-Iranian Treaty of February, 1921, a bloodless *coup d'état* was engineered by two men. One of them, Seyyid Zia ed-Din (Taba-Tabai), was a young politician in his early thirties, imbued with liberal reformist ideas. As editor of the Teheran newspaper *Ra'd,* he was in frequent contact with the British Legation. This led some to suspect that he had sold himself to the British; such a violently anti-British observer of Iranian affairs as M. Lesueur called him the "damned soul of the British Legation." [1] Others, like James Balfour, whose controversial book about Iran led to a lawsuit and its subsequent withdrawal from sale, believed that Zia ed-Din was an honest reformer as distinguished from pro-British reactionaries. Balfour called Zia's party a "party of legitimate reform, which had looked towards England for at least moral support in their struggle for freedom." [2] Zia ed-Din was the political leader of the coup; the military leadership was in the hands of Reza Khan. The latter was the commander of the Iranian Cossack Division, a military formation initially under tsarist Russian influence, from which White Russian officers were removed in October, 1920. Upon the successful completion of the coup Reza Khan was appointed Commander-in-Chief of the Army. In this capacity he exerted powerful influence upon public affairs.

The first official act of Seyyid Zia's government was the conclusion of the Soviet-Iranian treaty on February 26. The making of the treaty was not Seyyid Zia's achievement because negotiations between the two countries began in 1920 under Moshir ed-Dowleh's premiership

[1] *Les Anglais en Perse* (Paris, 1923).
[2] *Op. cit.,* p. 255.

and were conducted in Moscow. It was, however, within the power of Zia ed-Din to cancel or suspend the negotiations. His failure to use this power testifies to his readiness to re-establish normal relations with the northern neighbor. The next official act of his government was to repudiate the Anglo-Iranian Agreement of 1919 as not binding upon Iran because of the failure of the Majlis to ratify it. As Zia ed-Din put it, the agreement "has disappeared." Again it may be said that the repudiation was not his achievement, but rather the work of the nationalistically minded cabinet of Moshir ed-Dowleh; accordingly Zia was only reaping the fruit of the nationalist victory over British ambitions. The fact remains, however, that it was he who officially sealed the fate of the unpopular agreement by declaring the whole matter closed so far as Iran was concerned.

These two steps looked outwardly as if Zia were in favor of closer relations with Russia than with Britain. This was not the case, however. Zia ed-Din was not in favor of Communism, and his lengthy stay in the Caucasus during the revolutionary developments there did not make him an enthusiast of the Soviet regime. On the contrary there are good reasons to believe that Balfour's opinion about his mildly pro-British orientation was right, at least at the time to which Balfour refers. Nationalist above everything else, Zia ed-Din was the author of the refusal to permit the Soviet envoy Rothstein to enter the country before the Bolshevik troops were withdrawn from Iranian territory. His was also the idea to appeal to the British not to evacuate their troops.[3] All that did not tend to make him a *persona grata* with the Moscow authorities.

Anxious to carry out reforms speedily, and if need be forcibly, Zia ed-Din soon made himself unpopular in Teheran also. First of all, the arrest of several men who could be considered pillars of the *ancien régime* produced an undying hatred of him on the part of several influential families in Iran. His radical-sounding program of reforms, which he hastened to announce, met with opposition from many entrenched interests. The most important cause of his unpopularity was, however, his failure to cultivate the friendship of Reza Khan, to whose military aid he owed his advent to power. Without the support of the army Zia could not count on a lengthy period of office. Dif-

[3] See p. 47; also Balfour, *op. cit.,* p. 244.

ferences that arose between him and Reza Khan led eventually to his overthrow. On May 24, 1921, after barely three months' rule, Zia ed-Din had to escape from the country. He first reached Bagdad, and later settled in Haifa, Palestine. "Thus," writes Balfour, "terminated an honest and self-sacrificing attempt to save Persia from bankruptcy and to preserve her from foreign invasion."

Reza Khan remained sole master of the situation. He did not reach immediately for supreme power: he was satisfied with having control of the army in his new capacity of Minister of War. On the reorganization of the army Reza focused all his energies. After the World War Iran found her army in a sad state. The gendarmerie was Swedish-officered and during the war found itself under the preponderant German influence. In the south, to counteract German diversionary activities, the British had created the South Persia Rifles, a formation eventually recognized by the Iranian government, yet completely dependent on the British financially and organizationally. The Cossack Brigade, and later Division, was Russian-officered and was, till the late fall of 1920, commanded by Colonel Starosselsky. There were, to be sure, a few purely Iranian units; their effectives were, however, small and their organization corrupt and inefficient. The Cossack Division was, at the time of the coup in February, 1921, the only well-organized Iranian formation within easy reach of Teheran. To command the Division was to have almost unlimited opportunities in Iran. Reza Khan acted, however, slowly and cautiously. To establish himself as the supreme ruler of Iran, he would have to overcome much opposition as well as to decide the fate of the monarchy, now personified by the last representative of the Qajar dynasty, weak and pleasure-seeking Ahmed Shah. Reza's slow work in consolidating his influence was successful. In the eyes of the Shah and Iranian cabinets, he was indispensable because of the necessity of curbing revolts of provincial tribes and of separatist border movements. The pacification of Azerbaijan was mainly Reza's work. All foreign advisers, including the British, having been eliminated from the heterogeneous military formations, Reza Khan managed to unify all these forces into a closely knit, centrally controlled army. By 1923 Reza became Prime Minister, and after a period of hesitation whether or not to establish a republic he overthrew the last Qajar sovereign and in 1925 proclaimed himself Shah-in-Shah of Iran. The Majlis confirmed this decision, and thus a new Pahlavi dynasty was founded.

As the new ruler of Iran, Reza Shah resembled in many ways his Turkish fellow-dictator, Mustapha Kemal Atatürk. Nationalism and westernization were two main points in the programs of both men. Reza Shah was resolved to put an end to whatever foreign influence might threaten the sovereignty of Iran. This meant a suspicious and guarded attitude toward Soviet Russia and Communist infiltration, as well as a challenging attitude toward Great Britain. With regard to westernization Reza did not go so far as his Turkish counterpart. While Kemal was uncompromising in some of his reforms, the soberminded Reza realized that there was a line beyond which even an absolute ruler could not safely proceed. Iran was in many ways a much more isolated country than Turkey and had fewer western influences than her Ottoman neighbor. This produced a deeply ingrained conservatism in the masses of the population, and the influence of the Shia clergy tended to deepen it. It would be unsafe to be too radical, and the Iranian ruler rightly felt that there was a definite limit to the capacity of Orientals to absorb Western culture. Thus, while Kemal insisted on the word "secularism" for his new Turkey, Reza satisfied himself with only limited and gradual curbs on the influence of the clergy. While Kemal introduced the Latin script and revolutionized the whole fabric of education, Reza maintained the old Persian script. It was even said that Reza refused to introduce the Western alphabet because of fear lest it facilitate the circulation of Communist literature. He did not hesitate, however, to order the unveiling of women and to introduce Western dress and headgear for men. Like Kemal, Reza established a system of controlled economy, investing government funds heavily in industrial and commercial enterprises and setting up, eventually, a government monopoly of foreign trade. Economically Reza wanted to make Iran self-sufficient while laying foundations for the development of local industry and transportation. American, and later German, advisers were invited to reorganize Iran's finances, and a national Bank

[73]

of Iran, the so-called Bank-i-Melli-yi-Iran, was created, to which the privilege of issuing banknotes was granted, a privilege formerly enjoyed by the British-controlled Imperial Bank of Iran.

The building of a powerful national state free of foreign domination was in the forefront of all of Reza's policies. Reference was made earlier to the challenging attitude of the Shah toward England. This attitude can best be illustrated by three issues on which the ways of Iran and Great Britain parted. The first was the problem of advisers; the second, the Bahrein controversy; and the third, the oil dispute.

FOREIGN ADVISERS AND BAHREIN

As a result of the Anglo-Iranian Agreement of 1919 military and economic British missions arrived in Teheran. Although it is difficult to ascertain to what degree the Military Mission succeeded in influencing the reorganization of the army, it is certain that the Financial Mission headed by Armitage Smith and James Balfour did manage to introduce some semblance of order into Iranian finances. The nationalist propaganda against the agreement and the resultant failure of the Majlis to ratify it caused the withdrawal of the British missions and the disbandment of the South Persia Rifles by the fall of 1921. The evacuation of British troops earlier in the same year was an additional reason for the waning of British influence. By the beginning of 1922 Iran, at least insofar as the central authorities and the army were concerned, was entirely free of any British dictation. Later the Iranian government carefully avoided hiring British advisers. In 1922 an American financial adviser, Dr. Arthur C. Millspaugh, was invited to continue the interrupted work of the British mission. When his term expired in 1927, Iran turned to German advisers, again leaving the British out of the picture. In the great enterprise of the Transiranian Railroad, courageously undertaken by Reza Shah against heavy technical and financial odds, the British were treated like any other nation that could contribute technically to the construction. British firms, like the Richard Costain Company, were hired, but alongside with American, German, Italian, and other concerns. Furthermore, the line along which the Transiranian was constructed was not entirely according to what Great Britain might have wished if her commercial and strategic desiderata were to be satisfied. On the contrary, the Transiranian, conceived as a link between the north and the south of Iran, disappointed in many ways both Great Britain and Soviet Russia, because instead of facilitating economic or strategic penetration by these two neighbors, it served to strengthen the national unity of Iran.[4]

The Bahrein controversy was another example of the assertion of Iranian nationalism against the British. In 1927 the Iranian government began to claim that the Bahrein Islands situated in the Persian Gulf should return to Iranian sovereignty. The claim was based on historical grounds. The islands, the Iranians asserted, belonged to the Empire of Iran throughout history, and it was only in 1906 that the British, in violation of Iranian suzerainty, extended their protectorate over them. That the islands were inhabited by the Arabs and that their sheikh always enjoyed complete autonomy to all practical purposes did not deter the Iranians from launching energetic propaganda at home and abroad to right the wrong done to Iran by the alleged British perfidy. The Iranian government took special offense when it transpired that by the Treaty of Jidda concluded on May 20, 1927, between the Kingdom of Hejaz and Great Britain, the latter's claim to the Bahrein Islands was officially recognized (see Article 6). Between 1928 and 1936 Iran repeatedly appealed to the League of Nations, but to no avail. At the time of the outbreak of World War II the dispute remained unsettled.

Iran's claim to the islands was intensified by the circumstance that they turned out to contain oil reserves in their subsoil. Strangely enough, it was not the British but the Americans who eventually undertook oil exploitation there. Reluctant to invest capital in what seemed a very uncertain venture, the British in 1927 relinquished their original concession of 1925 in favor of the Gulf Oil Company (American). This concession passed, in 1928, into the hands of Standard Oil of California. Following the discovery of oil in 1932, the Bahrein Oil Company was created. Since 1936 it has been owned

---

[4] A revealing analysis of Big-Power maneuvers with respect to the construction of a railway in Iran is contained in L. P. Ellwell-Sutton, *Modern Iran* (London, 1941), pp. 90 ff.

by Standard of California and the Texas Company. Bahrein's production soon reached the figure of approximately one million tons a year.

Despite these rebuffs from resurgent Iranian nationalism, Great Britain did not relinquish all her interests in Iran. The concession exploited by the Anglo-Iranian Oil Company continued as a powerful link between the two countries. It constituted also an instrument of British influence in that region and, naturally, like any foreign-held concession it contained seeds of disagreement between the host nation and the concessionaire. It was mainly in the field of oil exploitation that the nationalist policy of Reza Shah clashed with British interests, and it may be said without contradiction that the behavior of the Iranian ruler in this field constituted the best test of his true attitude toward Great Britain.

THE STORY OF OIL

The exploitation of oil in Iran is so linked with the Big Powers' competition for influence in that country that it may be useful to recapitulate briefly the events that led to the development of the British concession in the south.

As far back as 1872, as has been stated earlier, Baron Julius de Reuter, a British subject, had obtained from Nasir ed-Din Shah a concession that gave him, among many other privileges, the exclusive right to exploit all the natural resources of Iran with the exception of gold, silver, and precious stones. A year later this concession had been canceled because of the hostile attitude of Russia. Reuter, feeling wronged, had appealed to his government for protection. Official British intervention had brought about the granting of a new concession to Reuter, as a compensation. This time (1889) it was a permission to create a bank as well as to exploit oil deposits in the country. As a result the Imperial Bank of Iran was founded, an institution that still plays an important role in the economic life of the country. The oil rights were taken care of by the Persian Bank Mining Rights Corporation, which began prospecting but, failing to obtain tangible results, soon renounced its rights.

In 1891 the Governor of Kermanshah requested M. de Morgan, head of the French archeological mission, to try to find oil in his province. The mission acceded to this request and some time afterwards its work gave gratifying results. In 1892 M. de Morgan published in *Les Annales des mines* (Paris) a report indicating the existence of oil in the subsoil of the region Qasr-i-Shirin, situated near the Iranian-Mesopotamian border.

As a result of this report an Australian financier, William Knox D'Arcy, expressed a desire to invest funds in prospecting works. In 1901 two representatives of D'Arcy appeared in Teheran and obtained from Mozaffar ed-Din Shah the desired concession. The concession was valid for sixty years and covered the whole territory of Iran except the provinces of Azerbaijan, Gilan, Mazanderan, Astarabad, and Khorasan. Thus five northern provinces of Iran, a traditional area of Russian influence, were excluded from the grant. The concession gave D'Arcy the exclusive right to construct pipe lines and gave him gratis all noncultivated lands belonging to the state that might become necessary for the work of prospecting. A special clause protected the concessionaire against an unjustified rise of prices of privately owned land that might be necessary for oil exploitation. On his part D'Arcy undertook to found within two years one or more companies for oil exploitation. He was to pay the Iranian government 20,000 pounds sterling in cash, another 20,000 pounds in shares of the company, and 16 per cent of the net profits made by the company. Besides, D'Arcy undertook to pay an annual sum of 2,000 tomans as a compensation for the yearly tax levied by the Crown on royal estates put at the disposal of the concessionaire. The government, in turn, would have the right to watch the activities of the company through a Commissioner whose salary was to be paid by the company itself. In case of a dispute between the contracting parties, a commission of three arbiters would be called upon.

Following the terms of the concession D'Arcy founded the First Exploitation Company, which undertook prospecting work. After seven years of trials the first geyser of oil burst out in 1908, at Masjid-i-Suleiman. As a consequence the Anglo-Persian Oil Company was created and it absorbed the First Exploitation Company. The new company set to work energetically, and by 1912 quantities of oil began to be exported from Iran. This great organizational effort was not free of complications. The main problem during the initial work was security. The oil deposits in southwest Iran were situated in territory inhabited by seminomad tribes that only nominally recognized the authority of the central government. To obtain the concession from Teheran and to exploit oil in Khuzistan were two different things. With all the characteristic realism of their race, the British—company people as well as consular authorities—entered into negotiations with the local tribes to secure their friendliness or at least noninterference with the company's work. Agreements were negotiated between the British Residency in Bushire on one side and the Sheikh of Mohammera (Khorramshahr today) and the Bakhtiyari tribe on the other. In order to protect the oil installations at Masjid-i-Suleiman against any unforeseen encroachments, a small detachment of Sikhs, commanded by a British officer, were brought in with the knowledge of the Iranian government.

These details are mentioned in order to stress the importance of the discovery of oil in Iran for the whole British policy in the Persian Gulf area. To watch the company's operations and to maintain friendly relations with the local potentates, a number of able public servants had to be employed by Great Britain in these regions. This meant deeper penetration of British consular and intelligence authorities into the area, the establishment of certain customs and usages, and generally a greater influence.

The development of the company was spectacular. Without much delay pipe lines were laid down linking the oil fields with the island of Abadan, where one of the largest oil refineries in the world was constructed. The most important event, however, in the story of the company was the decision of the British government, in 1913, to replace coal with oil as a fuel for the navy. This decision resulted in the purchase by the Admiralty of the controlling stock of the company, and so, since 1914, the British government has been directly interested as an investor in the exploitation of Iranian oil.[5] A detail, perhaps not without significance, is that it was Winston Churchill who headed the Admiralty at that time.

[5] Today the British Treasury owns 1,000 pounds sterling of shares of first privilege and 11,250,000 pounds sterling of ordinary shares, which represent a majority of 52 and 55 per cent of the votes in the company's Assembly. The capital of the Anglo-Iranian Oil Company is 32,843,752 pounds sterling (M. Nakhai, *Le Petrole en Iran* [Paris and Brussels, 1938], p. 42).

The production of the company was of great importance for the successful prosecution of war by Great Britain. As soon as the first World War ended, it became clear that the company's relations with the Iranian government were not cordial. The crisis was precipitated by the refusal of the company to pay royalties to the government. This refusal occurred because the company held the government responsible for manifold property damage that the government's neglect had allowed local tribes to perpetrate. On the other hand, Iranian public opinion realized by that time that the profits of the company were enormous and that only a small portion was going to the Iranian treasury. The unfortunate Anglo-Iranian Treaty of August, 1919, only worsened the situation. Both parties finally agreed to submit the matter to the arbitration of Armitage Smith. The arbitration led to a provisional agreement of December 22, 1920, which, however, was not ratified by the Majlis. The advent of Reza Shah to power found relations between the company and the government in a state of irritation. The tension increased as time went on. In 1932 the showdown came. According to the calculations of the Iranian government, the total sum paid by the company to Iran between 1901 and 1932 was 11,000,000 pounds sterling. If the company, instead of paying the royalties, had paid the normal taxes in force in Iran, the total sum due the Iranian treasury would have been 22,000,000 pounds sterling. In addition the government accused the company of certain manipulations detrimental to the interest of Iran. On November 27, 1932, the government notified the company that the concession had been annulled.

British reaction was quick and energetic. In a note sent to the government on December 2, 1932, the British Legation threatened to use force in case of need. The threat was supported by the appearance near the Iranian coast in the Gulf of a few British naval vessels. This was followed by an exchange of notes rather violent in character. Great Britain appealed to the Permanent Court of International Justice in The Hague; Iran, however, protested against this procedure, considering the dispute a purely domestic one between the government and the company. The matter was eventually brought before the Council of the League of Nations. There, after hearing eloquent pleas by Sir John Simon and by Mr. Davar, Iranian Minister of Justice, the Council decided to appoint a rapporteur. The latter informed the Council in February, 1933, that the disputing parties had entered into direct negotiations, and thus the matter was dropped from the agenda. On May 28, 1933, a new concession was granted to the Anglo-Iranian by Iran.

The new concession is valid for 60 years and is much more favorable to Iran than was the old one. The new terms provide for an annual payment to Iran of 20 per cent of the dividend on ordinary shares in excess of 671,250 pounds sterling. The company is also bound to pay 4 shillings a ton sold or exported. It is exempt from taxes, but it must pay Iran during the first fifteen years of the concession 9 pence for each of the first 6,000,000 tons of oil and 6 pence for each ton in excess of this sum. During the next fifteen years these dues will increase up to 1 shilling a ton and 9 pence a ton, respectively. The total sum of all dues cannot in any case be lower than 1,050,000 pounds sterling a year. Another important stipulation is that the territory of the concession is to be limited to 100,000 square miles, which may be chosen by the company south of the line drawn on the map attached to the document of the concession. This line runs approximately from the point north of Qasr-i-Shirin (Zohab region) on the Iranian-Iraqi frontier, through the area north of Kermanshah, then south of Yazd and Kerman, through Saidabad and Irafshan to the frontier of Indian Baluchistan. The new concession foresees also gradual "iranization" of the company's personnel and training of Iranian students at its expense. The Iranian Government Commissioner is maintained, and the Anglo-Iranian continues to pay his salary. A special clause deals with the price of oil in Iran with a view to protecting Iranian consumers. Finally the concession agreement contains clear and precise provisions concerning the procedure of arbitration.

Compared with the previous concession, the new agreement gave so many more benefits to Iran that its conclusion could justly be regarded as a great victory for Reza Shah's bold foreign policy and as a final act in the process of development and assertion of Iranian independence. By this act perhaps more than by any other, the new regime demonstrated that, far from being a tool in the hands of

Western imperialism, it was ready and able to put up a stubborn resistance against it.

THE NORTHERN OIL IMBROGLIO

While Reza Shah was thus emancipating Iran from inconvenient Western influences, he took care not to fall at the same time under Russian tutelage. It may be recalled here that his early military career was linked with the exploits of the Cossack Brigade, and the Brigade had a distinctly anti-Soviet record, having been commanded by the White Russian officer Colonel Starosselsky and having played an important role in curbing the Gilan revolt of Kuchik Khan. Later, when Reza Khan became a dominating force in Iranian politics, it was again his task to quell the disturbances that broke out in Iran's provinces adjoining Soviet Russia, like Khorasan and Azerbaijan. In both of these disturbances Soviet agents were implicated to a greater or lesser degree, and that complicity further estranged Reza Khan from the Soviets. What had troubled Soviet-Iranian relations since 1921 more than everything else was the problem of oil in Iran's northern provinces. The Soviet-Iranian Treaty of February 26, 1921, it may be recalled, provided for total renunciation of all former Russian concessions in Iran with the stipulation that these concessions could not be granted by Iran to any third party. Actually, as regards oil resources, only one concession was granted in 1916 to a Russian subject, Akakiy Khoshtaria. This concession was in turn based on an earlier grant made in 1896 by Mozaffar ed-Din Shah. It covered the provinces of Azerbaijan, Gilan, Mazanderan, Astarabad, and Khorasan. Owing to the war the oil was never exploited there. In 1920, before the conclusion of the Soviet-Iranian Treaty, the Anglo-Iranian Oil Company purchased Khoshtaria's concession for the sum of 200,000 pounds sterling. As a result, a branch of the Anglo-Iranian, the North Persian Oil Company, was created.

This British penetration into the north of Iran was greatly resented by Soviet Russia and did not meet with the approval of either the Iranian government or of interested American oil companies, the latter also desirous of obtaining concessions in the northern region.

[81]

Pressed by the Soviets and reluctant to admit the validity of the British concession, the Iranian government refused to recognize it. It stated that the title of 1896 could not be regarded as valid, having been granted by the Qajar dynasty; and since the Qajars were recklessly squandering the natural wealth of Iran, their harmful acts could not be binding upon the present Iranian government. As to the direct concession of 1916, it was not valid either, because, the government asserted, it was never ratified by the parliament and thus did not fulfill the requirements of Article 24 of the Constitution. Moreover, the Iranians argued, the Soviet-Iranian Treaty of 1921 annulled all concessions previously granted to the tsarist government or Russian subjects; hence Khoshtaria's title was also canceled. The Anglo-Iranian replied that Khoshtaria was not a Russian subject but a citizen of the free Republic of Georgia and that, therefore, the provisions of the treaty did not apply to him. This was true, because Khoshtaria had, in the meantime, acquired Georgian citizenship. The conquest of Georgia by Soviet Russia, which occurred in 1921, complicated again the problem of Khoshtaria's citizenship and made it difficult for the Anglo-Iranian to press this argument.

Besides these purely legal considerations, the Iranian government had other good reasons to oppose the British concession in the north. The first was the fear that the British would come into possession of all the natural wealth of Iran. The second was the desire to grant the concession to citizens or corporations of a more distant country less dangerous to the sovereignty of Iran. It was with this aim in mind that the government entered into negotiations with the Standard Oil Company. They were conducted through the intermediary of Morgan Shuster, former American financial adviser to the Iranian government, and resulted in an authorization to grant a concession, voted by the Majlis on November 22, 1921. The concession was to be valid for fifty years, and the Iranian government had to receive without any expenses 50 per cent of the oil produced. The details of the concession would have to be worked out between the government and the company and ratified by the parliament. The fifth article of this agreement provided that the concession could not be ceded by the company to any third party. Even the adherence of a new capitalist to the company would have to be confirmed by the

Majlis. Any violation of this clause would cancel the concession automatically.

This act of the parliament provoked immediate opposition from both the British and the Soviets. The British Legation in Teheran lodged a protest invoking the acquired rights of the Anglo-Iranian Oil Company. In turn, the American government invoked the Open Door principle and demanded equal recognition for American companies. A direct note, said to have been couched in sharp words, was also sent from Washington to London. This exchange of notes led to a compromise between the British and the American companies. Both renounced exclusivity and agreed to share the concession equally. It may be added here that the reason why the American company was compelled to make a deal with the Anglo-Iranian was the monopoly of oil transportation held by the latter for the whole original territory of the D'Arcy concession, i.e., for most of central and southern Iran. This agreement, however, never went into operation because of the protest of the Soviet government. On January 15, 1922, Rothstein, Soviet Minister in Teheran, declared that Russia would oppose any concession granted to foreign capitalists for the exploitation of northern oil. As a result, the Iranian government broke off negotiations with Standard Oil and the Anglo-Iranian Company.

Despite this disappointment Iran did not abandon further endeavors to grant a concession for the exploitation of northern oil. Such a concession would contribute greatly to the solution of Iran's financial difficulties. After some lapse of time the government started negotiations with the Sinclair Consolidated Oil Corporation. At that time Sinclair was on speaking terms with the Soviet government, from which it had received an oil concession on Sakhalin Island and also the right to sell Soviet oil products in world markets. The Iranians hoped that Russia would not object to the granting of the concession to Sinclair. In June, 1923, the Majlis passed the bill authorizing the government to grant the new concession to the American company. To make it quite sure, the Majlis stated that no other valid concession or claim existed with regard to the oil in the northern provinces.

Simultaneously with the negotiations in Teheran, Sinclair Oil conducted parleys with the Soviet government for permission to transport north Iranian oil through Soviet territory, via the Baku-Batum pipe line. In return for this permission Sinclair would pledge itself to buy Soviet oil in quantities equal or larger than the amount of Iranian oil in transit. These talks were unsuccessful. To add to the failure, Sinclair's Sakhalin concession was annulled by the Soviets, and the company lost also the sales agency of Soviet oil products.

In Teheran, in the meantime, a few significant incidents took place. On the day that the Majlis voted the bill authorizing the concession, a fire broke out in the parliament building. The deed was intentional, and the perpetrator was arrested. More important was the murder of the American vice-consul in Teheran. There was a strong suspicion that both acts were in some way connected with the question of oil. As a consequence, in the summer of 1924 the Sinclair Company representative left Teheran, informing the Iranian government that the attitude of Soviet Russia did not permit the continuation of negotiations.

During the next thirteen years nothing was done to revive the problem of northern oil. In 1937, however, American oil interests showed a renewed interest in it. On February 4, 1937, the Majlis voted to grant the concession to the Amiranian Oil Company for the exploitation of oil in the northeastern province of Khorasan. The Amiranian Oil Company (owned by the Seaboard Oil Company of Delaware) obtained in addition the nonexclusive right to process and transport oil on the entire territory of Iran. The clauses of the concession resembled closely those of the new concession granted in 1933 to the Anglo-Iranian. Simultaneously the Iranian Pipe-Line Company, affiliated with Seaboard of Delaware, obtained a concession to construct pipe lines in Iran.

This time it seemed that the new concession would endure, untroubled by opposition from any side. Reza Shah's position was strong both internally and externally, and it was doubtful whether any foreign pressure would be able to cause the cancellation of the new agreement. Despite that, the new concession came to an end in 1938. It was the Amiranian Oil Company that, on its own initiative, gave notice of renunciation to the Iranian government. In a letter addressed to the government, the company explained that its

decision was due to commercial reasons as well as to the general
political uncertainty that prevailed in the world in 1938. This statement was no doubt true: the pipe line that would carry the northern
oil would have to run from the north to the south of Iran, the Soviet
territory being naturally nonavailable, and that would make the
whole operation too expensive. Moreover, the successful development of production by the Arabian-American Oil Company in the
tidelands of southern Arabia introduced a new factor of prime magni-
tude. In such circumstances the Amiranian, with its territory so far
inland, could not hope to withstand competition. It is interesting
to note, however, that eventually the Russian press was not loath to
attribute this withdrawal to Soviet pressure on the Iranian government.

Thus ended the last attempt to exploit the oil resources of the
north in the interwar period.[6] The problem was not revived until
the fall of 1944, of which more will be said later.[7] Of all the vicis-

---

[6] Aside from the big oil concessions in northern and southern Iran, still another,
though of minor importance, was granted by the Iranian government in the dis-
trict of Semnan. In 1878 Nasir ed-Din Shah awarded this concession covering the
district of Semnan east of Teheran to one of his subjects, Haji Ali Akbar Amine
Ma'aden. In 1924 this concession was confirmed by the Iranian Minister of Public
Works. The acquired rights of the late Amine Ma'aden were represented by Haji
Mirza Ali Akbar Khan Sotudeh and Mirza Abdol Hosein Khan Amine Ma'aden.
This concession was also subjected to the vicissitudes of Anglo-Soviet rivalry. The
Anglo-Iranian Oil Company claimed that the concession was invalid because the
Semnan district was located within the area of the original D'Arcy concession of
1901. The Iranian government managed to prove, however, that in 1901 the district of Semnan constituted a part of the province of Khorasan, which together
with four other northern provinces was excluded from the D'Arcy concession. In
this controversy with the British Iran was supported by Russia. This happened because the Soviet government had meanwhile bought a share of this concession from
the heirs of the late Amine Ma'aden. A detail that adds flavor to this intrigue was
that the middleman who arranged this deal was none other than the old rival of
the Soviets, Khoshtaria himself. According to this deal, an "Iranian" company,
Kavir-Khurian, was set up in 1925 to exploit the oil resources there. Its capital was
50,000,000 rials divided into 100,000 shares worth 500 rials each. Sixty-five per cent
of the stock was owned by the Soviet government. In 1926 following an agreement
between the Iranian and Soviet governments, French capital was invited to participate in this enterprise. As a result an Iranian-French syndicate was created to
carry on prospecting. (For more details see Zangueneh, *Le Petrole en Perse* [Paris,
1933], p. 209.)

[7] See p. 216.

situdes of northern oil concessions, one thing may be said with certainty: they left a bitter memory in the minds of Soviet leaders. American and British attempts to secure a concession there were regarded as a proof of encircling capitalist imperialism, while the Iranian attitude was considered as disloyal and full of duplicity. The legal arguments advanced by Iran during some of these controversies made little impression on Soviet authorities. While restraining themselves from having a showdown with Reza Shah's government, the Russians were carefully registering the various manifestations of Iran's behavior in their minds. The deterioration of Western-Soviet relations in 1945 gave many evidences that Soviet leaders had a long memory. For Iran this fact proved to have, perhaps, more ominous significance than for anyone else. For reasons of its own, however, Moscow was not in a mood at this time to make immediate use of these proofs, as it considered them, of Iranian hostility.

THE SOVIET ATTITUDE TOWARD REZA SHAH

Why did Soviet Russia practice self-restraint toward Iran? The first reason that seems quite plausible is that Russia was too busy with her internal affairs in the 1920's and '30's to afford an expansionist policy abroad. Stalin's proclamation of "Socialism in one country" would lend support to this explanation. Yet this was not the only reason, as we are led to believe by an analysis of contemporary Soviet writings. Something much more profound, something of a basic theoretical character, was involved in determining Soviet attitude toward her southern neighbor. As long as Iran was ruled by the weak and degenerate Qajar dynasty, she had a well-defined place in Marxist thinking: this was a typical semicolonial country, passing through the epoch of feudalism in its historical development and, naturally, being subjected to the exploiting practices of Western capitalism, itself in its final stage—that of imperialism. The concrete tasks facing Soviet Russia in relation to the Iran of the Qajars were thus relatively simple: precipitate a revolution, which would immediately put an end to the antiquated feudal structure of the society, and use the downtrodden masses of Iran as a great "reserve of the proletarian revolution" with a view to ousting the imperialist influences of Western capitalism. With this end in view an experiment was made in Gilan in 1920–1921, and Ambassador Rothstein, on the other hand, tried to influence the Iranian internal situation from the strategic point of Teheran. In the eyes of Soviet leaders the coup of February, 1921, that swept Zia ed-Din into power did not radically alter the picture. Zia was regarded as a tool of British policy, and his regime meant to the Soviets only a reaffirmation of British imperialist influence in Iran. Zia's denunciation of the Anglo-Iranian agreement left Soviet leaders unimpressed. His proclamations of liberal-radical reforms were branded as hypocrisy and as a cloak for more sinister British designs on Iran. The fact that Zia was aided in his coup by Reza Khan did not attract enough notice from the Soviet leaders. Not even the overthrow of Zia ed-Din by the latter was immediately considered as of deep significance. Eventually Reza's emergence as the dominant power in Iranian politics, especially when he assumed the premiership in 1923, caused the Soviets to give greater attention to the role that the former Cossack trooper might play in Iran's history.

The great news to Moscow was, however, Reza's overthrow of the Qajar dynasty in 1925 and his formal assumption of royal—and dictatorial—powers. The time was then come to analyze Reza's actions with "scientific" precision, to revise, if necessary, the attitude toward his regime and Iran as a whole, and, on the basis of the correct interpretation of the new historical phenomenon, to draw practical conclusions as to the strategy and tactics to be employed.

The change of regime in Iran in 1925 gave rise to an open controversy among Soviet Marxists—so open as to be almost unbelievable to all those who are accustomed to the efficient streamlining of Soviet policy since the emergence of Stalin as an undisputed ruler of Russia. The years of 1924–1927 were, we must remember, the years of interregnum in Russia: Lenin's death left the Communist party divided and uncertain of its future. The rivalry between Stalin and Trotsky was ripening to lead to a final showdown at the Fifteenth Party Congress toward the end of 1927. For a few brief years the party members, if not the Russian people, enjoyed a semblance of freedom of thought and speech. Controversies among the party factions ranged from the question of the correct attitude toward collectiviza-

[87]

tion to the problem of what should be the tactics in China. The debate on Iran found its place among those quarrels.

Two schools of thought actually developed with regard to the Iranian problem. One, represented by Vissanov, maintained that (a) Reza Khan gained power chiefly owing to British intervention and not as a result of changing social conditions in Iran; (b) Reza Shah and his army represented reactionary forces, economically linked to the traditional feudal strata of the society, and (c) therefore Reza's coup did not constitute a social revolution, but was just a change from one dynasty to another. This being the case, argued Vissanov, Iran was still in the midst of her feudal epoch and needed a radical change that would bring her into the capitalist epoch and the ensuing industrialization. To achieve this change it was first necessary to carry out a radical agrarian revolution that would result in the division of great estates among the peasantry. In other words, insofar as internal tactics were concerned, chief attention was to be focused on the peasant sector. Externally, on the other hand, Marxists should not forget that Reza Shah and his regime were essentially the tools of Great Britain.

The theses of Vissanov met with violent opposition from the other school, represented by V. A. Gurko-Kriazhin, F. Raskolnikov, and others. This school believed that the coup of Reza Shah was a manifestation of a revolutionary change in Iran's history. Owing to it Iran passed from a semifeudal into a semibourgeois phase of development. Thus the coup was in reality a bougeois revolution. To support this thesis Raskolnikov, a onetime commander of the Caspian Red Fleet that invaded Enzeli, pointed to the composition of Reza Shah's army; this army, he asserted, was mainly composed of nationalistically minded elements of the intelligentsia and middle class of both antifeudal and anti-British tendencies. It followed, therefore, that Reza's advent to power was, from the Marxist viewpoint, a step forward.[8] Gurko-Kriazhin, who in his *Critical Meditations on the Coup in Persia* quoted Raskolnikov as an authority, criticized Vissanov for his abandonment of the Marxist platform with regard to the Iranian army. Vissanov, stated Gurko-Kriazhin, has committed a grave mistake in calling the army a "mobile force"

[8] F. Raskolnikov, "Imperialisty na Vostoka," *Pravda*, no. 158/3387, 1926.

[88]

standing above the social classes (*nadklasovaya*) and in denying it a special sociohistorical role. Reza Shah, asserted Gurko-Kriazhin, was allied with the so-called progressive bloc and carried out a number of far-reaching reforms. On the other hand, his struggle against the feudal nobility, the clergy, and the British should not be overlooked. Although the establishment by Reza Shah of the new Pahlavi dynasty was a manifestation of "Bonapartism," nevertheless this did not detract from the basic fact that the coup marked the beginning of the capitalist epoch. "Summing up our remarks," wrote Gurko-Kriazhin, "we can observe the politico-economic weakening of the class of landed nobility and the simultaneous strengthening of the commercial capital, which penetrates at the present time into industry and into village economy." [9]

Another author, Iransky (a pseudonym), whose name appears in many Soviet and Comintern publications over a quarter of a century on the subject of Iran, expressed a similar view. Praising Reza Khan as a "plebeian" and a "former trooper," Iransky made it clear that the new regime was a welcome step toward the transformation of Iranian society. "A strong central state authority," he wrote in *Novy Vostok*, "relying on a unified national army, assures commercial, industrial, and cultural development of Persia and secures her transition from the feudal into the new forms of economic and political existence." [10]

This view on Reza's regime was supported by another writer, hiding his identity under the pseudonym Irandust. In the article "Remarks on the Change of Regime in Persia," the latter stated that there was in Russia a greatly increased interest in Iranian affairs due to the dynastic coup. He stressed the necessity of "detailed analysis of the character of the Persian coup" because "a defective theoretical analysis may lead to harmful practical conclusions." He took issue with Vissanov concerning the priority of agrarian revolution. Vissanov, stated Irandust, based his prescription for agrarian revolution on the theses of the Baku Congress of Oriental Peoples of

[9] V. A. Gurko-Kriazhin, "Kriticheskiye Razmyshlenia o Perevorotie v Persyi" (reply to Vissanov), *Novy Vostok*, no. 15, pp. 17–34.

[10] "Cinq ans de rapports du Gouvernement Soviétiste avec la Perse," Part II, *Novy Vostok*, IV, 218.

September 6, 1920, but he was mistaken in doing so because much had changed in Iran since then. Since Reza's advent to power had created an entirely new situation in Iran, it would be dangerous to apply to it the precepts that were good for another period. Iran, according to Irandust, has entered the epoch of capitalism with absolutist monarchy as her political form. Hence she faced new problems. "The main problem of Persia's development," concluded Irandust,

turns out to be the question whether she can skip the phase of a slow ripening of capitalism and the period of absolutist monarchy . . . and pass directly to the democracy of her working classes. The theses on the national and colonial question of the Second Congress of the Comintern foresee the possibility of such a skipping if the popular masses of the backward countries are given help by the enlightened proletariat of advanced countries. Persia, no doubt, presents a typical picture of a delayed development caused by imperialism. And it remains to . . . diagnose how much the existing international situation favors the solution of the Persian problem by way of such a "jump." [11]

This controversy among Soviet orientalistic experts is revealing in many ways. The impression one obtains is that the second school of thought seems to get an upper hand. *Novy Vostok,* an officially sponsored Soviet publication, never gave Vissanov a chance to reply to his opponents, whereas the latter were given ample opportunity to express their views. Thus, according to the Soviet viewpoint, Reza Shah's regime represented a national liberation movement of anti-imperialist and semibourgeois character. As such, the regime had to be supported by Soviet Russia, particularly wherever it happened to clash with British interests. In practice this was more or less the attitude that the Soviet government adopted. Self-restraint was practiced in the whole northern oil controversy, and Soviet displeasure over Iran's dealings with American and British companies never went beyond the limits of diplomatic protests. On the other hand, Russia either overtly supported Iran or at least sided with her in such Iranian-British controversies as those over Semnan oil or the Bahrein Islands. Naturally the best solution for Russia would have been

[11] "Zametki o Smenie Rezhima v Persyi," *Novy Vostok,* no. 15, p. 63.

to see Iranian nationalism express itself *only* against the West and *never* against Russia herself. Such an attitude would presuppose a strong Soviet influence on the Iranian government, and, as we shall see from a review of economic relationships, Moscow was not loath to use economic weapons to secure this end.

SOVIET-IRANIAN ECONOMIC RELATIONS

In her commercial relations with Iran, Soviet Russia followed a policy that could best be described as a combination of traditional tsarist principles with new Soviet devices. The policy of Imperial Russia was characterized by a desire to acquire exclusive economic advantages in Iran as against Western commercial penetration, and to make northern Iran entirely dependent on her northern neighbor. As a result of this policy Russia secured for herself a predominant position in Iran's foreign trade. Prior to World War I two-thirds of this trade was in Russian hands.

The Soviet State developed a special system for its trade relations with the East, which differed substantially from the pattern followed in the case of the West. When, in 1920, the Soviet foreign trade monopoly was established, the neighboring countries from the Black Sea to Mongolia were exempted from its provisions. In 1923 an official document called *Principles of Eastern Trade* codified all rules pertaining to Russia's commerce with her Asiatic neighbors. These principles were as follows: (a) Soviet industrial goods had to be exchanged for Eastern raw materials; (b) Eastern merchants individually were permitted to sell their goods in Russia; (c) Russia would not insist on a favorable balance of trade with the East; (d) mixed Soviet-Eastern companies were to be promoted; (e) Soviet industrial goods were to be sold in the East at lower prices than they were in the West.[12]

In its practical application to Iran this general Soviet policy passed through several stages, dictated more by the economic needs and power of the Soviet State than by an altruistic regard for the needs of renascent Iranian nationalism. From the opening of Soviet-

[12] A detailed analysis of Soviet trade methods may be found in Violet Connolly, *Soviet Economic Policy in the East* (London, 1933). A special chapter deals with Iran.

[91]

Iranian diplomatic relations in 1921 till 1927, trade between the two countries was not regulated by any special convention. Profiting from the general exemption from the Soviet foreign trade monopoly, Iranian merchants traveled throughout Russia, transacted commercial deals with Soviet institutions or Russian individuals (this was possible in the period of the New Economic Policy), and participated actively in the fairs of Nizhni Novgorod and Baku, which were permitted to function at that time. The result of this liberalism was that Iran enjoyed a favorable balance of trade, mainly due to the export of raw materials and foodstuffs to exhausted and famished Russia. Simultaneously protracted negotiations for the conclusion of a trade agreement were taking place. Two main difficulties prevented an early conclusion of the agreement. These were the Soviet demand for diplomatic immunities for their official trade organs in Iran and insistence on very low import duties on Russian oil products entering Iran. It may seem strange that Russian oil supplies should have been discussed at all, but we must not forget that, owing to the lack of properly developed communications in Iran, it was easier for the northern provinces to obtain oil from Baku than from Iranian sources in Khuzistan. While these negotiations were carried on, the deliberate Soviet policy of low tariffs on Iranian nonmanufactured goods was making Iran's Caspian provinces more and more dependent on the easily accessible Russian market. This was convenient for Iranian exporters, but it also was dangerous, for Iran, too much linked to Russia economically, might one day be forced to accept dictated solutions. According to the well-known doctrine of Frederic List, "a country exclusively agricultural, destined to sell its raw materials in order to obtain manufactured goods, is bound to be in a subordinated position." This adage proved to be only too true in the case of Iran. Insisting on the recognition of her demands, Russia put an embargo on Iranian imports to the Soviet Union in 1926. This step was catastrophic for Iran's Caspian provinces, whose production of fruit, rice, livestock, hides, and fish was dependent upon sales in Russia. The embargo was strict, and only in exceptional cases did the Soviet government accord import licenses to Iranian merchants. If such licenses were granted, they were used as a political weapon to obtain the services of individuals for the Soviet cause, including, not infrequently, espionage activity for Soviet secret police.[18] The result of this Soviet pressure was quick: in 1927 Iran concluded a commercial treaty with Russia. The treaty, accompanied by a fisheries convention, established a net-balance principle in the trade between both countries and introduced a system of barter transactions. Fifty per cent of Iranian exports to Russia could be handled by private Iranian firms, but at least 25 per cent of these had to be offered first to the Soviet trade organs in Iran. The other 50 per cent of Iranian exports were reserved exclusively to the Soviet trade representations. As regards imports from Russia, several categories of goods were expressly reserved for marketing by Soviet trade organs in Iran. They included such important items as oil and oil products, grain, manufactured metal goods, valuable skins and furs, and arms and munitions.

In this way Soviet trade authorities in Iran obtained quite a privileged position, which enabled them to exert a strong influence on conditions in the Iranian market. The Soviet share of Iranian foreign trade rose from 23 per cent in 1926–1927 to more than 38 per cent in 1928–1929. On the whole, Iranian merchants were irritated by these restrictions and complained that their interests were jeopardized. The most common complaint was that Soviet trade representatives were holding merchandise so long as to cause undue increases in prices. When, owing to great demand, Iranian merchants turned to other countries and signed contracts, the Soviet trade organs would release suddenly their commodities, dictate their prices, and severely hurt those merchants who had already entered into deals with foreign firms.

On the other hand, artificially reduced Soviet prices (sometimes below the cost of production) ruined the development of native Iranian industry. In Iran both private concerns and the government attempted to found sugar, textile, cement, match, and other industries, but difficulties were encountered owing to Soviet dumping practices. As a concrete example a match factory in Tabriz was quoted. Artificial Soviet competition compelled the factory to shut down, but, as soon as the native industry was eliminated, the price of Soviet imported matches rose perceptibly.

[18] Georges Agabekov, *OGPU, the Russian Secret Terror* (New York, 1931).

Furthermore, the Soviet authorities usually demanded cash payment from Iranian merchants, without reciprocity so far as their own purchases were concerned; they obstructed transit of goods through Russia to Iran; and they asked exorbitant prices for certain imported goods, above the level permitted by the Commercial Treaty.[14]

The Fisheries Convention concluded simultaneously with the treaty provided for a mixed Soviet-Iranian Company to exploit the fish and caviar resources of the Caspian Sea. The ownership was equally divided, with Iran receiving in addition 80,000 tomans per annum and 15 per cent of the gross profits (less the expenses of administration) as royalties. This arrangement seemed to favor Iran, yet in reality the contrary was true: the lack of precise provisions on marketing permitted Russia to gain disproportionately high advantages from this convention to the detriment of her Iranian partner.

The Treaty of 1927 expired in 1929, and the next two years witnessed commercial exchanges between both countries without any conventional basis except for a tariff agreement. By the beginning of 1931 the Iranian government came to the conclusion that private traders were unable to withstand the pressure of the Soviet centralized system. Accordingly, in February of that year Iran instituted a foreign trade monopoly, mainly as a protective measure against Soviet economic domination. This was followed by the conclusion of a new trade agreement with Russia in October, 1931, which established the principle of net balance, fixed contingents of goods, and a most-favored-nation clause. This clause gave rise to many misgivings, as the reciprocity that it provided for seemed to be doubtful in practical application. In view of domestic Soviet legislation such rights as the acquisition of property, the residence of nationals in either country, or free practice of trade would in reality not be available to the Iranians.[15]

The new treaty, which, by the way, coincided with Soviet centralization of Eastern trade through the creation of the *Gosvostorg* ("State Eastern Trading Company"), was not entirely satisfactory

14 Connolly, *op. cit.*, pp. 70 ff.
15 *Ibid.*, p. 69.

to Iran, as it left a margin in Soviet exports to Iran that was not to be included in the net balance principle. Besides, the principle of the exchange of Iranian raw materials for Soviet manufactured goods did not correspond to Iranian interests in the long run. A good example was textile goods. In 1929 Iran would sell cotton to Russia for 52 million rials and buy textiles from Russia at a cost of 200 million rials.[16] The difference was the penalty that Iranian people had to pay for lack of their own industries. Aware of this painful situation, Reza Shah took energetic steps to develop a native textile industry. His work was crowned with success: imports of Russian cotton goods fell from around 21 million rubles in 1930 to about $8\frac{1}{2}$ million rubles in 1932.[17]

In 1935 a new trade treaty was signed, which expired in 1938. It was also based on the net balance principle with certain exceptions. On the whole, it permitted the Soviet Union to maintain a favorable balance of trade with Iran, which amounted between 1935 and 1938 to 142 million rials.

Throughout the 1930's Russia occupied first place in Iran's foreign trade, and her share amounted to about one-third of the total. Reciprocally, trade with Iran constituted an important part of Soviet foreign trade, amounting in 1931–1932 to 17 per cent of Russia's total. Only in the year preceding the second World War did Russia cede her predominant place to Germany. Between 1938 and 1939 the Soviet share in Iran's foreign trade fell from 34 to 11.5 per cent, while the German share rose from 27 to 41.5 per cent. This was due partly to the fact that the Soviet-Iranian Commercial Treaty of 1935 was not extended and partly to the intense economic activity of Germany in preparation for war. It is worth while to note in this connection that during the first year of the war, in 1939–1940, when Soviet trade with Iran fell almost to zero and German trade amounted to 39 per cent of the total, most of the Iranian exports to Nazi Germany went in transit through Russia.

To conclude this brief review of Soviet-Iranian economic relations in the interwar period, it may be stated that the Soviet Union consistently strove to maintain Iran in a state of economic subjection

16 *Ibid.*, p. 73.
17 *Ibid.*

by dumping on her markets Russian manufactured goods to the detriment of both foreign competitors and the native industry; that, profiting by the fact that she was the only important market for the northern provinces, Russia did not hesitate to take advantage by compelling Iran to conclude trade agreements often prejudicial to the latter's interests; and that Russia's predominant position in Iran's foreign trade waned only when she met with the more determined centralized system of Germany and with the energetic action of Reza Khan to put order into the affairs of Iran. The introduction of a foreign trade monopoly has already been noted. Another action of epochal significance was the construction, by 1938, of the Transiranian Railway, which finally linked economically the long-separated northern and southern parts of the Iranian Empire. The Transiranian, whose completion was due to the stubborn resolve of Reza Shah and whose financing was based on a special tax on tea and sugar, without foreign help, was an outstanding achievement of Iranian nationalism. But contrary to the early hopes of Soviet rulers, this oriental nationalism was opposed as much to Soviet ambitions as to Western imperialism.

That much can be said about external Iranian-Soviet relations. With regard to internal matters, Moscow would never forget, as is attested by the above-quoted writings, that Reza's regime was only a transitional period, which had, according to the Marxist view, to lead to the final stage of historical development, Socialism, and eventually Communism. The official school of thought having rejected the immediate priority of the agrarian revolution, it followed that, by contrast, Moscow would favor the concentration of efforts upon the industrial workers and the radical intelligentsia. In practice that meant agitation and organizational work among these two classes. Following Lenin's precept that any ruse was good to achieve the ends of the proletarian revolution, there should be both overt and covert activity to promote Communism in Iran. Four instruments should be utilized for that purpose: the official Soviet diplomatic representatives, the Communist party of Iran, the G.P.U., and the Comintern. The initial activities of such Soviet envoys as Rothstein and Shumiatsky have already been reviewed briefly. During the period following Curzon's ultimatum the Soviet Embassy in Teheran behaved in a less conspicuous and provocative way than had been the case under the first two envoys. Yet the Embassy was too convenient a place, owing to its extraterritoriality, to ignore completely its advantages as a safe liaison or even directing center. There were fluctuations in Soviet policy as to the degree to which the services of the Embassy should be utilized for the promotion of revolutionary work, but this institution was never completely eliminated from the over-all plans. The real field work had to be done, however, by instruments able to come into more direct touch with the population. And it was here that the Communist party and the Comintern came to the fore.

THE COMMUNIST PARTY OF IRAN

Organizationally the Communist party of Iran was not a spontaneous Iranian creation. It had its beginnings in Russia. After the Russian Revolution of 1917 a Bolshevik group called *Adalat* ("Justice") was formed among the Iranian workers employed in the oil fields of Baku. At that time about 300,000 Iranians lived and worked in the border regions of Russia, the Caucasus and Turkestan. The original Adalat group in Baku counted about six thousand members. Its influence radiated to Turkestan and Iran. Its leader was Haidar Khan Am Oglu, a veteran of the Tabriz revolt against Mohammed Ali Shah of 1908–1909. Agents sent to Iran by Haidar Khan founded local committees of the party in Tabriz and in the Caspian provinces, as well as in Teheran. In Tabriz the movement was supported chiefly by the Baku Tatars and by the Armenians. Many of them pretended to be refugees from the Bolshevik rule in the Caucasus, and the general chaos that had prevailed in the Caucasian and Transcaspian borderland since 1917 greatly facilitated their infiltration into Iran. The invasion of Gilan by the Red forces in the spring of 1920 and the subsequent proclamation of the Soviet Republic there gave impetus to the development of the party. Haidar Khan arrived from Baku and became a member of Kuchik Khan's Soviet. The movement was greatly strengthened by the fact that among the Soviet Azerbaijani troops operating in Gilan were units composed of indoctrinated Iranian oil workers from Baku. On July

23, 1920, a congress of the Iranian Communists was called to Enzeli, at that time within Kuchik Khan's area. It was attended mainly by Communists of Iranian nationality from Turkestan, and it did a considerable amount of work in regard to the program and the organization of the party. In Gilan, where it was under the protection of the Red Army and where it co-operated with Kuchik Khan's regime, the party could act openly. In the remainder of Iran, however, it had to be conspiratorial.

Sultan-zadeh, Chief of the Near Eastern Section in the People's Commissariat for Foreign Affairs in Moscow and simultaneously representative of the Iranian Communist party in the Third International (Comintern), wrote the following about the party in *Pravda*, July 16, 1921:

> The Communist party tries to rally around it the most advanced elements among the peasants and the workers, to organize them, to elevate them under the inspiration of the Third Communist International, and to create simultaneously trade unions in all cities and the unions of agrarian workers in the villages.

Praising the work done by the Enzeli Congress, he said:

> Thanks to our efforts the Communist party of Persia counts now 4,500 members. . . . During the past year we had more members, but due to the provocations of a group of adventurers who pretended to be Communists, our party's work ceased in some regions. It was necessary also to suspend for some time the publication of the Central Committee's paper *The Communist*. These events have obliged us to become excessively cautious and to increase the secret of our organization. Despite this we have succeeded in creating trade unions of workers and artisans which count now around 4,000 members. The Iranian Communist party has a good understanding of the almost feudal environment in which it has to work.

> The Communist party has adopted in its *minimum program* as its aim the overthrow of the authority of the Shah and of big landowners as well as the liberation of Persia from the economic and political oppression exercised by the English bandits, while trying to achieve a democratic regime in order to be able to augment the Communist propaganda.[18]

In February, 1921, at the time when the Soviet government was

[18] Quoted from Ducrocq, *op. cit.*, pp. 145 ff.

[98]

concluding a generous and anti-imperialistic treaty with Iran, an interesting document was seized from the Tatar Bolsheviks in Tabriz. It was a set of instructions for the committees of the Iranian Communist party Adalat with a view to promoting a revolution in Iran. It read as follows:

The progress of the revolution depending in Persia on the formation of the local Communist committees *Adalat,* it is necessary to engage in organizing them as soon as possible in order to intensify the action of the Persian Communist party in the provinces and in the cities.

   I. The following are the aims of the local committees of the Communist party:

(a) Adherence to political revolution: war on English colonial imperialism. Overthrow of the present government. Establishment of a new government.

(b) Preparation of armed uprising of the party groups and organizations in order to accomplish the revolution.

  II. Immediate tasks of the local committees:

(a) Creation in the sphere of activity of the local committees of a central committee composed of the most zealous, most disciplined members, respected and loved by these committees.

(b) Preparation of new sections of party members.

(c) Awakening of the revolutionary forces and their organization under the auspices of the central committee.

(d) Preparation of local groups with a view to revolutionary struggle and to an immediate uprising on the orders of the Central Committee.

 III. Tactics of a local committee to realize the above-mentioned objects:

(a) In the papers, in the discussions, and at the meetings of the circles make propaganda to save the Orient from the clutches of English imperialism and against the present government, which is one of the principal obstacles to the salvation of Persia.

(b) Make propaganda immediately to reorganize the guilds created by the workers of the same trade, the importance of which is considerable for the grouping of workers; awake class feeling among the workers and spread agitation among them in the country.

(c) Prepare a youth union, which is one of the important auxiliaries of any revolutionary action.

(d) Organize a regular service of information and of liaison with other party groups in the zone of action.

(e) The local committees must send every month reports on their activity and on the political and economic situation of their district through the intermediation of the provincial committee.

(f) A local committee must be composed of a secretary and of two directors who will call party meetings. A certain number of intelligent members shall be designated to organize other groups in the region.

(g) The organization of the sections in the region shall be analogous to that of urban groups.

Signed: Haidar Khan

Seal: Central Committee of the Communist party of Persia Adalat.[19]

The above document, somewhat verbose in its phraseology, reveals the far-reaching ambition and hope that the party will play its due role in Iran. As a matter of fact, at the time when these instructions were written, the prospects for revolution looked bright in Iran. The Gilan Republic enjoyed virtual independence from the central government and could serve as a lever for the further spread of revolution. The unfortunate Anglo-Iranian Treaty was being denounced by practically everybody in Iran, and the prevailing climate in politics was decidedly anti-British. The Soviet government was on the point of executing a bold propaganda maneuver by formally renouncing old tsarist privileges. The disruption of economic life in Iran as the result of the war and the suspension of normal trade with Russia had produced great unemployment and discontent among the masses. This induced the Soviet leaders to cherish fond hopes for an early radical change in Iran. In September, 1920, Haidar Khan participated in the Congress of the Peoples of the East in Baku and, together with Sultan-zadeh,[20] actively represented the Communist party of Iran. In those days of enthusiasm no attempt was made to conceal the fact that the Russian and Iranian Communist parties had an organizational link with each other. Sultanzadeh, as mentioned earlier, could combine without embarrassment the functions of an Iranian party representative and a responsible official of the Moscow Foreign Commissariat.

To Sultan-zadeh we owe, perhaps, more frank information about the early activities of the party than to any other source. In his book *Sovremennaya Persya* ("Contemporary Persia"), published in Mos-

19 Ducrocq, *op. cit.*, pp. 144–145. Reproduced from French by permission of the publisher, Presses Universitaires de France.

20 For the identity of Sultan-zadeh, see p. 224.

cow in 1922, he revealed that after initial successes the Communist movement in Iran suffered serious setbacks and that it followed closely the orders of the Comintern:

> A party that had not gone through a phase of long years of organization, a party in whose ranks no doctrinaire experts were to be found, a party that was working isolated in a region dominated by semicolonial policy could not in a short time strengthen itself and stand on its own feet. The organizers committed numerous errors and turned to recrimination and to internal dissensions. At the beginning of 1922 energetic intervention of the Executive Committee of the Communist International re-established peace. In substance, the party had remained faithful to its principles. [21]

By 1922, according to Sultan-zadeh, the party had shrunk to only 1,500 members, yet it seemed that this shrinkage was beneficial from the organizational and ideological viewpoint. Soviet press and publications were at that time quite optimistic about the success of the Communists in Iran, because the party managed to organize a number of trade unions and faithfully followed the plan elaborated in Moscow by the Oriental Bureau and by the International Trade Unions Council (Mezhsovprof).[22]

On September 17, 1922, *Pravda* analyzed a series of demands formulated in Teheran by the pro-Communist paper *Haqiqat*. They were:

(1) Immediate ending of martial law in all regions of Iran.

(2) Release of all political prisoners.

(3) Reappearance of all the newspapers that were suspended without previous judgment.

(4) Lifting of censorship.

(5) Freedom of assembly and association.

(6) Freedom to bring to justice officials guilty of embezzlement and also ministers, parliamentary deputies, and foreign advisers.

(7) Adoption of laws regulating the relationship between labor and capital.

(8) Prohibition of the use by estate owners of violent methods against peasants and the adoption of laws to protect the peasantry.

(9) Distribution of state lands among the peasants.

[21] Pages 60 ff.
[22] V. Ossetrov, "Les Partis politiques en Perse," *Novy Vostok*, I, 147 ff.

(10) Adoption of income tax.

(11) Election of administrative officials in towns and villages.[23]

These demands, published openly by a newspaper, differed visibly in scope and intensity from the previously quoted secret instructions. One may presume that this was intentional. While proclaiming openly a liberal and relatively nonrevolutionary program in order to win over progressive elements of the intelligentsia to its cause, the party simultaneously conducted a revolutionary agitation among the workers. The preliminary step in this direction was to organize the workers into trade unions, and to this task the party gave particular attention. While on duty in Iran as Consul General, Tardov, a prominent member of the Soviet Orientalist Association, made a study of the existing Iranian trade unions and presented an analytical report to his government. This report as well as other sources served as the basis for an exhaustive article on Iranian trade unions that appeared in *Novy Vostok* in 1922 under the signature of V. Ossetrov. According to this author, trade unionism, which had begun in Iran during the 1906 revolution, was still in the early twenties predominantly in the form of artisans' guilds. In Isfahan at that time forty artisans' guilds formed the Artisans' Union. Their program, according to Ossetrov, was "permeated by petty bourgeois ideology of the narrow guild group, seeing in the constitution and in the parliament the only device for the defense of their exclusive interests." [24] In Tabriz there were also forty guilds, and in Kermanshah twenty. In Teheran the artisans belonging to a number of guilds were of a slightly different type than those in the provincial cities. Here the hired worker type predominated, in contrast to the generally independent artisan class in such a city as Isfahan. As time went on stratification became more and more visible among the artisans. This process, believed Ossetrov, would result in a split and a class struggle within the guilds themselves. Thus, he stated, "This form of organization turns out to be entirely antiquated and faces a period of disintegration."

It is this process of disintegration that the party desired to turn to its own advantage. In the years immediately following the revolu-

23 Ducrocq, *op. cit.,* pp. 142 ff.
24 "Le Mouvement syndical et ouvrier en Perse," *Novy Vostok,* II, 571.

tion in Russia, when Gilan and Mazanderan were controlled by Kuchik Khan, and especially during the existence of the Soviet Republic there, two real workers' trade unions were created in Enzeli: a porters' union and a longshoremen's union. This initial development of trade unionism among the workers of northern Iran was due, according to Ossetrov, "to their greater knowledge of workers' movements in Russia." By 1921 eleven workers' unions existed in Teheran.[25] They grouped 8,250 members and were composed of hired laborers only. In the same year a Council of Trade Unions was created in Teheran, to which each union was to send three delegates. The council promptly decided to affiliate with the Red Profintern and informed Moscow accordingly. In Tabriz, which is an important industrial center, a trade unions' association called Kargaran (800 members) was formed and seemed to enjoy a major political influence. It had its own press organ, *Takammol*. In contrast to the north, the south of Iran did not prove to be a favorable ground for trade unionism. The Teheran Council of Trade Unions, despite repeated attempts, could not establish a working relationship with the workers in the south. Ossetrov commented about it with regret, inasmuch as southern Iran with 47,000 workers employed in the British oil fields represented "a large field for the development of workers' organization."

The activity of the Trade Unions Council in Teheran proved moderately successful. One of its most important affiliates, the Printers' Union, succeeded in making a collective agreement with printing press owners that provided for the shortening of the workday to eight hours and for overtime pay and that covered several other points such as dismissals and medical care. The council was also politically active. It published the *Haqiqat* ("Truth"), a paper with a circulation of about two thousand, definitely Communist in tone.[26] *Haqiqat* insisted on denying that the trade union movement was caused by Bolshevik agitation. This did not prevent the govern-

[25] These were: (1) printers, 200 members, one of the oldest trade unions in Iran, first created in 1908 in Teheran; (2) bakers, 2,000; (3) telegraphers, 564; (4) post office clerks, 100; (5) government schoolteachers, 400; (6) pastry bakers, 400; (7) store salesmen, 80; (8) tailors, 1,000; (9) shop clerks, 120; (10) brass workers, 150; (11) shoemakers, 1,800.

[26] Ducrocq, *op. cit.*, p. 125.

ment, however, from closing it for revolutionary propaganda. Its place was soon filled by a new organ, *Eqtesad-i-Iran* ("Economics of Iran").

Work for the promotion of trade unionism did not exhaust the activities of the party. They spread to the press and to parliament, although usually in a more or less disguised form. With regard to the press, the propaganda conducted by Soviet Ministers Rothstein and Shumiatsky, mentioned earlier in this work, was of inestimable value. Encouraging any manifestation of nationalistic, democratic, or liberal spirit among the Iranian intelligentsia or merchant classes, the envoys succeeded in creating a number of pro-Communist or pro-Soviet papers, edited by all sorts of men ranging from genuine liberals disgusted with the antiquated system of government in their country to ardent Soviet sympathizers of the fellow-traveler type.

Communist influence in parliament was of a less tangible character. In the Fourth Majlis, which convened in the summer of 1921, the deputies were divided into so-called Majority and Minority groups. The latter was headed by Suleiman Mirza, who professed to be a Socialist. Suleiman Mirza had originally been a member of the old pro-German Democratic Party. After the war, he and Mussavat organized the Social Democratic Party (*Ejtemayun Amiyun*), in which were merged the Left Democrats and some Independent Socialists. Neither of these groups had strength among the masses, but after their unification by Suleiman Mirza, the new party sought active support among the trade unions. Thus it had a link with the Communist-influenced labor organizations. Suleiman's Minority defended in the Majlis the strike of teachers, which broke out in 1921, and organized mass demonstrations in the streets. Eventually this group became a front for the Communist party. Led by Suleiman Mirza and Reza Rusta it took a vigorous part in the electoral campaign to the Fifth Majlis in 1923 under the name of the National Bloc. Rusta's name was to reappear twenty years later in Iranian politics as one of the most active Communists. Although the National Bloc managed to gain some support among the proletarian masses in Teheran as well as in Enzeli, Kerman, and Tabriz, it was defeated in the elections. The government as well as the British accused it of being pro-Soviet and desirous of spreading anarchy and revolution.

As a result, many arrests were made among the Bloc's members and some of its more active leaders were killed.[27] We do not know what happened at that time to Rusta, although there are indications that he sought refuge in Russia and was later arrested and jailed in Iran under the regime of Reza Shah.[28] As to Suleiman Mirza, he continued as a deputy to the Majlis; and when Reza Shah overthrew the Qajar dynasty in 1925, he and his left-wing group of fifteen deputies voted in favor of recognizing Reza as Shah of Iran.[29] This seemingly strange behavior in favor of a man who had been instrumental in arresting their comrades two years earlier, can be explained by the fact that Reza's coup represented, after all, a bourgeois tendency opposed to the old feudal regime, and thus, despite everything, constituted a step forward.

The vote in favor of Reza Shah was apparently the last open act of a group working in liaison with or at least sympathetic with some of the aims professed by the Communists. Reza Shah might have been regarded with approval by Soviet theoreticians as the representative of a national liberation movement of anti-imperialist tinge, but that approval did not lead him to reciprocate in his attitude toward Communism. On the contrary, during his regime energetic measures were taken against the Communists and even against leftist liberals, who in Reza's thinking represented subversive groups dangerous to the unity of Iran. Gradually all political parties and groups disappeared to make way for the ever-growing military dictatorship of the new Shah. The same fate befell the press, so that ultimately only four newspapers were permitted to appear in Teheran, and none of them was allowed to express views critical of the government. Independent trade unions were also liquidated, which, incidentally, caused the International Labor Organization to question the genuineness of the Iranian workers' representation in that body. Under these conditions the Communist party was driven underground. In fact, to an outside observer it was difficult to see anything on the surface of Iranian life that pertained to Communism. The Soviet press and publications became very reticent about the activities of the party

27 Gurko-Kriazhin, *op. cit.*, p. 25.
28 As to his activities during World War II, see Chapters Eight and Eleven.
29 Gurko-Kriazhin, *op. cit.*, p. 25.

in Iran, no doubt because of fear lest their information might facilitate the task of the Iranian police.

Of that underground period in the party's history only a few
definite facts can be ascertained. It is known that the party relied
heavily upon the national minorities in Iran, especially the Armenians and to some extent the Assyrians. Its activities centered
mainly in the north of Iran, presumably because of the convenient
proximity to the Soviet border, but it extended also to Teheran. For
a number of years in the 1920's the presidency of the party was in the
hands of Sultan-zadeh, who was assisted in his work by Hasanoff and
Shareqi. The party held a congress with the Turkish Communist
party at Urumia in 1927 and there decided to send Hasanoff as
Iranian delegate to the ninth Plenum of the Comintern. Soviet
consular and diplomatic representatives, especially in the north,
aided the party. At one time the Soviet consul in Meshed, Apresoff,
was recalled to Moscow. George Agabekov, a former member of the
Soviet secret police, wrote in this connection in his memoirs:

> Apresoff's recall displeased the Persian Communists. A letter was sent to
> Chicherin, Stalin, and Djerzhinsky, expressing the hope of the Iranian Com-
> munist Party, of the Communist Youth of Iran, and of certain bodies of
> Persian workers, that the action in Apresoff's case would be reversed; for the
> origin and development of the Communist movement in Persia were entirely
> due to Apresoff.[30]

This laudatory tone toward Apresoff seems to be slightly exaggerated
as it is difficult to imagine how a consul in Meshed could be responsible for the whole of the Iranian Communist movement, yet it is eloquent of the role played by the Soviet representative in the region
of Khorasan at least.

Thus the party, despite all odds, continued its existence, and
whenever necessary its morale was bolstered up by the expert advice
of special Comintern agents dispatched to Iran. By 1928 even the
basically favorable attitude of Soviet oriental experts toward Reza
Shah did not prevent the principal organ of the Comintern from
flaring up in an outburst of indignation against the Iranian regime.
For example, in its traditional column "The White Terror," where

[30] *Op. cit.*, p. 76.

persecution against the comrades all over the world was regularly reported, *International Press Correspondence* in the fall of 1928 published the following article:

Appeal of the Young Communist Leagues of Persia and Great Britain against the White Terror in Persia.

One of the best and most fearless comrades in the Persian revolutionary working class movement has been murdered by the Persian Government. Comrade Hedjazi, a member of the illegal Communist Party and Young Communist League of Persia, was imprisoned for his activities. While in prison he was cruelly tortured in order to compel him to reveal information with regard to the revolutionary movement, its work and its members. This he steadfastly refused to do. His death came as a result of the police applying ice to his head for three successive days. The torture and death of this comrade is but one incident typical of the reign of terror being conducted by the Persian Government against the revolutionary movement. Many revolutionary workers are at present languishing in jail for such "crimes" as participating in the last May Day celebrations, or as "suspected" of being members of the Young Communist League. This brutal anti-working class terrorism is waged at the behest of and on behalf of *British Imperialism,* whose puppet the Persian government is. British imperialist oil interests in Persia and the plan to use Persia as a base for military operations against the Soviet Union are responsible for collaboration of the British and Persian bourgeoisie against the Persian revolutionary working class movement. The Young Communist Leagues of Britain and Persia unite in protesting against the murder of Comrade Hedjazi, the continued imprisonment of the Persian comrades and the White Terrorism exercised against the workers' organizations. Unitedly we demand the release of all imprisoned comrades and call on the working class youth of Persia and Britain to sharpen the struggle against the White Terror in Persia and against British Imperialist Domination. *Down with the White Terror in Persia.*

Young Communist League of Persia

Young Communist League of Great Britain [31]

In another resolution adopted by the Executive Committee of the League against Imperialism at its session in Berlin in 1928, an appeal was made to "fight for the overthrow of the Government of Reza Shah who enslaves the Persian people in the interest of British imperialism."

[31] VIII (Oct. 19, 1928), 1336.

These resolutions not only reveal the growing dissatisfaction with the regime that, on theoretical grounds, seemed acceptable to Communists. (This new trend, somewhat revisionist in character, had to find its final expression after the Sixth Congress of the Comintern.) They also indicate that the revolution in Iran and the interests of the Soviet Union were continuously identified in the minds of the Comintern leaders, who, on their part, never ceased to be vigilant over party activities there.

COMINTERN AND G.P.U. IN IRAN [32]

In the promotion of the revolution in Iran both the Third International and the G.P.U. were of prime importance. Theoretically the functions and aims of these two organizations were different. While the Comintern aimed at the ideological guidance of Communism all over the world and at organizational help to its national sections, the G.P.U. was to perform tasks of a more concrete character. In practice, however, the work of one body was parallel and closely related to the activity of the other.

The G.P.U., an undaunted "sword of the revolution," was an institution as old as the Soviet regime itself. It developed an elaborate organization, which extended not only throughout Russia but to foreign countries as well. Oriental matters were dealt with by two sections: the Eastern Section (V.O.) for work among the Asiatic peoples of the Soviet Union and the Foreign Section, which through its "Oriental Sector" was competent to deal with areas outside the U.S.S.R. The Foreign Section normally acted through agents called G.P.U. residents. These, in turn, were divided into "legal" and "illegal" or "secret" residents. A legal resident was one who nominally had another function for the Soviet government: that of consul, com-

---

[32] The information contained in this section is drawn from three chief sources: Georges Agabekov, *op. cit.;* Alexander Barmine, *op. cit.;* and Grigory Bessedovsky, *Revelations of a Soviet Diplomat* (London, 1931). All three authors had been high officials in the Soviet hierarchy and had escaped from Russia and written their memoirs. In some points their stories overlap. This fact helps to dispel doubts, if any, regarding the reliability of their extraordinary personal testimony. Agabekov's book is especially valuable because of the names and details mentioned in describing the G.P.U. and Comintern work in the Middle East. A number of these names may be found also in the official publication of the Comintern, the *International Press Correspondence.*

mercial representative, or attaché to the Soviet Embassy. Hence his official function served only as a disguise for his real duties. An illegal or secret resident was an agent who had no connection with official Soviet missions. He was expected to establish himself permanently in a foreign country, to adopt a trade or a profession, and thus to become independent of anything that might happen to the official Soviet mission. If as a result of the rupture of diplomatic relations a Soviet Embassy had to leave the country, the illegal resident remained and continued his work. In the early twenties there was a tendency to favor the system of legal residents as the facilities that an extraterritorial embassy or a consulate afforded were obvious. In 1927–1929, however, this practice was more or less abandoned because the Soviets expected a capitalist war of intervention and a possible rupture of diplomatic relations with several countries as a prelude to it. Consequently more emphasis was put on organizing a network of secret residents.

The Oriental Sector had a number of agents in Iran, Afghanistan, Turkey, Iraq, and several other Eastern countries. These agents were men of wide experience in the type of work to which they were assigned. They had usually passed, before their foreign appointments, through an apprenticeship in the domestic Eastern Section. Very often they were graduates of one of the Soviet academies of oriental languages, Tashkent and Moscow schools being prominent in this respect. Likewise many of them were oriental natives, recruited mainly from among the peoples of Turkestan and the Caucasus. The G.P.U. work in Iran was directed from the center in Moscow, but three provincial G.P.U. offices, those of Tashkent, Baku, and Tiflis, were specially concerned with Iran's border provinces.

Nominally the foreign policy of Soviet Russia was directed by the People's Commissariat for Foreign Affairs. Yet the G.P.U., which as a rule was better informed on the situation abroad, had much to say about it and often disagreed with the Foreign Commissariat. Ultimately quarrels between these two bodies were settled by the Politburo.

On the whole, the G.P.U. played an important role in the actual shaping and execution of Soviet foreign policy toward Iran. In 1925 a revolt broke out in Khorasan. It was headed by an army officer,

Salar-jang, and caused considerable trouble to the Teheran authorities. The G.P.U. immediately manifested great interest and its Ashkhabad office asked Moscow for permission to arm the rebels and assist them through instructors. The Ashkhabad G.P.U. appraised the rebellion as a popular movement of revolutionary character and considered that Soviet aid was imperative. Instead of acting promptly, Moscow delayed its decision and asked for further information to be obtained through an investigation on the spot. This procrastination proved fatal. Lacking adequate assistance, the rebellion was speedily crushed by the Iranian government. Yet despite the delaying action of the central authorities the zealous chief of the Ashkhabad G.P.U., Karoutsky, sent fifty disguised Soviet frontier guards, with a number of machine guns, as instructors to the rebels. This aid proved insufficient. Karoutsky was later reported to have complained bitterly about Moscow's lack of initiative and to have expressed fears as to the resulting loss of Soviet prestige among oriental peoples. Calling the Khorasan revolt a Persian "Canton," he said that such promising revolts close to Russia's borders should never be deprived of active Soviet help.[33]

In the spring of 1927 an agent by the name of George Agabekov was sent to Iran as "legal" Resident General of the G.P.U. (officially his function was that of an attaché at the Soviet Embassy). Agabekov was given a set of instructions that provided for (a) centralization of the G.P.U. activities in Iran in the hands of the Resident General, (b) organization of the G.P.U. apparatus in southern Iran with a view to facilitating contact with India and Iraq, and (c) special extension of activity to Arabistan, the area of the Anglo-Iranian Oil Company concession.[34] In practice this meant that hitherto independent G.P.U. agents in Tabriz, Pahlavi, and Khorasan-Baluchistan had to sever their direct links with Tiflis, Baku, and Moscow and come under the command of the Teheran resident. Such a change, as Agabekov related in his memoirs, was actually accomplished, although not without difficulties because of the professional jealousies

[33] Agabekov, *op. cit.*, p. 75.

[34] Bessedovsky, *op. cit.*, p. 200, corroborates this by saying that in 1927 the Comintern assigned a fund of $750,000 to promote revolutionary and trade union movements in India.

of the Tiflis and Baku branches. The subjection of the north-Iranian agents to the authority of Teheran was not without definite purpose: the G.P.U. wanted to intensify its activity in Iran and desired to combat more effectively the national movements of the Dashnaks and Mussavatists as well as to keep an eye on the Kurds. The Dashnaks were members of the Armenian party Dashnaksutiun, which in 1918 had been instrumental in proclaiming the free Armenian Republic and which in the course of the Republic's stormy two-year history had dominated its politics. As followers of evolutionary socialism, the Dashnaks were a special target of Communist hatred; they were regarded by Moscow as dangerous Mensheviks. When Armenia was overrun by the Red Army in 1920, many Dashnak leaders escaped abroad and conducted intense activity to restore freedom to their country. Concretely the Dashnaks worked for a revolt in Armenia against the Soviet regime. Spying on their activities or splitting their unity became, therefore, one of the principal tasks of the G.P.U. in Iran. As Tabriz was one of the most important Dashnak centers, the G.P.U. paid special attention to that city. The same could be said of the nationalist Mussavat party, which had represented Social Democracy in the free Republic of Azerbaijan. Its leaders in exile grouped themselves in Constantinople and were very active in promoting the unity of all peoples of the Caucasus suffering under the Soviet rule. They also had a representative in Tabriz. This nationalist movement of the Caucasian peoples was commonly known as Prometheism, and there were reasons to believe that several foreign countries, in anticipation of an ultimate clash between the West and Soviet Russia, assisted the movement morally and financially. Thus the French government continued to recognize the diplomatic missions of Georgia, Armenia, and Azerbaijan in Paris for a few years. After the conquest of Transcaucasia by the Red Army, the British, with their traditional interest in the Caucasus and Baku oil fields, were also interested in Prometheism, and not infrequently officers attached to the office of the British military attaché at Teheran were of Caucasian descent. Poland also manifested interest in Caucasian nationalism, as was testified by numerous articles in Polish orientalist magazines and by the friendly hospitality extended to Caucasian refugees, some of whom were even given commissions

[111]

in the Polish army.[35] By using *agents provocateurs* and infiltrating the Dashnak and Mussavatist organizations in Iran, the G.P.U. was able to obtain valuable data, especially the names of anti-Communist nationalists in the Caucasus, which in turn permitted Soviet authorities to effect a number of arrests there.

As to the Kurdish problem, Moscow seems to have inherited from tsarist Russia a great interest in it. Following old traditions Soviet Russia paid special attention to the Iranian Kurds inhabiting the Lake Urumia region. When the Khan of Maku rose in revolt against the government in 1923, Moscow promptly decided to accredit a Soviet consul to him.[36] In 1927 the Soviet government conceived a scheme to create an "independent" Kurdish republic within the Soviet Union, in the area inhabited by Kurds. The creation of such a republic would have effects similar to the creation of the Armenian Republic: Kurdish sympathies in Iran, Iraq, and Turkey would turn toward this little nucleus of Kurdish statehood and, in the event of war with other Powers, Russia would be able to count on support of these warlike tribesmen. Ultimately the Commissariat of Foreign Affairs pronounced itself against this scheme, because of the possible straining of relations between Russia, Iran, and Turkey. Thus the plan was abandoned. Instead it was decided to start an intense

[35] It was the magazine *Wschód* ("The East") that propagated the ideas of Prometheism in Poland. For typical articles see *Wschód,* no. 19, Nov., 1935, and no. 27, March, 1938. The latter article, "Russian Imperialism in Persia," by Bohdan Halajczuk, comes to the following conclusion it its English summary: "This is understood by Persia, who also knows that her independence can only then be assured and guaranteed when she succeeds in issuing from the status of a buffer State; this can take place only in the event that the ever potent threat of an insatiable Russia is removed from her frontiers, and when independent Caucasia and Turkestan will block the historical routes followed by Russian imperialism" (p. 25).

According to Agabekov (*op. cit.,* p. 100) the Polish government was subsidizing nationalist elements of the Caucasus at the rate of $1,000 monthly, but these subsidies ceased about 1927.

[36] Barmine, *op. cit.,* p. 135. The Khanate of Maku is the most strategically situated Kurdish area. It occupies the Sharur-Daralagez and Nakhichevan districts of Iran. Squeezed among Soviet Russia, Turkey, and Iran this tiny khanate provided a transit road for Turkish, Russian, and Dashnak armies in World War I as well as a center of political intrigue. An interesting account of political maneuvers in this area between 1914 and 1919 is contained in the article "Makiyskoye Khanstvo," *Novy Vostok,* I (1922), 334.

propaganda in favor of the Soviet Union among the Kurdish tribes of Iran, Iraq, and Turkey. After such preliminary activity a secret treaty was to be concluded between representative Kurdish chieftains and Russia, providing for mutual assistance. This plan was put into execution, and Sauj Bulaq (Mahabad) was selected as a center from which propaganda should radiate. The G.P.U. resident at Tabriz, Minossian, was chosen to direct this work.[37]

Watching the activities of groups hostile to the Soviet Union, the G.P.U. in Iran observed carefully the White Russian exile group known as The Fraternity of Russian Truth. The Fraternity, which had its headquarters in Paris, kept a branch office at Pahlavi. Using a former tsarist colonel by the name of Javahoff as a spy, the G.P.U. resident in Pahlavi managed to get the secrets of this organization and to intercept its correspondence regularly.

Apart from these special tasks the G.P.U. had to perform a number of routine duties. Among these may be mentioned interception of the correspondence of foreign diplomatic and consular missions, especially that of the British military attaché, Major Fraser,[38] and of British consuls; smuggling of arms and agitators through Khorasan and Baluchistan to India; spying on Iranian army activities; reporting on the Anglo-Iranian Oil Company; and interception of the correspondence between the Iranian government and its embassies abroad.

In order to carry out these multifarious tasks an elaborate network of agents was necessary. They were disguised under many trades and occupations, the Soviet commercial companies in Iran being an important haven for these men. Agabekov mentioned in his memoirs the Soviet Oil Syndicate, the Iranian-Soviet cotton trading company Khlopkom, and the wool trading firm Cherst as agencies whose officials served often also as G.P.U. agents. These firms were by no means the only disguise for them. An Armenian Orbeliani, who in the 1920's was Tass correspondent in Teheran, was described by Agabekov as a secret agent, while a number of officials in the Iranian

[37] Agabekov, *op. cit.*, p. 97.

[38] *Ibid.*, pp. 83, 109. Major W. A. K. Fraser enjoyed a long and distinguished career as military attaché in Iran. Promoted to the rank of Major-General, he continued in the same capacity throughout the second World War. He was reputed to have great influence among the tribes of southern Iran.

Ministry of Public Works were also on the G.P.U. payroll. Some of these agents, according to the same source, were relatives of the Minister of the Court Teymurtash, and the agent known as No. 16 was a prince of the House of Qajars. The G.P.U. scored quite a success when it engaged the services of the cipher expert of the Iranian Council of Ministers. Two Iranian consuls, in Khanaqin and in Mosul, who had served previously in Erivan (Soviet Armenia) and Nakhichevan (Soviet Azerbaijan), were also mentioned by Agabekov as G.P.U. informers, while the Iranian police chief in Tabriz was reported to have received bribes from the Tiflis G.P.U. The Iranian governor of the district of Baharz, south of Meshed, by the name of Saul as-Saltaneh was recruited by the G.P.U. to assist in smuggling arms from Russia through Afghanistan to India. Agabekov's revelations were corroborated in the main by such former Soviet diplomats as Alexander Barmine or Gregory Bessedovsky. Vincent Sheean, an American who had visited Iran in 1927 during the period described by Agabekov, wrote in this connection:

In Persia the Soviet Union interferes to an extent which would not be credible in western Europe or America. Russian agents are everywhere; Russian money pays for the most incongruous assortment of political movements, popular upheavals, dynastic flurries, tribal agitations. Most of the crop of rebellions which have been harvested by Reza Shah's seizure of the imperial crown have had legitimate and natural bases, of course; but in some of them—particularly those which have been taking place in the north, in Gilan and Mazanderan, and in the northeast, toward Turkestan—Russian influence is so obvious that it would be silly to disregard it.[39]

It is a point of interest to note that in its activity in Iran the G.P.U. made ample use of the Armenian minority, despite the fact that another Armenian group—the Dashnaks—was so hostile to Russia. The number of G.P.U. agents of Armenian nationality was astounding. Agabekov himself, his Teheran aide Makarian, the Tabriz resident Minossian, and several others were Armenians. It looked as if the G.P.U. had developed a special fondness for this race. Very revealing, in particular, were the G.P.U. approaches to the Armenian Orthodox hierarchy in Iran and elsewhere in the Middle East. Agabekov relates that as a principle Soviet authorities tried to win

[39] *The New Persia* (New York and London, 1927), p. 212. Copyright 1927 by The Century Company. Reprinted by permission of Appleton-Century-Crofts, Inc.

over to their cause bishops in Soviet Armenia. If they succeeded, the G.P.U. would seek an appointment for such a bishop to a post outside the confines of the U.S.S.R. so as to have a willing agent in a foreign country. These appointments were possible because the *Catholicos,* the head of the Armenian Orthodox Church, had his See in Echmiadzin, in Soviet Armenia, and it was on his orders that bishops and priests were appointed to such far-flung countries as Manchuria or India. This was also the reason why Soviet authorities were always anxious to have some bishop from Soviet Armenia elected to the supreme rank of *Catholicos.* In 1929, since the *Catholicos* was of very advanced age, there was speculation about his successor. Among the candidates, Nerses, Armenian Archbishop of Tabriz, stood a good chance of being called to the post. Nerses was known to the Russians as favoring the Dashnak liberation movement. If he were elected, Iran might become his country of residence in his new capacity. This would practically put an end to Soviet influence on the Armenian Church. Under these circumstances the Soviet authorities did all they could in order to get rid of Nerses and his candidacy. The choice of the G.P.U. (which was in charge of this "operation") fell ultimately on an Armenian Church dignitary in France by the name of Kitchian. Kitchian had previously been drafted into the service of the G.P.U. Under some pretext he was invited to visit Russia and there an arrangement was concluded between him and the G.P.U.: Kitchian was to go to Soviet Armenia and, assisted by the Soviet secret police, was to obtain consecration as Archbishop and appointment as Legate to Iran. Once in this post he was to work to remove Nerses from Tabriz and replace him with Archbishop Mesrop of Isfahan (or rather Julfa, which is the Armenian suburb of Isfahan) who was simultaneously head of the Indo-Persian Eparchy. Having achieved the transfer of Mesrop to Tabriz, Kitchian was then to try to obtain for himself the appointment to the former's place. By becoming Eparch for Iran and India he would be in a position to establish a good network of G.P.U. agents all over India. At the time when Agabekov wrote his memoirs (1931) Kitchian had obtained his appointment to Teheran as a Legate. Agabekov reported also that about that time a G.P.U. man, a former bishop of Harbin, Manchuria, was appointed to the Armenian bishopric in Bagdad and that

Basmatchian, a dignitary of the Church hierarchy in Constantinople, was compelled to co-operate with the secret police. In the latter case, Basmatchian had been about to be consecrated bishop and for that reason had had to appear personally in Echmiadzin. The Soviet Consulate at Constantinople, however, had stubbornly refused to issue him a visa unless Basmatchian promised that he would perform certain tasks for the G.P.U. upon his appointment as bishop. Playing thus on the man's ambition, Soviet authorities finally obtained the desired end: Basmatchian, according to Agabekov, entered into the service of the G.P.U.

Another example of the use of Armenians as G.P.U. agents is the bribing of Dr. Gazarian, ex-member of the Dashnak Central Committee, who was persuaded to edit in Teheran an Armenian newspaper *Gahapar* in which he was to praise the Soviet Union. The doctor was given as compensation, apart from his regular subsidy, an internship in the Soviet Hospital in Teheran. A Society for Aid to Armenians in Iran's capital was utilized as a convenient front for political and espionage activities. Agabekov reports that its president, Dr. Caro Minasian, was the personal physician of Sheikh Khazal of Mohammera (Khorramshahr), who in turn depended much on British support in his land claims against the Iranian government. Minasian, having easy access to the Sheikh, gained his confidence and was able to report to the G.P.U. the details of Khazal's dealings with the British.

As a result of the new program adopted by the Sixth Congress of the Comintern in 1928,[40] fresh instructions were sent to the G.P.U. Resident General in Iran. They provided for an increased study of the tribal affairs in Iran and an extension of work to southern Iran and India. The Anglo-Iranian Oil Company in Khuzistan was to be the subject of an intensified study. In compliance with these orders the G.P.U. Resident General undertook a round trip through southern Iran, visiting Qum, Isfahan, Shiraz, Bushire, Yazd, and Kashan. Soviet consulates in this part of the country were inspected and new agents recruited. The next development was the final change of the G.P.U. system in Iran from legal into secret. Agabekov, the legal Resident General, was recalled to Moscow. Triandophiloff,

40 See Chapter Five.

chief of the Oriental Sector in the Foreign Section of the G.P.U., was to be the first secret resident. He was preceded by another agent from headquarters by the name of Einhorn, who upon arriving under a false name in Teheran, established there a garage business. This Edelstein Garage soon increased its personnel by four other individuals, all of them working for the G.P.U.[41]

It was characteristic of many of these fantastic episodes that a number of men employed by the G.P.U. for work abroad were also agents of the Communist International. Pianitsky, Director of the Foreign Relations of the Comintern Executive Committee, was in constant consultation with the Foreign Section of the G.P.U., and many a campaign was planned together. Persons whose names appeared first as G.P.U. men emerged later as emissaries of the Comintern. In relation to Iran one such man, mentioned several times by Agabekov, was Reza-zadeh, whose colorful career included missions to Constantinople and other oriental centers under disguised names. In August, 1928,—that is, at the time of the Sixth Congress—a special delegate of the Comintern, whose name Agabekov failed to mention but who might possibly have been Reza-zadeh, arrived in Teheran in order to strengthen the links with the Iranian Communist party and help reorganize it. Agabekov described him as a Tatar about thirty years old.[42] He was very much interested in everything pertaining to the Anglo-Iranian Oil Company and also in the Armenians of Iran. The latter possessed an organization known as the Armenian Workers' party. It desired to change its name into the Armenian Communist party, to be affiliated with the Iranian Communist party, and through it to establish contact with the Comintern. One of the reasons for the delegate's visit was to ascertain facts concerning this party before the Comintern took action on its request.

Following the policy of courting the favor of national minorities in oriental countries, the Comintern also paid attention to the As-

[41] Agabekov, *op. cit.*, pp. 171 ff.

[42] In his memoirs written in 1931 the former Soviet diplomat Bessedovsky mentions a Tatar from Kazan by the name of Khakimov who acted as representative of the Comintern in the East. In 1927–1928 Khakimov was Soviet Consul-General in Hejaz and following a special Soviet mission led by Astakhov was also appointed trade representative to Yemen.

syrians, who were widely dispersed over Iran, Iraq, and Syria. A Communist party known as the Assyrian Section of the Third International was organized among this minority.

In concluding this review of the interwar era in Iranian politics, we would like to recall that we have given it the title of the "Period of Armed Truce." It is difficult, indeed, to consider this period as a genuine peace. On the surface, conditions inside Iran and Iran's foreign relations appeared calm and undisturbed. Iran was not in a state of war either with Russia or with Britain, nor was there any open conflict between the latter two states. In reality, powerful forces of Iranian nationalism, conservative British imperialism, and dynamic Soviet Communism were at cross purposes and were, to a large degree, mutually incompatible. The most disturbing factor was, of course, the Russian revolutionary proselytism, expressed by the zealous activities of Soviet and Comintern agents in Iran. We have purposefully devoted special attention to the account of these activities. They prove that despite the anti-imperialist phraseology of the Treaty of February 26, 1921, a basic conflict between Russia and Iran was ripening. Russia was grimly serious about her ideological principles, which were the mainspring of all her actions. In 1928 these principles in their special application to colonial countries were given new expression. It may be useful to take a glimpse at the theoretical foundations of Soviet activity before investigating further Big-Power rivalry in Iran.

CHAPTER FIVE

A Theoretical Interlude: Blueprint for Colonial Revolution

THE DOCTRINE

THE basic principles of the revolution in the East have been expounded by Lenin, Stalin, and the resolutions of the Soviet government and the Comintern either in the decade preceding the revolution in Russia or during the first five formative years of the Soviet regime. These principles dealt with (1) the role of colonies and semicolonies in the proletarian revolution, (2) the problem of historical development in these areas, and (3) the question of self-determination. Study of them is instructive in that it permits us to understand more adequately Soviet policies in the Middle East and to remove doubts that are bound to arise in view of some apparently contradictory Soviet tactics. We shall endeavor to sum up briefly the official Soviet doctrine in this field.

It will be proper, perhaps, to start this review by reminding the reader that world revolution has never ceased to be the ultimate aim of the Soviet leaders. "The victory of socialism in one country," writes Stalin, defending himself against the accusations of Trotsky's followers that he has betrayed the revolution,

is not a self-sufficient task. In the country where it is victorious, the revolution must regard itself not as a self-sufficient quantity, but as a support, a means for hastening the victory of the proletariat in all countries. For the

[119]

victory of the revolution in one single country,—in this case Russia—constitutes at the same time the beginning and premise of the world revolution.[1]

1. The Role of the East in the Proletarian Revolution

According to the Marxists, in the world dominated by imperialistic states colonial peoples belong to the masses oppressed by monopolistic capital. This oppression exists despite the fact that the colonies themselves may not yet have entered into the stage of capitalism, and it is intensified by another fact—namely, that the oppressor is a foreigner. Sometimes a country may be nominally independent, but its economic and political position may be semicolonial. A century or more of foreign capitalistic exploitation of colonies and semicolonies has produced an undying hatred on the part of the colonial peoples toward the conquerors. These peoples adopt a more and more rebellious attitude and strive to liberate themselves from foreign bondage. Because they aim at the destruction of the power of capitalistic states, their immediate aim coincides with the aim of the world's proletariat and in particular with that of the already established Proletarian State.

Thus, while the "antagonisms, conflicts, and wars between capitalist states" can be exploited by the proletariat to its own advantage as "indirect reserves" of the revolution, "the revolutionary movement in colonial and dependent countries" constitutes the "direct reserves." If great masses of Iranians, Chinese, Indians, Arabs, Indonesians, and Africans could be mobilized and their effort co-ordinated with the action of the Proletarian State, the prospects for world revolution would be much brighter indeed. Naturally, the participation of colonial areas in the world struggle against capitalism must not only be conceived as a tactical maneuver to help the proletariat, but it must lead also to the transformation of their own colonial societies. The authority of feudal chieftains, of superstitious clergy, and of local wealthy traders should be destroyed, and the masses of the laboring people should be emancipated from every form of exploitation.

[1] "The Tactics of the Russian Communists," in *The October Revolution*, pp. 122–129; quoted in *The Theory of the Proletarian Revolution* (New York, 1936), p. 85, and in J. Stalin, *Leninism* (London, 1932), p. 212.

2. Problem of Historical Development

This leads us to the second basic problem, that of the historical development in colonial areas. How can we reconcile the establishment of a socialist society in the colonies with the fact that these areas have not yet entered the capitalist epoch of their historical development? To a Marxist who believes in "scientific," immutable laws of history, it is difficult to admit that a given country may skip an entire epoch, pass from the feudal straight into the socialist society, and thus avoid altogether the capitalist stage.

To understand the practical implications of this problem we may realize that Soviet authorities had, from the beginning, to solve this very question in the oriental districts of the former tsarist Empire to which they had become heirs. Should Transcaucasia and Turkestan immediately become socialist after the revolution, or should they be permitted to develop capitalism, and only after a considerable length of time, be transformed into socialist communities? The Soviet government did not seem to have a very clear blueprint in this field, and the initial steps were somewhat confused. While the upper, more theoretically minded circles of the Communist party would not admit a sudden jump of a backward Moslem area into socialism, the men who were assigned to the concrete duty of strengthening the Soviet power in these districts ruthlessly displayed their zeal in converting Azerbaijanis, Georgians, Bukharans, Khivans, and Kirghiz, to Communism.

This produced acute tensions and required a clear formulation of policy. The task fell upon Stalin, who since his first study on *Marxism and the National and Colonial Question* in 1913 was regarded as a foremost party theorist in this field. No doubt with the approval of Lenin, Stalin solved this intricate problem by stating that it was possible for a feudalistic country to skip the capitalist phase and establish socialism. But such a process should be carried out with great caution and the tactics employed should be elastic. He expressed these ideas at the Tenth Congress of the Russian Communist Party in 1921:

The fact of the matter is that a number of peoples, mainly Turkic peoples—about thirty million in all—have not passed, have not had time to pass, through the period of industrial capitalism, and consequently have no industrial proletariat, and as a result will have to pass from primitive forms of economy to the stage of Soviet economy without passing through the stage of industrial capitalism. In order to effect this difficult *but by no means impossible operation,* we must take into account all the peculiarities of economic life and even the history, social life and culture of these peoples.[2]

This theme of caution as a concomitant to revolutionary action in the East frequently reappeared in Stalin's writings and speeches. Having warned the comrades on one occasion against "mechanical transplantation of the economic measures of Central Russia," on another he severely admonished them against ill-conceived haste in converting the conquered border regions into Communism. With truly Marxist approach he said:

If, for instance, the Daghestani masses, who are profoundly imbued with religious prejudices, follow the Communists on the basis of the Shariah, it is obvious that the direct method of combating religious prejudices in this country must be replaced by indirect and more cautious methods. . . .

In brief, cavalry raids with the object of "immediately communizing" the backward masses of the people must be discarded for a cautious and well conceived policy of gradually drawing these masses into the general stream of Soviet development.[3]

Combining the basic principle with necessary caution, Moscow devised the following stratagem: A backward area that had undergone a revolution would obtain a new political structure based on the institution of the Soviet and of the Communist party's monopoly of power. Economically, however, such an area, while skipping the capitalist phase, would not immediately become socialist. Instead, it would pass through a transitional period during which stress would be laid on the development of industry by the state and on the promotion of co-operatives. Industry would create an industrial prole-

[2] *Marxism and the National Question, Selected Writings and Speeches* (New York, 1942), p. 104. Italics mine. Reprinted by permission of the publisher, International Publishers. This book is a modified edition of *Marxism and the National and Colonial Question* (Marxist Library, Works of Marxism Leninism, vol. XXXVIII) published in the thirties by International Publishers, undated. The latter contains interesting chapters such as "The Political Tasks of the University of the Peoples of the East," which are omitted in the revised edition.

[3] *Ibid.,* p. 85.

tariat, thus guaranteeing the success of Communist doctrines among the class-conscious workers. On the other hand, improvement and advancement of "co-operative organization among the broad masses of the peasants and handicraftsman" would be "the most reliable way of bringing the Soviet republics of the East into the general system of Soviet economic development." [4]

Following these instructions some areas of the former tsarist Empire were made not into socialist republics, but into the so-called People's Soviet Republics. This was the case of the People's Republics of Khorezm and Bukhara, which, not being socialist, had temporarily to remain outside the U.S.S.R. when the union was created. As soon, however, as they had reached socialism in their economic development, they were incorporated into the Union as Soviet Socialist Republics.

3. The Soviet Attitude toward Self-Determination

The question of the transition from a feudal to a socialist society thus definitely solved, another problem remained to be answered, namely, the problem of national self-determination of colonies and semicolonies. Concretely the issue could be limited to two points: (a) should the Proletarian State grant only a moral support to a revolutionary movement in colonies or should it intervene actively, if necessary with a military force; and (b) should the Proletarian State agree, in the name of national self-determination, to the secession of an oriental, formerly semicolonial area, if the people of that area wished to secede? Both points could, in turn, be narrowed to a single one: should a proletarian revolution be imposed upon a foreign people unready or unwilling to accept it?

The reply that the Marxist-Leninist-Stalinist school gave to this problem was a positive one: yes, the revolution could and should be imposed even if the people concerned did not want it. This solution seems to run so definitely counter to the principle of national self-determination that some explanation is necessary. Lenin, it is true, proclaimed the principle of self-determination, because he believed that any struggle for national emancipation contributed to the weakening of imperialistic states. Stalin, who amplified and devel-

4 *Ibid.*, p. 194.

oped Lenin's ideas, also proclaimed the principle of self-determination, yet he made it conditional. In his thesis on the national question, he made it clear that while in principle Communists supported national self-determination, yet they would not back it under every circumstance. Wrote Stalin:

> The Trans-Caucasian Tatars as a nation may assemble, let us say, in their Diet and, succumbing to the influence of their beys and mullahs, decide to restore the old order of things and to secede from the state. According to the meaning of the clause on self-determination they are fully entitled to do so. But will this be in the interest of the toiling strata of the Tatar nation? . . . Should not Social-Democrats [5] interfere in the matter and influence the will of the nation in a definite way? [6]

Then he explained that the reason for opposing the self-determination of the Tatars is that by seceding they would make a retrogressive step in their historical development; they would thus tend to violate the natural, "scientific" laws of history. "It follows from this," added Stalin, "that the solution of the national problem can be arrived at only if due consideration is paid to historical conditions in their development."

As time went on, it became clear that the Soviet government, and Stalin in particular, had not abandoned the afore-mentioned attitude, but had maintained it and made it more precise. Writing in *Pravda* in 1920 on "The Policy of the Soviet Government on the National Question in Russia," Stalin stated:

> The demand for the secession of the border regions from Russia must be rejected . . . primarily because it is fundamentally opposed to the interests of the mass of the peoples both of the center and of the border regions. Apart from the fact that the separation of the border regions would undermine the revolutionary might of Central Russia . . . the seceded border regions themselves would inevitably fall into bondage to international imperialism. One has only to glance at Georgia, Armenia, Poland, Finland . . . in order to realize *the counter-revolutionary nature of the demand for the secession of the border regions* under present international conditions. When a life-and-death struggle is being waged and is spreading, between proletarian Russia and the imperialist Entente, only two alternatives confront the border regions:

[5] The name used by the Russian Marxists, including the Bolsheviks, at that time.
[6] *Marxism and the National Question*, p. 24.

Either they join forces with Russia, and then the toiling masses of the border regions will be emancipated from imperialist oppression;

Or they join forces with the Entente, and then the yoke of imperialism is inevitable.

There is no third solution. So-called independence of a so-called independent Georgia, Armenia, Poland, Finland, and so forth, is only an illusion, and conceals the utter dependence of these apologies for states on one imperialist group or another.[7]

Having thus made it clear that revolutionary Russia will resist as counterrevolutionary the separation of border regions from the center, Stalin formulates the program for federal ties and regional autonomy of these regions with Russia:

Soviet autonomy is not a rigid thing fixed once and for all time; it permits the most varied forms and degrees of development. It passes from narrow administrative autonomy (the Volga Germans, the Chuvashes and the Karelians) to a wider, political autonomy (the Bashkirs, the Volga Tatars and the Kirghiz); from wide political autonomy to a still wider form of autonomy (the Ukraine and Turkestan); and finally from the Ukrainian type of autonomy to the supreme form of autonomy—contractual relations (Azerbaijan). This elasticity of Soviet autonomy constitutes one of its prime merits, for this elasticity makes it possible to embrace all the various types of border regions in Russia, which vary greatly in their levels of cultural and economic development.[8]

Thus absorption by the Soviet State, **according** to Stalin, is not just another annexation of the imperialist-capitalist type. Instead the absorbed regions are promised Soviet autonomy, the highest form of which is *contractual relations.* Azerbaijan is quoted as an example of contractual relations, and we know that Azerbaijan, having been infiltrated by the Communists and conquered by the Red Army, had concluded a treaty with the Soviet Russian Republic in 1920. Tech-nically speaking, the Republic of Azerbaijan was independent when concluding this treaty. Yet virtually it was already a conquered state and its agreement to conclude a treaty was made under foreign pressure and dictation. Thus, in fact, the Soviet concept of autonomy and independence necessarily blurs a clear distinction between a Soviet-

[7] *Ibid.,* p. 77. Italics mine.

[8] *Ibid.,* p. 79. This and the preceding quotation are reprinted by permission of International Publishers.

dominated and a non-Soviet political unit. The Communists may, in view of this theory, be perfectly sincere when they infiltrate and impose their will in the form of an extorted treaty on a hitherto independent nation and at the same time pretend that this nation is free and is linked with Russia only by "contractual relations." The application of this theory to the Mohammedan countries adjacent to Russia may have far-reaching political consequences.

ORGANIZATION OF ORIENTAL REVOLUTION

Once the Soviet form of government was established in Russia, the Bolsheviks proceeded without delay to organize revolution in the Middle East, in order to avail themselves of the great "reserves" in colonies and semicolonies, of which Lenin so eloquently spoke. The first step was to convince the colonial peoples that in the new Russia they had a staunch friend and a disinterested ally. Two official proclamations served this purpose. The first was the "Declaration of Rights of the Peoples of Russia," issued in November, 1917, and signed by Stalin and Lenin. The second was the proclamation addressed "To All the Toiling Moslems of Russia and the East," and published under Stalin's and Lenin's signatures in *Pravda* on December 5, 1917.

These two declarations expressed the basic Soviet policy toward the East. While containing tactical slogans such as self-determination and religious freedom, calculated to win over the oriental masses to the Soviet cause, they also gave a frank statement of Soviet aims, namely, war on Western imperialism and the refashioning of the world.

Both declarations were significant and important, as enunciations of principles and strategy, yet they could not be regarded as all-sufficient. What was required was a constant stream of tactically well-conceived propaganda addressed to oriental peoples. A large team of professional propagandists and revolutionaries was needed to penetrate the nerve centers of the Moslem world and incite the masses toward anti-imperialist revolution. First, however, one had to train the agitators themselves. Toward this goal the Soviet State made impressive strides from the very beginning.

First of all there was a Commissariat for Nationalities headed by

Stalin. Under its auspices was created the Communist University of the Toilers of the East, the aim of which was to train Communist cadres. Headed in the beginning by Comrade Broido, famous for his rule of terror in Turkestan, the University was not designed to be an intellectual center of objective studies, but to be a propaganda center with the purpose of acquainting students with the principles of Marxism, the tactics of the proletarian revolution, and the customs and languages of oriental peoples. By the summer of 1922 the university had 700 enrolled students belonging to 57 nationalities. The course of study lasted four years and included, aside from theoretical preparation, interim assignments in various parts of the Soviet Republic. The university opened branches in Central Asia, in Irkutsk, and in Baku, the most important being the branch in Tashkent.[9] The latter played a very important role as a great radiation center of propaganda for Central Asia, Iran, Afghanistan, and India. The Soviet Turkestan Commission (*Turkkommissia*) and the Pan-Hindu Revolutionary Committee were located in Tashkent.[10]

Apart from the university and its branches, numerous schools of oriental languages were established. They were either autonomous or attached to other institutions of higher learning. In 1922 *Novy Vostok* published an impressive list of these schools, of which the most important were the Institute of Oriental Languages of Moscow, the Oriental Section of the Military College in Moscow, the Center of Practical Studies of the Orient at the Military College of Moscow, the Institute of Classical Orient at the Moscow Museum, the Institute of Living Oriental Languages in Leningrad, and the Institute of Oriental Languages at Tashkent.[11]

In addition, the Soviet government also sponsored genuine orientalist studies in order to have at its disposal a number of experts ready to supply it with necessary documentation and facts. Thus the Scientific Association of Orientalists of Russia was founded as a section in the Commissariat for Nationalities. Among the first collaborators in this association were Tardov, an expert on Iran, Raskolnikov and Nikulin for Afghanistan, and Lavrov and Astakhov

9 Castagné, *op. cit.*
10 Barmine, *op. cit.,* pp. 99, 100.
11 Castagné, *op. cit.,* p. 49.

for Turkey. In the 1920's the association published an orientalist magazine, *Novy Vostok* ("New East"), with M. Pavlovich (Weltmann) as editor-in-chief. Branches of the association were established in Tashkent, Baku, Tiflis, Irkutsk, and also abroad, Teheran being the first foreign seat. In many cases the same men had to act both as scholars and as officials of the Soviet government. Tardov, for example, on whose initiative the Teheran branch was created, was appointed Consul General at Isfahan. Raskolnikov skillfully combined the functions of a scholar, a military and naval commander, and a diplomat, acting in the latter capacity as Soviet Minister to Afghanistan. Lavrov and Astakhov were also employed in the Soviet foreign and secret service.[12]

With regard to the concrete execution of revolutionary propaganda, a body of prime importance was, of course, the Third International. Apart from its executive functions the Comintern was also a center of theoretical debates. As such it was a policy-making organ second only to the Soviet government. Its theses and resolutions were fundamental in guiding all those who had to perform various revolutionary assignments in the Middle East.

The Comintern's Second Congress in 1920 devoted considerable time to the formulation of oriental policies. It made an important contribution to Marxist theory by confirming the doctrine that a backward country might skip the capitalist phase. During this session the decision to call the Congress of Eastern Peoples to Baku was reached. Theses adopted at the Second Congress, together with the subsequent Baku resolutions, gave basic guidance to oriental Communists for the next eight years.

As time went on, however, these theses were gradually supplemented by various new directives. In the later twenties a need was felt to review, perhaps to revise and to codify, all these principles. Several reasons justified their reconsideration. First of all, the Soviet regime had passed through a period of ferment between 1924 and 1927, that is, between Lenin's death and the emergence of Stalin as the undisputed ruler of Russia. Behind the brutal contest for power was an ideological struggle between Trotsky's "Permanent revolution" and Stalin's "Socialism in one country." Stalin and his close

[12] Agabekov, *op. cit.*

associates felt the need of making their position quite clear to the comrades around the world in order to secure their support. Since the Comintern had not met for several years, it was thought advisable in Moscow to call a new Congress and expound the accepted views before it. Another reason for review and codification was that the execution of the early principles in colonial and semicolonial countries had given Moscow a wealth of experience and had created some doubts on points of the early program. The debate on Iran that raged among Soviet theorists after Reza Khan's coup was a good example of uncertainty in meeting concrete problems in the Middle East. What was needed was a clear-cut program that would contain not only the principles but also the tactics to be followed in various areas. Responsible agents of the Comintern should no longer be left in the dark as to which directives should be followed. Finally there was still another reason, perhaps more urgent than the first two: it was the fear, almost the panic, in Moscow in 1927–1928 that Russia was threatened with immediate armed intervention by capitalistic countries. History gave the lie to these apprehensions, but at that time the possibility of a concerted armed attack against the Socialist Fatherland was taken seriously by Soviet leaders. Hence arose the necessity of strengthening Communist forces all over the world and of issuing to them clear-cut instructions as to how to behave in case of emergency. A revolt in the colonies of capitalistic countries would, in such a case, be of inestimable defensive value to the Soviet Union by creating serious disorders in the enemy's rear. A careful elaboration of tactics in colonies and semicolonies was, then, of capital importance. The task of doing it fell upon the long-delayed Sixth Congress.

THE SIXTH CONGRESS OF THE COMINTERN

The Sixth Congress of the Communist International was called to Moscow in the midsummer of 1928 and sat there till almost the end of the year. Most of the Communist parties in the world sent their delegations, often headed by their top leaders. The East, including the Middle East, was well represented. The atmosphere of the Congress was marked by enthusiasm for Soviet internal achievement; the delegates worked generally in a serious mood and did not spare their efforts to elaborate a body of theses and rules to cover a wide range of subjects. The basic work of preparing the theses was entrusted to Bukharin, but the detailed elaboration of directives for the East was left to the Colonial Commission of the Congress. This commission was headed by the veteran Finnish Communist Otto Kuusinen, who had prepared in advance a draft of Colonial Theses. The debates following Bukharin's and Kuusinen's reports were frank and lively. They allowed the Eastern delegates to state the positions of their native Communist parties, to present concrete problems, and to give their criticism of the reports.[13]

The Communist party of Iran was represented by Sultan-zadeh and Shareqi. Both took an active part in the work of the Congress and felt free to criticize some points of Bukharin's and Kuusinen's reports. Shareqi was elected to the International Control Commission of the Comintern, a body composed of twenty-two trusted comrades. Iranian delegates discussed a number of topics, expressing their views on the agrarian question, the problem of the infiltration of non-Communist groups in the Middle East, organizational questions, and Pan-Islamism.

With regard to the agrarian problem, Shareqi complained that Bukharin's report dealt with it "only incompletely and without sufficient clarity." He urged further discussion to elucidate the matter and stated that in the interim between the Fifth and Sixth Congresses four mass uprisings of peasantry had occurred in Iran.

Shareqi was especially concerned with the question of co-operation with non-Communist groups and with the related problem of the composition of Communist parties in the East. The pertinence of this problem will become obvious if we realize that "united front" tactics had been recommended for oriental countries long before their introduction into Europe and the Western world. Communists working in the East have had frequent recourse to collaboration with other parties, particularly if the latter were of an anti-imperialist character. In concrete fulfillment of this policy, however, many practical difficulties had arisen. Consequently Shareqi voiced not only his per-

[13] A full record of these proceedings may be found in *International Press Correspondence*, vol. VIII (1928), nos. 38–92, pp. 691–1687.

sonal, but a general, worry of Communist emissaries in the Middle East when he declared:

In his Report Comrade Bukharin spoke about the attitude of West European Communist Parties towards the Social Democratic Parties. While we (in Iran) have no Social-Democratic Party, we do have similar parties, such as Socialist, Nationalist, etc. For a long time we were working in a bloc with the *Socialist Party*, but in recent times it has developed into a typical opportunist party and has frequently come out openly against the Communist Party and has betrayed it. . . . Unfortunately, the Comintern has no definite clear line in this question either.[14]

As to the composition of the parties, Shareqi elaborated on the thesis that colonial Communist parties should be proletarian. Accepting this thesis as a "correct line," he warned that "colonial parties have been crowded with opportunist and petty bourgeois elements" and cited the Iranian Communist party as an unfortunate example. Accordingly he recommended, on the one hand, purging undesirable elements from the Communist parties and, on the other, co-operation with and utilization of "the small and middle peasantry, the intelligentsia and middle traders."

The utilization of other groups as fronts has always been a vital problem for the Communists; hence Shareqi's remarks in this connection are of special interest. Urging the establishment "of labor-peasant parties, as auxiliary organizations for the Communist Parties," Shareqi paid special attention to the national revolutionary parties in the East. These parties, he admitted, do not have a class character, but are useful because they are dedicated to the fight against imperialism. As, however, "by themselves [they] are unable to organize the struggle, . . . *the Communist Party must assume control over them.*" "We are . . . confronted," said Shareqi:

We are . . . confronted with the question of creating such parties in countries such as Persia. We know, of course, that in China this party, i.e. the Kuomintang, has turned reactionary. On the other hand in Mongolia such a party has produced brilliant results. . . . Therefore, I personally consider imperative the organization of national-revolutionary parties in

[14] *Ibid.*, p. 843.

colonial and semi-colonial countries, but of course only when a strong Communist Party has been established there.[15]

No less eloquent was Sultan-zadeh. Displaying an imposing knowledge of Marxist dialectics in the field of economics, Sultan-zadeh severely criticized Kuusinen's report. To him the proposed division of oriental countries into separate categories seemed erroneous. He expressed it forcefully by saying:

Comrades, when I received the Theses and began to read them, I imagined for a moment that I was not in Moscow, but in one of the colonies with which Comrade Kuusinen's Theses are dealing. And as much as I endeavored to get Persia into this scheme which divides all colonial and semi-colonial countries into four groups, I did not succceed in this. How does it stand with Persia in reality? *Can Persia skip over the capitalist development?* [16] Is it possible to establish immediately the Soviet regime in Persia, or must one proclaim there on the day after the Revolution the democratic dictatorship of the proletariat and the peasantry? Can we develop in Persia the agrarian revolution, or should we abstain from this there also? Unfortunately, I have received no answer to these questions which are of such great interest to us.

I think that Comrade Kuusinen's scheme is on too general lines; there is no concretization whatever; the countries are grouped in a manner which makes it very difficult to give every country its proper place. . . . I am convinced that the Turkish comrades are in the same boat. I am sure that the comrades from the Arabian countries are as badly off in this respect as I. . . .

Having thus criticized Kuusinen's report on general lines, Sultan-zadeh appealed for greater precision:

What tactic must we adopt in Persia, which is situated between the country of proletarian dictatorship and the great colony, India? . . . These Theses must become an instrument in the hands of the oppressed colonial slaves with the help of which they will be able to enter upon the path of their liberation.[17]

In reply to this and other criticisms of Eastern delegates Comrade Vassiliev of the Communist party of the Soviet Union presented his views on the defects that are typical of the Communist parties in the

[15] *International Press Correspondence*, VIII, 1469.
[16] Italics mine.
[17] *Ibid.*, p. 1359.

colonial and semicolonial countries. These defects were as follows: First, "these parties are still to a large extent organizations made of leaders. They have no local rank and file organizations. . . ." Second, "as a rule, the influence of the Communist Parties . . . is based solely upon the personal influence of individual leaders of the Communist Party, but not upon the organizational activity of strong Communist factions. . . ." Third, "there is generally a lack of understanding among their leaders as to the proper tasks of the Communist Party and the other revolutionary organizations of their respective countries." "This question," concluded Vassiliev, "the development of the Communist Parties as such, as Parties relying upon strong local organizations and factory nuclei, the carrying on of extensive ideological activity to clarify the role of the Communist Parties—*this question is just now in the very center of the activities of the Communist International in the colonies.*" [18]

This debate was significant because it permitted the representatives of the East to air their opinions, and also because it influenced the ultimate formulation of the Theses. In the final stage of the Congress when Kuusinen presented the report of the Colonial Commission to the plenary session, he stated that his draft theses had been improved by amendments and addenda. Among them he listed as most important the following three:

(1) A recapitulation of incidents of the revolutionary movement in colonial countries was inserted.

(2) More concrete form was given to tactical questions, especially with regard to China, India, Egypt, and Indonesia.

(3) Much was added to the chapter on immediate tasks of the Communist parties in various colonial and semicolonial countries.

The report of the Colonial Commission was adopted unanimously by the Congress. It contained the "Theses on the Revolutionary Movement in the Colonies and Semicolonies," which, in turn, constituted a part of the larger whole called the *Theses and Resolutions of the Sixth World Congress of the Communist International.*[19]

The Colonial Theses were divided into four parts.

Part I, "Introduction," reaffirmed first of all the full validity of the

[18] *Ibid.*, p. 1361.
[19] See Appendix no. VII.

Theses on the National and Colonial Questions drawn up by Lenin and adopted at the Second Congress, but stressed the necessity of further development of these principles. It repeated the old Communist formula that the toiling masses of the colonies "represent a most powerful auxiliary force of the Socialist world revolution." Active support "in deeds" by the Soviet Union and the Comintern of the liberation movement of dependent peoples was reaffirmed. Lenin's original thesis admitting the possibility of skipping capitalism in colonies, provided the revolution there is aided by the Soviet Union, was upheld in the following words:

> Furthermore, the alliance with the U.S.S.R. and with revolutionary proletariat of the imperialist countries creates for the toiling masses of the people of China, India and all other colonial and semi-colonial countries the possibility of an independent, free, economic and cultural development, avoiding the stage of the domination of the capitalist system or even the development of capitalist relations in general.
>
> Thus the epoch of imperialism, of wars and revolutions opens an epoch in which the proletarian dictatorship arises, opens a quite new perspective for the development of the colonial peoples. Since the analysis of contemporary world economy as a whole in no way leads to the perspective of a new prolonged period of flourishing capitalism . . . this denotes the presence of the objective possibility of a noncapitalist path of development for the backward colonies, the possibility of the *"growing-over"* of the bourgeois-democratic revolution in the leading colonies into the proletarian socialist revolution with the aid of the victorious proletarian dictatorship in the other countries.

Part II, "The Characteristic Features of Colonial Economy and of Imperialist Colonial Policy," contained a long and careful analysis of economy and society in dependent areas. It paid special attention to the pauperization of the peasantry in these countries.

Part III, "On Communist Strategy and Tactics in China, India and Similar Colonial Countries," dealt chiefly with the transition from the bourgeois-democratic revolution to the proletarian revolution. It was admitted that the bourgeois-democratic revolution of a nationalist, anti-imperialist character constituted the first and a welcome step toward the attainment of Communist goals. The skipping of the capitalist epoch, envisaged in Part I, did not mean that there would be no democratic-bourgeois revolution. On the contrary, such a revolution was accepted as something inevitable. Once it took place (and the Communists should support it), the strategic and tactical problem would be how to transform it into the proletarian revolution without waiting for the long capitalist epoch to ripen.

Part III gave ample instructions to the Communist parties in this connection. Communist parties in colonies were warned that they must

from the beginning *demarcate themselves in the most clear-cut fashion,* both politically and organizationally, from all the petty bourgeois groups and parties. In so far as the needs of the revolutionary struggle demand it, a temporary cooperation is permissible, and in certain circumstances even a temporary union between the Communist Party and the national revolutionary movement provided that the latter is a genuine national revolutionary movement, that it genuinely struggles against the ruling power and that its representatives do not put obstacles in the way of the Communists educating and organizing in a revolutionary sense the peasants and broad masses of the exploited.

But the Communist parties must be wary of the so-called national reformist parties in the colonies and must struggle against their nefarious influence. As an example, the Theses cited the Swarajist and Wafdist parties, whose reformist character had to be exposed.

Another important instruction in this field was that the transition from the bourgeois-democratic to the proletarian revolution could be effected only if two basic conditions were fulfilled. The first was the existence of a strong Communist party. The second was the presence of certain objective circumstances described as an "unusually deep revolutionary crisis and an unusually high and persistent revolutionary wave." And to make it quite clear when this could be expected, the Theses said: "Such a possibility is most easily presented, for example, when the ruling imperialism is temporarily distracted by a long continued war outside the frontiers of the colonial country concerned."

Part IV, "The Immediate Tasks of the Communists," contained instructions of a concrete character as to what the Communist parties should do in colonies and semicolonies. The first task was to build up and strengthen the Communist parties themselves. This was urgent, because it was necessary to harmonize the objective factor and the subjective factor of the revolution. The objective factor was described as the revolutionary situation in the colonies. Inasmuch as the objective factor was largely independent of human will, Part IV urged the strengthening of the subjective factor, which meant a well-organized and disciplined Communist party. The party had to be well prepared whenever the objective situation, such as war or economic crisis, warranted a revolutionary coup. The disproportion between these two factors had to be removed and the parties strengthened. This represented, according to the Theses, one of the most important and primary tasks of the Communist International.

Following this introduction, Part IV gave several instructions how to strengthen the Communist parties. They can be summed up briefly as follows: give your parties a "genuinely proletarian" character by recruiting industrial and transport workers as well as "the semi-slaves in the plantations"; create party nuclei everywhere, including working class tenements and barracks; do not neglect work "among journeymen, apprentices and coolies employed in small handicraft workshops"; bring together the white workers from the metropolis and native workers and keep them in the same party organization; entice cautiously revolutionary intelligentsia into the party; promote trade unions; penetrate the existing peasant organizations; create mass Young Communist Leagues; and—in case of insurrection—promote the creation of elected soviets of workers' and peasants' deputies.

These general tasks were followed by a rather detailed enumeration of the immediate tasks for the Communists country by country. The following areas and problems were dealt with separately: China; India; Indonesia; Korea; Egypt; North Africa; the Negro question in the United States, the Union of South Africa, and the Central African Colonies; and Latin America. This review was in turn followed by instruction on how to struggle against the colonial policy of the Social Democratic parties. Iran was not mentioned separately; apparently the Iranian delegate's worry as to where to fit in his country was left unsolved. The reason why only certain countries were mentioned by name was the desire of the authors to divide colonies and semicolonies into several categories, and the countries expressly mentioned were to be considered as typical. The difference between these categories was dictated mainly by the degree of industrialization and capitalism existing in various areas. The list was headed by China, because there the bourgeois-democratic revolution had already been completed, and China clearly had to await only the next stage, the proletarian revolution. As to India, it entered on the path of industrialization more than any of the remaining areas, so that the tasks had to be adapted to the existing situation there. As to the problem where one could fit Iran into these divisions, the answer was not easy because in some respects Iran closely resembled China (the bourgeois-democratic revolution of Reza Khan was of an anti-imperialist character), in some India (there was a fair degree of industrialization in the province of Azerbaijan for example, with uneven land tenure) and in some even the backward Arab countries (elements of feudalism and nomad tribes were still much in evidence). Thus it could be assumed that the tasks enumerated with regard to China, India, and the Arab countries could all to some degree apply to Iran. As the tasks of the Communists in China were formulated in a more precise form than those for any other area, it may be useful to reproduce them here, as basically applicable to an area like Iran as well. They were:

The fundamental slogans through which the Party must seek to win over the masses, are the following:
1. Overthrow of imperialist domination.
2. Confiscation of foreign enterprises and banks.
3. Unity of the country, with recognition of the right of each nationality to self-determination.
4. Overthrow of the power of the militarists and the Kuomintang.
5. Establishment of the power of Soviet of workers' and soldiers' representatives.
6. The 8-hour working day, increase of wages, assistance to the unemployed and social insurance.
7. Confiscation of all lands of big landlords, land for the peasants and soldiers.
8. The abolition of all governmental, militarist and local taxes and levies; a single progressively graduated income tax.
9. Alliance with the U.S.S.R. and the world proletarian movement.

The Theses on the colonial question were thus one of the major achievements of the Congress. To enforce them in practice the Statutes of the Communist International were amended. In particular, a new paragraph (No. 19) was added which proclaimed: "The Executive Committee of the Communist International and its Presidium have the right to form a permanent bureau (West European, South American, Eastern and other bureaux of the E.C.C.I.) for the establishment of closer connection with the individual sections of the C.I. and of better guidance of their work."

Paragraph 20 said: "The Sections are obliged to carry out the instructions of the permanent bureaux. Against the decisions of the bureaux an appeal can be lodged with the E.C.C.I. or the Presidium of the E.C.C.I. The Sections are nevertheless bound to carry out their instructions."

To this paragraph 21 was added: "Apart from this, the E.C.C.I. and its Presidium have the right to send instructors to the individual Sections of the C.I. The rights and duties of the instructors are determined by the E.C.C.I., to which the instructors are responsible for their work."

These paragraphs took care of the organization: the principle of "centralism" was officially confirmed; the Sections, which means Communist parties, had to obey orders; and the instructors had to be the eye and ear of headquarters. Specialization was approved by the creation of an Eastern Bureau.

APPLICATION OF THE THESES TO IRAN

The blueprint being ready, one had to follow its lines. Agabekov, who had worked hand in hand with the Comintern representatives, testifies that in 1928 their work was intensified in the Middle East.

What were the effects of the Congress on Iran?

That there was an increase in Communist work and agitation is certain. The main problem, however, was what would be the attitude of the Comintern toward Reza Shah. Would his regime be regarded, as before, as something worth while supporting because of its predominantly anti-imperialist character, or should it be condemned because of its open persecution of Communists? Fortunately this was . still the era of frank diplomacy of the Soviet Union, and responsible

Communists were not loath to write openly about their aims and tactics. In 1932, on the occasion of the Iranian-British conflict about oil, a revealing article was published in the Comintern's organ, *International Press Correspondence,* under the title "The Fight for Persian Oil and the Tasks of the C.P. of Iran." It was signed by L. Magyar and is worth reproducing in its major parts:

The conflict which has arisen between British imperialism and the Reza Khan government, confronts the Communist Party of Iran, all revolutionary elements and all anti-imperialist fighters in the country with responsible tasks.

The C.P. of Iran regards as its chief task to mobilize the working masses for the fight against British imperialism and to *organize* them in the course of this fight, to set up a proletarian cadre in the anti-imperialist movement, and thereby win the hegemony of the proletariat in this fight.

In order to be able to solve this strategic task the Communist Party of Iran clearly takes into account the meaning, content and character of the conflict which has arisen and is still going on, between British imperialism and the Reza Khan government and also the perspectives of the struggle. . . .

Persia achieved its national independence as a result of the October revolution. . . . At the same time, however, the ruling classes of Persia succeeded in throttling the national revolutionary movement in its beginnings. The Ghilan revolution was crushed. . . . The anti-imperialist movement was not carried out to an end. The country became independent *politically;* *economically,* however, all the important key positions remained in the hands of the . . . British imperialists. . . .

Economically Persia remained a *semi-colony* of imperialism. . . . The most important key positions of the country—foreign trade, oil, banking, motor transport—remained under the control of British finance capital. This circumstance and the class character of the government of Reza Khan caused the latter to pursue the path of capitulation to imperialism. Many Persian comrades have put forward the view that Reza Khan is only an agent of British imperialism. Other comrades, on the other hand, maintained that Reza Khan is the bearer of national progress and is successfully solving the task of the national emancipation and centralization of the country. It is scarcely necessary to emphasize that both these points of view are incorrect. . . .

The fight which Reza Khan is conducting over Persian oil is nothing else but *a national-reformist fight,* and there is every prospect of his capitulating

[139]

to British imperialism. For the government of the Shah this fight is *not* a revolutionary fight for winning back the greatest source of the wealth of the country—oil. It is a case of bargaining at the cost of the working population of Persia. The Shah and his government wish to come to an agreement with the Anglo-Persian. *It is only a question of the price.* . . .

In Persia itself a broad anti-imperialist mass movement is growing: a national movement against British imperialism. This movement is not organized, and the broad masses of the people who are taking part in it have not yet got rid of their illusions regarding the role of the government of Reza Khan.

The masses of workers, peasants and petty bourgeoisie still believe that Reza Khan is conducting a consistent *fight* against imperialism, and do not yet perceive that he is only bargaining with British imperialism over the price of the new capitulation. Reza Khan wants to obtain a higher price for Persian oil; the masses are fighting to win back the oil wells from British finance capital.

This situation determines the tactics of the C.P. of Iran.

Reza Khan only wants a higher price for the oil. The masses want the restoration of the oil fields to Persia. The Communists therefore set up the slogan of confiscation of the oil wells. This demand is directed against British imperialism, but it also exposes the government of Reza Khan to the masses.

England has occupied the Bahrein Islands. The Persian government has already demanded the handing back of the Bahrein Islands. The C.P. of Iran demands the handing back of the Bahrein Islands and is opposed to any negotiations until the Bahrein Islands are given back. England sends warships to the Persian Gulf. The Communist Party of Iran demands that there be no negotiations with England so long as English warships threaten Persia. Next to the naphtha works the Saschi-Sach Bank [20] constitutes the most important key-position of English finance capital in Persia. The C.P. of Iran demands the cessation of activity of this bank in Persia and the annulment of the concessions held by this bank. At the same time the Communists demand the cessation of debt payment to England.

Foreign Trade in Persia is under State control. The C.P. of Iran demands the breaking off of trade relations with England. Its slogan is: "Boycott English goods, banks and undertakings."

In order to support these anti-imperialist slogans, in order to be able to take over the leadership of the anti-imperialist movement, the C.P. of Iran is fighting for the setting up of anti-imperialist unity committees which shall

[20] This is the Russified name for the Imperial Bank of Iran.

unite the masses of workers and peasants and the urban petty bourgeoisie for common fighting actions. These committees of action shall lend weight to the anti-imperialist fighting slogans by means of demonstrations and protest strikes.

From the point of view of the whole movement it is of the greatest importance to mobilize the workers employed in the oil works. The oil workers of Persia already proved their fighting capacity in the big strike in the year 1929. . . . The C.P. of Iran considers it its most important task to develop the strike movement in the oil region. . . .

The C.P. of Iran is endeavoring at the same time to . . . bring to the masses the fighting slogans for democratic liberties (freedom of political organization, freedom of the press, right of combination, right to strike, release of proletarian prisoners, repeal of anti-communist laws). . . . Needless to say, the C.P. of Iran is continuing its fight for the everyday demands of the workers. . . . It goes without saying that the Communists also voice the demands of the peasantry. . . . There is no need to say that the C.P. of Iran also propagates its final slogans (overthrow of the monarchy, workers' and peasants' government).

The Communist Party of Iran is confronted with responsible tasks. It depends upon the solution of these tasks whether the C.P. of Iran will succeed in arriving on the broad path of the mass movement, whether the Party will succeed in emerging from the narrow circles to which its work has hitherto been confined, and in penetrating into the broad anti-imperialist movement of the masses.[21]

THE SEVENTH CONGRESS OF THE COMINTERN

To complete this survey of the Comintern's attitude toward Iran and the Eastern countries in general, one may legitimately ask how far the Theses applied in the later thirties and forties. To reply to this question it is necessary to look at the debates of the Seventh Congress of the Comintern, which was held in 1935 in Moscow. This Congress, called after a lapse of seven years, was held in unusual circumstances so far as the Soviet Union was concerned. The rise of the Hitlerian menace led Moscow to change tactics abruptly and to seek friends among the Western democracies. This change of attitude was marked by the entrance of Russia into the League of Nations in 1934 and by the conclusion of a series of nonaggression or friendship treaties, including the pacts of mutual assistance with France and Czechoslo-

[21] *International Press Correspondence*, vol. XII (1932), no. 58, pp. 1239 ff.

vakia in 1935. On the home fronts Communists had to be given new instructions to adapt themselves to the new conditions. Hence the necessity of calling a new Congress, which, because of the dictatorial policy of Moscow in all matters pertaining to the Comintern, had gone into disuse as a method of co-operation.

Because of the new political climate in the midst of which the Congress was called, it was obviously necessary to stress that fascism and nazism were the two chief enemies of Communism, and not imperialism in general. Care was taken, however, not to change a line in the old Theses on colonial problems. Oriental questions, generally speaking, occupied less place during the debates than the main problem of new Communist tactics in Western European countries. There a new line was adopted—that of tactical co-operation with the socialists and even with the petty bourgeois parties that were ready to combat fascism. This was the genesis of the "popular fronts," which were created in France and Spain and which played such an important role in the political drama before the second World War. As to the Eastern countries, the interesting feature of the Congress was the tendency to adapt the old colonial "united front line" to the new circumstances. This meant co-operation with anti-fascist elements in those areas and struggle against Italian and German influence rather than an open fight against French and British imperialism.

The obvious preoccupation of the Congress with European problems could be best measured by the fact that only four Eastern representatives spoke during the debates. They were delegates of the Communist parties of Syria, of "Arabian countries," of Indonesia, and of Palestine. Characteristically these were mostly the colonial areas properly speaking, namely, those of Great Britain, France, and the Netherlands. Such "semicolonies" as Iran and Turkey did not participate in the debate, although there is no reason to believe that their delegates were not present at the Congress.

The basic attitude toward imperialism was clearly not abandoned, as was testified by the report of Comrade Georgi Dimitrov, freshly covered with glory as a result of the Reichstag fire trial. Dimitrov reaffirmed that "the proletariat of the imperialist countries has possible allies not only in the toilers of its own countries, but also in the oppressed nations of the colonies and semi-colonies," and reminded the Congress that "the Communists have to support, extend and participate in anti-imperialist mass activities, not excluding those which are under national reformist leadership." [22]

The new lenient attitude toward the national reformist elements was accentuated by the stress laid on combating anti-French and anti-British brands of imperialism. This was eloquently expressed in the speech made by Comrade Nadir from Syria. While reminding the delegates that his country was a "colony of French imperialism," he concentrated on a description of German and Italian fascist activities as especially dangerous to the Soviet Union. "We have developed," said Nadir, "great activity in the struggle against imperialist war and for the defense of the Soviet Union. There was not one campaign conducted by the Party which was not linked with these two questions." [23]

It was evident that the security of the Proletarian State in this grave hour of German resurgence overshadowed all other aspects of the colonial question. An imperialist war, which, according to the Sixth Congress, was welcome as an "objective factor" providing a "deep revolutionary wave," was now vigorously condemned since it might threaten Russia. Nadir's admission that "the defense of the Soviet Union" was in the forefront of party activities left no doubt that the cause of world revolution was subordinated to and identified with the interests of the Proletarian State. The evidence that the Communist parties and the Comintern were treated primarily as tools of Soviet foreign policy could not be clearer.

Thus the Seventh Congress neither repudiated the Theses adopted in 1928 nor did it deviate to any considerable degree from the tactics elaborated by the Sixth Congress. The sharp edge of revolutionary agitation had to be turned primarily against those imperialist countries that seemed to threaten the Soviet Union at that time, but the basic anti-imperialist struggle was not to be forgotten. It seemed that

[22] A full record of the Seventh World Congress of the Communist International may be found in *International Press Correspondence,* vol. XV (1935). This quotation comes from p. 963.
[23] *Ibid.,* p. 1299.

such a decision was, from the Soviet point of view, timely in 1935. Germany, under Hitler's leadership, emerged again as a powerful rival in Middle Eastern politics. Her penetration, both economic and political, was clearly visible in this part of the world. In Iran it assumed proportions that might easily have destroyed the existing status quo and have affected the security of both the Soviet Union and the British Empire.

CHAPTER SIX

The Growth of
German Influence in Iran

THE present study embraces the period between 1918 and 1948. During this period Germany made an intensive effort to subject Iran to her influence. This spectacular release of Teutonic energy was, however, based on a tradition that it would be unwise to underestimate. Hence, we have found it necessary to precede the story of recent German penetration by an account of earlier activities.

BEFORE AND DURING WORLD WAR I

Germany, as an imperialist competitor, appeared on the horizon of Iranian politics later than Russia and Great Britain. The unification and strengthening of Germany under Bismarck was not accompanied by interest in the Middle East. It was only after the retirement of the Iron Chancellor that German policy definitely turned toward that area. The visit that Kaiser Wilhelm paid to the Ottoman possessions in 1898 can be regarded as a turning point in German policy. After that time Imperial Germany made persistent efforts to secure a "place under the sun" in the Persian Gulf area. In 1903 the Deutsche Bank obtained the famous concession to construct the railroad that would link Berlin with Bagdad. The B-B railway was to be the main artery for German influence in Mesopotamia and the Persian Gulf. It was eventually to be extended to Basra. This railway development was accompanied by the establishment on the Gulf shores, including the territory of Iran, of a number of German import-export firms, of which the largest were Robert Wonckhaus and Company, from Hamburg, and F. Undutsch and Company, from Bremen. The Wonckhaus Company, founded in 1904, established branches in Bushire, Bandar Abbas, Bahrein, Basra, Bagdad, and other cities. It tried to monopolize pearl fisheries in the Persian Gulf and to obtain several concessions from the Iranian government. Die Persische Teppichgesellschaft A.G. (Petag) from Berlin, with a capital of ten million marks, was active in the production and marketing of Persian rugs.

In 1907 the Hamburg-Amerika Linie inaugurated service between the ports of Germany and the Persian Gulf. This introduced a dangerous element of competition to the hitherto unchallenged position of British shipping in these waters. In the same year after protracted negotiations the Deutsche Orient Bank obtained from the Iranian government a concession to open branches in Iran with the privilege of issuing silver bullion. Russian and British opposition kept this concession from materializing. However, German banks subsequently attempted to gain influence in the National Bank of Iran, the creation of which had been proposed by progressive politicians of the first revolutionary Majlis.

The German attempts at penetration caused considerable anxiety and alarm in Great Britain. On May 5, 1907, the British government was compelled to issue a warning to Germany. In reply to an interpellation in the House of Lords, Lord Lansdowne, Foreign Secretary, declared that the establishment of a naval base or of a fortified port in the Persian Gulf by a foreign power would be considered a grave menace to British interests. "We should certainly resist it," he said, "with all the means at our disposal." [1]

The Anglo-Russian agreement of 1907 temporarily concluded the rivalry between these two powers and consequently rendered German penetration into Iran more difficult. The Germans explicitly recognized this agreement following British and Russian intervention in Berlin. In 1908 Prince von Bülow, German Chancellor, issued a public statement in which he accepted the Anglo-Russian agreement and reaffirmed the German hands-off policy in Iran. This statement, made to satisfy Russo-British diplomatic susceptibilities, apparently was not sincere, for Germany continued to penetrate Iran economi-

[1] M. Nakhai, *L'Evolution politique de l'Iran* (Brussels, 1938), p. 40.

[146]

cally and politically. She supported the Iranian Democratic party, which was composed of liberal intelligentsia and merchant classes. This party grew steadily more and more pro-German and at the same time gained ascendancy in the Majlis. Moreover, the traditional British influence exercised on Iranian constitutionalists waned as a result of the 1907 agreement. This feeling of disappointment and resentment against British and Russian imperialism was exploited by German diplomacy. Consequently, a large part of the Majlis, including its President, became pro-German. The same was true of a number of important ministers in the cabinets that preceded the first World War. A German school was founded in Teheran, offering excellent education to the sons of the most prominent Iranian families, who not infrequently continued their higher studies at German universities.

Prewar attempts at appeasement, due to the tense international atmosphere, resulted only in giving Germany a better opportunity to pursue her aims. Thus, as a result of the Potsdam conference between Wilhelm II and Nicolas II, an agreement was signed in 1911 in St. Petersburg that opened new vistas for the success of the Berlin-Bagdad railway. According to the agreement Russia was to ask Iran for the railway concession from Teheran to Khanaqin. Upon completion, this line was to be linked with the Berlin-Bagdad railway. The Russian government undertook to consider the wishes of Germany regarding the exact tracing of the new line. It promised, moreover, that if the concession were left unexploited by Russia for four years, the latter would cede it to Germany. In this way Iran became an integral part of the master plan of the Berlin-Bagdad railway and became subject to all its political implications. However, the outbreak of the first World War put an end to these schemes. But by that time Germany had managed to secure an important influence in Iran.

When the war broke out, German's preparatory activities in the Middle East were crowned with a large measure of success, for the Ottoman Empire followed the lead of Berlin and Vienna. If Iran were won to the same cause, German strategic triumph would have been complete. Hence, after the beginning of the war, feverish efforts were made to induce Iran to side with the central powers. German activity was both diplomatic and military. With respect to the first, Prince von Reuss, the German Minister to Iran, tried to influence the government and the parliament. He seemed, by 1915, to be nearing a diplomatic triumph. The elections to the Majlis, which were held in that year, gave a majority to the pro-German Democratic party.[2] This party and the Majlis as a whole strongly protested against the violation of Iranian territory and neutrality by Russian and British troops (although the German-officered Turks were the first to violate this neutrality in the region west of Lake Urumia). The government, though less openly, leaned to the German cause. Mustaufi ul-Mamalek, the Prime Minister, even signed a secret treaty, by which Germany was promised the full support of the Iranian government.[3] Rumors concerning this alliance and an impending *coup d'état* swept Teheran in the fall of 1915 and precipitated strong diplomatic intervention by Russian and British ministers. The Iranians were warned as to the possible consequences of such a Germanophile policy. To add weight to her Minister's words Russia was about to order her troops, which were already in occupation of some points in the Caspian provinces, to march on Teheran. Fearful lest the capital be taken by the Russians, the German and Austro-Hungarian legations left and established themselves at Qum. A number of pro-German Iranian politicians headed by Suleiman Mirza followed them. In Qum under the auspices of Prince von Reuss they created a Committee for the Defense of Islam (otherwise called *Ittihad-i-Islam*) to rally the patriotic and devout Iranians for the coming struggle against the infidel Russians and British. The choice of Qum for headquarters of this movement was an astute political move, because of the role the divines of that stronghold of Shiism played in Iran. In fact, German propaganda strove persistently to convince the Iranians that Germany was the only friend of Islam. The Kaiser's visit to Damascus in 1898 was cited as an example of his warm feelings toward the Moslem world, and his professions of friendship were skillfully exploited by German agents. The Sultan-Caliph's alliance with the German Emperor added new fuel to these arguments, and rumors were even circulated that the Kaiser had accepted

[2] Nicolson, *op. cit.*, p. 130.
[3] Sykes, *op. cit.*, p. 544.

Mohammedanism. The ingenuity of German propaganda knew no bounds. For example, the Iranians were even told that the German race had its origins in the province of Kerman (German-Kerman). Despite the differences between the Sunni and Shia sects the declaration of a holy war (*jihad*) by the Sultan-Caliph against the British and their allies had its effect on a part of the Iranian clergy. A number of mullahs actively agitated in favor of a jihad. With the advance of the Turkish army, commanded by General von der Goltz Pasha, into the Iranian Kurdistan, Prince von Reuss moved his headquarters to Kermanshah and was followed by his Iranian allies. There these pro-German leaders eventually established a temporary "government" and thereby began to challenge the authority of the legitimate Teheran cabinet.

Such was the "diplomatic" activity of the German Minister and his agents. Coupled with it, military action was undertaken by the German General Staff. Count Kanitz, military attaché to the German Legation in Teheran, worked assiduously to provoke uprisings against the Allies in the provinces. To that end he employed German and Austrian prisoners of war who had escaped from Russian internment camps and found refuge in Iran. He armed them and maintained a small military force of his own that was prepared to fulfill dangerous assignments. He was also aided by special missions sent from Germany for diversionary and sabotage purposes. Of these missions three deserve special mention, namely, those conducted by Wassmuss, Zugmayer, and Niedermayer. Before the war Wassmuss had been consul in Bushire and there had established excellent contacts with the neighboring nomad tribes. Recalled to Germany at the beginning of the war, he was now sent by the General Staff to southern Iran to provoke a general uprising of tribes against the British. His task was twofold: to sabotage the supply of oil to the British navy and to divert British forces from their main campaign in Mesopotamia in order to weaken them in the face of the Turko-German adversary. Wassmuss, whose daring exploits gained him the nickname of "the German Lawrence," did his best to carry out the assigned task. By extraordinary feats of energy and shrewdness he managed to provoke a rebellion of Tangistani tribes in the south, to enter into alliance with the powerful tribe of Qashqais in Fars, and to win over a number of traditionally pro-British Bakhtiyari chieftains. German consuls and commercial agents in southern Iran co-operated with him. In fact, even before his arrival Wonckhaus had made an abortive attempt to blow up British oil installations in Abadan and Basra. Wassmuss, leading a force of tribal warriors, attacked Bushire and immobilized in this port British Resident Sir Percy Cox and a force of eight hundred Indian troops. Aided by Consul Wüstrow in Shiraz, Wassmuss entered that city and there captured the British consul together with the manager of the Imperial Bank of Iran and fourteen other British subjects. He later kept them as hostages in the clay fortress of Ahram in southern Fars. The British, in order to protect their oil fields and pipe lines in Khuzistan, were compelled to dispatch forces to southern Iran. The result was a considerable weakening of their offensive in Mesopotamia, and in April, 1916, General Townshend and his twelve thousand troops had to surrender to the Turks at Kut el-Amara.[4]

The expeditions led by Zugmayer and Niedermayer operated in northern Iran and were actively supported by German consuls in Kermanshah and Hamadan. Like Wassmuss, these agents managed to win over to their cause some tribes. They were particularly successful among the Kurds, who, as followers of the Sunni sect, co-operated with the Turks and their allies. Niedermayer's mission was not limited to Iran. He was instructed to proceed to Afghanistan and to extend his activities there to the gates of India. After a dangerous and arduous journey Niedermayer reached Kabul and tried to induce Emir Habibullah to side with Germany. But the Emir was noncommittal, and, reluctantly, Niedermayer was forced to leave the country. Nevertheless his companions von Hentig and Röhr remained in Afghanistan for some time, reaching the Pamir Plateau and Hindu Kush. There they rallied around them numerous German and Austrian prisoners of war who had escaped from Russia. Although both of them had to leave Afghanistan in due time, their efforts were revived toward the end of the war when the Kaiserliche and Königliche Ost-Indische Abteilung was formed in that country.

While all these diversionary activities were taking place, the

---

[4] For detailed description see Christopher Sykes, *Wassmuss, the Persian Lawrence* (London, 1936).

Iranian government in Teheran was neither willing nor able to do anything to restore order and respect for law. Thus, even Russo-British intimidation of the Iranian cabinet and their outward diplomatic successes in Teheran were of little value to the Allies. The chief aim of their policy was to keep Iran strictly neutral and free of enemy military activities. This end was not attained. To add to their difficulties, the only organized military force in Iran—the gendarmerie—turned pro-German and refused to obey government orders. Its Swedish officers felt an affinity with the cause of Germany despite a denunciation of their attitude by the strictly neutral Stockholm government. Having offered their services to Prince von Reuss, the gendarmes co-operated with Wassmuss and liberally helped themselves to the funds of the captured branch of the Imperial Bank of Iran in Shiraz. All in all, order in Iran could be maintained only in the areas that were subject to either Russian or British military occupation. This was not what the Allies desired, for it diverted forces essential in other theaters.

Despite these successes, the Germans failed to fulfill their military and political objectives. Iran neither declared war on the Allies, nor was she opened for further advance to India. Yet German intrigue and diversion constituted a major headache to Russia and Britain and interfered with the efficacy with which the Mesopotamian campaign was prosecuted. It intensified anti-Russian and anti-British feelings in the country and left the seed for future German influence.

GERMAN INFLUENCE IN IRAN AFTER WORLD WAR I

The end of the war saw a momentary eclipse of German influence. By the middle twenties, however, it was gradually revived. Step by step the Weimar Republic regained the lost position of Imperial Germany and prepared the ground for the further expansion of the Nazi period. The characteristic feature of this penetration was the tendency to gain a foothold in the field of communications. One is tempted to see a sort of meticulous method or master plan pursued by Germany in the Middle East. This plan, which will be elaborated more fully below, may be briefly described in the following manner: first, prepare the way by dominating the transport system; second, use it for your capital investments and flow of goods; third, with the economic situation well in your grip, gain political influence; fourth, absorb the country within your military sphere.

In all these fields German policy was characterized by consistency and dynamism. In this respect it is difficult to differentiate clearly between the general activities of the Weimar and the Nazi periods. Hitler's advent to power in 1933 added only new impetus to the already existing policy. In his bid for world hegemony the German dictator assigned an important role to Iran. During the Nazi period German methods were simply bolder than before, but the over-all aim—to entrench the Germans in Iran—remained essentially the same.

One may well ask, How was it that Iran, a sovereign country, with strong nationalistic leadership, allowed herself to be treated as a territory for somebody's expansion, especially in view of her success-ful emancipation from British and Soviet influence? The reply is that Iran was psychologically prepared to accept the friendship and support of any strong third Power sufficiently distant not to en-danger her political integrity. Such a Power could be, for example, France, the United States, or Germany. In fact, the latter two figured prominently in the plans and policies of Reza Shah, with America given the priority. This was expressed in the willingness of the Iranian government to grant oil concessions to American companies and in the engagement of Dr. Millspaugh as financial expert between 1922 and 1927. The United States might have superseded all other countries in Iran by offering its disinterested friendship and prac-tical business opportunities. But basic American isolationism pre-vented it. Accordingly, Reza Shah, fully conscious of the political implications of such an attitude, turned again to Germany.

Following the pattern to which we referred above, we shall attempt to review the four sectors in which Germany secured an uncontested supremacy in Iran.

1. *Germany and Iranian Communications*

Communications are a key problem in Iran. The economic and political unity of the country, the volume of its foreign trade, and its military preparedness depend to a considerable degree on the solution of the transportation problem. Hence many attempts were made by the Big Powers to gain supremacy in this vital sector.

In the Weimar era, Germany scored two notable successes in this connection. Having obtained an exclusive concession, the German Junkers Company operated all internal airlines between 1927 and 1932. German firms and technicians participated in the construction of the Transiranian Railway. A German company built the Bandar Shah-Shahi sector in 1928, and many German technicians were employed in the Scandinavian Consortium Kampsax, which in 1933 took over all the remaining construction work of the railroad. The higher personnel of the railroad was recruited in Germany and supplemented by several Iranians who had studied and practiced in Berlin. In 1937 the Iranian Ministry of Roads and Communications awarded ten scholarships for the study of railway operations in Germany. Important orders for locomotives were placed with German firms, one of which provided a parlor train for the use of the Shah. In 1939–1940 German firms supplied to Iran the bulk of imported rolling stock.[5]

Germany exported to Iran automobiles and airplanes. She had a virtual monopoly for the supply of motorcycles. For instance, in 1939–1940, of 326 imported motorcycles 321 came from Germany and only 5 from Britain.

The field of maritime communications was not forgotten either. Regular service between Hamburg and Bremen on the one side and the ports of the Persian Gulf on the other was maintained by the German steamship company Hansa Linie, whose ships visited Iran twice a month. Branch offices of the line were established in Teheran, Bushire, Bandar Shahpur, and Ahwaz. In the last years before World War II the German flag in Iranian ports was second only to the British. It overtook the Soviet and Norwegian standards.

The Third Reich paid special attention to air transportation in Iran. Reviving the traditions of the old Junkers Company, the Deutsche Lufthansa inaugurated, in 1937, an airline that linked Berlin with Bagdad, Teheran, and Kabul via Tirana, Athens, Rhodes, and Damascus. It was possible to reach Teheran from Berlin

[5] Unless otherwise indicated, statistical data in this chapter are quoted from the *Statistique annuelle du commerce exterieur de l'Iran.*

in forty-one hours. The new airline aimed to link Germany with the Middle East countries that figured in her expansionist plans. It was to serve as a main artery of German penetration into the Persian Gulf area exactly as the old Berlin-Bagdad railway did a quarter of a century before.

The whole enterprise was not without military implications. The government of Reza Shah granted the Lufthansa the right to fly over and to land on the Iranian military airport in Meshed, not far from the Soviet border. As this privilege was given at the time of Nazi-Soviet tension, it did not fail to produce uneasiness in Moscow and a strong reaction in the Soviet press.

2. German-Iranian Investment and Trade

Without much exaggeration it may be said that Germany was the virtual founder of the young Iranian industry. This process of industrialization was convenient for her, for (a) it increased German exports and contributed to the favorable trade balance; (b) it compelled the Iranians to purchase spare parts in Germany.

In the twenties and thirties the Iranian government decided to establish a number of foundries. In order to buy all necessary machinery and materials, an official mission was sent to Berlin in 1938. On its return the government proceeded to recruit personnel for the construction and management of the foundries. Candidates possessing a knowledge of the German language were given priority.[6]

Only a few years before World War II Iran started to mine coal by modern methods. Machinery for that purpose was supplied by a German firm. Also all factory installations for the production of coke and related coal products were purchased in Germany by the Iranian Ministry of Mines and Industry.

Imposing government buildings were an object of special fondness to Reza Shah. His reign was characterized by a frenzy of house-building in Teheran and in some showy places of Iran. Most of this program was carried out by German builders and architects. The magnificent building of the Bank-i-Melli in Teheran, in neo-Achaemenid style, was built by a German architect—to mention one example.

[6] *Journal de Tehran,* no. 1019, Dec. 1, 1938.

The construction of many public buildings necessitated the development of a cement industry. In 1936 the Iranian government gave a contract to a German firm to reconstruct the only existing factory. In 1937 its capacity reached the figure of three hundred tons daily.

German firms constructed and supplied machinery for textile factories in Isfahan and Kerman, a paper factory in Isfahan, packing and drying establishments for tea in various parts of Iran, and the only ice factory in the country.

In the field of electrical motors and light installations the famous Siemens Company enjoyed supremacy on the Iranian market, and Ernst Leitz of Vetzlar (the world-famous producer of Leica cameras) attempted to monopolize trade in microscopes and other equipment with hospital and industrial laboratories.

The armament industry also owed its development to German technical assistance. A machine-gun factory in Teheran and an airplane factory at Shahbas were established. According to the *Orient Nachrichten*,[7] the airplane factory was capable of producing a squadron of smaller fighter planes every two months. They were convertible into light bombers. German-Iranian co-operation in the armament industry was only beginning before the second World War. It was interrupted in 1941.

The description of German industrial expansion in Iran would be incomplete without mentioning the role played by Czechoslovak industry, and especially by the great Skoda works. The dismemberment and absorption of the Czechoslovak state by Germany in 1938–1939 made the Skoda, for all practical purposes, a German factory. Skoda introduced itself to the Iranian market in 1932 and in the following years its activity increased. Its achievements included the construction of numerous bridges, roads, and buildings; the regulation of rivers; and the construction of various industrial plants.

With regard to trade between the two countries solid foundations were laid during the Weimar period and continued throughout the Nazi era. In 1928 Germany and Iran concluded a trade treaty that contained a most-favored nation clause. It was followed in 1929 by a

[7] No. 16/17, Sept. 1, 1938.

treaty of friendship and by several conventions regulating tariffs, trade, navigation, and the reciprocal settlement of nationals. By that time the old Wonckhaus Company had reappeared in the south.

German expansion was, however, more noticeable in the north. The main route of German merchandise was the Trebizond-Tabriz line rather than the Gulf. An Iranian observer of German penetration remarked that the British favored German economic expansion in northern provinces because of its political significance. This, according to him, was especially visible after the conclusion of the Locarno treaties.[8]

In 1932–1933, the last year of the Weimar Republic, Germany's share in Iran's foreign trade amounted to 8 per cent. This was smaller than the shares of the Soviet Union (28 per cent), Great Britain and her Empire (23 per cent), and the United States (12 per cent). At first glimpse Germany's percentage does not look very impressive; yet it should be borne in mind that during the first World War Germany was completely cut off from the Iranian market and, accordingly, was compelled to start from scratch after the end of hostilities. In attaining fourth place, Germany regained the position that she had held before the war and thus in terms of trade successfully reinstated herself.

In the Nazi period, as a result of a skillful commercial policy Germany attained an amazing success in her trade with Iran. Within nine years after Hitler's advent to power the German-Iranian trade increased almost ninefold.[9] From a poor fourth in 1932, Germany reached the second place on the Iranian trading list in 1937. She was then topped only by the Soviet Union, and even that did not last long. In 1939 she overtook Russia and maintained her supreme position through the three years preceding the German-Soviet war.

Germany's percentage of Iranian foreign trade also increased rapidly. From 8 per cent in 1932–1933 it rose to 21 per cent in 1936–1937. It reached 41.5 per cent in 1938–1939 and attained the imposing figure of 45.5 per cent in 1940–1941. Thus, according to Iranian statistics, Germany secured for herself almost half of the Iranian

[8] Gussein Zade Meshti, "Germanskoye Proniknovenye v Persiyu," *Novy Vostok*, no. 13–14, pp. 92–93.

[9] See Appendix no. VI.

foreign trade. In reality, the trade between the two countries was even greater. This was due to the fact that most German goods imported via Trebizond and Istanbul or via England and India were not counted by Iranian authorities as German, but as Turkish, British, or Indian merchandise.[10]

German-Iranian trade possessed the characteristics typical of trade between a highly developed industrial country and an agrarian semi-colonial area. Germany naturally exported to Iran all sorts of machinery and tools. In the year preceding the German-Soviet war Germany supplied Iran nearly 80 per cent of all the machinery imported by the latter, i.e., almost four times as much as all other countries combined. In the field of motors and electrical machines Germany's share was even larger, almost monopolistic. Germany exported to Iran important quantities of metals, paper, and chemicals (the I. G. Farben Industrie dominated the trade in aniline colors for carpets). Despite her role in building up Iranian textile industry, Germany was also able to export her own textile products. During the last four years before the outbreak of the German-Soviet war she supplied more than 50 per cent of all imported textiles. In 1938–1939 alone, her exports of woolens to Iran constituted 75 per cent of all woolens imported by the latter. Characteristically, Germany imported from Iran raw wool and exported finished products.

Germany's increasing domination of the Iranian market was also illustrated by the fact that by 1937 registered German trademarks in Iran were more numerous than the trademarks of any other country (German—351; British—285; American—177; Soviet—143; French—118).[11]

In contrast to German industrial exports, Iranian exports to Germany were mostly of an agricultural or raw material type. Of finished products, only carpets were significant. By 1940–1941 Germany's purchases of Iranian cotton were almost 60 per cent of the total. Since Japan was another important buyer, the two Axis powers monopolized almost 90 per cent of Iranian cotton exports. German purchases of wool were even more impressive, especially after the begin-

---

[10] According to Haji Gholi Khan Ardalan, *Die Stellung Persiens in der Weltwirschaft* (Teheran, 1929).

[11] *Orient Nachrichten*, no. 22, Dec. 1, 1937, p. 336.

ning of the war in Europe: In 1939–1940 Germany purchased more than 90 per cent of all Iranian exported wool.

In the field of food supplies Iranian exports to Germany included grain, fruit, and rice. In 1940–1941 Germany purchased in Iran nearly 1,700 tons of wheat and barley. These vital food supplies reached Germany in the first years of World War II when the Reich was blockaded by the Western Allies. Russia served as a transit route.

In order to facilitate commercial exchange between Germany and Iran a clearing agreement was concluded in 1935 and renewed in 1939. According to this agreement Iranian importers of German goods were to pay the price of purchased merchandise to the Bank-i-Melli in Teheran, whereas German importers were to pay to the Deutsche Verrechnungskasse in Berlin. German and Iranian exporters were, in turn, entitled to receive money from these two institutions. The general Iranian regulation that importers had to obtain import licenses did not apply to their dealings with Germany. The only document required in this case was the certificate of origin of merchandise. Thus the German-Iranian clearing agreement gave a privileged position to the trade between the two countries.

To stress the importance attached to this trade in Berlin and Teheran, special institutions dedicated to it were established in both countries. An Iranian-German Clearing Office was created in the Iranian Ministry of Trade. In Berlin the German-Iranian Chamber of Commerce published a monthly *Mitteilungen* and a quarterly *Bulletin der Deutsch-Iranischen Handelskammer*. In 1937 a commercial company, *Afshar A. Shoyegan,* was created in Teheran with a capital of 1,000,000 rials. It devoted itself exclusively to the trade between Germany and Iran.

3. German Cultural and Political Penetration

In addition to commercial exchanges Nazi Germany laid great stress on cultural and political influence in Iran. This constituted a part of a wider program embracing the whole of the Middle East. This program was carried out with particular intensity in the middle thirties, when an impressive number of German cultural institutions devoted their time to the study of Eastern problems.

The most important among these institutions was the Deutsche

Orient Verein founded in 1934 soon after the Nazi advent to power. The Verein published the widely circulated *Orient Nachrichten*. In the Iranian sector it was valiantly seconded by the Deutsch-Persische Gesellschaft, which sponsored various publications, organized lecture tours, and generally facilitated cultural exchanges between the two countries. At the same time a number of periodicals such as the *Zeitschrift für Politik,* the *Koloniale Rundschau,* and *Der Neue Orient* devoted their columns to Eastern problems arousing the interest of experts and laymen alike.

With the establishment of the Nazi regime the curricula of German universities likewise were enriched by a greater number of courses devoted to the East and colonial questions. In 1933 the number of such courses was 196; by 1936 it reached the figure 341, of which 24 dealt with the problem of *Deutschtum* outside Europe. In 1935 alone 41 theses were written on colonial topics.[12]

Apart from stimulating interest in Eastern affairs within Germany (two thousand conversions to Islam were registered in Berlin in 1938), the Nazi government became intensely active in dispensing propaganda proclaiming its role and achievements in the East. This propaganda stressed that, politically, German's intentions were pure, that, in contrast to other powers, Germany had no imperialistic designs in the Middle East. The Nazi political system was asserted to be superior to others, as one that did not produce the class struggle because of its excellent social balance. It was pointed out that a similarity existed between the German awakening under the impact of National Socialism and the awakening of the East. Aware of Eastern respect for authority, German propagandists underlined the beneficial role of the *Führerprinzip* and drew analogies among Hitler, Reza Shah, Kemal Ataturk, and Ibn Saud. They described them as forceful and God-sent leaders. The *Hitlerjugend* was cited as an example of youth's enthusiasm for national revival. Accordingly, similar youth organizations were encouraged in the Middle East. With all that, care was taken to impress the Orientals with the military might of resurgent Germany. A weak Germany would not find sympathy among Eastern nations; a strong one was sure to enlist a number of friends. During the Nazi period Berlin became more than

[12] Bernard Vernier, *La Politique islamique de l'Allemagne* (Paris, 1939), p. 27.

ever a meeting place of Orientals in Europe. Furthermore, owing to Hitler's openly anti-Soviet policy until 1939, the German capital became a center of the Pan-Turanian Prometheist movement, which strove for the liberation of oppressed Turkic groups from Russian domination.

With regard to Iran, emphasis was laid on a number of points on which the Iranians were particularly sensitive. Aware of their sensibility about economic exploitation by foreigners, the Nazis stressed that Iran should get rid of foreign technicians and should acquire her own equipment under the guidance of German experts. Despite their dubious logic, these persuasions fell on fertile ground, especially since they were supported by good precedents. In the twenties, the Iranians had employed German experts in technical, economic, and cultural capacities and were appreciative of their services. As early as 1927, soon after Dr. Millspaugh's dismissal, a German financial adviser, Dr. Bötzke, had been engaged by the Iranian government. He had been followed in 1928 by Dr. Lindenblatt, who had become Director of the newly founded Bank-i-Melli-yi-Iran. Later the number of German advisers in various government departments had considerably increased. Even the Ministry of Education, this always sensitive organ under authoritarian governments, availed itself in the middle thirties of the services of a German adviser.

The Germans made quite an effort to gain a foothold in the Iranian school system. Successful arrangements were made to staff higher and specialized schools with German teachers. Professor Londhoff became the head of the technological department in the Industrial School in Teheran. By 1939 seven German professors were engaged in the same school. The policy of bringing young Iranians to study at German universities was not without effect on their subsequent pro-German orientation. The doctoral dissertations of these students were characteristically Germanophile in tendency.[13]

To remove any causes for misunderstanding under the Nuremberg Racial Laws, a special decree of the Reich cabinet in 1936 exempted the Iranians, as "pure Aryans," from their restrictive provisions. In

[13] For example: Ardalan, *op. cit.;* Dr. Kaviani Reza Khan, *Das Verkehrswesen Persiens und seine Ausgestaltung* (Berlin, 1930); Dr. Abdollah Molekpur, *Die Wirtschaftverfassung Irans* (Berlin, 1935).

fact, great use was made of the Aryan legend to encourage friendship between both nations. The adoption of the swastika as a symbol of the Nazi party was interpreted as pointing to the spiritual unity between the Aryans of the north and the nation of Zoroaster. The German architects who constructed the railway station in Teheran adorned its ceiling with a discreet yet clearly recognized pattern of swastikas. After the visit to Teheran in 1937 of Professor Fritz Höger, of the Nordic Academy of Arts in Berlin, Iranian architecture fell under considerable German influence.

In 1939, following the initiative of the Nazi cultural "expert" Alfred Rosenberg, the German government presented Iran with a collection of books called the German Scientific Library, composed of 7,500 volumes. These carefully selected books were destined to convince Iranian readers of the cultural mission of Germany in the East and of the kinship between the National Socialist Reich and the "Aryan culture" of Iran.

This constant stressing of spiritual community was not without effect on political *rapprochement* between the two "Aryan" nations. In 1936 Dr. Hjalmar Schacht, President of the Reichsbank and economic "wizard" of Nazi Germany, paid a visit to the Iranian government. As a result of this journey a trade agreement (see p. 158) was concluded. In 1937 this visit was reciprocated by an official trip to Berlin made by the President of the Majlis, Hasan Esfandiyari, in the company of Mr. Karagozlu, of the Protocol Division of the Iranian Ministry for Foreign Affairs. Esfandiyari was received by Hitler, Goering, Schacht, and other high-ranking members of the Nazi hierarchy. In the same year Baldur von Schirach, chief of the Nazi youth organizations, was ceremoniously received in Teheran. He reviewed a parade of Iranian boy scouts and spoke sympathetically of national emancipation.

Apart from these official visits large numbers of Germans traveled to Iran. In the single year 1936–1937, 778 Germans arrived there under various pretexts. In the same year only 446 Germans left the country, which means that the number of Germans in Iran increased by 332. More than a hundred of them were "tourists." In 1937–1938, 819 Germans came to Iran, and again many of them remained in the country. This "tourist" traffic continued even after the outbreak of war in Europe. By August, 1941, the number of Germans in Iran reached two thousand. The Deutsches Haus on the elegant Qavam as-Saltaneh Avenue became a social center for German citizens.

The main center of Nazi political activity in the Middle East was the German Legation in Bagdad under the able leadership of Dr. Grobba. Compelled to leave Iraq after the outbreak of war between Germany and Britain, Grobba moved with his personnel to Teheran and there, in the spacious quarters of the new legation, was able to continue his work. During the short-lived Rashid Ali's revolt in Iraq in 1941 Grobba went again to Bagdad, to return to Germany through Syria. The defeated rebel Rashid Ali, however, fled to Iran, seeking refuge in a country with pro-German orientation.

THE GERMAN FIFTH COLUMN IN IRAN

To experienced observers it was obvious that Germany was building a powerful fifth column in Iran. The penetration or outright control of railways, airlines, and a number of vital industries placed the Germans in an important strategic position within the country and promised effective action in the event of some emergency. The menace that this well-organized body of Germans represented to the Allies was especially alarming in the spring and the summer of 1941. The revolt of Rashid Ali in Iraq, which broke out early in that year, permitted Germany to make a bold thrust into the Middle East. Rashid Ali, having installed himself as a pro-Axis premier in Bagdad, asked Berlin for assistance, which was readily given to him. The French administration in Syria, under the Vichyite General Dentz, granted the right to German aircraft to use Syrian airfields in transit to Iraq. Soon German planes were landing in the oil-rich Mosul and Kirkuk areas. British subjects, including the Embassy and consular staffs, were detained by the rebellious authorities and kept under close arrest. The success of German enterprise in Iraq would have permitted them to establish a direct link with the fifth column in Iran, and to exert even more powerful influence on the not unwilling Iranian government. Although this success did not materialize as a result of energetic British counteraction, the presence of German agents in Iran still remained a threat to Allied interests. With the

German invasion of Russia in June, 1941, this fifth column assumed tremendous importance. It would, if possible, wreck the Transiranian railway, the only available road of supplies to Russia.

Details of what happened in the British-Soviet-Iranian relations as a result of the Nazi attack on the Soviet Union will be related in the next chapter. Here it is enough to say that, following an ultimatum, Britain and Russia occupied Iran in August of 1941 and promptly interned the majority of the German citizens residing in the country. Despite this drastic action the apparatus of the German fifth column was not entirely destroyed. On the contrary, a few enterprising agents managed to revive their secret organization and seriously to imperil the Allied war effort in Iran.

The story of their initial success and ultimate failure goes back to October, 1940, when two German secret service men, Roman Gamotta and Franz Mayr, arrived in Iran ostensibly to work for the transport firm, Nouvelle Iran Express. They were followed by another agent, Major Julius Berthold Schulze, who in April, 1941, arrived in Tabriz as consular secretary.

The internment of German citizens in August, 1941, brought temporary havoc to their plans, but Gamotta, Mayr, and Schulze managed to escape arrest. Gamotta fled to Turkey and thence proceeded to Berlin. Schulze fled from Tabriz just before the Red Army entered the town and subsequently reached Teheran. From there the German Minister, Herr Ettel, dispatched him as a diplomatic courier to Afghanistan. Before crossing the border, however, Schulze and his wife were arrested by the Iranian authorities and brought back to Teheran. Pending an official investigation into the question of his diplomatic status, Schulze was allowed to live in the German Legation. Some time afterward he and his wife escaped to the south. There he initiated an intrigue among the Qashqai tribesmen with the view of dividing Iran into two puppet states.

Meanwhile Mayr, aided by an Armenian friend, managed to live in hiding throughout the winter of 1941–1942. In January, 1942, he established contact with an Iranian anti-Allied group. Under his guidance this group was to act as a revived fifth column. It was organized as a national movement called *Melliyun-i-Iran* and was headed by a committee including two Iranian generals. Its task was to incite the Kurdish and other tribes to revolt in the north, while Schulze's mission was to conduct parallel activity in the south.

In his daring enterprise Mayr found a valuable ally in the Japanese Minister in Teheran. The latter, before leaving Iran in the spring of 1942, changed Mayr's dollars into Iranian currency, gave him five wireless transmitter sets, and introduced him to various Iranians possessing influence with the tribes.

Mayr's chief worry was to establish effective contact with Berlin, which had been severed following the events of August, 1941. The Japanese transmitters were of no use as long as he had no operators to handle them. Hence his efforts were centered on establishing liaison with Germany through Ankara. For this purpose he sent several couriers to Turkey. For a long time, however, none of them were able to reach their destination. One was even arrested by the British. Eventually, in July, 1942, a smuggler recruited by Mayr managed to get through to Ankara and there to explain his chief's need for wireless operators.

In the meantime the Melliyun committee suggested that Mayr should go to Isfahan and help there in the unification of tribes on behalf of the Germans. This Mayr did. Arriving in Isfahan he presented a prominent Iranian general with two radio transmitters and set to work with local members of the Melliyun. Mayr's plans included a coup by the Iranians, the subsequent deposition of the Shah, and the carrying out of military operations against the Allies behind their lines. They provided also for close co-operation between the southern tribes and the German army, once it broke through the Caucasus and reached the frontiers of Iran. Final details of this conspiracy were to be elaborated after the expected German victory at Stalingrad. Mayr's plans were modeled on the German invasion of Norway.

German reverses at El Alamein and Stalingrad in the fall of 1942 complicated the execution of these schemes and brought about some defections among Mayr's Iranian collaborators. One of them handed over to British intelligence agents a suitcase containing 250 documents. These seriously incriminated a number of prominent Iranians

[164]

including the well-known mullah Seyyid Abol Qasim Kashani and the deputy Habibullah Nobakht.

Informed of this betrayal Mayr hurriedly left Isfahan and reappeared in Teheran. There, by a courier from Ankara, he received information that his secret service chiefs had decided to send him the requested wireless operators. The message contained details as to the time and place of their parachuting into Iran.

Following these arrangements, six German agents were parachuted near the salt lake northeast of Qum on March 30, 1943. They were amply equipped in money and weapons. Upon reaching Teheran they informed Mayr that their orders provided for the establishment of wireless liaison with Berlin and for the sabotage of the Allied war effort.

The German secret service, promptly informed of the success of the first mission, decided to send another to southern Iran. The second mission, composed of three Germans and one Iranian, was parachuted near Shiraz on July 15, 1943. There they joined Schulze.

Despite some earlier reverses at Isfahan, Mayr managed to preserve the Melliyun organization relatively intact. Melliyun's task now consisted in influencing the coming elections to the Fourteenth Majlis with a view to creating an anti-Allies bloc of deputies. This bloc would have to prevent Iran's entry into the war on the side of the Allies and to conduct a general anti-Allies policy.

The main objective of Mayr's fifth column was, however, to hinder the flow of supplies to Russia. "Our aim," he telegraphed Berlin in August, 1943, "would thus be the creation of an independent and neighboring war zone with the object of interrupting supplies and keeping the occupying troops busy." [14]

By the middle of August, 1943, these plans were well under way. The Melliyun, which included responsible railway officials, was busy sabotaging the Transiranian line. Accidents multiplied, security in the provinces deteriorated rapidly, and election maneuvers were at their height in the capital.

Meanwhile the British intelligence organs (the Counter-Intelligence Corps Iran) were gradually gathering clues to the whole

[14] Quoted from the *Tehran Daily News,* March 16, 1945, which, following the British Embassy's release, published the story of the fifth column.

plot. With the intensification of the fifth-column activity in August the British decided to strike a blow. In the night of August 14–15 Mayr was arrested in Teheran by the British. Other Germans in the capital were also rounded up and interned. Those agents whom Mayr had sent to the Bakhtiyari country were subsequently lured to Teheran and captured. At the same time, following the Allied request, the Iranian police arrested some 170 Iranians as proven or suspected German collaborators. The list included a number of higher army officers, several editors and deputies, as well as many railroad officials. Of these, some were released soon afterward, but many were detained in the internment camps until the end of the war.

Thus owing to British vigilance the fifth column was smashed at the moment when it was about to fulfill its hazardous task. Only Schulze and his collaborators remained free for a number of months. Eventually, in the spring of 1944, the Qashqai chieftains surrendered them to the British authorities.

The defeat of German intrigue was complete when Iran declared war on the Reich on September 9, 1943.

CHAPTER SEVEN

Iran's Policies during the Second World War

FOREIGN RELATIONS

G ERMANY could not have been so successful in her policies if Iran had not responded to her advances. Hence, it was not surprising that Iran decided to remain neutral when the second World War broke out. Such a policy was beneficial to both Germany and Iran, because it permitted them to continue and even to increase their mutual trade. An outright alliance between the two countries would have presented unnecessary inconveniences to both of them. Iran might have become a theater of hostilities because of possible British action, and consequently Germany would have lost a valuable source of supplies. Outwardly Iran observed neutrality faithfully. Her press published war communiqués of German, French, and British agencies without discrimination as well as the communiqués of Tass, the Russian news agency. At the same time German goods, tourists, and technicians poured into Iran in even greater numbers.

The German invasion of Russia in June, 1941, suddenly changed the whole situation. The British government ranged itself on the side of Russia and declared its readiness to assist her in every possible way. In order to deliver war supplies to her Russian ally on a large scale Britain had to send them in transit through Iran. But the presence of a large German fifth column in that country might have prevented any such plan from succeeding. Accordingly, on July 19 and August 16 the Soviet and British diplomatic missions in Teheran presented to the Iranian government memoranda demanding the expulsion of a large number of Germans. Simultaneously Russia and Britain launched a vigorous propaganda of intimidation. Broadcasts from London, Delhi, and Baku in the Persian language accused the Iranian government of sheltering a German fifth column, gave exaggerated numbers of Germans in Iran, and spread false rumors about tribal unrest, dissatisfaction in the army, and so forth. This propaganda irritated the Iranians enormously. Their government insisted, in notes of August 7 and 21, that its record of impartiality toward the belligerents was of the strictest character and that to expel the Germans would be tantamount to the violation of neutrality. In conversations with foreign diplomatic representatives, the Iranian ministers asserted that all the Germans were closely watched and that the government had the situation well under control, so that no danger from the Germans existed. In thus temporizing with the issue, the Iranian government was apparently unaware of the seriousness with which the Allies treated the whole problem.

On August 25 the final Allied notes were presented. On that day the Soviet and British envoys appeared together at 4 A.M. at the private residence of the Iranian Prime Minister to submit their message. The parallel notes expressed disappointment that Iran had not complied with Allied requests, voiced regret that the Allies were now compelled to take unilateral action, gave assurances that the Allies had no designs on Iran's territorial integrity and independence, and expressed the hope that Iran would not resist Allied advance.

Simultaneously, at dawn August 25, Soviet and British forces invaded Iran. The Soviet army entered Iran in three columns: the first heading from Julfa to Tabriz; the second marching through Astara toward Pahlavi and Resht; and the third invading the northeastern border province of Khorasan. Soon such important centers as Tabriz, Meshed, and the Caspian coastal towns were under Soviet occupation. On August 31 Soviet forces effected junction with the British group under Brigadier-General Aislewood in Qazvin. On September 17 they entered Teheran. These land operations were accompanied by naval action at Pahlavi, where on August 25 the Soviet navy shelled the town and harbor. The Soviet air force also bombarded several Iranian towns, such as Tabriz, Pahlavi, Hamadan, Qazvin, Meshed, and, as late as August 31, Teheran.

The British advanced from two points. One of their columns entered Iran from Khanaqin and proceeded through Kermanshah and Hamadan up to Qazvin. Another invaded the southwestern province of Khuzistan, also from Iraqi territory. British naval action was centered at Bandar Shahpur, which soon fell in their hands, together with eight German and Italian merchant vessels. The Royal Air Force bombed a few military objectives at Ahwaz but otherwise showed restraint.

Iranian opposition to this invasion was negligible. Despite the Iranian Staff's communiqués, which boasted of the excellent morale of the army, the reverse was true. Iranian military resistance crumbled. Many officers deserted their units; many units abandoned their arms and melted away. The Pataq Pass lying across the British line of advance from the west was left open, although it might have been a formidable obstacle if defended. Except for an engagement in Khuzistan, where the Iranians under General Shahbakhti managed to inflict fifty-five casualties on the British, the Iranian army surrendered easily and made it possible for the Allies to take quick possession of most of the strategic points. A general breakdown of morale among the Iranian troops was evident. Their lack of courage was perhaps best symbolized by the fact that when the surrender decision was taken at Pahlavi, no Iranian of consequence ventured to approach the Soviet navy to announce it. Eventually a Belgian harbor employee volunteered to act as intermediary.

The military occupation of the country was completed within a few days. Simultaneously important political developments were taking place in Teheran. On August 27 the cabinet of Ali Mansur resigned. It was clear that the complexion of the government would have to change to meet the new situation. On the same day the Shah appointed Mohammed Ali Furuqi to head a new government. Furuqi acted quickly: his new cabinet was presented to the Majlis on the following day and it obtained a vote of confidence. Except for two shifts in portfolios the cabinet members remained unchanged. On the same day, August 28, the new Premier announced that orders were given to the army to cease resistance.[1] This was a gesture of purely political character inasmuch as the army had ceased to be a

---

[1] *Journal de Tehran*, Aug. 29, 1941.

fighting force before the announcement. Martial law and a curfew were proclaimed in Teheran. Marshal Ahmadi was appointed Military Governor of the capital.

These events were followed by an exchange of notes between the Allies and Iran that brought about a new political settlement. Three of these notes deserve special mention. In the first parallel notes presented by Russia and Britain on August 30 the two Allies reiterated that they had no designs against the independence and territorial integrity of Iran and that their military action had been necessitated by the German menace and the non-co-operative attitude of the Iranian government toward their proposals. This note contained the following demands:

(1) The Iranian government must order its forces to retreat to the east and north of the following line: Khanaqin–Kermanshah–Khorramabad–Masjid-i-Suleiman–Haft Kel–Gachsaran–Bandar Dilam; and to the south of the following line: Ushnu–Miandoab–Zanjan–Qazvin–Karaj–Babolsar–Semnan–Shahrud–Aliabad. The zones thus traced would be occupied by the Allies, with the center of the country left to the Iranians.

(2) The Iranian government must expel within one week all German citizens except those that had taken refuge in the German Legation and certain indispensable technicians and furnish a list of all Germans to the Allied diplomatic representatives.

(3) The Iranian government must undertake not to admit any more Germans to Iran for the duration of war.

(4) The Iranian government must facilitate the transport of Allied war materials by road, rail, and air.

(5) The Iranian government must agree to remain neutral and refrain from any hostile acts against Britain or Russia.

In return the Allies offered the following guarantees:

(1) The British promised to continue payment of oil royalties.

(2) Iran was assured of economic assistance.

(3) The Soviet and British advance would be halted and their forces withdrawn from Iran when the military situation permitted.

The Soviet note of August 30 differed from the British in the following points:

(1) Iran was asked to facilitate the task of the Soviet government

in developing the oil resources at Kavir-Khurian as well as the fisheries on the Caspian.

(2) The Soviet government agreed to continue payment of royalties for fisheries on the Caspian as provided by the Treaty of October 1, 1927.

One day later, on August 31, the British hastened to send a second, additional note to the Iranian government in which they demanded the handing over to British and Soviet forces of all Germans except the bona fide members of the German Legation and certain technicians. This demand was thus to replace the previous demand for expulsion only.

In its reply to these notes on September 1 the Iranian government complied with Allied demands and made a number of requests and observations, of which the following were most important: Iran—

(1) Requested the evacuation of British forces from Khorramabad and Dizful and of Soviet forces from Qazvin, Semnan, and Shahrud; asked for permission to station Iranian troops in Kermanshah.

(2) Requested that the occupation troops should have as little contact as possible with the Iranian population.

(3) Asked the Allies to consider an indemnity for the loss of Iranian life and property and the return of captured arms and munitions.

(4) Stated that no mention of Kavir-Khurian oil deposits was made in the treaties with the U.S.S.R. and added that any agreements made with the Soviet Union concerning these deposits were considered as abandoned since no action to exploit them had been taken. The Iranian government declared its willingness, however, to enter into friendly discussions concerning this matter with a view to protecting the rights of both parties.

This communication was followed by the third parallel Allied note on September 6. This time the Allies demanded the expulsion of German, Italian, Rumanian, and Hungarian legations and immediate cancellation of their code, radio, and pouch privileges. They drew the government's attention to the change in the situation caused by the conduct of Axis and satellite nationals and stressed that the enemy legations took advantage of the Allied failure to occupy Teheran to indulge in obstructive tactics and hostile propaganda. From that point on the British and Soviet notes again differed in their tenor. The British note approved in principle of the Iranian request to evacuate Dizful, Khorramabad, and Kermanshah and expressed readiness to discuss these withdrawals with the Iranians; it promised that Iranian administration in occupied provinces would continue; and it expressed willingness to consider the return to Iranians of captured war equipment as well as the payment of indemnity upon the final evacuation of British troops.

The Soviet note, in contrast, refused any alteration of the Soviet occupation line; it refused to accept the request to separate the Soviet troops from the people of Iran; it expressed appreciation of Iranian willingness to reach a new agreement with regard to Kavir-Khurian oil deposits; and it refused any payment of indemnities or the return of captured arms and munitions.

By its note of September 8 the Iranian government accepted the Allied terms and stated that there could be no pretext for occupying Teheran. Meanwhile the rounding up of Axis nationals was well under way. They were handed over to British and Soviet forces and sent either to Russia or to India. Eventually Iran was asked by the Allies to expel the Bulgarian Legation as well (not previously included in the list because of Soviet hope that Bulgaria could be saved from the Nazi clutches). Later a request came to cancel the pouch and code privileges of the French and Japanese legations and to break off formal diplomatic relations with all the Axis countries.

There was a certain amount of confusion in connection with the arrest and internment of Axis nationals. This, as we know from the preceding chapter, permitted some Nazi agents to escape and continue their secret activity in Iran. The Iranian government could not, however, be blamed for it. In fact, it co-operated loyally with the Allies in this respect. The blame should be put rather at the door of the Allies, who failed to formulate clear-cut demands from the outset. Their notes asked first for expulsion of the Germans by the Iranian authorities, and only later insisted on the internment of all Axis nationals by the Allied forces. Their hesitation in occupying Teheran permitted a large number of Germans to escape from the provinces to the capital and to seek refuge in the German Legation. It was reported that the number of those seeking diplomatic asylum exceeded nine hundred. The evacuation of Axis diplomatic missions went altogether smoothly and due courtesy was shown their representatives except for an unfortunate incident on the Turkish border toward which the Axis diplomatic convoy had been directed. There all the heavy luggage of the Axis diplomats was suddenly confiscated by the Soviet authorities.

During these days of feverish activity one more crisis was ripening. The position of Reza Shah became obviously very uncomfortable. The change of cabinet signified a change in policy, and it was difficult to imagine that the ruler who had so closely collaborated with the Germans during the past decade could continue on his throne in the new circumstances. Yet, paradoxically enough, there was widespread conviction among the Iranians that, despite all his pro-German leanings, Reza Shah was a friend and perhaps a tool of the British. Such a popular feeling was, of course, most inconvenient to the British government. It decided, therefore, to disassociate itself completely from the person of the Shah. Consequently a vigorous radio campaign beaming from New Delhi and London was inaugurated in the beginning of September. These broadcasts stressed the tyrannical rule of the Shah, his injustices and exploitation of the people. As a result the ruler whom nobody had dared to criticize openly for the past two decades became subject to more and more pronounced attacks among the people. His prestige fell rapidly. Yet the Shah clung tenaciously to his throne and refused to believe the gravity of the situation. On the evening of the day of the Allied invasion (August 25) the Shah asked the United States Embassy to use its good offices between Iran and the invading states. This request was accompanied by a direct telegram to President Roosevelt. On receipt of the President's reply the Shah, on September 6, summoned the American Minister to his palace. During the conversation that ensued, he thanked the President for his declaration of friendship and good will and expressed his appreciation that the President was closely following events in Iran and his satisfaction that the American government had taken note of British and Soviet statements that they had no designs against the independence of Iran. The Shah stated, furthermore, that he had no sympathy with the Germans and said that Britain and Russia could have satisfied their desires by friendly negotiations instead of the use of force.

[173]

These statements were made, apparently, with the conviction that some accommodation could be reached with the British and the Russians and that the Shah's person would not constitute an obstacle. It was generally believed in Iran that the Shah's mistaken hope was due to his misinformation about the real state of affairs. A theory, quite plausible, was advanced that his advisers did not dare to inform him fully about the seriousness of the situation and thus led him to draw erroneous conclusions.

By the middle of September it became obvious that the incessant hostile propaganda made his position untenable. On September 16 Reza abdicated in favor of his son, Mohammed Reza Pahlavi, who was proclaimed Shah by the Majlis on the same day. Significantly the British and Soviet forces entered Teheran on the following morning, September 17. The deposed monarch left Iran for Isfahan and on September 28 embarked at Bandar Abbas on a British vessel *S.S. Bandera*, which took him to the island of Mauritius. The ex-Shah, who had hoped to sail to one of the Latin-American countries, found himself an exile in British custody. Later he was transferred to Johannesburg in South Africa. He died there in 1944.

The accession of the new ruler was followed by a general amnesty to political prisoners. A large number of opposition politicians including radical left-wing elements were released.

Iran became divided into three zones: the British zone, including the southern and central parts of the country; the neutral zone, including Teheran and Meshed; and the Soviet zone, embracing, with some exceptions, the provinces of Azerbaijan, Mazanderan, Gilan, Astarabad, and Khorasan. The Teheran–Hamadan–Kermanshah–Qasr-i-Shirin road was retained by the British, but Qazvin, lying on the northern branch of this route, found itself in the Soviet zone. No British or Soviet troops were to be kept in Teheran, but this rule was not strictly heeded. The civil and military airports in and around Teheran were taken over by the British and Soviet forces. Military and passenger communications with Russia were established by Soviet air forces. The British Overseas Airways Corporation, acting under the supervision of the Royal Air Force, assured communications with other countries in the Middle East. Soon passport control of all in- and out-going passengers was in the hands of the occupying powers.

On January 29, 1942, this *de facto* situation was confirmed by the conclusion of the Tripartite Treaty of Alliance between the Soviet Union, Great Britain, and Iran. Britain and Russia undertook to defend Iran from aggression on the part of Germany or any other power. They pledged to "respect the territorial integrity, sovereignty and political independence of Iran" and promised to withdraw their forces "from Iranian Territory not later than six months after all hostilities between the Allied Powers and Germany and her associates have been suspended." Britain and Russia engaged themselves to "safeguard the economic existence of the Iranian people against the privations and difficulties arising as a result of the present war" and not "to conclude treaties inconsistent with the provisions of the present Treaty." In return Iran undertook to co-operate with the Allies. It was understood, however, that assistance of her army was to be "limited to the maintenance of internal security on Iranian territory." Iran promised the Allies free passage and facilities, including recruitment of labor. A censorship that would apply to all communications was also provided for. The Allies were permitted to maintain military forces on the territory of Iran with the understanding that their presence would not constitute a military occupation and would disturb as little as possible the administration and economic life of the country.[2]

The treaty was signed on behalf of Iran by Premier Ali Soheily, who had succeeded Furuqi in office and who continued his conciliatory pro-Allies policy. He was replaced later in 1942 by Qavam Saltaneh, only to reappear on the political scene at the beginning of 1943. The sudden catapulting of Iran from a markedly pro-German attitude into the Soviet-British alliance was accomplished smoothly but not without some tension. In fact, many Iranians deeply resented the occupation of their country by two traditional enemies. Some were convinced of ultimate German victory, and a number were ready to continue their clandestine work in favor of the Nazis. Others masked their true feelings and pretended to be pro-Ally. With the exception of some radical elements, the majority

[2] For the full text see Appendix no. II.

of the population was fearful of Russia and of the consequences of her occupation in the north.

When Iran formally declared war on Germany in September, 1943, it was not so much a manifestation of hatred against the Reich or of friendship toward the Allies. By this act Iran expressed her conviction that the Germans had lost the war and ensured her position on the winning side.

That was about as much as Iran could do on her own initiative in the field of foreign policy. Iran's impotence was well illustrated at the time of the Russo-British-American Conference, which took place in Teheran in November, 1943. The Allies chose Teheran for their meeting place without consulting the Iranian government. Premier Soheily was even not informed of the exact time of Stalin's, Roosevelt's, and Churchill's arrivals. In fact he learned of this event by mere accident. He was notified officially by the Allied embassies of the event only after gossip of the presence of the Big Three had made the rounds of the town.

The conference was primarily devoted to European problems and war strategy. Hence it was not unnatural that the presence of Iranian representatives was not required. Yet, even at the time when the problems of Iran were discussed, the Iranian government was not invited to participate.

As it turned out, the conference, so tragic in its decisions concerning eastern Europe, proved to be of inestimable benefit to the Iranians. The Declaration on Iran, signed by Stalin, Roosevelt, and Churchill, recognized the assistance that Iran had given in the Allied war effort; promised economic aid; reaffirmed Iran's independence, sovereignty, and territorial integrity; and reiterated the Allies' adherence to the principles of the Atlantic Charter.[3]

To speak of Iranian foreign policy during the war years is to use something of a misnomer. Occupied by Russia and Britain and harboring American troops as well, Iran obviously had limited freedom of movement. Theoretically she could have tried to sabotage the Allied war effort, but such a policy would have been suicidal and, at any rate, could not have been of long duration. Within the limited range of possibilities Iran's foreign policy chiefly was linked to her

[3] For the full text see Appendix no. III.

internal situation. The crucial difficulty in this connection was the degree to which it was safe to protest abuses of power by the occupying states without incurring the odium of being anti-Ally. Among the more positive tasks for the Iranian government stood the problem of economic adjustment to the war situation. In this field much again depended upon the good will of the Allies, and Iran, necessarily, was in the position of a petitioner. But towering above all these problems remained the supreme task of ensuring the prompt evacuation of the Allied armies and the return to full sovereignty at the end of the war. The Iranian government, indeed, was obliged to play the unwilling role of a tightrope walker without an appreciative audience.

To cope with this difficult situation Iran should have possessed certain qualities which, alas, she lacked. There was no strong government enjoying the confidence of the country. Discipline among the people was nonexistent. The loyalty and devotion of public servants was questionable. Due to her unfortunate involvement with Germany Iran could not avail herself of a strong moral argument in case of a dispute with foreign Powers. Finally, courage, necessary in every situation, was not conspicuous among Iranian statesmen and officials.

THE AFTERMATH OF DICTATORSHIP

There was an evident lack of strong leadership in the country after the deposition of Reza Shah. A prolonged period of dictatorship, no matter how beneficial, invariably leaves a country without prominent leaders. Those who appear on the scene after the passing of a dictator either lack idealism or, if idealistic, lack practical experience of independent government. This was the case of Iran after September, 1941. Furthermore, the new government was committed to democracy—a natural reaction against the former dictatorship. But democracy could not be implanted at once, and the war era, together with the occupation of the country by foreign Powers, was hardly a propitious period for the gradual introduction of a new, more liberal system of government. On the one hand, a number of political parties and newspapers sprang into existence. On the other, there were necessary restrictions on the freedom of press and assembly, necessitated by the war conditions and by specific pledges contained in the Tripartite Treaty.

Iran was pledged to liberalism, but instead she obtained something that resembled anarchy. Various political groups vented their feelings of hatred and revenge against the old regime, and particularly against the deposed ruler. At the same time they heaped abuse upon their rivals, upon the governments actually in office, and upon particular cabinet ministers. The level of political dispute was low. The invectives and vocabulary used by the newspapers would normally in the West lead to a series of libel suits. The internal situation was marked by growing instability and constant shifting of forces. The lack of traditional political parties with clear-cut programs and aims only confused the picture, for often the issues were purely personal among the competing politicians. The consequences of the removal of Reza Shah were soon felt in the provinces where the tribes, hitherto kept in submission to the central authority, now raised their heads to defy the government. The sudden liberalizing of internal conditions also released forces of an antiliberal character, either of the extreme right wing, such as the resurgent Shia clergy, or the Communists.

Simultaneously economic conditions in the country were worsening.[4] The sudden stoppage of normal sources of supply and of normal outlets for produce caused shortages of many necessities. The purchases that were made by the foreign armies contributed to an unhealthy stimulation of the market. The Allies monopolized the Transiranian Railway as well as the motor transport and confiscated almost all the trucks in the country. This produced havoc in the Iranian transportation system, and normal economic exchange between outlying parts of the country was greatly impeded. The division of the country into two zones of occupation only deepened these difficulties. Prices rose. Before long Iran suffered acutely from wild inflation, surpassed in its intensity perhaps only by that in China.

[4] This study being devoted chiefly to the presentation of political issues affecting Iran, it would be outside its scope to describe fully all the vicissitudes of Iranian wartime economy. Readers interested in more technical aspects of the economic problems should acquaint themselves with A. C. Millspaugh's *Americans in Persia* (Washington, 1946), which contains the fullest account yet presented of that subject.

In these circumstances all sections of the population with fixed income, especially the government employees, were greatly victimized. Bribery, not an uncommon phenomenon in the East, often became a necessary device for a government official to survive. The morale of public servants was lowered considerably, and this opened the road to foreign intrigue. It was not difficult for a foreign legation to "buy" a newspaper, an editorial writer, or an underpaid employee in one of the administrations.

With all these changes in Iran, one factor, however, remained rather constant, namely, the ruling class. This class was composed of wealthy landowners, wealthy merchants, and higher army officers. The deposition of Reza Shah might have eliminated from office a number of individuals, but those who replaced them did not represent a different social stratum. Thus many criticisms that could be addressed to the former ruling clique likewise could be maintained against the new cabinets. The selfish and economically unprogressive attitude of the ruling circles did nothing to endear them either to the masses, despite new official liberalism, or to facilitate their position vis-à-vis the Soviet-sponsored extremist elements.

Yet with all these inadequacies and handicaps the government still might have played a positive role if it had been ready to show determination in the event of foreign pressure. But this was seldom the case. There was marked reluctance among the politicians to becoming martyrs. And this general phenomenon overshadowed the courage and public spirit displayed by a few patriotic individuals.

THE ROLE OF THE MAJLIS IN WARTIME

In order to understand fully internal conditions in Iran during the war, an analysis of the role played by the parliament and the political parties is necessary. Although the cabinet changed after the deposition of Reza Shah, the Majlis remained unchanged for some time to come. It was filled with deputies who, in fact, often had been nominees of the late ruler. With the passing of the dictator the Majlis emerged as an independent force with which the government found it necessary to reckon. The role played by the parliament was not constructive in the Western sense of the word. There was little of which the Majlis could boast in the way of solving urgent national problems. Its debates were often acrimonious. Accusations of dishonesty and graft made from the floor against other members, the government, or its ministers were not an infrequent feature. Before the first wartime election one could speak of the Majlis as one compact group undivided into political parties. Dr. Millspaugh, in his *Americans in Persia,* refers constantly to the parliament as one body without differentiating between parties, although a new parliament was elected in 1943–1944. To be sure, groups and factions existed, but they were of a rather personal character, with no concrete programs and ideology to render them fully distinct from one another. Fluidity characterized these groups, and yet to the outside world the parliament could be presented as an almost indivisible entity.

The Majlis proved too slow and inefficient to contribute actively to foreign or domestic policy. Yet it had the power to confirm or to reject important government measures and, occasionally, did come forth with significant initiative. A few examples of action by the Majlis can be cited. When the government invited the American financial mission in 1942, the Majlis confirmed the invitation. It also passed the law confirming the contract and the powers of the head of the mission as well as the engagement of further personnel. When the mission arrived, its difficulties were largely due to the hostility of the parliament. The role of the Majlis was also of importance in the question of oil concessions during and after the war. It was the parliament that in 1944 imposed limitations on the government's right to negotiate oil concessions, and again in 1947 it was the parliament that refused to ratify an oil agreement with the Soviet Union. One should mention finally the role that the Majlis played at the time of cabinet crisis. Not only was the deputies' vote decisive but the selection of a new prime minister came to be the Majlis' privilege. In this respect, the Majlis differed not only from the American Congress, but also from its original model, the western European parliament, which may confirm or reject the premier, but which usually leaves the choice to the head of the state. In the Majlis as much as two weeks were sometimes spent in debate as to who should be recommended to the Shah as prime minister. In view of the close connection between the making or unmaking of the cabinets and the powers of the Majlis, it is paradoxical that the Constitution of 1906 (and the supplementary law of 1907) prohibits a cabinet minister from being a member of the Majlis. Thus, if a deputy was invited to join the cabinet he first resigned. In most cases the deputies gladly exchanged their positions for that of a cabinet member, but there were a few cases when a more prominent deputy did not want to lose his seat for the sake of participation in the government. This may indicate, to some extent, that in the opinion of some people the role of the Majlis was not altogether negligible.

In 1943 elections to the Fourteenth Majlis took place. Iranian elections are not held on a single day but last for a considerable time. Six months were required to complete the elections in 1943. In view of the dictatorial practices of the old regime, politically conscious public opinion had been agitated over the issue whether the elections would be really free. Rumors that the government would try to influence the elections by illegal means arose, and several papers even hinted that soldiers, disguised in civilian dress, might be employed by the government to ensure electoral victory. To combat these rumors Premier Ali Soheily issued several strong denials and assurances. The real issue in these elections was not, however, the presence or lack of government intervention. Such intervention undoubtedly existed, and will probably exist in Iran for some time to come. In this respect the Iranian system does not differ significantly from Latin-American democracy.

The problem that concerned the government more than anything else was that of representation from the northern provinces. Would the traditional ruling class win the elections in the Soviet zone or would new men, with different ideas and loyalties, emerge from obscurity? Until the time of the 1943 elections no strong anti-Communist center had been organized. Thus the entire burden of combating Russian or Communist influence in the elections fell to the government. The elections were conducted in an atmosphere of rivalry among Great Britain, the Soviet Union, and the Iranian groups vying for power. Except for the Communist Tudeh party the contenders fought for seats on a personal rather than an ideological basis. There were no party machines to back up the candidates. Very often the electoral struggle was reduced to the amount of money a candidate could distribute among the voters. These expenses, it was publicly claimed, would be refunded to the deputies during the two-year tenure in the parliament. This would come about through various intercessions with government departments in favor of their business-minded clients. Toward the end of the election period one of the papers stated bluntly: "The newly elected deputies are not representatives of the nation. They have been elected either by bribery or through the intervention of the authorities." [5] Another paper added somewhat later: "In Iran the personality of the candidate plays a greater role than his program." [6]

When the parliament was finally elected at the beginning of 1944, it differed from the former in one important respect. It seated a bloc of eight Communist deputies who knew what they wanted and who behaved like a disciplined group. The rest of the deputies, 60 per cent of whom were new and 40 per cent re-elected, divided themselves into a majority and a minority, the latter being led by Dr. Mosaddeq. Yet neither the majority nor the minority could be regarded as fixed in character, for a marked instability in their composition prevailed. This, in turn, resulted in instability of the cabinets, which could never count upon consistent and prolonged support of any parliamentary majority. To be sure, there were voices demanding reform of the chaotic situation in the parliament. The daily *Kushesh* of April 18, 1944, for example, published an article under the title "Parliamentary Debates and the Need for Reform" in which it drew attention to the fact that the lack of crystallized political parties in Iran created confusion in the Majlis and prevented the creation of a stable majority. *Etella'at,* a paper of moderate tone and wide circulation, also appealed for the creation of blocs within the Majlis that could be distinguished and identified in terms of the positions they would espouse on various issues.[7]

Soon after the election of the new Majlis the following groups were formed among the deputies: *Ettefaq* ("Unity"), *Melli* ("National"), *Mihan* ("Fatherland"), *Iran,* Democratic, and Independent. These were not, however, stable groups in that their membership was of

[5] *Mihan Parestan,* Dec. 19, 1943.
[6] *Ettela'at,* April 23, 1944.
[7] *Ibid.*

a highly fluid character. Evidence of concrete programs that would indicate political differences was totally lacking. However, in the course of 1944, when political cleavage between the growing Tudeh party and the conservative elements of the nation became more acute, one could perceive a gradual tendency toward crystallization of the blocs and a movement toward greater stability in the Majlis. It seemed that the Communist menace awakened the deputies to the necessity for stronger organization. Hence in August, 1944, the parliamentary factions *Azadi* (Liberal), *Mihan* (Fatherland), and *Ittihad-i-Melli* (National Union) formed a common bloc in order to create a stable majority. It was estimated to comprise eighty deputies. The new bloc did not publish any program, but one could assume that its members represented conservative elements. Despite this fact the conservative and nationalist group of Seyyid Zia ed-Din did not join the bloc, although it was reported that some of Zia's partisans belonged to each of the above-mentioned factions. The creation of the bloc was commented upon favorably by the press as an indication of progress in the parliamentary life of Iran. The *Journal de Tehran,* published and edited by the deputy Javad Massudi, wrote on September 24, 1944, that for the first time in the history of the Majlis an "official" majority had been created.

The new bloc played an important role in the government crisis in August, 1944, when it showed unanimity in opposing Premier Mohammed Sa'ed's cabinet and in according a vote of confidence to the new cabinet headed by the same premier. In 1945 the bloc made common cause with Seyyid Zia's group. Both constituted a powerful anti-Communist majority opposed to Soviet influence. The minority included then the Tudeh group and a number of deputies amenable to Soviet persuasion. The latter were mainly those whose estates or business establishments were under Soviet occupation.

In the spring and the summer of 1945 the issues before the Majlis centered around the candidacy for premiership. The Soviet-influenced minority tried to obstruct the proceedings of the Majlis, especially at the time of cabinet crises, or to oppose those candidates for the post of premier who were unacceptable to Russia.

A weapon commonly used by the minority was abstention from the meetings of the Majlis whenever the majority was about to carry

[183]

through some important decision. Such an absence often deprived the parliament of the legally required quorum of three-fourths of the deputies, and as a result decisions could not be made. The number of deputies in the Majlis was only 136. Thus, determined action of at least 35 deputies could prevent the parliament from acting at decisive moments. During prolonged cabinet crises throughout the spring of 1945 frequent absences of the minority deputies paralyzed all government activity and presented the danger of anarchy to the country.

One of the peculiar characteristics of the Majlis is that it acts in its plenary sessions as a credentials' committee. In practice this means that the parliament, after constituting itself, reviews the mandate of each deputy and decides whether the election was legally conducted. If irregularities are discovered, the Majlis may, by a majority vote, nullify the mandate of a newly elected deputy. This strange practice is dangerous in that it consumes considerable time, which could be spent more constructively, and places too strong a weapon in the hands of the majority. Theoretically no legal limit to the invalidation of mandates by the majority exists. Naturally, there must be an irregularity as the basis of accusation, but it is difficult to see where the line between an illegal procedure and a generally accepted custom may be drawn. In the Fourteenth Majlis a number of mandates of Communist deputies were rejected. This fact created an uproar in the Tudeh party ranks and led to violent demonstrations in the north. There was no doubt that in several cases the question of confirmation or rejection was predominantly political in nature, with legal considerations strictly subordinate. In the case of the questioned mandate of Deputy Habibulla Dorri (Tudeh), thirty-two deputies voted for the confirmation of his seat, but the majority decided to invalidate it. In the case of the hotly debated mandate of the rightist leader Seyyid Zia ed-Din, twenty-nine deputies voted for its invalidation, but the majority resolved to confirm it. With few exceptions the deputies who voted in favor of Dorri voted against Zia ed-Din, which throws some light on the numerical strength of the minority (open to Soviet influences) in the beginning of the Fourteenth Majlis. Later the minority could occasionally muster more voices.

In short, we may say that the parliament in the main was represented by conservative elements, essentially nationalist, who were reluctant to approve of any radical changes in the country and ambitious to assert their authority after a long period of dictatorship. In a period characterized by lack of strong leadership the parliament's role increased in importance. With reference to both the internal and external problems of Iran the Majlis had become a force to be reckoned with.

THE POLITICAL PARTIES

Cutting across the groups and factions in the Majlis were the political parties. The collapse of the Reza Shah regime acted as a powerful stimulant for the creation of a number of political groups ambitious to carry out reforms. These parties had practically no past and no tradition upon which they could rely. True, various political parties existed between 1906 and 1921, i.e., between the Iranian revolution and the coup made by Zia ed-Din and Reza Khan. But that was a generation ago. In 1942 political life had to begin anew.

The urge toward some form of political expression was strong. The number of parties formed in 1942 and 1943 testified to the traditional individualistic spirit of the Iranians. It would be beyond the purposes of this study to review the composition and activity of all the parties that were created then. Suffice it to say that in 1943 some fifteen appeared on the political horizon of Teheran. Many of them had either ceased to exist or suspended their activities by 1944. Many were replaced by others. Some splits and fusions took place. The year 1944 was one of considerable political crystallization. In that year the most important parties were the Tudeh, Eradeh-yi-Melli, Mihan, Iran, Mardom, Socialist, and Adalat parties. Two of them, the Tudeh and the Eradeh-yi-Melli, stood apart because of their close connection with Russia and Great Britain. Accordingly, we propose to study them more thoroughly in the chapters dealing with British and Soviet policies. With respect to the remaining five, it would be well at this point to indicate briefly their common features and to examine their impact on Iranian political life.[8]

None of these parties possessed a regular faction in the parliament. The previously mentioned parliamentary groups had nothing to do

[8] For a more detailed description of these parties, see Appendix no. V.

organizationally with the political parties, although in some cases they bore the same names and occasionally there existed an overlap-laping of leadership. No political party could claim to represent a real mass movement. All of them, even those that could boast of membership of prominent government or Majlis leaders, were ephemeral in character and were apt to disappear from the political scene of the nation without leaving any traces whatever. Their programs, with the possible exception of that of the Socialist party, did not contain anything to permit political and ideological differentiation among them. Nevertheless they could not be ignored. While it is true that separately none of them exercised important political influence, yet, combined, they represented a significant political awakening. Their very existence meant that more educated Iranians were tired of dictatorship and were anxious to see democracy flourish. Although the acquaintance of the average Iranian with democratic procedures was superficial and often indicated an eager expectation of full civic rights without the corresponding responsibilities, yet these parties were dedicated to liberalism and social justice. This statement does not mean that the parties were completely disinterested. On the contrary, many of their members experienced a feeling of personal frustration due to the methods of the antiquated and conservative regime that did not offer too many opportunities to young talents. But these younger men were ready to identify the general liberalization of the regime with their own success.

It is important to note in this connection that all of these parties were essentially nationalistic and, with a few exceptions, hostile to any form of foreign interference. It was public opinion as shaped by these groups that dictated the tenor of editorials in the press of Teheran. The fact that in many cases members of the parties were recruited among the civil servants meant that important sections of the Iranian bureaucracy were dissatisfied with existing conditions. On the other hand, certain cliques were being formed among government officials to promote their own interests. The Adalat party had a particularly large representation of officials in its ranks. In the case of the American Financial Mission government employees played the role of a pressure group. A political party was a good platform on which one could ventilate one's grievances. The parties also served as a springboard for more ambitious politicians who, not content with their seats in the Majlis, tried to rally around themselves an organized group of supporters.

From the viewpoint of the development of Iranian democracy one must admit that these parties, despite all their shortcomings, were playing a useful role. They kept alive interest in public affairs and encouraged independent thinking among their members. One of the younger and more prominent deputies in the Fourteenth Majlis, Farmand, declared in 1944 that the young Iranian democracy stood in need of political parties. Since these parties adopted similar programs, he believed that it would be wise to fuse them into one single party.[9]

Farmand's statement was not devoid of wisdom. All these political parties possessed the common feature of nationalism and espoused the common end of democracy. Lacking good organization and discipline, they would have gained by uniting their efforts. As small groups they failed to have a mass following. Consequently their political action was largely ineffective.

THE PRESS

The collapse of the old regime also acted as a stimulant to all those who wanted to express their opinions in writing. If the number of political parties was unusual, even more amazing was the sudden growth of the press. From the time of the entry of the Allies into Iran approximately one hundred and fifty newspapers and periodicals appeared within two years. They were even more ephemeral than the parties. Many of them were liquidated for lack of funds; many were suspended by the government, which possessed the right under martial law to prohibit any publication. In 1944–1945 the number of newspapers and periodicals published in Teheran alone was approximately fifty. Some of the papers were the organs of political parties, for example, *Mihan Parestan* (Mihan party), *Shafaq* (Iran party), *Shiam* (Hamrahan party), *Neda-yi-Mellat* (Mardom party), and *Adalat* (Adalat party). But the majority of newspapers had no stable political affiliation. Sometimes they were created with the sole object of securing income for their publishers. Since the circulation of these

[9] *Journal de Tehran*, May 11, 1944.

papers was never large (it often did not exceed 300 to 500 copies), the subscriptions alone were not sufficient to cover the minimum costs of printing and paper. Advertisements could bring some additional funds, but the merchants in Iran were not so publicity minded as their American counterparts, and, moreover, there was not much sense in advertising in a new periodical, which could disappear from the scene in a few days or weeks. In these circumstances, the publishers were forced to have recourse to special practices. The most notorious was blackmail. Placing oneself at the disposal of some foreign legation or mission constituted another device. Subsidies from such a source were, perhaps, the commonest means used to guarantee the regular appearance of a newspaper. In some cases the service thus rendered to a foreign Power was done with the conviction that the cause was just and honorable; but often the matter was merely a business proposition.

The level and quality of articles in the papers was generally low. If a political adversary was attacked, one could be sure that an array of vile epithets would be used. Dishonesty constituted the most frequent charge. The journalistic vocabulary abounded in such blunt words as "stealing" or "thieving," and—by way of contrast—the greatest compliment that could be paid by the press to a politician or cabinet member was that he was honest. Because of the inevitable connection of Iranian internal politics with outside influences, the papers often accused various persons and groups of treason. Iranian readers were accustomed to this sort of language and the rather lenient laws did not act as a deterrent to these practices. Consequently, libel suits very rarely resulted from such attacks—except in the case of Seyyid Zia ed-Din, who was in almost constant legal wrangles with the Communist papers over invectives addressed to him.

The government was sensitive to press criticism and made frequent use of its powers of suspension. In some cases such a suspension acted as a deterrent to further publication. More often, however, the suspended paper reappeared on the next day under a changed name. Often as many as ten or twelve newspapers were suspended by the government on a single day. Since the cabinets did not possess any papers to defend their policies during the war, suspensions became the government's only weapon. At one time in December, 1942, the government suspended all newspapers published in Teheran, and for several weeks the only paper appearing was *Akhbar-i-Ruz,* on this occasion published by the government itself. This radical step was dictated by violent disturbances that took place in Teheran toward the end of 1942. Angered by a serious shortage of food a mob attacked and put fire to the house of Prime Minister Qavam Saltaneh. The troops machine-gunned the populace, and further bloodshed occurred near the parliament buildings. The press poured out a torrent of insults against the Premier and his cabinet. The result was its wholesale suspension for an indefinite time. Eventually Qavam resigned and was replaced by Ali Soheily.

At this time the Majlis adopted a law setting forth certain conditions for the publication of newspapers. The law provided that a university diploma was to be required of prospective editors and that a paper could be founded only after a permit was issued by the Department of Press and Propaganda. But soon after the law was passed approximately thirty newspapers sprang into existence. Their number gradually increased. The restrictions were of little value. In view of the anarchistic conditions prevailing in the press, the government of Ali Soheily proposed in June, 1943, a new law that would limit the number of newspapers to seven in Teheran and to one, two, or three in the provinces. A storm of protest broke out in the Majlis, and during a secret session Soheily was compelled to withdraw his project.

Although most of the papers naturally were published in Persian, several were published in foreign languages. In Teheran alone three newspapers were published in Armenian. Of these, *Veradzenund* had the largest circulation. In Tabriz *Vatan Yolunda* was published in Turkish. The brothers Massudi in Teheran, owners of two Persian-language newspapers, the daily *Ettela'at* (circulation 15,000) and the weekly *Ettela'at-i-Haftegi,* published also the *Journal de Tehran,* a daily in French, with a circulation much larger than the average Iranian newspaper. In 1944 a weekly literary and political review, the *Journal de Tehran-Samedi* was added. It was sponsored unofficially by the French Legation. The Soviet Embassy published a daily, *Novosti Dnia.* The British Embassy had its *Tehran Daily News,* which, though originally a one-sheet bulletin, eventually became a well-edited newspaper of six pages. A rather unusual innovation in Teheran was the appearance of a number of periodicals in the Polish language, such as *Zew* and *Polak w Iranie*. These periodicals found their *raison d'être* in the presence of a large Polish refugee colony and, for a time, of a Polish army in Iran.[10]

In addition to all these publications, several legations were issuing bulletins that were not available at the newspaper stands and distributing them among the politically conscious Iranians and to the foreign colony in Iran. Thus, the American Embassy distributed a mimeographed bulletin, and the Belgian and Polish legations published printed bulletins, *Les Nouvelles de Belgique* and *La Nouvelle Europe,* respectively. As a source of information for Iranians anxious to learn the truth of international developments, these foreign-language publications played a useful role. Since they were largely exempt from the restriction of government censorship, they contributed much to the clarification and elaboration of political controversy then prevalent.

The editorials in the Iranian press generally reflected strong criticism of the old regime and of present conditions. Frequent demands for improvement in every field of national life appeared. But in those years the press generally avoided any debate on foreign policy. The joint invasion of Iran by Britain and Russia received cautious treatment in the editorials, for no one openly dared criticize these countries. If any reference was made to either Britain or Russia, it was usually under the all-embracing name of the Allies, to whom affirmations of loyalty were lavishly extended. With the exception of a small group of Communist newspapers, which adhered to a consistent

10 Between 1939 and 1941 these refugees, both men and women, had been arrested by the Soviet authorities in eastern Poland and deported as slave laborers to Siberia and Turkestan. Of the two million Poles who met this fate, nearly 45,000 were permitted to leave Russia under the terms of the Sikorski-Stalin agreement of 1941. They were evacuated to Iran by the British authorities. Furthermore, about 80,000 former Polish prisoners of war in Russia were permitted to join the Polish army established on the territory of the Soviet Union in 1941–1942. Under the command of General Anders, who had just been released from the Lubianka prison after two years of captivity, this army was moved by inter-Allied agreement to northern Iraq. There it was to defend the Middle Eastern oil fields at the time of the German thrust toward the Caucasus. It passed in transit through Iran.

policy, political divisions among the Iranian press were still not clearly defined as late as 1943. Gradually, however, a change took place. By the fall of 1944 the oil crisis between Iran and Russia provoked greater crystallization of political opinions. The press aligned itself either with pro-Soviet or pro-British sentiment, and started to discuss foreign policy issues. In time the Iranian press became the most sensitive barometer of Russo-Western relations in this part of the world. The artificial truce was broken, and in the winter of 1944–1945 the press began to indulge in open attacks against Great Britain and Russia. Somewhat earlier two press camps were established: the Freedom Front, a pro-Soviet coalition of newspapers created in 1943, and the Independence Front, a nationalist and pro-British journalistic coalition grouped around Zia ed-Din.

Any discussion of the press during the war period should include the question of its influence on political life. In this instance the reply is that the role of the press was somewhat similar to the role of political parties. With very few exceptions an individual newspaper did not exert significant influence, but the effect of approximately fifty dailies and periodicals, taken as a whole, could not be ignored. The press played an important role as a supplier of news and as a molder of public opinion. And public opinion, even in a country with as much illiteracy as Iran, was not a negligible factor. True, a backward peasant of Farsistan or a nomad of Luristan was quite oblivious to what the newspapermen in Teheran might write and, of course, his traditional way of life could not be affected by it. But the newspapers were not destined to serve him. They were addressed to the town population. Teheran, a metropolitan center, numbered 700,000 inhabitants, Tabriz around 350,000. Isfahan with its textile industries, Meshed, Hamadan, and Shiraz constituted important population centers. In these towns literacy was greater than in the villages. Merchants, traders, artisans, government employees, policemen, soldiers, and a number of workers were anxious to read the news. The widespread custom of reading a book or a newspaper aloud to a number of people by an accidental or planted "lector" increased the number of news consumers. It may safely be asserted that the material printed in these fifty-odd papers was ultimately penetrating the consciousness not only of the educated but also of the masses in the big cities. After the downfall of Reza Shah the masses became more conscious politically and more easily excitable. Mobs attacked and burned the residence of Qavam Saltaneh in December, 1942. Mobs demonstrated at the time of the oil crisis in 1944. Workers in textile factories or in the Teheran silo influenced events by their strikes. A good slogan, a clever word, might have kindled the imaginations of these people and prompted them to action. And it was the press that was the carrier of words. Thus, despite the weakness of individual newspapers as contrasted with the strength of such traditional groups as the aristocracy, the bazaar merchants, the Court, the army, or the clergy, the press as an entity had to be reckoned with. The sensitivity of the government to the editorials, the frequent suspensions and legal restrictions —all these factors testified that the government of Iran did not fail realistically to appraise the importance of the press. And there is evidence that foreign Powers also fully realized its significance and potentialities.

To sum up these observations on the position of Iran during the war period, one may say that between 1941 and 1945 the country passed through a state of ferment. With regard to foreign policy, her freedom of movement was limited. In this respect Iran was compelled to adopt a passive attitude for fear of further blows at her independence. Internally the lack of strong leadership was felt as an aftermath of dictatorship. Democratic tendencies were clearly visible, but the time was hardly propitious for the development of democracy. The presence of foreign troops in the country had an upsetting effect on economic life and permitted free exercise of foreign intrigue. There was danger that the political ambitions of various groups might be channeled into the wrong direction and that Iran might deviate from the necessary road of reform. There was danger also that the country might be deprived entirely of her sovereignty. In short, the destiny of Iran ceased to be shaped by the Iranians alone. The rivalry of the Big Powers and their diplomatic and military activities constituted the main substance of political life during this stormy period. This rivalry, however, was conducted in an Iranian setting, and, therefore, what the Iranians did or did not do was not altogether without effect on the course of history.

His Imperial Majesty the late Reza Shah Pahlavi.

His Imperial Majesty Mohammed Reza Shah Pahlavi.

Mohammed Sa'ed.

Qavam as-Saltaneh.

Former Premier Ibrahim Hakimi and (at left) former Chief of Staff General Arfa.

Foreground: Former Empress Fawzia, Shah Mohammed Reza Pahlavi, and Governor of the Bank Melli, Abol Hasan Ebtehaj. Behind Ebtehaj is Minister of the Court Hosein Ala.

Foreground: Sir Reader Bullard, former British Ambassador, and the Shah.

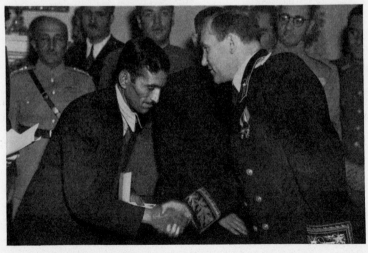

Ambassador Sadchikov at a reception in the Soviet Embassy.

Some Kurdish chieftains with the officers of the Second Division in Teheran.

Qazi Mohammed (in white turban), head of the autonomous Kurdish Republic, and Deputy Sadraq Qazi (holding hat). Both were hanged after the collapse of the Kurdish Republic.

Louis Saillant (left), Secretary of the World Federation of Trade Unions, and Reza Rusta, Tudeh agitator.

Sepah Square in Teheran with a statue of Reza Shah. The Post Office is in the background.

CHAPTER EIGHT

Soviet Policy in
Iran in Wartime

T HE outbreak of World War II gave Russia an opportunity to revive her long-cherished ambitions with regard to Iran. Documents on Nazi-Soviet relations published by the American government revealed that Moscow was seeking, at the time of the Soviet-
Nazi friendship, formal recognition of her special interests in the
Persian Gulf area. The draft of a Four-Power Pact, drawn up in
Berlin between Hitler and Foreign Commissar Molotov on November 13, 1940, provided for the division of the world into spheres of
influence. It had to be submitted for adoption to Germany, Russia,
Italy, and Japan. According to the secret Protocol No. 1 Germany
secured for herself a sphere of influence in Europe and central Africa;
Italy, a sphere in northern and northeastern Africa; and Japan, in
southeastern Asia. As to Russia, paragraph four of the Protocol provided: "The Soviet Union declares that its territorial aspirations
center south of the national territory of the Soviet Union in the direction of the Indian Ocean." [1]

This draft agreement was supplemented by a more exact formulation of the Soviet sphere of influence made to the German Ambassador in Moscow by Molotov on November 26, 1940. In this
conversation Molotov stated that the Soviet government was prepared
to accept the draft of the Four-Power Pact, provided—inter-alia—
"that the area south of Batum and Baku in the general direction of

---

[1] *Nazi-Soviet Relations 1939–1941, Documents from the Archives of the German
Foreign Office* (Department of State, Publication 3023; Washington, 1948), p. 257.

[193]

the Persian Gulf is recognized as the center of the aspirations of the Soviet Union." [2]

Consequently, from the Soviet point of view the invasion of Iran in August, 1941, was something more than just the opening of a transit road for supplies of war matériel. It marked the end of the armed truce that had prevailed between Iran and Russia since the withdrawal of the Red Army from Gilan in 1921. After long years of ideological preparation, of training and indoctrinating the cadres of Communist agitators, an opportunity had come to put into practice the program so long conceived. For the first time after twenty years of self-restraint did the Red Army in large formations enter an oriental Asiatic country. The stage was open for bold moves. Britain, a traditional rival in the East, was in alliance with Russia and was not expected to put up obstacles to Soviet activities in northern Iran. There was no other Big-Power opposition. The mortal danger that the German attack presented to the Soviet State was not to distract the latter from careful execution of its plans in the Iranian "semi-colony."

CONDITIONS IN THE SOVIET ZONE OF OCCUPATION

From the very beginning there was an obvious difference between conditions in the Soviet and British zones. Whereas the British considered their presence in Iran a temporary expedient and treated the country as a transit road to be kept in order and free from enemy menace, the Russians gave early signs that they were embarking upon a long-range policy that would effect basic changes in the political, economic, and social life of the provinces under their occupation.

In contrast to the British zone, wherein complete freedom of travel applied, the Soviet zone was closed to foreigners. Special passes difficult to obtain were issued by the Soviet Embassy in Teheran to those who wished to travel to the north. This limitation did not apply to the Iranians, but because of the many foreign advisers employed by the Iranian government it proved to be very onerous. Allied diplomats accredited to the government of Iran were barred from traveling and reporting on conditions prevailing in the most pros-

[2] *Nazi-Soviet Relations 1939–1941*, p. 259.

perous industrialized provinces. Between 1942 and the end of the war no foreign newspaperman was permitted to enter the Soviet zone. The accredited correspondents of the Associated Press, the United Press, and Reuters could move freely only in Teheran and in the south. For them the north was a mysteriously sealed area. The Iron Curtain was thus hung in Iran long before the English-speaking democracies learned of its existence.

The arrival of the Red Army resulted in panic among the more prosperous elements of the northern provinces. Many left hurriedly and settled for the duration of the war in Teheran or in the south. Foremost among them were big landowners. Their estates were left to caretakers; hence their absence permitted the Soviet authorities to take over some of their lands. Some landowners remained, but they also felt the impact of the presence of the Red Army. There was no evidence of any immediate land reform in the north. But the Soviet authorities instituted three measures that affected the economy and structure of agriculture. These were as follows: first, the issuing of new regulations that would favor the peasantry as opposed to the landowners with regard to the sharing of crops; second, the confiscation or compulsory purchase of large amounts of grain from private individuals and government stores alike; third, the taking over of some estates and the establishment of model farms to be operated by the Red Army. The latter measure was rarely applied and could not be considered as typical for the whole of the north. However, it was important as a precedent-setting device and as a propagandist move. The farm run by the Red Army experts was intended to be a model of modern agricultural efficiency and to provide excellent material conditions for the farm workers.

A ban imposed on the export of staple foodstuffs from the Soviet to other zones separated the northern provinces from the rest of the country even more than travel limitations. This ban primarily affected grain and rice and proved to be almost disastrous to the rest of Iran inasmuch as central and southern Iran represented a food-deficit area. In the fall of 1942 Teheran and some other centers faced starvation, and by the end of the year some deaths actually resulted from famine. The riots that broke out in the capital in December, 1942, referred to in the previous chapter, were caused by the acute food shortage. Yet the fear of Soviet reprisals kept the Iranian press silent about Russia's part in this crisis. The only voices that were heard in this connection were those that praised the situation in the north in contrast to that in the south.[3] To many observers it was clear that Russia by artificially restricting the transfer of foodstuffs was attempting to embarrass the British in their zone. The lack of food in Teheran and in the south had its logical effect on the already existing inflationary trend, and soon it became known that prices in the Soviet zone were lower than those in the rest of the country. The press did not neglect to stress this fact.[4]

In order to help Iran in her difficult food situation the United States and Great Britain early in December, 1942, promised to supply 25,000 tons of grain to the Iranian government. This pledge did not receive much publicity. It was not easy to transport this quantity of grain quickly for the lack of shipping space compelled the Allies to assign priority to combat theaters. In the meantime the food situation was deteriorating. At this juncture Russia took a step typical of her policy in Iran. In March, 1943, Ambassador Smirnov visited Premier Ali Soheily and declared that in view of the needs of Iran the Soviet government had decided to present 25,000 tons of wheat as a gift to the Iranian nation. Praising the generosity of the great northern neighbor the Soviet-influenced newspapers gave much publicity to this gesture, and even the neutral papers were obliged to devote some space to this sensational news. The editor of the *Journal de Tehran,* Javad Massudi, in a move typical of some Iranian newspapermen, hastened to pay a call on the Prime Minister in order to obtain an interview and hear his comment, which, naturally, was nothing less than a tribute to Russia.

The British Embassy felt the sting. In a news item published on April 10 in the *Tehran Daily News* and entitled "Iran to receive wheat supplies from Russia," the following acid comment appeared: "This wheat will not only take the place of supplies of wheat *which in a normal year would have been sent to Teheran from Azerbaijan,* but will enable the Ministry of Supply to build up a reserve. . . ."[5]

[3] *Khorshid-i-Iran,* Feb. 23, 1943, in an article "Moans from the Cemetery."

[4] *Emruz-o-Farda,* July 28, 1943, stated, for example, that prices in Teheran were much higher than those in Qazvin in the Soviet zone.

[5] Italics mine.

On April 15, Mr. Casey, British Minister of State for the Middle East, arrived in Teheran and at a press conference did his best to impress his audience with the amount of help given Iran by Britain and the United States. He issued a warning to the press that their one-sided unfriendly attitude to the West would only harm the interests of Iran. He forcefully pointed out that the lack of shipping space was the result of bulky supplies of war materials to the Soviet Ally. The Minister's sudden visit and his energetic talk were generally regarded as a diplomatic countermove against the Soviet gesture. It proved that the British were on their guard, but it did not stop the Soviet Union from continuing relentlessly her long-range policy.

Aside from the economic inconveniences to Iran resulting from the division of the country, political consequences even more important developed. Shah Reza had been working assiduously to restore the unity of Iran. Now this unity was jeopardized. After 1941 the authority of the government extended, for practical purposes, only to Teheran and to the south, and even in the south it was limited by the resurgence of nomad tribes. In the north Iranian governors and officials could do nothing that might displease the Soviet authorities, and in many instances they were reduced to the role of puppets. In 1944–1945 it was impossible for the government to appoint a provincial governor to the Soviet zone if he was not acceptable to the Russians.

The Soviet authorities had recourse to political terror from the very day of their entry. A number of political refugees from the Caucasus, such as the Dashnaks or the Mussavatists, were arrested. Others mysteriously disappeared. This happened not only in the north but also in Teheran, although the capital was in the neutral zone.[6] Freedom of the press, enjoyed in Teheran, only partly applied to the northern provinces. An open letter written in 1945 by the editor of the nationalist paper *Hur* to the editor of the Communist *Darya* vividly described the press restrictions in the Soviet zone. The letter said:

[6] Among those who were thus spirited away in Teheran can be mentioned Salim-zadeh (Salimoff), an octogenarian, who in the early twenties had co-operated with Sir Henry Deterding in the latter's Caucasian oil enterprises. Sir Henry had been a particular target of Soviet enmity.

In the south of Iran there are newspapers which sometimes attack Great Britain and America, and they fear no reprisals. But try to go to the north of Iran with the newspaper *Hur*. You will be promptly arrested! Yes, my dear editor! The editor of *Hur* has not made money, and he has no special mission except to defend 15 million Iranian citizens from the slavery of the dictatorship of the proletariat.[7]

As time progressed Soviet control of political activity in the north tightened. By 1944 and 1945 it was unsafe to profess allegiance to the rightist party of Zia ed-Din or to edit or distribute any nationalist papers. Incurring the displeasure of Soviet consuls or Red Army commanders resulted either in periods in jail or in expulsion from the Soviet zone. A number of such cases were recorded in the Teheran press toward the end of the war period.[8] Among the expelled were Iranian government officials.[9] Fear and uncertainty were characteristic of the people's feelings under the Soviet occupation.

It was generally agreed that the Soviet authorities exerted pressure during the elections to the Majlis in 1943, and that those Communist deputies who were elected owed their success to the presence of the Red Army in the north.[10] As pointed out earlier, the fact that a number of deputies owned land in the Soviet zone rendered them amenable to Soviet persuasion. For example, rumor had it that the attitude and political alignments of former Premier Qavam as-Saltaneh were largely dictated by the fact that his estates were situated in the Caspian provinces.

There is no doubt that from the time of their arrival the Russians persistently prepared the ground in the north with a view to making

[7] *Nasim-i-Shomal,* Jan. 25, 1945.

[8] *Ra'd-i-Emruz,* Dec. 5, 1944, wrote that on the orders of the Soviet consul in Rezaieh three Iranian citizens, Eqtesam Va'ez, Ibrahim Sam-Sam, a lawyer, and Haji Mirza Ghulam Fegi, were expelled from the Soviet zone. See also *Ra'd-i-Emruz,* Nov. 22, 1944, on the numerous expulsions from Gilan and Mazanderan; similarly *Tehran-i-Mossavar,* Nov. 17, 1944, on the expulsion of Vatan party members from the north.

[9] *Arzu,* April 28, 1944, contains a photographic reproduction of a Soviet order of expulsion.

[10] To be fair it is proper to say here that the British on their part did not neglect to influence the elections in the south. Yet, although their involvement in the pre-electoral intrigue might have been more pronounced than that of the Soviet in 1943, their methods differed widely and could hardly be described as intimidation. For more detailed analysis of British policies, see Chapter Nine.

a radical political change at an appropriate time. The events of 1945 vindicated this opinion.

SOVIET PROPAGANDA: ITS ORGANIZATION

But Soviet activities were not limited to the north exclusively. The Soviet Embassy in Teheran put into motion formidable propaganda apparatus to obtain as many adherents to the Soviet cause as possible.

The center of propaganda was located in the Soviet Embassy under the direction of the press attaché. It employed a considerable number of officials many of whom were natives of Soviet Central Asia or the Caucasus and most of whom had an excellent knowledge of the Persian language. The post of press attaché was entrusted during the major part of the war to Comrade Danil S. Komissarov, whose face will never be forgotten by Iranian editors.[11] Komissarov maintained direct and constant contact with a host of newspapers in Teheran, and his frequent receptions and press conferences were destined to bring the Soviet Embassy and the press ever closer. One of the major tasks of the Press Office was to secure in the Iranian press as much space as possible for Tass Agency items. Tass dispatches were released free of charge to newspapers. Essentially the matter reduced itself to competition between Tass and Reuters for dominance of news space in the Iranian press. In this duel Tass usually had the upper hand and often the privilege of the first page and larger headlines. The one-sided policy of outright Communist papers published in the Persian language was, of course, pronounced. Non-Communist papers, which did not dare to refuse, also printed the Tass material in abundance. In the *Journal de Tehran,* for example, three-quarters of the news items published were often Tass dispatches.

Except during the last phases of the war, when more open opposition to Soviet moves was voiced by the nationalist press, the servility of the Iranian newspapers toward Russia was extreme. Even the papers that indulged in open polemics with the Communist Tudeh party were careful not to say a word against the Soviet Union. Instead they competed with each other in praising the "great and gen-

[11] He was assisted by Sobhan Ulov (radio), Orestov (Tass), Ivanov (Tass), and Petrov (editor of *Duste Iran*). At a certain period Grigory I. Rassadine was in charge of propaganda.

erous Northern Neighbor." Good examples of this attitude, dictated either by fear or by caution, can be found on such occasions as the anniversary of the Red Army, of the November Revolution, or of Lenin's death. For instance, *Setareh,* a newspaper regarded as consistently pro-American, wrote on one such occasion:

Today in all the Soviet republics the Red Army anniversary is celebrated. . . . In the name of the Iranian nation and in view of the good relations which exist between us and the Soviets, we congratulate the Soviet Republics on the occasion of the twenty-sixth anniversary of the Red Army and we wish them success in the struggle for security and independence of all the Soviet nations.[12]

Anxious to appear as friendly as possible and borrowing even the words from the conventional Soviet dictionary, the *Journal de Tehran* wrote on the same occasion:

And for us Iranians who from the first day have been the sincere friends of the Soviet peoples and for us who are at present active allies, it is a joy to assist in the triumphs of this Red Army without which very certainly the freedom-loving nations would have succumbed long ago under the boots of the fascist hordes.[13]

Such statements can be considered as typical. Apart from exerting various pressures and inducements, the Soviet Embassy had one very important weapon: it supplied newsprint to some newspapers. The general consensus was that the *Journal de Tehran* was among the recipients.

In the fall of 1943 another center of propaganda was established, the Irano-Soviet Society for Cultural Relations. The pompous ceremony of inauguration took place in the presence of Premier Ali Soheily, Iranian cabinet ministers, the Soviet Ambassador, and many other notables. The society constituted a branch of the well-known Soviet institution V.O.K.S., which specializes in dispensing propaganda abroad through cultural mediums. It manifested great vitality in Teheran and in the provinces. It established libraries of Soviet publications, conducted courses on Russian language and literature, organized innumerable lectures, concerts, receptions, art exhibitions,

[12] Feb. 23, 1944.
[13] Feb. 23, 1944.

and sponsored shows. It also provided travel scholarships for some Iranian artists and regularly brought Soviet professors and academicians, sometimes of high caliber, to speak to Iranian audiences. Hardly a day passed without the press giving notice of some cultural or artistic event at the society. The House of Culture, the headquarters of the society, was a meeting place for many Iranians. These were mainly students and younger intellectuals who were attracted by the prospect of free tuition and the stipends offered by the society and who were generally eager to hear something about Soviet life, economics, and government. Some of these Iranians were either outright Communists or sympathizers with Soviet doctrine, but the majority came simply to learn and hear something new.

It is difficult to judge exactly what motivated some Iranians in prominent positions to associate themselves with Soviet propaganda, but whether it was money, threats, self-insurance against future risks, or genuine friendship, some well-known figures were in close touch with the Cultural Society. Professor Said Nafisy, Secretary-General of the Iranian Academy of Arts and Letters, gave, apparently, both body and soul to the cultural *rapprochement* between Russia and Iran. He became Secretary-General of the Irano-Soviet Cultural Society and worked relentlessly for its success. In the winter of 1944–1945 Nafisy together with a few other professors was invited to visit Uzbekistan and there to participate in the ceremonies of the twentieth anniversary of that Soviet Socialist republic. Due publicity was given to this visit. After their return the professors launched an offensive of lectures praising Soviet achievements. In August, 1944, the society began to publish its own organ, *Payam-i-No* ("New Messenger"), devoted exclusively to the cause of Soviet-Iranian friendship. Its editor was Madame Fatima Sayah, professor of the University of Teheran. She was a member of a well-known family and a relative of Hamid Sayah whose public career included such positions as Minister to Poland and frequent cabinet posts during the second World War. In 1943 Madame Sayah had founded a Women's Party, the aim of which was to raise the position and dignity of women in Iranian society. In view of her record and her prominence Madame Sayah's appointment as editor of the Soviet-sponsored publication was very significant. The society's activities were growing

[201]

apace, and before long it was found that larger premises were needed for its offices. In January, 1945, new and sumptuous quarters were inaugurated in the presence of Premier Bayat and the usual array of Iranian and Soviet notables. Eventually three large buildings, easily accessible to the Iranian public, served the aims of Soviet propaganda in Teheran. These were the House of Culture, the standing Soviet Exhibition, and the V.O.K.S. branch headquarters.

Radio constituted another powerful means of disseminating news favorable to Moscow. The Iranian government was obliged to grant to the Allies a certain amount of time on Radio Teheran for war propaganda. The time was divided between the British and the Russians, but the British ceded part of their time to smaller Allied nations such as France, Poland, Netherlands, and Belgium. The legations of these countries devoted their time to programs concerning their own war efforts. The Soviet programs were longer and, as the war progressed, more and more hostile to the West. After the crisis in Soviet-Iranian relations created by the oil problem in 1944, Soviet radio programs from the Teheran station were occasionally devoted to criticisms of the Iranian government itself. At one time such procedures resulted in dramatic tension. As soon as the Soviet spokesman finished his tirade against the Iranian authorities, another voice was heard from the same station. It was the Iranian Director of Propaganda, Safavi, who denied Soviet accusations and stated that Teheran radio would not be permitted to become an instrument of anti-Iranian propaganda. For an Iranian official this was, under these circumstances, an extraordinary feat of courage. Shortly afterwards Safavi was replaced without explanation.[14]

The distribution of Soviet publications to Iranian libraries and newspaper stands was well organized. *Izvestia, Pravda, Krasnaya Zvezda,* and *War and the Working Class* were available at the most important points of Teheran. A bookstore on one of the principal thoroughfares, Avenue Firdausi, was almost exclusively devoted to Soviet books and pamphlets published in Russian, Persian, and other languages.

[14] *Shahbaz,* July 29, 1945; *Journal de Tehran,* July 15, 1945; for the Soviet interpretation see *Pravda,* July 26, 1945.

Nor was the motion picture forgotten as a powerful means of propaganda. The Soviet authorities owned Setareh ("The Star"), a movie theater situated in the most conspicuous spot on the main Avenue, Shahabad. A mysterious fire in 1944 did much damage to the building, but the theater was restored without delay. Two other well-known theaters, Mayak and Teheran, presented considerably more Soviet films than movies received from other countries. A certain sector of the main street was so plastered with Soviet film posters that it practically resembled a city in one of the Asiatic republics of the Soviet Union. In addition, the Soviet Embassy or the Cultural Society were indefatigable in presenting motion pictures at large official parties. Such parties were held in the wintertime in the spacious rooms of the Soviet Embassy, which inherited the premises from the Imperial regime. In the summer they were held in Zargandeh, a summer residence with magnificent parks, located about seven miles from Teheran. Five hundred to one thousand guests were usual at these parties at which lavish entertainment with a buffet dinner, vodka, wines and champagne was customarily offered. Soviet military bands or orchestras and artists brought from Russia for this special purpose added to the glamor of these receptions. Thus, apart from giving substantial meals to the invariably hungry multitude in which grandees and suspicious-looking minor Tudeh agents elbowed each other energetically to obtain access to the table, these parties impressed the guests with the wealth and power of the northern neighbor. They contrasted with the wartime austerity prevailing at British Embassy receptions.

A propaganda center of inestimable value to Russia was the Soviet Hospital in Teheran. It was conducted by Dr. Baroyan, an Armenian, who was believed to hold an important position in the Foreign Section of the N.K.V.D., and whose travels to Cairo were undoubtedly a riddle to many an intelligence agent of the Western powers. Since medical services were greatly needed, the hospital possessed an excellent reputation. Iranians were permitted to use this hospital, and many prominent members of Iranian society took advantage of it. Iranian medical circles were drawn into collaboration with the hospital, under whose auspices a *Medical Review,* published in Persian and Russian, began to appear in December, 1944. The Soviet Hospital was generous in distributing necessary vaccines to the population in case of epidemics.

The Red Army, although in principle assigned to technical and security tasks, proved to be an instrument of propaganda as well. In the main, unless political circumstances dictated otherwise, its behavior was correct. This was especially true of the Teheran area. Soviet privates were rarely granted passes to the city, and whenever they appeared in Teheran, they behaved quietly. They seldom walked alone, but usually appeared in small groups. They did not indulge in drinking and did not molest the population. Their conduct thus contrasted with the British and American soldiers, who freely mingled with the population, bought souvenirs in antique shops, frequented restaurants and night clubs, and enjoyed their liquors. In some individual cases Western soldiers, unaccustomed to the strong effects of the local vodka, committed acts that brought no credit to their armies. Such conduct would invariably serve as an excuse for a slanderous whispering campaign, inspired no doubt by Soviet sources, with a view to blackening the Western reputation. And although the Western soldiers were not altogether disliked by the populace and merchants, yet pro-Soviet newspapers had a strong point when they emphasized the good behavior and discipline of the Red Army. To the more discriminating Iranians these matters were not so simple. They saw the contrast between the Red Army officer who was always smartly dressed and able to buy watches, furs, golden British sovereigns, and tsarist rubles and the Soviet private whose shabby uniform, unhealthy pallor, and complete lack of money often made him a miserable and subdued figure.[15] In contrast, American enlisted men looked free, healthy, and prosperous, and this, in turn, did not fail to impress the Orientals. Moreover it was common knowledge that Red Army discipline was maintained by exceedingly harsh methods, inconceivable in Western armies. Drastic penalties, including death sentences, were known to be applied to soldiers guilty of excess in

---

[15] The Soviet private's pay is 10.5 rubles per month; the second lieutenant receives 900 rubles. In Iranian currency the purchasing power of 10.5 rubles was about 3 tomans. A bottle of locally made beer cost 1.5 tomans in Teheran in wartime.

town. These strict measures, while producing desirable results, could not, however, inspire more discerning Iranians with confidence in the publicized Soviet humanitarianism.

The Red Army was used as an active weapon of propaganda in performing certain services for the Iranian population. Red Army ambulances busied themselves distributing medicines and helping the people in the northern provinces; Red Army engineers occasionally repaired a broken well in an Iranian village; Red Army units fought the plague of locusts in Iranian wheat-producing provinces. These actions, to be sure, could be explained as undertaken in the self-interest of the Soviet Union. The prevention of epidemics, the purification of water, or the extermination of locusts near the Soviet border could not fail to redound to the benefit of the Russians themselves. Yet Soviet publicity took care to depict these actions to the Iranian public as pure altruism.[16]

Charitable activities were not limited to the Red Army alone. When an earthquake occurred in the province of Gorgan in 1944, the Soviet Embassy displayed considerable generosity in presenting money and goods to the stricken population. On the other hand, Russia was glad to benefit from reciprocal generosity from the Iranians. Thus, for example, a Committee of Aid to the Soviet Victims of War was created in Teheran and in many provincial towns. It was presided over by General Ahmadi, the Minister of War at one time or another, and included the most prominent statesmen, officials, and aristocrats of Iran. The meetings of this committee were given tremendous publicity. The sums contributed by various persons were published, and participation in the work of the committee or a donation to the Soviet cause was essential in establishing one's loyalty to the great northern Ally. This artificial enthusiasm was carefully fanned by the official Soviet representatives, and steps were taken to extend it to some special groups. In the fall of 1943 it was announced that a Zoroastrian Committee to aid the Soviet Victims of War had been established. The Armenian community in Teheran

---

[16] The pro-Soviet paper *Iran-i-Ma* wrote on Jan. 22, 1945: "During the three-year stay of the Red Army in Iran we became convinced that the behavior of Soviet soldiers was very correct and decent and that everything propaganda told about Communism was a lie. . . ."

competed with the Zoroastrians for Soviet favors by organizing fiestas for the Red Army soldiers and gathering funds for Soviet charitable purposes. In order to obtain funds the main Committee of Aid and its subsidiaries were active in organizing musical shows, dances, and even a nation-wide lottery. It was obvious that these sums, however large from the point of view of individual donors, were insignificant in comparison with the vast destruction in the Soviet areas. Their significance lay in the field of propaganda. The more that people gave to the Soviet cause, the greater the impression that friendship toward Russia was spontaneous.

No field was neglected and no opportunity was lost to further Soviet publicity. Even the drivers transporting lend-lease supplies to Russia through Iran were given proper attention. In the summer of 1944 the Soviet Embassy gave medals to thirty-five Iranian truck drivers for their good performance. The ceremony was attended by the Iranian Minister of Communications and the Deputy Minister of Foreign Affairs.

THE CENSORSHIP

While all these means were used as positive mediums of Soviet propaganda, care was simultaneously taken to prevent the spread of information unacceptable to the Soviet authorities. The instrument that served the latter purpose was the Anglo-Soviet-Persian Censorship created in accordance with the provisions of the Tripartite Treaty of January 29, 1942. The censorship worked on the principle of unanimity. The veto of any one of the three censors was sufficient to bar the news from publication. In practice, the veto was a privilege of the Soviet censor, because the Iranian censor was only a figurehead and the powers of the British censor were limited by special circumstances. This limitation on the British censor was due to the fact that censorship, according to the inter-Allied agreement, was to apply only to news released by private news agencies and not to government-published statements. As Reuters was a privately owned agency (the British government always took pains to insist upon it), censorship applied to its releases. Since, on the other hand, Tass was a government-owned agency, the Soviet censor took the stand that all Tass releases represented official Soviet government communiqués and, therefore, were not subject to censorship. The situation thus created clearly favored the Soviet Union from the very beginning, and in the battle of propaganda with the British Russia had an obvious legal superiority. The consequences of this unequal arrangement were felt by the British, by the Iranians, and by the smaller Allied nations whose legations conducted information programs.

Between 1941 and 1944 the Soviet censor generally did not attempt to put a stop to incoming Reuters dispatches. Toward the end of 1944, however, after the oil crisis, and throughout 1945, the Soviet censor freely used his veto prerogative. Thus, in the period of gradually mounting tension between the West and Russia, the Iranian press was receiving a rather one-sided presentation of facts from Soviet sources and was refused adequate British comment on various events.

The censorship of outgoing dispatches was also prejudicial to British interests. The Reuters correspondent in Teheran was compelled to submit his dispatches to censorship. The Soviet censor stubbornly refused to pass anything that might describe Soviet activities in Iran too openly and especially those in the northern provinces. The same applied to any other corespondent residing in Teheran. As a result, the American public was also deprived of an unimpeded news service from this strategically vital area. The only way legally to avoid Soviet censorship was to leave Iran and send a dispatch from another area in the Middle East not subject to Soviet control. Bagdad in Iraq was the nearest place to Teheran, but an overland journey would normally take three days. By plane this distance could be covered in two and a half hours but to obtain a priority on a military airplane was not an easy matter. No matter how quickly a Western correspondent might arrive outside the boundaries of Iran, the Tass release from Moscow concerning Iranian affairs would always precede his account. For this reason neither American nor British correspondents accredited in Teheran ever left the country to send a dispatch.

A few good examples of such Soviet obstruction can be cited. In 1943 Archbishop Spellman of New York, as Chaplain-General of the United States Army, visited Iran to inspect the installations of the Persian Gulf Command. He also paid a visit to a Polish refugee camp in Teheran. There in a sermon he asserted that free Poland would be restored despite all the misfortunes that had befallen her and that the American people in their hearts were at one with the gallant Polish Allies. In view of the fact that this visit happened shortly after the rupture of diplomatic relations between the London Polish government and the Soviet Union, the Archbishop's speech was not devoid of political implications. Leopold Herman, Associated Press correspondent; John Wallis, Reuters correspondent; and Oscar Guth, United Press correspondent, filed dispatches to their agencies covering this event. The Soviet censor stopped all three dispatches with no explanation whatever. No amount of pleading helped. One may add here that censorship was supposed to be applied only so far as the security of the Allied war effort was concerned. No legal justification existed, therefore, in this particular case, for censoring the prelate's statements.

Another striking example was furnished at the time of the oil crisis in the late fall of 1944. When the Iranian government refused to grant the Soviets an oil concession, Communist-led mobs demonstrated in the streets of Teheran. The outside world obtained most of the news about the crisis and the demonstrations from Soviet sources. The Tass Agency said, for example, that about 20,000 people demonstrated against the government. In reality the number was much smaller. When Western correspondents wanted to send news to this effect, their dispatches were again stopped by the Soviet censor. Thus the public in the West received an altogether distorted picture of a situation that should have served as a good case study of Soviet expansionism.[17] In connection with the same crisis the difficulties of the Iranian government in the field of censorship were revealed. Premier Mohammed Sa'ed, who had to weather the oil storm, attempted to keep in constant touch with Iranian envoys abroad in order to inform them and be informed himself of various reactions. He was prevented, however, according to his own admission, from communicating by telegraph with his diplomatic representatives, for the Soviet authorities controlling the telegraph link at Pahlavi stopped his messages at the most critical moment.[18]

17 See p. 216.
18 *Ra'd-i-Emruz,* Dec. 20, 1944. See also Appendix no. IV.

When growing tension was manifested in the north of Iran in the summer of 1945, an urgent need arose to keep Western public opinion properly informed. Yet nothing could be done since foreign correspondents were paralyzed by constant Soviet vetoes. Sir Reader Bullard, the British Ambassador, took the matter so much to heart that he extended a special invitation to Alexander Clifford, a correspondent of the *Daily Mail,* to visit Iran and to report to the British public upon leaving the country. Clifford's visit bore fruit. In an article on Iran he bluntly warned the readers that "queer, sinister things have been happening [in Iran] lately and the Persians are badly scared." Among the "queer" things he mentioned Soviet censorship, Russia's reluctance to quit northern Iran, and her open backing of the antigovernment Tudeh party. His article was quoted in the American press,[19] and for the first time after a long period of darkness, some light was shed on the disturbing situation in this region.

With regard to Iran herself the immunity of the Tass Agency from censorship produced most unfortunate effects. It often made ineffective the working of Iran's own censorship, which, as described earlier, applied *post factum* in the form of suspensions of newspapers by government order. A normal course of events was as follows: An Iranian newspaper would publish an article containing violent criticism of the government as dishonest, "fascist," and "reactionary." The government would suspend the paper in order to keep spirits calmed. A few days later Tass would release an article published in *Izvestia* or *Pravda* in which the accusations against the Iranian government were repeated almost word by word from the Iranian paper. As the Iranian and British censors could not veto Tass dispatches, the Soviet article could be released to the whole of the Iranian press, and consequently it would be very unsafe for the government to suspend all papers that published it.

A word may be added about the position of smaller Allied nations in this connection. It was evident that from 1943 on a crisis was mounting between the governments-in-exile of Poland, Yugoslavia, and Greece on the one hand and Russia on the other. This crisis was of great interest to the Iranian public inasmuch as the handling

[19] *Time,* Aug. 13, 1945.

of the dispute by the United States and Britain provided a test case of the Allies' attitude toward small nations. The politically conscious Iranians were eager to learn as many details as possible about the controversy and its solution. They could not learn a great deal from Reuters (American agencies did not service the Iranian press) as considerable reluctance prevailed in Great Britain during the war against discussing these matters too openly. Tass, on the contrary, was eager to publish news concerning these inter-Allied disputes, and much material in which the Soviet view was presented with force and volubility was released to the Iranian newspapers. The Iranians were thus receiving a biased description of the controversy and often outright false factual material. The Tass dispatches were filled with invectives directed against the governments-in-exile. The Poles were frequently called fascists and "lackeys of Hitler." Descriptions of Mikhailovitch's Chetniks or the Royal Yugoslav government were of a similar nature. It was obvious that to restore some balance in the minds of the Iranian public, some counteraction was necessary. The Polish Legation in Teheran defended the position of the London government in its monthly bulletin, *La Nouvelle Europe,* which devoted most of its energies to factual presentations of the Polish war effort on land, sea, and in the air. It avoided as often as possible polemics with the Soviet Ally. Because the bulletin was an official release of a foreign diplomatic mission, it was not liable to censorship, and thus for a long time it evaded the rigors of Soviet control. In the winter of 1944–1945, however, one printing press after another gradually refused to print it. The printers, as has been shown in the preceding chapters, were members of one of the earliest trade unions in Iran organized under Soviet influence. Pressure on the union with an added threat to the printing press owner was sufficient to stop the publication of any material displeasing to Russia. The Parliament Printing Press resisted Soviet pressure longer than any other establishment but eventually it gave way also.

To all those informed about these proceedings the lesson was clear. Russia's influence was stronger than anybody else's. These conditions could not continue without seriously affecting the prestige of the West and of Great Britain in particular. The Iranians knew that London was a seat of the governments-in-exile, and they understood that Britain was timid and unable to defend the smaller nations. Nor were their fears relieved by the official American indifference in these matters. The result was a growing servility of journalists, statesmen, and deputies toward Russia.

SOVIET PROPAGANDA: ITS SUBSTANCE

The substance of Soviet propaganda in Iran fell into two categories. The first consisted of that type of propaganda that every belligerent government usually spreads concerning its contribution to a war, the heroism of its soldiers, the devotion and patriotism of its population. In this field Soviet publicity did not differ greatly from the publicity of any other Allied country save in the volume of information presented. The second category, however, differed from the established wartime pattern, and could be described as specific political action directed toward ulterior objectives. Sometimes it became difficult to distinguish between the two kinds inasmuch as both ultimately served the same long-range Soviet policy. The Red Army victories were enormously publicized in the Iranian press. Because Russia bore the brunt of the German attack for a long time, this did not seem objectionable. But often it happened that routine occurrences on the Russian front were given much more prominence than important victories in the West. If one were to judge by the Iranian press, Anglo-American strategic bombing of German cities and war industries was a poor second to Soviet victories. Soviet-owned or Soviet-influenced movie theaters presented an amazing number of films exalting the prowess of the Red Army. This process definitely relegated all Western war effort to a subordinate plane. Minor facts testifying to the devotion of Soviet citizens to the regime were given prominence, as, for example, a news item that a *kolkhoznik* from some distant village donated one million rubles to the Soviet government to help the war effort.

Another salient feature of this propaganda was the constant stressing of Soviet achievements in economic, social, artistic, and political spheres. The type and quantity of news released to the Iranian press seemed to prove that the articles were to serve other aims than war publicity. Prominence was given especially to the regime's achievements in the Asiatic border regions of the Soviet Union. Information thus supplied was clearly designed to contrast the poverty of Iranian masses with the alleged happiness, freedom, and prosperity of the Soviet citizens of the Caucasus and of Turkestan. Hardly a week passed without the release by Tass of two or three items of this kind. The following table illustrates the kind of news that the Iranian press received with monotonous regularity in this particular sector of propaganda.

Sample of News Items Released by the Tass Agency
and Published by the Journal de Tehran *on*
Soviet Developments in Regions
Bordering on Iran

February 2, 1944—Theater Art in Kazakhstan
February 7, 1944—Armenian *Kolhozniks* Drying Up Marshlands
February 9, 1944—The Development of Uzbekistan
February 10, 1944—The Kirghiz Fighting German Invaders
February 13, 1944—Progress of Irrigation in U.S.S.R. (Erivan, Armenia)

June 16, 1944 —Enthusiasm in Kamardo-Balkan Republic
June 19, 1944 —Oil Industry in Kuban
June 23, 1944 —Art in Soviet Azerbaijan
June 29, 1944 —Oriental Motifs in Russian Music

July 3, 1944 —Council of Cults in U.S.S.R.
July 3, 1944 —New Electrical Power Plants in Kirghizia
July 9, 1944 —Protection of Public Health in U.S.S.R.
July 11, 1944 —Soviet State Aid to Mothers
July 19, 1944 —New Institutions of Higher Learning in Uzbekistan

While these features were stressed, care was also taken to point out the kinship existing between Iran and the Soviet Asiatic republics. Emphasis was put on the affinity between Soviet and Iranian Azerbaijan and on common links between Iran and the Tajik S.S.R. (a

Persian-speaking area). Tass dispatches were replete with news about serious work in Iranology conducted by Soviet scholars. Some of these scholars, like Pavlovsky, were brought to Iran for lecture tours. Films depicting Soviet scientific expeditions in Iran were shown. A troupe of artists from Tajikistan toured Iran, presenting ninety shows in sixteen towns. An impressive exhibition of architecture of the Soviet Asiatic republics was organized.

Conscious of the average Iranian's pride in the artistic achievements of his country, Soviet agencies did not neglect this field either. Various exhibitions showing Soviet contributions to the discovery and study of Iranian art were repeatedly presented. Perhaps the most successful of these was a great art exhibit organized in the winter of 1946 under the auspices of the Irano-Soviet Cultural Relations Society. The exhibit was devoted in large part to Iranian art of the modern period and did not fail to produce a deep impression in the capital. Implicitly it served two purposes: to prove the seriousness of the Soviet approach to cultural problems and to show their solicitude for the "free" development of national characteristics. It was an excellent medium with which to refute hostile criticism that under the Soviet system all culture is leveled down to a common proletarian denominator. In this, as in many other cases, Soviet tactics displayed an amazing elasticity. While proclaiming at home that culture should be "proletarian in content and national in form," Soviet propaganda abroad pushed the "national" element to the fore and covered the remainder with discreet silence.

In view of Iranian devotion to Islam, Soviet propaganda took pains to publicize "freedom of religion" in Russia. Tass carried news about the activities of the Moslem hierarchy in the Soviet Union and its devotion to the regime. On the other hand, attempts were made to counteract the hostile propaganda of the Shia clergy among Iranian masses and to win them over, if not actually to the Soviet cause, at least to the position of neutrality. For this purpose an Iranian mullah, Lankorani, a native of the Caspian provinces, was recruited. Collaborating with the Tudeh party, he was useful in spreading news of the friendly relations between the government and the Moslems in the Soviet Union. In November, 1944, four mullahs from the Uzbek Soviet Socialist Republic arrived in Teheran on their way to

Mecca. Their visit was seized upon as testimony of the religious freedom existing across the border. When the Iranian University professors returned home in January, 1945, from their visit to Uzbekistan, they brought back a greeting from Ishan Baba Khan, Grand Mufti of Tashkent, to the Director of the Moslem Theological College in Teheran.[20]

The greatest efforts to dispense Soviet religious propaganda in Iran were made in 1945. In the summer of that year Sheikh ul-Islam Ali zadeh, the Chairman of the Moslem Board of Transcaucasia, and a group of leading Moslems from Soviet Azerbaijan visited Iran. Soviet sources [21] maintained that the visit was in response to an invitation from Sheikh ul-Islam Malayeri of Iran, but no confirmation ever came from the Iranian side. Ali-zadeh and his aides visited Tabriz, Qazvin, and Teheran, and in the latter city were received by the Shah. According to reports circulating at that time in Teheran the Soviet Moslems endeavored to impress their Iranian colleagues with the freedom they enjoyed in the Soviet Union and with the benevolent attitude of the government toward them. Malayeri and his entourage were reported to have listened attentively to these persuasions and to have acknowledged politely their faith in the information conveyed. At that time many Iranians were still interned in Erak for their co-operation with the German fifth column, and the end of the war with Germany raised a popular clamor for their release. Since some of these internees were under Soviet guard, the Soviet government was in a position to set them free. The Iranian divines, anxious to see them liberated, addressed on their behalf a plea to the Soviet theologians. With a truly oriental cunning they endeavored to convince their Soviet colleagues with reasoning which, if reconstructed, might have sounded like this:

"You say that your relations with the government are excellent. We are glad to hear that. We here also enjoy very good relations

---

[20] The members of the Iranian delegation included Academician Said Nafisi; Majlis Deputy Gonabadi; a newspaper editor, Fernemsh; Deputy Governor General Farrukhi of the province of Khorasan; and others. The delegation "made special note of the tremendous organizational successes that have been achieved by Soviet Moslems" (*U.S.S.R. Information Bulletin*, Washington, August 14, 1946, p. 19).

[21] *Ibid.*

with our government. And this fact permits us to exert quite a bit of influence. Do you mean that you have as much influence with your authorities?"

"Yes, certainly we do."

"Well, in that case why don't you do us a favor? As you know poor innocent Iranians are still kept in jail for their alleged connivance with the Germans. The war with Germany is over, and, of course, it is a shame that good Moslems should languish in captivity for no reason whatever. Can you use your influence with the Soviet Ambassador to effect their speedy release? If you do, you will give us an irrefutable proof of the position you enjoy with your authorities."

Reportedly, the result of this conversation was an immediate visit of the Soviet Moslem chief to the Soviet Ambassador in Teheran to request the release of the internees. The Soviet government, sensing good propaganda potentiality for both the Iranian masses and the Iranian clergy, gave the order for release. Soon afterwards the internees were set free. It is open to doubt whether the Iranian public felt any gratitude toward Russia or whether the clergy was convinced of the influence of Islam in Russia. But one thing was certain, namely, that the British government was involuntarily placed in the role of villain, for it had not released the internees that were under British guard at the same time. The Soviet authorities obviously acted in bad faith, purposely avoiding consultation with the British in the matter. The British were eventually obliged to release their own contingent of prisoners,[22] but the harm had already been done.

To an observer of the Iranian political scene it was clear that Soviet propaganda was being stepped up and was becoming more and more anti-Western as time progressed. Even at the time of greatest Soviet weakness when German armies pressed toward the oil fields of Mozdok and Grozny in 1942, the Soviet agencies in Iran relentlessly carried on their proselytizing activity. Until the fall of 1944 the anti-Western attitude of Soviet propaganda had, however, a veiled character. After that time it was openly directed against Britain and the United States. The turning point proved to be the conflict between Russia and Iran concerning oil concessions.

[22] For the British explanation see the *Tehran Daily News,* Aug. 15, 1945.

THE OIL CRISIS OF 1944

At the time when the war spread to Iran there were only two valid oil concessions in the country: the first was operated by the Anglo-Iranian Oil Company and the second, of minor importance, was operated by the Kavir-i-Khurian Company and owned conjointly by Russia and an Iranian group. The Anglo-Iranian possessed a limited, though not small, area in southwestern Iran. The Kavir-i-Khurian Company's terrain near Semnan was negligible in size. The remaining territory of Iran was free from foreign concessions. Thus not only the northern provinces in the Soviet zone but also the southeastern area, especially the Iranian province of Baluchistan, were potential areas of oil exploitation. In the fall of 1943 the British Shell Company sent a representative to Iran to negotiate an oil concession for the southern area. In the spring of 1944 he was followed by the representatives of two American companies: Standard Vacuum Oil Company [23] and Sinclair Oil Company. The first official news about these negotiations was given by Premier Mohammed Sa'ed to the Majlis in August, 1944. The Premier promised to give further information to the deputies in due time. In the meantime two American petroleum geologists, A. A. Curtice and Herbert Hoover, Jr., were engaged by the Iranian government to survey the oil reserves in various parts of the country. During the parliamentary debate in August the Communist deputy Radmanesh criticized their presence. He stated that, if Iran was to grant an oil concession to the Americans, impartiality demanded the engagement of experts of another nationality. In the same speech Radmanesh went on record as opposing, on behalf of his party, any foreign concessions. He argued that if Iran managed to construct by her own means the Transiranian Railroad, she should also be able to exploit oil resources without any foreign aid.[24]

In the second half of September, 1944, a new element was injected into the oil negotiations. In a surprise move the Soviet Assistant People's Commissar for Foreign Affairs, Sergei I. Kavtaradze, arrived in Teheran at the head of a large mission of diplomatic and technical experts. After a few days of silence during which Teheran was a prey

[23] Owned jointly by Standard Oil of New Jersey and Socony Vacuum Oil Co.
[24] *Journal de Tehran*, Aug. 11, 1944.

to the most fantastic rumors concerning the real aim of the Soviet visit, it was revealed that Kavtaradze had come to discuss the exploitation of oil in Semnan, in the territory held by the Soviet-controlled Kavir-Khurian concession. Although a number of people had serious misgivings in this connection, the prevalent trend was that of avoiding alarmistic deductions. It was argued in private conversations that any discussion concerning the Semnan oil could only be of a technical nature. It was pointed out that the matter of the concession itself had been settled a long time before and that nobody had questioned the acquired Soviet rights in this particular case. Although no Iranian source claimed that the Commissar's visit was the result of an official invitation, both press and government circles competed initially in their affirmations of friendship toward Russia. A nationalist paper, *Rastakhiz,* commented favorably on Kavtaradze's speech at the Premier's reception during which the Soviet official complimented the Iranians on their contribution to the Allied war effort. "We are very happy that this mission has arrived," added the paper. "It proves that our relations with Russia are good and will be even better." [25]

Soon, however, this mood of expectant servility underwent a change. This was due to the revelation that the Soviet Commissar had suddenly changed the avowed purpose of his visit and, instead of discussing the Semnan oil, demanded a new oil concession that would cover all the five northern provinces of Iran bordering on the Soviet Union.

This information, revealed to the public some two weeks after Kavtaradze's arrival, threw a number of people into consternation. Of the various interpretations given to the new Soviet move, two deserve special mention. One was that the real aim of the Soviet demand was not to obtain an oil concession but to prevent the granting of concessions to the American companies, which were reported to be on the verge of successful conclusion of their negotiations with Iran. Realizing fully Iranian reluctance to grant oil concessions to the Soviets, Moscow thus would compel the Iranian government to refuse *all* concessions rather than incur Soviet hostility for its discriminatory policies. According to this interpretation, Russia did not begrudge America the oil so much as the fact that an oil concession

[25] Sept. 25, 1944.

[217]

might link the United States and Iran politically. Russia's main aim, it was asserted, was to keep America at arm's length from Iran, so that Soviet schemes might not be frustrated by the presence of a powerful newcomer in this part of the world.

Another interpretation was that Russia really wanted oil and believed that the war period was most propitious for obtaining a concession. Such a concession, it was argued, would place Russia not only in possession of a coveted raw material, but would also serve as an instrument of Soviet influence on Iranian politics.

Whatever the real motive of Soviet action at the time, the fact is that on October 16 the Iranian government rejected all offers for concessions, i.e., American, British, and Soviet. Thus the first interpretation of the Russian action seemed to have been vindicated. However this was not the end of the drama. Six days later *Trud*, organ of the Soviet trade unions, published an article headlined "The Words and Deeds of Mr. Sa'ed" in which the policy of the Iranian Prime Minister was strongly attacked. The Iranian government was accused of neglect for not punishing the "harmful actions of certain evil-intentioned elements" who had sabotaged the regular flow of Allied supplies to the Soviet Union through Iran and for not opposing the "intensification of subversive work of profascist elements." The Premier himself was criticized for having rendered Iran's relations with the Allies "strained and tense." The well-known technique of reproducing Iranian editorials was used when *Trud* quoted the Tudeh-affiliated *Shahbaz* as saying: "Reactionaries have set Premier Sa'ed to the task of smashing workers' and democratic organizations, and for this purpose he has introduced a bill for the militarization of industry." *Trud* revealed that a number of Iranian newspapers were inquiring why Premier Sa'ed did not resign and concluded by stating that the "continuation of Premier Sa'ed's policy is harming the interests of Iran and of the Iranian people." [26] On the same day *The War and the Working Class* significantly cited American statistics in order to prove that the United States controlled 57 per cent of the world's oil resources, Great Britain 27 per cent, and the Soviet Union only 11 per cent.[27]

[26] Quoted in the *New York Times*, Oct. 23, 1944.
[27] It is interesting to note that on other occasions Soviet propaganda asserted

These articles were followed by dramatic developments in Teheran. On October 24 Vice-Commissar Kavtaradze received a large number of Iranian newspaper editors in the Soviet Embassy. He stated that Iran's decision to refuse oil concessions made a very unfavorable impression in Moscow and that "the disloyal and unfriendly position taken up by Premier Sa'ed toward the Soviet Union excluded the possibility of further collaboration with him." Foreseeing the deterioration of relations between the two countries as a result of Sa'ed's attitude, Kavtaradze appealed to the Iranian public to bring pressure on the government "for a favorable solution of the dispute." He pointed out the advantages that would accrue to Iran if the Soviet offer were accepted. These advantages would be, first, greater employment in Iran; second, the training of Iranians for skilled jobs; third, the development of Iran's natural resources and wealth; and fourth, a larger market for agricultural produce in the areas under concession. He also assured the audience that the Soviet government would guard the health and welfare of the workers and their families. The Vice-Commissar was pleased to note that the "majority" of Teheran newspapers supported the Soviet position.[28]

This unprecedented attack by a foreign official on the government of the country to which he was sent on a mission created a great deal of tension and fear in Teheran. Premier Sa'ed hastened to call a press conference at which he said that his government had only decided to postpone all negotiations concerning oil until the end of the

that the Soviet Union was rich in oil. In the *U.S.S.R. Information Bulletin,* published by the Soviet Embassy in Washington, Oct. 2, 1946, p. 7, we read under the title, "Fuel Resources of the U.S.S.R.": "Nature has lavishly endowed the Soviet Union with minerals, especially with coal and oil. For ascertained deposits of coal the U.S.S.R. is second to the United States, and for oil it holds first place in the world. In 1937 the estimated total coal reserves in the U.S.S.R. were 1,654,-000,000,000 tons, which constituted nearly a quarter of the world's reserves. In the same year the oil reserves in the Soviet Union were estimated at 6,376,000,000 tons, or 55 percent of the world's visible reserves." In the same article we find the following figures on Soviet oil production: 1913, 9,000,000 tons; 1940, 31,000,000 tons; planned for 1950, 35,400,000 tons; planned for 1965, 60,000,000 tons.

28 The story of this interview was published in the *New York Times,* Oct. 30, 1944, p. 5, and was entirely based on the Tass dispatch published in Moscow the day before, dated Teheran, Oct. 25, 1944. Owing to Soviet censorship no direct dispatches from Teheran were available to the American public despite the presence of American correspondents.

war. His action, he said, was not directed against the Soviet Union. Oil concessions were temporarily refused to all those who asked for them, including the Americans and the British. The Premier listed the following four reasons for the refusal: (a) the presence of foreign troops in Iran, (b) the uncertain economic situation due to the war, (c) the fact that some questions remained unsolved during the recent Anglo-American oil conference in Washington, and (d) advice from Iranian diplomatic representatives abroad not to grant concessions.[29] Finally the Premier declared that this decision was taken as a result of negotiations with the British and American companies before the arrival of Vice-Commissar Kavtaradze in Teheran.

Kavtaradze's appeal to the Iranian public through the "free press" of Iran did not remain unanswered. Suddenly reversing their recent attitude of opposing all grants to foreigners, the Tudeh and affiliated papers launched a vigorous campaign in favor of the Soviet oil concession. They accused the Iranian government of reaction, fascism, and hostility to Russia. They repeatedly emphasized the theme that after the war and the liquidation of Allied installations in Iran the resulting unemployment could be combated only by such measures as the development of natural resources in collaboration with the Soviets. They identified the interests of the Soviet Union with the welfare of Iranian workmen and unanimously insisted on an early resignation of Premier Sa'ed.[30] Moreover, the Tudeh organized mass demonstrations in the parliament square. A throng, reported by Tass as twenty thousand strong (in reality not exceeding four to five thousand), assembled before the Majlis and menacingly demanded Sa'ed's dismissal. The revealing fact about this demonstration was that its participants were brought to the square in Soviet trucks and that Soviet Army detachments happened to march through the area at the very same time. The Iranian troops called to secure order were thus paralyzed, as any step taken against the demonstration could be interpreted as directly anti-Soviet. According to reports that were given general credence in Teheran each demonstrator was paid a day's wages by the Communist party for his participation. A wave

[29] *Journal de Tehran*, Oct. 30, 1944.

[30] *Rahbar*, Oct. 26, 1944; *Zafar*, Oct. 27, 1944; *Razm*, Nov. 8, 1944; *Azadegan*, Nov. 18, 1944; *Azhir*, Nov. 26, 1944.

of similar mob demonstrations took place in most of the important cities in the Soviet zone of occupation. Tass reported, for example, that in Tabriz alone twenty-five thousand workers protested in a mass rally against Sa'ed's policy.

If this mob pressure was conceived by the Soviets as likely to modify the negative attitude of Premier Sa'ed, it did not achieve the desired result. To make matters worse, from the Soviet viewpoint, the American Ambassador, Leland B. Morris, revealed the United States' stand on the matter. The American government, he said, recognized the sovereign right of Iran to refuse the granting of oil concessions and did not reproach the Iranian government on that account.

On November 4 *Izvestia,* the official organ of the Soviet government, renewed its attack on Premier Sa'ed, whom it linked with former Premier Zia ed-Din. Zia was described as a "man who long ago took up the profession of trading with the honor and independence of his country in the interests of his foreign masters." *Izvestia* asked

how the presence of troops of another State on Iranian territory without any treaty with Iran tallies with Iran's sovereignty and independence. As is known, apart from Soviet and British troops that are on Iranian territory in conformity with the treaty of alliance, there are also American forces in Iran. But these forces stay there entirely without a treaty with the Iranian government.[31]

It was clear that a new element was introduced into the oil debate, namely, the Soviet view that British and American influence stood behind Iran's refusal. The Soviet attack on American troops in Iran elicited an acid reply from the State Department, which said that they were there "in connection with the running of the railroad for the delivery of lend-lease supplies through that country to Russia." The statement added that American troops were invited to enter Iran by the British forces of occupation and that negotiations had recently begun between the United States and Iran "to cover their presence." [32]

A United Press dispatch from Washington, published in the American press on November 6, said in this connection:

[31] Quoted in the *New York Times,* Nov. 5, 1944.
[32] *Ibid.,* Nov. 5, 1944.

No one here is hiding his apprehension about the explosive potentialities of the Soviet-Iranian dispute which also involves Great Britain and the United States. . . . Iran could make Poland look almost picayune as a United Nations problem. The United States and Great Britain are willing to compromise for a satisfactory settlement of the Polish question, but Britain will never compromise her position in Iran. . . . American officials are gravely concerned by the fact that most of the news about the dispute has been coming from Moscow.[33]

Despite the refusal Kavtaradze stayed in Teheran. Events were succeeding each other now with great rapidity. On November 6 the official Tudeh organ *Rahbar* demanded, in the name of the twenty-seven papers of the Freedom Front, the dismissal of Sa'ed. The next day the Tudeh party called a mass meeting to celebrate the anniversary of the Russian revolution and to protest against the government policy. The meeting was prevented by Iranian police and the army, which entered the headquarters of the Tudeh and temporarily arrested all those present there. A day later, November 8, Premier Sa'ed resigned. A two-week interregnum followed. In the second half of November the Majlis expressed its "inclination" toward Morteza Quli Bayat, who was asked by the Shah to form a new cabinet. The Iranian Communist press greeted the new government with reservations. It stressed the absolute necessity of accommodating the Soviet Union if the government were to continue. A new wave of anti-government demonstrations swept the north of Iran. The Tudeh deputies in the Majlis strongly attacked the new government. It looked as if the pressure were too strong for any Iranian cabinet to withstand Soviet cajolings.

In this atmosphere of tension one of the leading deputies in the Majlis, Dr. Mosaddeq, introduced a law that would make it a punishable crime for any cabinet minister to enter into negotiations or to grant oil concessions to foreigners without a previous approval of the parliament. The law was promptly adopted by the Majlis on December 2, 1944. Six days later Kavtaradze invited Premier Bayat and a number of deputies and newspapermen to the Soviet Embassy. There he issued a declaration strongly critical of the new law. He stated that the adoption of the law was a thoughtless step and a great

[33] *New York Times*, Nov. 7, 1944.

mistake. The main factor in the passing of the law, said the Vice-Commissar, was the section of the press that wanted to hinder good relations between Iran and the Soviet Union. In the light of the fact that the old concessions in the south remained untouched the ban on new oil concessions was illogical. It is the view of the Soviet government, he declared, that the Majlis must reconsider the whole problem. The Soviet concession proposals were very favorable to Iran and did not contain any features of imperialism. Kavtaradze concluded by saying that because of the deterioration of Soviet-Iranian relations he was obliged to leave Iran promptly. The next day, December 9, the Vice-Commissar left Iran for Moscow.

The first round of the Iranian-Soviet duel was over. In reality it was also a Soviet-Western duel. The tone of the Communist press in Iran after Kavtaradze's visit testified to this fact eloquently. These points of disagreement between the Western democracies and Russia that had been simmering throughout the war now flared up into the open as far as the Iranian press was concerned. The civil war in Greece, which had just begun, the Polish problem, and the over-all problem of oil in the Middle East were now volubly discussed, first by the Communist press and then, as a countermeasure, by the nationalist press. As time went on Great Britain found accusations of imperialism thrown at her. She was charged with aiding the fascist-reactionary regimes throughout the world, with oppressing India, and with exploiting Iran cruelly through the medium of the Anglo-Iranian Oil Company.

In contrast, however, to the direct action characteristic of Kavtaradze's visit, Soviet policy reverted to indirect methods. The main instrument of this indirect Soviet action was the Communist party Tudeh.

A TROJAN HORSE: THE TUDEH PARTY

The Tudeh Party was a reincarnation of the old Communist party of Iran. As pointed out in previous chapters, under the regime of Shah Reza the Communist party was obliged to go underground, and official persecution never permitted it to exert important influence in the country. In 1938 mass arrests by the Iranian police threw many Communists or Communist sympathizers into jail. There they languished until the entry of Soviet troops into Iran in 1941. Released as a result of foreign invasion and the subsequent amnesty to all political prisoners, the Communist leaders proceeded quickly, with apparent Soviet aid, to organize the new Communist party. The name given it this time was *Tudeh,* which means "the masses." The party was officially created in January, 1942, and was, of course, an open and legal political organization enjoying the freedom of the new Iranian wartime "democracy." Among the founders of the party were Reza Rusta, released from jail, to become famous later through his activities among the workers of the Anglo-Iranian Oil Company; Abol Qasim Assadi; Iraj Iskandari; Dr. Morteza Yazdi; and Dr. Reza Radmanesh. Somewhat later they were joined by twenty other leftists, among whom Ja'afar Pishevari became widely known as a result of the role he was to play in Azerbaijan. Pishevari had a long and stormy career as a Communist. Born in Iranian Azerbaijan in 1888, he went to Baku in 1904 and stayed there until the revolution. In 1918 he arrived in Iran with the Red Army under the name of Seyyid Ja'afar Badku Bayi. In 1920 he became Minister of Interior of the Revolutionary Gilan Republic. After its collapse he went to Russia and became active in the Comintern under the name of Sultan-zadeh. His Comintern errands took him to a number of countries in the Middle East including Abyssinia. Pretending to be a victim of Soviet purges in 1936, Pishevari reappeared in Iran. The Iranian government watched him closely and kept him in protective custody in Kashan. As a result of the amnesty in 1941 Pishevari was released. He went to Teheran, became editor of the daily *Azhir,* and helped found the Tudeh.

The organization of the party followed the pattern of other Communist parties. It had a Central Executive Committee of ten members [34] and a Control Commission of eight members.[35] Its affairs were

---

[34] Members of the Central Executive Committee elected in August, 1944, were Nur ed-Din Alamuti, Parvin Gonabadi, Ardeshir (an Armenian deputy), Ehsan Tabari, Iraj Iskandari, Ali Amirkhazi, Dr. Reza Radmanesh, Mahmud Boghrati, Abdosamad Kambakhsh, and Dr. Keshavarz.

[35] The Control Commission as of August, 1944, was composed of Dr. Morteza Yazdi, Dr. Jowlal, Abdol Hosein Nushin, Ali Alavi, Reza Rusta, Ahmad Qasimi, Dr. Kianuri, and Zia Alamuti.

[224]

run by three secretaries.[36] The party's main press organ was *Rahbar*, edited by Iraj Iskandari. In case of suspension by government order it was replaced by the daily *Razm*, whose editorship was then assumed by Dr. Keshavarz. In addition, the party's policy was represented by the papers *Azhir*, edited by Pishevari; *Mardom*, an organ of "antifascist organizations of Iran," edited by Dr. Radmanesh; *Rasti*, edited by Deputy Parvin Gonabadi; *Zafar*, edited by Reza Rusta; and *Damavand*, edited by Fatahi. The last two claimed to represent the trade unions and the Azerbaijani Turks, respectively.

In its official program the Tudeh avoided giving the impression that it might have revolutionary aims. Following the pattern adopted later in some eastern European countries, it did not call itself Communist. It demanded neither the nationalization of private property nor the collectivization of land. On the contrary, its platform included all the essential features of traditional liberalism, exactly as did the other Iranian parties. The Tudeh demanded progressive labor legislation, including social insurance, which would cover large groups including army officers, soldiers, and their families; the legalization of trade unions; improved standards of living for the peasantry; strict price controls to curb inflation; free education and general health services; the elimination of reactionary elements from public life and the restitution of democratic practices; equality for minorities; reform of the administration and of the judicial system; disarming of nomad tribes and promotion of order and security; national industrialization; friendly relations with all of Iran's neighbors; and the elimination of foreign interference. The one factor that might distinguish this program from that of other political parties was its stress on the welfare of the workers and of the peasantry.[37]

The first year of the party's existence was devoted to organizational activities. The party press was established. A network of local

[36] Iraj Iskandari, Dr. Mohammed Bahrami, and Nur ed-Din Alamuti.

[37] These points were compiled on the basis of the following party pronouncements: an editorial in *Rahbar*, June 25, 1943; an appeal to the electorate published by the official party organ, *Razm*, Sept. 9, 1943; the party's declaration containing instructions for its deputies in parliament, *Rahbar*, Feb. 28, 1944; the resolutions of the Tudeh Congress, *Rahbar*, Aug. 3–15, 1944; *Journal de Tehran*, May 11, 1944.

branches was spread in major cities throughout the entire country, particularly in the northern Soviet-occupied zone. Tabriz, Zanjan, Ardebil, Maragheh, Maku, Rezaieh, Khoi, Meshed, Semnan, Shahrud, Damghan, and Qazvin figured prominently in the Tudeh press reports as centers of the party's activities. In the south the most important gain for the Tudeh was the organization of labor in Isfahan textile factories. The party's influence even reached some distant places on the Persian Gulf coast. Attempts were made to influence labor employed by the Anglo-Iranian Oil Company, but the British authorities resisted strongly. Eventually, however, the Anglo-Iranian Company felt the impact of the Tudeh agitation. Quite naturally the party focused attention on organizing industrial workers. Trade unionism was encouraged and a central trade union organization was established in Teheran. The leadership of the latter overlapped to such an extent with the central authorities of the Tudeh that it became difficult, for all practical purposes, to distinguish between the two organizations. The number of party members was not officially disclosed. Government estimates were modest. According to them, the party numbered no more than three thousand members. At the other extreme were reports that the party numbered two hundred thousand, with *Rahbar* claiming forty thousand for Teheran alone.[38] Although party regulations provided for subscriptions of 30 rials per month per male member and of 15 rials per female or child member,[39] it is doubtful whether these rules were strictly followed, and therefore whether it was possible to distinguish between members in good standing and mere sympathizers. Actually the party's numerical strength could best be measured by the number of those willing to take part in party-sponsored demonstrations. These demonstrations ranged from simple strikes of factory hands to bloody riots definitely political in character. Naturally the party possessed a hard inner core of seasoned Communists. Some of them were veterans of the heroic period under the Reza Shah regime. Others were brought at one time or another from Russia.[40] There is no

[38] *Rahbar,* July 8, 1943.

[39] *Ra'd-i-Emruz,* April 27, 1944.

[40] In 1938 about 3,500 Iranians, mostly Azerbaijani Turks, re-emigrated to Iran from the Soviet Union. In contrast to the 8,000-strong Mussavatist emigration

doubt that this inner core constituted a closely knit organization well indoctrinated and disciplined.

The party's tactics consisted first in enlisting the support of the working class and then that of the intelligentsia. Younger Iranian intellectuals, often western-trained and frustrated in their ambitions because of the outmoded social system, constituted a chronically discontented class. Following the prescriptions of the Comintern congresses, the party did not neglect to appeal to them. In this action the party was applying the classical Communist tactic of forming a coalition with the liberal, anti-imperialist bourgeoisie in semicolonial areas. But in so doing, the Party carefully avoided purely Communist slogans that might have alienated the Western-minded intelligentsia. This is the explanation why the party's program included such a wealthy array of liberal and nationalist slogans. Following the prescribed line of a coalition, the Tudeh found it necessary to establish a working relationship with the socialists, and it managed to effect a split in the ranks of the socialist Hamrahan party. An originally independent socialist paper of Menshevik tinge, *Giti,* was also eventually converted into a tool of the Tudeh. In July, 1943, the Tudeh sponsored the formation of the so-called Freedom Front, a coalition of newspapers dedicated to liberalism and progress. It was characteristic of the Communist tactics that at the time of its formation the Freedom Front included, aside from the Tudeh organs, a number of wholly non-Communist papers.

Such were, for example, *Setareh,* considered an unofficial mouthpiece of the American financial expert, Dr. Millspaugh, or *Bakhtar,* belonging to one of the pro-British Isfahan deputies. These two papers, as well as some others, later left the front and became definitely hostile to Communist infiltration. In their place others, how-

---

of 1918–1923, these immigrants were mostly poor, representing such classes as laborers, small artisans, drivers, and mechanics. Their orientation was generally pro-Soviet and in Iran they found it difficult to establish themselves on a sound economic basis. The government of Reza Shah was definitely suspicious of these immigrants and in some cases applied stern measures against them. It is not quite clear why the Soviet government permitted such a large body of people to leave the U.S.S.R. at that time. Yet, since the immigrants formally enjoyed Iranian citizenship, Iran had to admit them. From among these, many Tudeh adherents were recruited.

ever, joined the coalition.[41] The original number of the Freedom Front members was fourteen. Its membership grew rapidly, reaching twenty-seven by the time of the oil crisis in 1944 and nearly forty in 1945.

By 1944, however, it was clear that the Freedom Front had ceased to be a coalition of various political shades and had become an outright tool of the Tudeh and, consequently, of Soviet policy. At the time of the oil crisis the Freedom Front behaved in a disciplined way, staunchly supporting Soviet demands. The purpose in creating the Freedom Front seemed to be not only to draw a number of newspapers into collaboration with the Communists, but also to create the impression both in Iran and abroad that a broad section of the country's public opinion sided with Russia on many controversial issues. For example, in September, 1945, the Soviet press and the Moscow radio announced that a group of twenty-six Iranian editors had sent a telegram to the Council of Foreign Ministers of the Five Big Powers then deliberating in London, requesting intervention to secure drastic internal reforms and to assure a foreign policy based on friendly relations with the Soviet Union. The editors had denounced the Iranian government as "fascist and reactionary." Characteristic of the role played by the press in Iranian politics during that period was the fact that soon after the release of this news, the Iranian Embassy in London hastened to make an announcement that it had received a cable from "fifty-six genuine editors of the leading daily newspapers" in Iran who had declared that the "Iranians have always been politically progressive people who would be sorry to see any interference in their internal affairs and are in opposition to any interference from outside." [42]

In August, 1944, the Tudeh held its first national congress in Te-

[41] At one time or another the following papers adhered to the Freedom Front: from Teheran—*Azadegan, Azhir, Hallaj, Hajat-i-Javid, Damavand, Razm, Rahbar, Zaban, Shu'levar, Shahbaz, Zafar, Farman, Kar, Kayfar, Mardom, Maslahat, Nejat-i-Iran, Neda-yi-Haqiqat, No Bahar, Darya, Iran-i-Ma, Rah-i-Nejat;* from Isfahan—*Ateshgah, Spenta, Donya-yi-Emruz, Rah-i-Nejat;* from Kermanshah—*Bisutun, Sa'adat-i-Melli;* from Ardebil—*Jodad;* from Tabriz—*Khavar-i-No, Vatan Yolunda, Setareh-yi-Azerbaijan, Shahin, Adabiyat-i-Sahifeh;* from Meshed—*Rasti;* from Resht—*Surat, Alborz;* from Qum—*Ostavar;* from Shiraz—*Surush.*

[42] *New York Times,* Sept. 21, 1945.

heran; this was an overt manifestation of its strength and influence. One hundred sixty-nine delegates from all over the country participated. The congress went on record as favoring a number of progressive reforms, struggle against fascism, and a friendly policy toward Iran's neighbors. The resolutions contained a denunciation of foreign advisers (this had its anti-American implications) and strongly anti-imperialist accents. The work of the party was reviewed and officers to the party's central posts were elected. The old ruling clique remained in power.

Earlier in the year the parliamentary elections gave eight seats to the Tudeh deputies.[43] In the chapter dealing with the parliament we have pointed out how this little group could influence the work of that body. Suffice it to say here that the Tudeh deputies, in contrast to all the rest of the Majlis, behaved in a disciplined way, stressing in their speeches that they represented an organized party. The election of the Tudeh candidates was not without its dramatic sidelights. Among those elected from the Soviet zone were deputies Pishevari and Khoi. Claiming, however, alleged irregularities in their election, the Majlis, by a majority vote, refused to seat the two men. This step infuriated the Tudeh. A number of mass demonstrations were organized at which the populace demanded the recognition of the two mandates in the Soviet zone. In some cases these meetings, terminating in clashes with local government authorities or hostile political elements, resulted in injuries and deaths.

Generally speaking, mass demonstrations and resulting accidental or premeditated violence were characteristic of the Tudeh. The party differed from others more in its real methods than in its avowed program. In comparison with the Tudeh other political parties were relatively inexperienced. Dedicated to liberalism and democracy, they naturally resented any use of force by the government or by their own members. The Tudeh was mature from the very start and frequently displayed mastery of all the techniques typical of totalitarian parties. Articles and speeches by Tudeh leaders were, as a rule, demagogical and violent. Slogans were adapted to a particular

[43] These were Dr. Keshavarz (Pahlavi), Ghazar Simonian, Valiolla Shahab (Khorasan), Dr. Radmanesh (Resht), Iraj Iskandari, Parvin Gonabadi, Ardashir Ovanessian (Tabriz), and Fidakar (Isfahan).

audience. Mass meetings or marches were often organized. Political adversaries were mercilessly criticized. Tudeh henchmen regularly attacked meetings of hostile organizations or persons known for their enmity to Communism. Strikes, often for purely political reasons, were organized, and special anniversary days, normally those connected with official Soviet holidays, were noisily celebrated.

It was typical of the party that to swell its ranks it accepted the collaboration of virtually anyone who wished to co-operate. A few examples may be cited here. During one of the roundups by the Anglo-Soviet forces of those suspected of fifth column pro-German activities, a young editor by the name of Tafazzoli was arrested. Tafazzoli edited an independent liberal paper, *Iran-i-Ma,* which was known for its pure nationalism and which was, therefore, implicitly anti-British and anti-Soviet in character. On some occasions it openly criticized the Tudeh,[44] although, in line with most Iranian newspapers before the oil crisis, it did not attack Russia directly. Upon his arrest Tafazzoli was sent to the Soviet prison at Resht. There a notable transformation took place in his political philosophy. Released after some months of captivity, Tafazzoli gradually reoriented his newspaper into a pro-Soviet organ. By the time of the oil crisis, which was the decisive test of the patriotism of the Iranian press, *Iran-i-Ma* unswervingly went on record as favoring Soviet demands.

Another example was Qavam as-Saltaneh. A wealthy latifundist from the north, Qavam was Prime Minister in 1942 until the bread riots at Christmas time forced his resignation in January, 1943. For a short time thereafter he remained politically inactive, but when the Freedom Front was created, Qavam emerged as its supporter. In the light of his postwar record it is not quite clear what motivated Qavam. Some have said that it was his desire to protect his property in the Soviet zone that prompted him to play the game with the

44 *Iran-i-Ma,* July 5, 1943, wrote: "When the Soviets entered Iran, many wealthy Iranians fled to the south. But many put on the mask of Communism. Such were Abbas and Soleiman Iskandari. They raised red standards and proclaimed themselves defenders of the people. They created the Tudeh party. When Abbas Iskandari embezzled some funds, he fled to America. Such is the Tudeh party of Iran!"

[230]

Tudeh. Others have maintained that Qavam was a patriotic Iranian who used the technique of friendliness toward the Tudeh as a subterfuge against the Russians. Whatever the correct answer, the fact remains that the Tudeh, despite all its anti-compradore philosophy, was glad to avail itself of Qavam's support. Such support was not to be scorned, for it meant a split in the ranks of the very class that naturally would be considered hostile to Soviet influence.

Still another example, more colorful perhaps, was that of Mozaffar Firuz. Firuz, a member of an ancient and influential family, was not too successful in the early years of his career. He was sent to Washington as a secretary of the Iranian Legation before the war but became involved in some embezzlement affair. This eventually compelled him to resign from the diplomatic service. Some members of his family suffered persecution and death under the regime of Shah Reza, and this fact made him bitter toward the dynasty. When the exiled former Premier Seyyid Zia ed-Din returned to Iran in 1943, Firuz offered him his services and became editor of *Ra'd-i-Emruz*, Zia's official organ. The editorship and the active role played in Zia's party kept him, of course, fully employed and probably well recompensed, but he did not become wealthy. Rumor had it that he faced financial difficulties. For some time his association with Zia was cordial despite a basic disagreement in their attitudes toward the Shah. Then in 1944–1945 Firuz gave signs of going to the other side of the fence. Although never officially a member of the party, he emerged eventually as a collaborator of the Tudeh. He was to become notorious by virtue of the role he played in the Irano-Soviet crisis of 1945–1946. In the postwar period his change of heart brought him for a short period to the summit of influence in Iran and culminated in his appointment as Ambassador to Moscow in 1946. In 1947 on his way to Iran he mysteriously disappeared. No news has been heard of him since.

Direct Soviet propaganda was supplemented by that of the Tudeh whenever need arose for indirect action. Iranian nationalism could, of course, be best stressed by the Iranians themselves. Hence the Tudeh assumed the role of protector of the Iranian nation against Western imperialism. In its attempts to stir up hatred against the

British, the Tudeh brought to the fore the long-forgotten issue of the Bahrein Islands.[45] The Tudeh persistently opposed the incorporation of foreign advisers in the government, whether American, British, or French.[46] It was most vociferous in criticizing the American financial administrator, Dr. A. C. Millspaugh. Its press frequently attacked the Anglo-Iranian Oil Company.[47]

In internal affairs the Tudeh doggedly opposed every government with accusations of indifference to the welfare of the people, inefficiency, and hostility to the Soviet Union. The formula employed was a simple one and was succinctly put by the official *Rahbar:* "Every government which fights against the workers' movement is fascist, [and] every government which acts against the Soviet Union is fascist." [48]

Among the political parties that were special objects of Tudeh denunciation was, of course, the nationalist and pro-British party of Seyyid Zia ed-Din. The Tudeh heaped vilification and abuse upon him. Called a traitor and "chief of quislings," [49] he was compared to Hitler and branded "fascist" and "reactionary." In the spring of 1945 *Rahbar* went so far as to demand that Zia be punished, threatening that "if the government will not do it, then the Tudeh will take matters into its own hands."

The Communists have recognized a potential source of strength in the minority groups of Iran. They have persistently appealed to them as loyal and worthy citizens and have won a measure of support from such groups as the Armenians and the Assyrians. Regionally concentrated peoples, such as the Kurds and the Azerbaijanis, are of peculiar importance to Communist plans. Although propaganda

---

[45] *Rahbar,* May 29, 1945, in an article entitled "Bahrein Is a Part of Iranian Territory."

[46] Even M. Godard, French Director of the Teheran Archeological Museum, and an utterly nonpolitical figure, was made an object of Communist attack. He was called "Dr. Millspaugh No. 2" by *Iran-i-Ma* in two articles on March 1 and 4, 1945.

[47] Typical article in *Darya,* Jan. 6, 1945, analyzing conditions of labor in the Abadan refinery. For a standard Soviet attitude toward the Anglo-Iranian, see the following articles in *New Times,* Moscow: "Through the Oil Districts of Southwestern Iran," nos. 11 and 12, 1946; "Three Weeks in Iran," by Vera Inber, no. 17, 1946; "Southern Iran Again," by M. Sergeyev, no. 20, 1946.

[48] Nov. 19, 1944.

[49] *Mardom,* March 8, 1944; *Rahbar,* May 7, 1945; *Mardom-i-Kar,* May 6, 1944.

among the Kurds has apparently produced no lasting results and has been left rather to the direct action of Soviet agents, the Azerbaijanis have proved more susceptible in view of their pronounced regional aspirations. As we shall see later, it was in Azerbaijan that the greatest effort of the Tudeh was focused in 1945. In this connection it is worth while mentioning that the Tudeh deputies in the Majlis invariably posed as defenders of the northern provinces anxious to eliminate government inefficiency and corruption. Acting in this manner, they endeavored to monopolize northern representation although they constituted only a minority of the deputies from the Soviet zone.

Perhaps the most ambitious of all Tudeh moves before the Azerbaijan crisis in 1945 was the attempt to extend its influence in the south. In 1944 increased agitation of the party led to bloody disturbances in Isfahan and occupation of the factories by the workers. This, in turn, led to the suppression of the Tudeh in Isfahan during the spring of 1945.

In all circumstances the Tudeh unswervingly maintained its loyalty to the Soviet cause. On no point did the party press editorials differ from the Soviet point of view. As long as Soviet policy manifested its restraint in criticizing the West (1941–1943), the Tudeh press was also cautious in its tone. When disagreements between the Soviets and the West became more conspicuous, the Tudeh increased its anti-Western hostility and began to indulge in more open attacks against the Anglo-Saxon powers. At the same time the Tudeh steadfastly denied that any contact existed between it and the Soviet authorities. For example, *Rahbar* asserted on May 7, 1944:

There seems to be an established opinion that the Tudeh Party is an organ of Soviet Communists. . . . Why conduct a one-sided policy? Why think that every Communist wants only the incorporation of other countries into the Soviet Union? The Tudeh works for the Iranian nation, for the maintenance of our own constitution, for the defense of Iran's independence, for the freedom of Iranian citizens. The Tudeh wants to introduce in Iran democratic principles such as they are in America. If our Party publishes pro-Soviet articles, it is because the Soviets fight well against the fascists. We are sure that the Soviet government neither intends to introduce Bolshevik government in Iran nor to occupy Iran.

Powerfully supported as it was by the presence of the Red Army in Iran and by parallel Soviet official propaganda, the Tudeh between 1942 and the fall of 1944 gained more and more adherents and increased its influence. To be sure, it never gained the confidence of the majority of the people, nor could it ever dream of achieving this goal, but as a disciplined and determined group it was able to exert influence incommensurate with its actual numbers. The antiquated social and economic system of Iran, the great need for agrarian reform and for curbing the privileges of aristocracy, certainly created ideal conditions for the development of any extremist movement. If the Tudeh had been a genuine nationalist-patriotic party, not affiliated with foreign interests, perhaps it might have had better chances of ultimate success. As an instrument of Soviet policy, it obviously made enemies not only among the reactionaries but even among those who desired a radical reform in the country. The turning point in the party's popularity was undoubtedly the oil crisis of 1944. The open manner in which the party press supported the Soviet viewpoint opened the eyes of a number of previously misguided individuals. Many of those who initially were not too sure of their loyalties deserted the party. To remain in the Tudeh ranks after the Kavtaradze visit signified an indoctrinated Communist or a bribed sympathizer. Patriotic Iranians, even of a radical tinge, could see no reason why progress and reform should demand the alienation of national property to foreign hands.[50]

Despite this "crisis of confidence," the party was not discarded by the Russians. On the contrary, continuous and even more intensive use was made of its services culminating in the Azerbaijan revolt in 1945. Of these things more will be said in the last chapter.[51]

[50] In this sense *Neda-yi-Adalat,* Jan. 25, 1945.

[51] The author is indebted to the *Middle East Journal* for permission to quote, in the above section, from his article, "The Communist Movement in Iran," which appeared in the January, 1947, issue, pp. 29–45.

CHAPTER NINE

Elements of Opposition

to Soviet Schemes

NATIVE CONSERVATISM AND NATIONALISM

ELEMENTS of opposition to the Soviet policy were manifold. The first important element was the Iranian government itself. Whatever may be said about its efficiency or the honesty of its employees, the fact remains that it was the government that shouldered the burden of maintaining security, collecting taxes, and securing adequate supplies whenever food was scarce. Thus it was the government and its provincial representatives that daily had to face all the complications resulting from direct Soviet obstructionism or from anarchy produced by the more violent activities of the Tudeh. The responsibility of the government will appear even more pronounced if it is realized that until the arrival of Seyyid Zia ed-Din from exile in the fall of 1943 there was no organized political movement that opposed Communism ideologically. The small political parties that had been formed prior to Seyyid Zia's arrival could not be considered a match for the Tudeh, closely knit itself and fully conscious of its aims. The absence of organized political opposition to the Communists became very obvious during the parliamentary elections in the fall of 1943.

Government action against Soviet influence expressed itself in many ways. Of course, most drastic was direct army or police intervention against the Tudeh. In Teheran and in the south the government was generally successful in applying force against the Tudeh demonstrations. Police would break up some of the menacing meetings or even occasionally raid the Tudeh headquarters and temporarily detain unruly individuals. In the north, however, the police were practically powerless in view of the generous protection assured to the Tudeh by Soviet troops. Suspension was, as we know, another weapon of the government. But recourse to this means was not always free from foreign interference. The Soviet Embassy intervened actively in these press matters and itself often demanded the suspension of a paper hostile to Communism. Thus despite the basic community of interests with the nationalists, the government was obliged to suspend many a newspaper belonging to Seyyid Zia ed-Din's party. These suspensions were only a temporary expedient, and in the foregoing chapter we have seen how they could be evaded. Nor could police action be considered as adequate to combat Communism. It was clear that an ideology or an organized political action could be fought only by another ideology represented by properly organized groups.

Several forces contributed to the "ideological" anti-Communist front. Starting from the summit of the Iranian hierarchy, we may mention the Court. The Court not only exerted a political influence; it also acted as a symbol. The institution of monarchy is deeply ingrained in the Iranian mentality of both the lower and the upper classes. The young Shah himself was reputed to be endowed with quick intelligence and a perceptive mind. He lacked, of course, the strength and experience of his father, but he managed to maintain his prestige. His influence was said to be strongest among army officers.

Pursuing a policy designed to enhance his prestige, the young Shah undertook three important journeys during the war period. Accompanied by numerous court attendants, he went to Isfahan in 1943. He was received in this ancient capital with due pomp and ceremony. His trip was linked to the difficult situation prevailing at that time in Isfahan's textile factories, wherein Communist propaganda had made important headway. His journey resulted in the creation of several company unions. Temporarily, at least, this curbed the Tudeh's hold on the workers. Later, in the fall of the same year, the Shah traveled to Meshed, capital of the northeastern province of Khorasan. According to the Anglo-Soviet agreement of 1941, Meshed was to be in a neutral zone, but in fact it was occupied by the Red Army. Khorasan thus faced the same troubles from Soviet occupation as did other northern provinces. The sovereign's journey into this "forbidden area" was, therefore, a rather daring exploit. The trip certainly did not please the Soviet authorities, who were persistently trying to lower the prestige of the traditional institutions among the populace. Yet an outright refusal to permit the Shah to travel through this territory could only be of doubtful value. News of it would have reverberated throughout the country, probably causing much indignation. Moreover, Meshed is a holy city of pilgrimages and the site of the tomb of one of the Shiite Imams as well. Therefore, a journey to it had not only an administrative but also a religious character. And, as we have pointed out earlier, Soviet propaganda tried to create a favorable impression with regard to religious tolerance in the Soviet Union. The third journey was undertaken in the summer of 1944. The Shah then visited Shiraz, and again passed through Isfahan, which for the second time was a scene of grave disorders provoked by the Tudeh.

The Shah also made efforts to gain more influence with the administration. Until the winter of 1942–1943 no special machinery for maintaining liaison between the Court and the cabinet existed. Ceremonious functions were taken care of by the Chief of Protocol, Mohammed Bahador, who combined his duties in the Ministry of Foreign Affairs with those of master of ceremonies at the Court. Upon his death toward the end of 1942, however, a new position of Minister of the Court was created. It was entrusted to Hosein Ala, former diplomat and Governor of the Bank-i-Melli Iran. Ala rapidly asserted himself as an important personage in public life. Furthermore, a faithful servant of the crown, Ibrahim Zand, former Controller of Royal Palaces, was entrusted with the portfolio of War in December, 1943. Through these appointments the Shah was reputed to have secured personal influence both in the government and the army.

Perhaps the weakest link of the Court was with public opinion. Whereas scores of newspapers worked for the Soviet or British cause, one paper only could be described as a mouthpiece of the Court. This was the daily *Kayhan,* edited by a young professor of law at Teheran University, Paris-trained Dr. Mesbah-zadeh.

The nationalist newspapers did not support the Shah as much as could be expected. Although devoted to the preservation of the basic state structure as a defensive measure against foreign encroachments, they did not necessarily identify the youthful ruler with the institution of monarchy. Thus the anti-Soviet *Ra'd-i-Emruz* wrote on January 31, 1944, in an article entitled "The Shah and Ourselves":

> The cardinal mistake of our rulers was the fact that they never paid attention to public opinion. When the present Shah ascended to the throne, the nation hoped that he would not continue his father's policy, because he had been trained abroad. We are not against the present policy of the Shah. But if he surrounds himself only with people who misinform him, people of the old regime, no advantages will accrue to the nation. At present there is no man in the Shah's environment who enjoys the love, respect, and confidence of the nation. The Shah must part with these men who do not care for the welfare of the people.

The army, as a force loyal to the sovereign, was naturally another strong center of anti-Communist feeling. Its social composition predestined it to represent a conservative viewpoint. Despite its well-known failure to oppose the Anglo-Soviet invasion in 1941, the General Staff stubbornly refused to consider any reduction of its effectives. The Iranian Military Academy commissioned large numbers of officers every year. For example, in September, 1943, 515 cadets were promoted to second-lieutenancies. This number would be considerable even in a country much larger than Iran. On the whole the army, notwithstanding obvious abuses by some greedy officers, presented a rather coherent unit, which could act as a deterrent against Communism.

From the Communist angle the proper policy would have been to exploit class differences in the army ranks. Yet the reported Tudeh endeavors in this direction met with no apparent success.

In contrast, the definite attempts made by Soviet agents to woo officers to their side did bear fruit. This clandestine work took place mainly in garrisons stationed in the northern provinces. It resulted in a small-scale revolt of several younger officers of the Khorasan Division in the late summer of 1945. The officers equipped themselves with a number of trucks, stole a quantity of arms and munitions, and joined hands with two thousand armed warriors of the Turkoman Yamut tribe. In a few localities small army detachments followed them. Thus reinforced, the rebels began operations for control of Khorasan. Regular army units were sent to quell the revolt. A few tense days of uncertainty followed, insofar as it was not known what the reaction of Soviet authorities would be. The *Journal de Tehran* expressed the prevalent mood with the usual caution and servility:

> If freedom of action is given to the Khorasan garrison, it will be able by concentrating forces at dangerous points to put an end to this sedition rapidly. It is the duty of the Minister of Foreign Affairs to solve this problem as soon as possible. We are absolutely certain that our neighbors, who are animated towards us by perfect friendship and sincerity, do not in any way desire the forces of disorder to flare up in this region.[1]

It is not quite clear what degree of freedom was enjoyed by the Iranian army in this connection. At any rate an engagement took place between the rebels and the army on August 21 at Gonbad-i-Kabus, a locality where the rebel force tried to capture gendarmerie headquarters. The army had the upper hand. This skirmish seemingly put an end to further rebellion. According to a communiqué of the General Staff, the rebellious officers were to be degraded and court-martialed. In addition, a light purge affecting twenty-four other officers was carried out. These men were transferred from the north to the south. A military investigating commission under General Hedayat was also dispatched to Meshed to report on the whole affair. During the next few days the press was replete with news of the army's reaction to these events. Officers of various divisions and garrisons sent telegrams to the Shah expressing disgust with what had happened and renewing solemnly their oath of fealty toward the sovereign and the country.

Another element of strong anti-Communist opposition was the Mohammedan clergy. The old government of Reza Shah pursued a

[1] Aug. 20, 1945.

policy of thinly disguised hostility toward the clergy, but it did not succeed in dispersing the Shia organization or in killing the spirit of devotion and fanaticism. As a result, as soon as the old regime collapsed, the clergy raised its head.

Opposed both to Westernism and to Communism, the Shia divines strove, throughout the war, to restore their influence and prestige among the masses. Consequently they waged a campaign against European dress and for the reintroduction of veils for women. They opposed secular education and insisted upon the revival of religious training. In some cases they appealed to the faithful not to read newspapers, which too often represented antireligious or indifferent tendencies. They also worked for the revival of ancient customs such as the ceremonious self-flagellation that had been forbidden by Reza Shah. In this offensive the Shiite hierarchy was generally successful. Step by step it gained new positions or regained old ones.

By and large the government tried to accommodate them. Several official measures may be mentioned in this connection. First of all, Mohammed Sadr, an elder statesman and a former mullah, was appointed Minister of Justice in the Soheily cabinet in 1943 and from that time continued to play an important role in succeeding cabinets throughout the war. In September, 1943, Sadr was appointed administrator of the great Sepah Salar mosque in Teheran while retaining his ministerial functions. At the same time a Theological Faculty was inaugurated in the same mosque, and it was given the status of a department of Teheran University. This important decision was followed by the granting of official permission to hold a self-flagellating procession on September 22, the anniversary of the death of Amir-al-Mu'minin, one of the Shiite martyrs, and a day of national religious mourning. The next step was taken in December of the same year when by government decree a Council of Ten on Religious Studies was formed. The council was composed of various government and Court dignitaries. The protection that the government bestowed on religion was well illustrated by an incident that took place toward the end of 1943. An Iranian pilgrim went to Mecca to prostrate himself before the Holy Temple of Kaaba. Exhausted by the long journey he suddenly became sick in the presence of the devout crowds assembled near the Kaaba. The reaction of the mob was violent. The unfortunate pilgrim was accused of sacrilege, dragged before a local religious judge, summarily tried, and promptly beheaded in the presence of his despairing wife. When the news reached Teheran in January, 1944, indignation was widespread among both the Iranian press and Shiite clergy. Mullah Ayatollah Isfahani, one of the leading dignitaries of the Shiite hierarchy, appealed directly to the Shah for protection of the Iranian faithful. Consequently the Iranian Ambassador in Cairo was instructed to lodge a strong protest with the Saudi Arabian government and to ask for indemnity as well as for adequate guarantees against the repetition of similar incidents.

Throughout this period the Shia dignitaries maintained a lively contact with the government. In 1943 a famous doctor of Shiite theology, Haji Aga Hosein Qumi, arrived in Teheran from Iraq. Qumi had been *persona non grata* under the old regime and was obliged to live in exile in Najef and Karbela, the two Shiite centers of Iraq. Upon his arrival in the capital he was greeted enthusiastically by a number of clerical and lay dignitaries and was visited personally by Prime Minister Ali Soheily. The head of the Moslem hierarchy in Teheran, Malayeri, as well as several Grand Ulemas from the provinces were frequently received by the Shah.

Thus encouraged by the friendly official attitude, the Shia hierarchy did not hesitate to intensify and expand its activities. In 1942 a Society for the Propagation of Islam was founded with branches in all cities of Iran. Between 1942 and 1944 alone the Society published eleven large volumes of religious works totaling 60,000 copies. Its press organ was *Nur-i-Danesh* ("The Light of Knowledge"), a richly illustrated periodical. Under the auspices of the society a new weekly entitled *Islam* began to appear in March, 1944.[2] Following this trend, in May, 1945, the daily paper *Vazife* inaugurated special weekly editions exclusively devoted to matters relating to the Mohammedan religion and ethics.

The clergy also combated the Communist offensive vigorously. We have pointed out earlier the line Soviet propaganda adopted in the matter of religion. This propaganda trying to present the Soviet Union as a country of tolerance and freedom for all denominations

[2] For details of the society's activity see *Islam*, March 25, 1944.

did not fit well with the activities of the Tudeh, whose policy in this respect was vacillating. Sometimes the Tudeh openly attacked the mullahs.[3] On other occasions, however, the party made attempts to approach the Shiite hierarchy in a friendly manner and to proclaim its positive attitude toward religion. It is not improbable that the Communists managed to win over a few individuals, but there is no evidence that they made any headway with the bulk of the clergy. On the contrary, the Shia divines were the first to see through Soviet and Communist tactics and were the most persistent and uncompromising in their opposition to Communist influence. Mullah Qumi from Najef and Karbela made it quite clear upon his arrival in Teheran that he disapproved of the Tudeh because its activity was contrary to Islam.[4] The nationalist papers, especially those affiliated with the party of Seyyid Zia ed-Din, frequently took issue with the Tudeh on account of its antireligious stand.[5]

SEYYID ZIA ED-DIN

Considering the hold that the clergy had on the Iranian masses, their anti-Communist attitude was an important element in the political game. If all Iranians had shared the religious devotion of the peasantry, ideologically the opposition of the clergy alone would have been sufficient to present the Russians with a truly united front. But this was not the case. Many Western-trained individuals had become skeptical in matters of religion, and some indifference prevailed among city dwellers. If Communist propaganda was to be met with effective countermeasures, a definitely anti-Communist political party was needed. Between 1941 and 1943 no such party existed, and the burden of opposing Communism fell upon the shoulders of the elements previously mentioned. But in 1943 the gap was filled. In September of that year former Premier Seyyid Zia ed-Din returned from exile and began to rally around himself anti-Communist elements. When the news of his impending return spread in Teheran, some papers greeted him with effusion. *Setareh,* for example, a daily reputed later to be close to Dr. Millspaugh, wrote an article entitled,

[3] *Rahbar,* Nov. 29, 1944.
[4] *Tehran-i-Mossavar,* Sept. 9, 1943.
[5] A typical article in *Ra'd-i-Emruz,* March 12, 1944.

"A Ray of Hope in the Darkness," which praised the exiled leader and welcomed his promised return.[6]

Upon Seyyid Zia's arrival a new political party called *Vatan* ("Fatherland") was created. Its press organ was first *Karavan* and later *Ra'd-i-Emruz*. In the fall of 1943 Seyyid Zia ran for parliament and was elected deputy by a substantial majority from the Yazd constituency. His campaign was made on a personal basis, and no other deputies in the Majlis were known as officially representing Vatan. After more than a year Vatan changed its name to *Eradeh-yi-Melli* ("National Will"), which was officially inaugurated as a new party in January, 1945. Seyyid Zia ed-Din established his headquarters in the sumptuous building of the former Club Iran on Sa'di Avenue in Teheran. Soon its offices and lobbies were full of functionaries and visitors. Large rooms equipped with "functional" conference furniture constituted an ideal setting for party meetings.

Eradeh-yi-Melli established a specific organization different from that of other small Iranian parties, and similar perhaps only to the Tudeh. Its basic unit was a "circle" (*halqeh*) composed of nine men and a chief. Nine such circles constituted a "group" (*rabet*) under a higher chief. Chiefs of groups were appointed by the Secretary General of the party. They were to meet in monthly conferences called "the little parliament" in every city where the party existed. In March, 1945, the first national congress of the party, called "the great parliament," was held in Teheran. Eighty-one delegates, primarily from Teheran, were present. The congress elected party officers. The rather honorary position of President was bestowed upon Reza Quli Hedayat (Nur ol-Molk), a former cabinet minister. Seyyid Zia retained for himself the key post of Secretary General.[7] The program of Eradeh-yi-Melli reflected all the characteristics of liberal progressivism. It included equality and freedom for all Iranian citizens; a higher standard of living; reform of education; reform of administration and justice; improved health standards; advanced agrarian reform including the division of state domains among the

---

[6] April 7, 1943.

[7] Other members of the Central Committee were Hosein Kashef and Ali Ashgar Fruzan, vice-presidents; Sadig Sarmand, editor of the *Seda-yi-Iran;* Baha ed-Din Pazargad, editor of the *Khorshid-i-Iran;* Samad Issa Beiglu; and Hasan Mo'asser.

peasants and revision of the share-cropping system; agricultural improvements and irrigation, and establishment of a state agrarian bank; development of industry and natural resources; reform of the financial system; reform of the armed forces, and the like.

Aside from these points common to most of the political parties, Eradeh-yi-Melli advocated a few more unusual policies. These were: stronger defense of the political and economic independence of Iran; friendly treatment of the tribes; defense of Islam; introduction of religious teaching into the school programs; and a foreign policy of eternal neutrality for Iran, following the Swiss pattern.[8]

Seyyid Zia did not make a secret of his anti-Communist feelings. His press organs waged a relentless struggle against the Tudeh, accusing it of treason, subversive activities, antireligious propaganda, violence, sabotage, hooliganism, and hypocrisy.[9] The invectives used by Seyyid Zia's press against the Communists were as strong as those addressed to him by the Tudeh. But it is noteworthy that until the oil crisis of the fall of 1944 Seyyid Zia's newspapers carefully avoided direct attacks on the Soviet Union. *Ra'd-i-Emruz* took pains to stress the basic friendliness of Iran toward Russia, pointing out that it expected honest reciprocity in this respect. These newspapers lamented the activities of the Tudeh, which they claimed confused good relations between the two countries. Regrets were expressed that an utterly irresponsible group endeavored to monopolize friendship toward the great northern neighbor.[10] Hope was occasionally voiced that the Soviet authorities would not give undue credence to the Tudeh and thus prevent unnecessary complications.[11] Such differentiation between the Tudeh and the Soviet Union could not fail to be rather artificial. From the practical point of view, however, it provided a good cloak to hide disapproval of Soviet policies without incurring the blame for directly attacking an Ally.

Increased Soviet pressure on Iran in the fall of 1944 finally provoked an open counteroffensive by Seyyid Zia ed-Din. *Ra'd-i-Emruz*

[8] *Ra'd-i-Emruz*, Feb. 19, 1945; *ibid.*, May 27, 1945. See also the pamphlet *Eradeh-yi-Melli* (Teheran, 1945).

[9] *Ra'd-i-Emruz*, Dec. 31, 1944, accused the Tudeh of having put fire to the Teheran silo and to the building of the A.I.O.C.

[10] *Ibid.*, Sept. 22, 1944.

[11] *Arzu*, Nov. 28, 1944.

and affiliated organs began to publish vivid descriptions of conditions prevailing in the Soviet zone of occupation, as well as protests against expulsions, deportations, or killings of Iranians in that area. The Soviet Embassy was accused of undue interference in internal affairs. Attention was drawn to "suspect types" armed by a foreign power and imported in great numbers to Teheran to prepare for revolution. The most obvious point of criticism was, of course, the behavior of Kavtaradze and the Soviet oil demands. In an impressive declaration published in December, 1944, Seyyid Zia lashed the Soviet emissary and forcefully attacked Communist methods. He accused Russia of seeking *Lebensraum* and threatening Iranian integrity and expressed the conviction that no foreign intrigue would induce the Iranians to change their religion and loyalty.[12]

The strong stand taken by Seyyid Zia during the oil crisis increased his popularity and the number of his adherents. The resentment that many "independent" Iranian nationalists felt against him for his pro-British attitude gave way now to an appreciation of his political realism. Even for those who disliked the British it became more and more obvious that in the Big-Power rivalry in Iran the Russians were on the offensive and that unless Iran sought support from the West it eventually would share the fate of eastern Europe. Seyyid Zia himself seized this opportunity to expose his views more candidly. One of his papers made the following statement under the title, "What Is the Meaning of the Word 'Freedom'?"

There are two imperialisms: British and Soviet. The British imperialism does not seek further gains and is satisfied with the *status quo*. The Russian imperialism, on the contrary, desires to enlarge Russia's dominance. . . . If our nation is resolved to resist illegal Soviet influence and its interference in internal affairs, Great Britain will certainly be faithful to her pledges and will defend Iran's independence. If, however, we shall cede without resistance before force, then Great Britain will also try to secure some gains for herself at the expense of Iran. If we allow our northern provinces to be overpowered by Communism, Great Britain will take over our southern provinces, and then Iran will be partitioned.[13]

12 *Ra'd-i-Emruz*, Dec. 20, 1944. For text see Appendix no. IV.
13 *Sargozasht* (published temporarily in place of the suspended *Hur*), Jan. 16, 1945.

On another occasion Seyyid Zia indicated that it may be necessary to ask not only Great Britain but also the United States for active military help. Invoking the guarantee of Iranian independence given by the Big Three in Teheran in 1943, *Ra'd-i-Emruz* wrote on January 10, 1945:

Mr. Iraj Iskandari, Professor Gonabadi, Prince Kambakhsh, and you, the celebrated Professor Radmanesh: Tell us under whose protectorate did you organize the demonstration of Aban 5th? Do you think that after so many scandals and intrigues we shall allow you to carry out a revolution? . . . No, my dear sirs, the Iranian nation will not permit it, and if need arises, we shall ask the American and British armies to come to our aid. We will not be ashamed to ask others for help. France, Belgium, Norway, Poland and other states requested aid from their Allies, and some of these countries have already regained their independence.

The first half of 1945 witnessed a growing bitterness in the mutual denunciations of Seyyid Zia's camp and the Communists. The end of the war in Europe placed a new weapon in the hands of the nationalist leader, the demand for speedy evacuation of Iran by foreign troops. On this point his voice could be heard unchallenged as the pro-Soviet press maintained stubborn silence.

What was the basis of Seyyid Zia's strength? Was it only British support? To make such an allegation would be to ignore completely Iranian nationalism and the fear of Soviet domination prevailing in the country.[14] Concretely, Seyyid Zia derived his main strength from alliance with the clergy, merchants, landowners, and tribes.

Nor did he ignore the Majlis. A deputy himself, he worked steadily among the deputies. By the spring of 1945 he enjoyed the support of a substantial voting block numbering about thirty-seven members. It is noteworthy, however, that this block did not include the name of Dr. Mosaddeq, author of the anticoncession oil law. Hence,

---

[14] Seyyid Zia was supported by a coalition of newspapers called first the "National Front" and later the "Independence Front." The following dailies and periodicals belonged to it: *Karavan, Qanun, Ra'd-i-Emruz, Sargozasht, Keshvar, Hur, Ettela'at-i-Iran, Tehran-i-Mossavar, Bakhtar, Mard-i-Emruz, Setareh, Asr-i-Eqtesad, Khorush, Vazife, Yo-Yo, Nameh-yi-Azad, Azad, Neda-yi-Asemani, Arzu, Nasim-i-Shomal, Khorshid-i-Iran, Ṣeda-yi-Iran, Kuṣhesh, Nahid, Sa'ad-i-Bashiar, Taqadaqi,* and *Nasim-i-Sabah,*

Seyyid Zia was not able to rally around himself all opposition against Soviet influence.

THE TRIBES

One-fourth of the Iranian population still lives in a state of tribal nomadism. The exertion of the central government's authority over these tribes has been a chronically difficult problem. Shah Reza managed, with his ruthless determination, to make them at least outwardly obedient to the government. Yet despite his determined policy the basic social structure of the tribes remained unchanged; nor were they entirely deprived of arms. His regime's collapse permitted the tribal chieftains to reassert their position. The defeat of Iranian armies at the hands of the Russians and the British in 1941 allowed the tribesmen to buy or capture substantial quantities of arms and munitions from the demoralized Iranian units. Hidden weapons were also recovered from the caches, and thus by 1942 the tribes re-emerged as a powerful force that no government and no foreign power interested in Iran could ignore.

In time of peace the survival of tribal structure obviously provided an impediment to the progress and modernization of Iran and as such constituted a source of serious weakness. But in time of stress the tribes could be regarded as a source of national strength. The tribal social structure was, despite all attempts to destroy it, stronger and more durable than the official fabric of the Iranian state. In the chaos, anarchy, and uncertainty that has characterized Iran since 1941, the tribes have remained relatively untouched by the general collapse and in some measure could be relied upon as a factor of stability.

Such a statement gives a somewhat oversimplified picture. In reality, despite their basic "stability," the tribes contributed in no small degree to the general confusion and disorder. Their clannish narrow-mindedness, tribal rather than national loyalties, greed, and readiness to resort to violence were the essential factors in this respect.

Their stabilizing influence could be felt on a local provincial scale rather than on a national scale. In other words, nothing or little could be done in certain areas without the approval or co-operation of the tribes. With regard to those foreign powers with special interests in Iran, such a state of affairs necessitated a second diplomacy, that of tribal relations, in addition to the normal Teheran diplomacy conducted on government levels. In fact, each contender for influence in the Middle East was compelled to reckon with this powerful tribal factor.

The Iranian government had to face the tribal problem following the Anglo-Soviet invasion. Both in the British and in the Soviet zones some tribes revolted. The government attempted to bring them to submission. In the south the powerful tribe of Qashqais, led by two members of the old Ilkhani family, Nasir and Khosro Khans, rebelled in the spring of 1943. The tribe demanded from the government the restitution of those tribal land properties illegally confiscated as a punitive measure by Reza Shah. The tribe, whose "capital" is Firuzabad in the province of Fars, lives and wanders in the vicinity of Shiraz, but in this rebellion it extended its operations to the area adjacent to Isfahan. Trying first to settle the quarrel by diplomacy, the government sent General Firuz to negotiate with the rebels, but the mission failed. In June, 1943, the Qashqais inflicted a heavy defeat on the army, capturing the fort of Samirom and killing its garrison of 200 men including three colonels. Following this episode, the government once again resorted to diplomacy. By August, 1943, agreement was reached, and the rebellion died down. Negotiations with the rebels were conducted in co-operation with the British Legation. Major-General W. A. K. Fraser, British military attaché, was actually known to have been in touch with both sides in his attempts to bring about a peaceful solution.

The north was also a scene of tribal unrest. There the Kurdish tribes challenged government authority all through the war and frequently raided villages on the Azerbaijan Plateau, especially in the vicinity of Lake Urumia. In 1943 violent riots broke out in and around Rezaieh, and in 1944 Kurdistan suffered the turmoil of a large-scale revolt conducted by Hama Rashid. Eventually the rebellion was quelled, with the aid of some Kurdish tribes such as the Javanrudi that co-operated with the government. Rashid saved himself by crossing the Iraqi border. He was to reappear after the end of the war and to play a prominent role in the dramatic developments of 1945–1946 in Kurdistan.

Thus the government was never free from worry and complications with regard to tribal affairs. More important, however, was the connection of the Big Powers with the tribes and their attitudes toward the tribal rebellions.

During the war Russia played a somewhat more limited role than Britain with regard to tribes. But this role should not be overlooked. First of all, the Russians controlled Azerbaijan with her Kurdish centers all along the Iraqi border. Important Kurdish towns such as Mahabad, Baneh, Saqqiz, Khoi, and Maku were in their zone. Secondly, the Russians extended their control over Iranian Turkoman tribes located east of the Caspian Sea. Of these two groups the Kurds were politically more important because of their sheer numbers in the Soviet zone and because of their well-known and traditional aspirations for independence. In addition, anything done in Iranian Kurdistan was bound to have repercussions in the Kurdish areas of Turkey and Iraq and could thus vitally affect international relations. The Big Powers' activity among the Kurds during the second World War would deserve a special study. It suffices to say here that this activity was full of complicated intrigue that made it difficult in some cases to discern who was the real source of inspiration behind one or another Kurdish move. The Russians consistently endeavored to woo the Kurds to their side and to render them hostile to the British and the Iranian governments. In 1942 several Kurdish chiefs were invited to visit Baku. After their return it was asserted that some of them were ready to play the Russian game. As compensation the Russians dangled before them the promise of Kurdish autonomy. The Soviet Consulate at Rezaieh was very active. The importance attached to the Kurdish question by the Russians could be measured by the fact that the chief of the Soviet Embassy's propaganda section, Press Attaché Danil Komissarov, was detailed to Rezaieh as consul for eight months in 1944. The Russians seemed to attach prime importance to the Kurdish tribal center of Mahabad (formerly Sauj Bulaq), seat of the influential chieftain Qazi Mohammed. In Mahabad an irregular paper, *Nisht Man,* was published in the Kurdish language under Soviet auspices.

[249]

The fact that the southern part of Iranian Kurdistan was in the British zone added special flavor to the Kurdish question. Through their consulate in Kermanshah the British maintained constant contact with the tribes. A number of experienced agents served British interests in this area. Colonel Fletcher and Major Lyons acted as political officers. Major Oakshot, manager of the Sanandaj branch of the Imperial Bank of Iran, was also reputed to apply his knowledge of local conditions to further official British policies in this area. The success of British and Soviet policies in their respective zones could, to some extent, be measured by the fact that Sadraq Qazi, deputy from Mahabad in the Majlis and brother of Mohammed Qazi, revealed a pro-Soviet orientation whereas three deputies from the British zone, Abbas Gobadian, Salar Sanandaji, and Dr. Moiaven, were definitely pro-British and belonged to the block supporting Seyyid Zia ed-Din in the parliament. It was asserted that the relative ease with which the British forces marched into Iran along the Qasr-i-Shirin–Kermanshah line in 1941, and the rapid disintegration of Iranian resistance, were in no small part due to the preliminary work of British agents among the Kurds.

The British had good reasons to cultivate Kurdish friendship. The area in question was strategically important. If the Nazis were to break through the Caucasus range, a grave possibility in 1942, the Kurdish regions would have had to be crossed. On the other hand, any Soviet thrust to the Persian Gulf would lead through the Kermanshah-Khanaqin line, which also runs in the Kurdish territory. In both cases, if only for defensive purposes, it was in the highest interest of the British to be on friendly terms with the local tribes. The British-controlled oil installations situated in the Kurdish areas of Iraq and Iran afforded an additional reason. Both the security of these installations and the success of labor-management relations depended on the success of the British tribal policy.

What has been said about the British cultivating friendship with the Kurds may be applied also to the British policy among other tribes of Iran. The stability of the tribes in contrast to the weakness of the Iranian government determined British policy in this respect. In Teheran governments might change, undergo strange convulsions, and become subject to foreign pressures occasionally inimical to the

British. But as long as tribal structure was preserved, these developments did not seriously affect the tribes and the areas under their control. This was especially obvious in the southern tribes. The British traditionally kept an eye on the tribes on the Iranian and Arab sides of the Persian Gulf. British diplomacy in this region radiated from the Residency in Bushire.

The region to which the British traditionally gave most of their attention was Khuzistan, a province inhabited largely by Arab tribes and the area of the Anglo-Iranian Oil Company's concession. At the time when the concession was established it was unthinkable to do anything in the area without the knowledge and approval of Sheikh Khazal of Mohammerah. It was also necessary to keep in friendly touch with the powerful tribe of Bakhtiyaris, who, if hostile, were apt to endanger the security of oil installations. The pro-German attitude of some Bakhtiyari chiefs during World War I resulted in the puncturing of a number of pipe lines and taught the British a lesson. It impressed upon them the necessity of exercising a skill in their relations with the tribes. To cope with this situation the British arranged with the Bakhtiyaris to grant their chiefs a regular subsidy amounting to 3 per cent of the Anglo-Iranian's income. This was intended to eliminate Bakhtiyari mischief and to make them the guardians rather than saboteurs of the pipe lines. The policy toward the Sheikh of Mohammerah was that of supporting him whenever he wanted to assert his autonomy both vis-à-vis Iran and, later, Iraq. The advent of Reza Shah spoiled this mutually profitable arrangement, and because of the ruthless centralizing policy of the Shah, Sheikh Khazal was obliged to flee Iran. He was given sanctuary in British-controlled Iraq. He never ceased to dream about his return and the future autonomy of his area. We shall see him reappear on the political scene of Iran in the winter of 1945–1946.

The support extended to Khazal was often criticized as an example of British perfidy and basic insincerity toward the Iranian government. Soviet sources were especially outspoken in this respect. The accusation as formulated was that, while pretending to defend the independence of Iran and to support the authority of its central government, the British were really sapping the very foundations of the Iranian state by promoting tribal identity. Such an accusation

[251]

does not seem, however, to be quite fair. British moves were acts of sheer political realism. In their transactions with Iran they dealt with central or local authorities. If the central authority proved to be unreliable and weak, negotiations with local authorities were conducted. Since this authority was frequently centered in the tribes, it became necessary to deal with them. There is no evidence of any long-range British policy to weaken purposely the central Iranian government in order to increase the strength of the tribes. The support given to Sheikh Khazal may seem to prove the contrary. Yet one should remember that, apart from giving him refuge in Iraq, the British were not prepared to challenge Reza Shah's authority in Khuzistan once it was firmly established. One should bear in mind also that any obvious extension of British control over the southern provinces would be tantamount to inviting Russia to do the same thing in the north. And such an eventuality was distinctly unpleasant to British diplomacy. To be sure, twice in the twentieth century the British were obliged to compromise with their principles by dividing Iran into two spheres of influence. This happened in 1907 and in 1941, but in both cases this solution was imposed by the *force majeure* of German aggression. During World War II British policy seemed to be dedicated definitely to the strengthening of the central government of Iran as a counterweight against Soviet infiltration. If they cultivated friendship with the tribes at the same time, they were seeking reserves to rely upon in case of the government's collapse. The events of 1946, which will be described in the last chapter, seem to support this thesis.

Apart from the consular-political center of Bushire, the British operated through a network of consulates and agents in the whole of the Iranian south. An assistant military attaché of the British Embassy, Colonel H. J. Underwood, was in special charge of tribal affairs and normally resided in Khorramshahr. Major T. Jackson and a number of political officers operated in the Qashqai and other tribal areas and kept a watchful eye on any foreigners that happened to travel there. In Luristan similar duties were discharged by Colonel Noel, famous for his encounters with Wassmuss during the first World War and with the Jangalis in Gilan in 1920. The appointment of Alan Charles Trott, a diplomat of long experience in Iran, to the post of Consul-General at Ahwaz in 1945 was generally interpreted as signifying British determination to keep Khuzistan free from the troubles besetting the Teheran authorities.

This cultivation of friendship with the tribes paid direct dividends to the British: one instance was the surrender of the German spies by the Qashqai chiefs. But the indirect gains were even more significant. The tribes, imbued with conservatism, resented radical change. The Soviet policy and the Tudeh stood for change. Hence, the tribes were naturally inclined to be hostile to Communism. The British encouraged this attitude and assisted the tribes in asserting authority whenever the central government failed to assert its own. This policy seemed to be successful.

The same considerations dictated Seyyid Zia's tactics. The nationalist leader persistently defended the cause of the tribes in the Majlis, even declaring that the tribes were fully justified in keeping arms. The tribes reciprocated. *Ra'd-i-Emruz* of April 27, 1944, published an open letter of the Qashqai and Bakhtiyari chiefs to Seyyid Zia with an acknowledgement and expression of gratitude for his action in their behalf.

The Communist press, Soviet or Iranian, repeatedly voiced criticism of these alliances. It blamed the British for arming the tribes [15] and accused the tribal leaders of separatist and anarchistic tendencies.[16] Both British intrigue and Seyyid Zia's tribal policy were subjected to a particularly strong attack by *Iran-i-Ma* on May 14, 1945, in an article entitled, "The Role of the Pro-German Qashqai Khans and Their British Friends."

Iran-i-Ma's outburst was typical of the general tendency displayed by the Communist press in 1945. This tendency represented an attempt to identify a conservative and nationalist attitude with pro-Nazi feelings and to accuse the British of fanning anti-Soviet spirit. Great Britain was thus regarded as chief villain and as the mainspring of all opposition to Soviet schemes. What had been said indirectly by Soviet agencies for the previous three years was stated openly in 1945.

[15] *Rahbar,* Jan. 24, 1945.
[16] *Ibid.,* Jan. 28, 1945; also *Darya,* Dec. 28, 1944.

BRITISH POLICIES IN IRAN DURING THE WAR

The above remarks concerning the tribes provide a convenient approach to an analysis of British policy in Iran. The tribal sector reveals several features typical of general British attitudes. These features may be listed as follows:

(1) Having occupied Iran to assure a smooth flow of supplies to Russia, the British, in the immediate sense, were primarily interested in maintaining order and security in the country. Hence they favored all conservative elements and opposed all elements threatening change, disorder, and confusion.

(2) Since oil supplies for the Royal Navy were vital in the prosecution of the war, the British opposed any radical labor tendencies that might have impeded the production of oil in Khuzistan. By the same token the British were prepared to establish agreements with the tribes to ensure the security of wells, pipe lines, and refineries.

(3) Faithful to their traditional long-range policy of treating Iran as a buffer between Russia and their possessions, the British regarded their occupation only as a wartime expedient. The permanent division of Iran into British and Soviet spheres of influence or zones of occupation did not suit their purposes. They had more to lose than to gain by such forceful division. Their losses would be: (a) the drain on the treasury of maintaining the requisite military forces; (b) the danger of Soviet proximity to India and the Persian Gulf; (c) the danger that Soviet occupation of the north might permit infiltration and bolshevization of the whole of Iran; and (d) the charge of aggressive imperialism by public opinion in the Middle East. There would be no gains to compensate these losses. Hence British policy sought to assure speedy evacuation of *all* foreign troops at the conclusion of the war.

(4) Since the British were interested in the independence of Iran, they favored the strengthening of the Iranian government. This did not keep them, however, from supporting elements that would strongly oppose subversive activities and Soviet encroachments in the event of government failure.

(5) Because Soviet policy was dedicated to forceful change, and

[254]

British favored return of the *status quo ante bellum,* the policy of the latter ran parallel to native Iranian nationalism and patriotism. The pro-British tendencies, therefore, of Seyyid Zia ed-Din or other circles could hardly be described as treason. This was in contrast to the Tudeh activities, characterized by complete subservience to Moscow as evidenced in the oil crisis.

Somewhat in contrast with Americans, the British gave plentiful evidence that they were fully conscious of the real issues involved from the very beginning of the occupation. The British realized that direct Soviet propaganda and infiltration must be counteracted by direct British action, and that indirect Soviet activities must be met by similar indirect measures. Thus, despite the outwardly cordial co-operation on higher government levels, a local but very important "cold war" was being waged in Iran between Russia and Great Britain during World War II.

In the following section an attempt will be made to describe British methods of activity, the problems confronted, the advantages and handicaps under which the British labored, and the mistakes they made.

Little needs to be said here about the indirect methods of British policy in the country during the war. In fact, all manifestations of Iranian nationalism and conservatism described in the preceding section may be regarded as an indirect method of British diplomacy, if one considers the degree of British support and encouragement of them. Iranian public opinion ascribed to the British the initiative for bringing Seyyid Zia back from exile. He was considered their anti-Communist trump card. This may not be far from the truth, especially in view of the fact that Seyyid Zia lived in British-controlled Haifa prior to his return and had to pass through equally British-controlled Iraq. Rumor also attributed to the British heavy financing of Seyyid Zia's campaign. Evidence of this is obviously lacking in view of the secrecy inherent in any such dealings, but such financial aid is highly probable. It is worth while mentioning, however, that Seyyid Zia's Vatan party appeared on the scene only in late 1943. This means, if we credit the British with the sponsorship of this movement, that they were reluctant to have recourse to such an ob-

[255]

viously anti-Communist device for a considerable period. The increasingly aggressive attitude of the Tudeh prompted them to take this decisive step.

More should be said about British direct diplomacy and propaganda. British interests in Iran were very ably represented throughout the war by Sir Reader Bullard, a diplomat of long experience in Middle Eastern and Russian affairs. Intelligent and erudite, firm and yet friendly, Sir Reader personified in his simple and unassuming manner all the best traditions of British diplomacy. Above all the British Minister (after the spring of 1944 Ambassador) knew how to impress the people with that undefinable quality that is known as prestige, his own and that of the country he represented. The wisdom of the British Foreign Office in keeping him in Iran throughout the war was uncontestable. Bullard was able to establish and maintain personal contacts with Iranian statesmen and politicians and to stand alone, in contrast to the envoys of other Powers, as a pillar of stability and permanency. In this way he could by his very presence and personal qualities repair much of the damage inflicted upon British interests in Iran by the vacillating and none too dignified policy conducted on higher levels toward Russia.

A good word could be said for the Embassy's personnel as well. It was composed partly of Foreign Office diplomats possessing world experience and culture that could not fail to impress anyone who knew them, and of men from the Indian Political Service who were area experts. The latter possessed an excellent knowledge of local conditions, customs, and language and constituted the hard core of the Embassy. Most prominent among them was perhaps Mr. Trott, the Oriental Secretary later appointed to Ahwaz. Trott was generally credited with extraordinary influence in Iranian politics. The Tudeh press chose him, among all the British, as its special personal target for criticism.

The Embassy's work was quietly conducted through the cultivation of personal contacts and through an excellent information service that experienced intelligence organs provided. The general impression that an outsider received was that of good teamwork among the Embassy, the army, and other governmental agencies. Occasionally this work was highlighted by large diplomatic receptions in Embassy rooms or gardens, but these were never so lavish as those of the Soviets.

In 1944 the Iranian Minister of Communications, Hazhir, journeyed to London. This was interpreted by observers as a manifestation of British-Iranian friendship and as an indication of postwar British interest in the railway development of Iran. The Embassy encouraged contacts between the Iranian army and air force and the British military services. Official visits to the fighting fronts and to Great Britain were organized for Iranian generals and younger officers. The British manifested their willingness to help Iran economically in the difficult war period. A special agreement between the Anglo-Iranian Oil Company and the Iranian government provided for the payment of a certain minimum of royalties, although the company was not officially obliged to pay the whole sum thereby stipulated because of the curtailment of exports in wartime. The grain supplies to Iran have already been mentioned in connection with Soviet policies. In 1943 the British Embassy presented the Iranian government with a thousand-bed hospital at the time of the typhoid epidemic. The Middle East Supply Center, an Anglo-American institution which had its branch office in Teheran, was instrumental in solving basic supply problems of Iran. It was headed in Teheran first by Lt.-Colonel Hobson, an Englishman of the A.I.O.C., and later by Colonel Harold Hoskins, an American industrialist. In the eyes of merchants and manufacturers its activity contrasted pleasantly with Soviet obstruction in north-south trade and shipments.

A word must also be said of various British charitable enterprises such as aid given to victims of the Gorgan earthquake, Red Cross activity, and the promotion of health and welfare among the tribes. With reference to the latter the activities of a Miss Palmer-Smith were notable, although rumor ascribed to her political and intelligence tasks in addition. The charitable activities of the British received less newspaper publicity than did those of the Soviet. Yet, under the specific conditions of wartime Iranian politics, it was difficult to determine in each case where charity ended and propaganda began.

This leads us to the organization of British propaganda apparatus.

All British information services were handled by the Public Relations Bureau, which was attached to the Embassy and constituted a branch of the Ministry of Information. Normally its head possessed the rank of First Secretary of the Embassy, and its ranking personnel also enjoyed diplomatic status.[17] The Bureau was divided into a number of departments such as press, photographs, exhibitions, and films. Its press section was headed by Miss A. K. Lambton, press attaché, a person with an excellent knowledge of the Persian language and politics. The Bureau was, itself, one of the most active departments of the British Embassy. It organized lectures and exhibitions. It released news to the local press and conducted a radio program. It also issued a newspaper, the *Tehran Daily News,* the only English-language paper appearing in Iran. It publicized primarily the Allied war effort and naturally stressed the British contribution. It also drew attention to the wealth and resources of the British Empire and the humane ways of British democracy. This propaganda was neither aggressive nor arrogant. No monopoly of achievement was claimed by Great Britain and even more than due share was given to other Allies, including Russia. Thus, for example, the exhibition window of the P.R.B. was more than once available to the Soviet Embassy for the display of war photographs from the Russian front. No direct criticism ever emanated from the P.R.B. with regard to any Ally. On the contrary, British propaganda endeavored to impress the Iranians with the unity and harmony prevailing in the Allied camp. The only villains were the Germans. Yet in the very stressing of British achievements and methods there was an implicit suggestion that British ways were better than the Russian. The only section of the P.R.B. that was conducting a counteroffensive against Soviet propaganda was the Press Office. This office had to handle the nationalist papers of Iran with skill and care in order to influence their editorial policies. In this sector the British seemed to be as eager as the Russians to secure the support of as many newspapers as possible. It was through newspaper editorials that the British had the opportunity to reply to Soviet attacks and to make known their own views.

[17] The P.R.B. was headed during the war by a succession of five directors, of whom Major C. A. G. Savidge of the Indian Civil Service, Lt.-Col. D. P. S. Graham, and G. Wilfrid Seager held the longest terms of office.

The Public Relations Bureau was valiantly seconded by the British Council. The latter, whose central headquarters are in London, is an institution dedicated to the spread of British culture among foreign nations. It had a permanent representative in Teheran, first in the person of J. S. Bingley and later in that of C. H. Owen. The council worked through the network of the Anglo-Persian Institutes that had been established in the capital and in some larger towns of Iran, especially in central and southern provinces. Concerts, exhibitions of British art, lectures by prominent British scholars, and excellent classical plays presented by the Anglo-Iranian Dramatic Society were frequently organized under the council's auspices. At the same time the Anglo-Persian Institutes conducted regular language courses attended by impressive numbers of the younger generation.

British propaganda carefully avoided any direct anti-Soviet references. But the very intensity of this propaganda and the large array of means to disperse it would make no sense whatsoever unless it was employed as a counterweight to the Communist offensive. It aimed at registering in Iranian minds that Great Britain was a powerful factor to be reckoned with and that she had no intention of liquidating her imperial responsibilities in the Middle East. And, despite the modesty prevailing at social gatherings in the British Embassy itself, the Public Relations Bureau was indefatigable in neutralizing any Soviet propaganda move by its own countermove. Repeated receptions, press conferences, film showings, and the like were held by the P.R.B. At times this Soviet-British competition would appear as a mad scramble for the privilege of preaching to and feeding an ever greater number of Iranians.

Unlike the Russians, the British worked under severe handicaps. Their propaganda efforts were hampered by the fact that London conducted a policy of friendship to Russia almost at any cost. This meant a readiness to accommodate Russia in many political matters and to ignore patiently many pinpricks from Moscow. In Iran it prevented the British from replying with adequate candor and firmness to Soviet anti-British moves. British propaganda, in contrast to Soviet, appeared to be on the defensive. As such it had to play second fiddle to Russian propaganda because an offensive, especially in psychological warfare, always secures better results. The British thus faced a most difficult position. They ardently desired to avoid any complications with the Russians that would vitiate the grand alliance and yet they wanted to prevent the Russian bear from eating the Persian lamb. Another handicap was the ownership of South Iranian oilfields. It made them vulnerable to the accusation of economic imperialism and labor exploitation. Again any counter-arguments were bound to be of defensive nature.

Furthermore, something in the British psychological make-up, partly inherited and partly resulting from colonial experience, prevents the British from mingling freely and fraternizing on an equal footing with Asiatics. An Englishman, whether in Egypt, India, or Iran, usually appears to the native as somewhat aloof, even if he takes pains to be courteous and friendly. This aloofness may perhaps increase his prestige with the average Iranian, but at the same time it prevents him from establishing a real communion. The net result is that the British may be respected, admired, and sometimes feared, but they are seldom loved and frequently disliked. In all fairness it should be said that heroic attempts were made by some members of the P.R.B.'s staff to remedy this situation. But these were exceptions.

Working under these handicaps, the British found it imperative to conduct a consistent, well-conceived policy and to avoid costly mistakes. Unfortunately, this was not achieved. Serious blunders erased many hard-earned gains. These mistakes, however, can hardly be ascribed to the British Embassy in Iran. They were rather the result of general attitudes prevailing in London. The first mistake was trying to convince the Iranians that perfect unity of purpose and action existed among the Allies, in particular between Russia and the West. The second was that the main if not the only war aim was to defeat Germany. Such propaganda did not appeal to the Iranians, and, with reference to the defense of the British position against Soviet action, it was definitely harmful. The politically conscious Iranians realized perfectly well that no real unity of purpose and action existed between Russia and the Western democracies. Long years of proximity to the Soviet Union and the British Empire had had its effect upon their minds and made them disillusioned and realistic. The British pretense, nay, almost maniacal insistence, that nothing divided the Allies could have only one effect upon Iranian public opinion, namely, to convince it that Britain was ready to purchase her harmony with Russia by making political compromises and concessions. This alone greatly lowered British prestige in native eyes; and, as British propaganda was restrained and defensive, Iranians deduced that the British were obviously in a weaker position and were not to be fully trusted.

The story of the Atlantic Charter is a case in point. The Charter had a tremendous effect on all smaller and oppressed nations. Originally both British and the American propaganda strongly upheld its reassuring provisions. The statement that the Western democracies sought no territorial aggrandizement and that they opposed any forceful changes was greeted as a promise and guarantee of a better future. The great merit of the Charter was that it did not blame any special country in particular, but that it enunciated general principles. In the early stages of the Allied occupation of Iran the Atlantic Charter was given due publicity. When, however, serious disagreements arose between Russia and the West over Polish and other European questions, propaganda in favor of the Charter was dropped and was replaced by emphasis upon Big Three unity. Definite instructions were sent to the Public Relations Office by the British Ministry of Information to soft-pedal Atlantic Charter publicity and to shift, instead, to a more vague "four freedoms," while insisting on the unity of the Allies.[18] As a result the Iranians, who were uncertain of their future, received artificial clichés that filled them with distrust and fear instead of reassurance that their country would be free again. The servility of many individuals toward the Soviet Union may find its psychological explanation in this fact. The noisily trumpeted enthusiasm of Allied victories over Germany, together with the complacent abandonment of half of Europe to satiate Soviet ambitions, hardly could give encouragement and hope to the Iranians. Hence in many instances instead of finding loyalty and courage, the British found treason and sheer cowardice.

It took skill on the part of local British representatives to reconcile the two contradictory tendencies of their policy: friendship with Russia on a higher level and firmness toward Russia on the Iranian

[18] Sidney Morrell, *Spheres of Influence* (New York, 1946), p. 72.

level. In such circumstances the importance of properly trained and politically conscious personnel could hardly be exaggerated. The assignment of a responsible position to an intemperate Russophobe or to a fellow-traveler could be equally dangerous. It was the misfortune of the British Embassy that for quite a long time the editorship of its official organ, the *Tehran Daily News,* was entrusted to a man with little journalistic experience and definitely appeasing tendencies. The manner in which the *Daily News* was edited should have brought a citation from the Soviet Embassy. Soviet victories on the eastern front were regularly given prominence in news of the war to the detriment of the Western war effort. Such touching stories as "Ivan the Killer" appeared not infrequently, probably with a view to encouraging Iranian love for the Russians through the medium of an English paper. Fortunately for British propaganda the editor was recalled, and the post was filled by an experienced journalist, Sidney Morrell, who was fully conscious of the issues at stake.

To conclude this chapter we may say that the opposition to Soviet schemes in Iran was greatly furthered by the British. The latter were fairly successful in those fields where liaison with native elements was required, but were in a weaker position in the field of technical propaganda. Their efforts might have been more successful if they had been properly co-ordinated with American policies. However, this co-ordination was not obtained. In Iran American moves and attitudes were apart from those of the British, although in basic wartime policy Washington and London seemed to be in complete harmony.

CHAPTER TEN

The American Role and
American Attitudes in Wartime

E VENTS of 1941 abruptly put to an end German penetration in
Iran, and a kind of vacuum was created. Under these circumstances it was only natural that the Iranians began looking for a
new partner and protector. This time the choice fell on the United
States. American policy seemed to have permanently abandoned
its old ways of isolationism. American aid to Britain and Russia
was a good augury. With the entry of the United States into the
war, no more doubt existed as to American involvement in world
affairs.

This constituted the background of Iranian-American relations in
wartime, at least so far as Iran was concerned. The *rapprochement*
between the two countries was expressed by the engagement by Iran
of a number of American advisers. Furthermore, the presence on
Iranian soil of American troops sent to speed up supplies to Russia
afforded an additional point of contact. Finally, the interest that
the United States quite formally manifested by signing the Teheran-
Iranian Communiqué was a factor of prime importance in Irano-
American relations.

AMERICAN ADVISERS

Soon after the Anglo-Russian occupation of the country, the
Iranian government invited Dr. Arthur C. Millspaugh to organize
the disordered public finances. Dr. Millspaugh, at that time sixty-
two years old, accepted what was to be his second mission to Iran

and arrived in Teheran at the end of 1942. He soon realized that to be of any aid his powers had to be extended to include not only financial but over-all economic responsibilities. He was given the title of Administrator General of Finances, which meant that his work was an executive and not merely of an advisory character. In fulfillment of his wish, the Majlis, by the so-called Law of 13th Ordibehesht 1322 (May 4, 1943), granted him the necessary powers. He was also permitted to engage sixty American economic experts. Because of technical difficulties this number was never employed at any one time, but as many as thirty-five experts were actually recruited.

Dr. Millspaugh could thus fill responsible positions in the Iranian government with Americans. Harold Gresham was appointed Director General of Customs, W. K. LeCount Treasurer General, Rex A. Pixley Director General of Internal Revenue, and William Brownrigg Director General of Personnel. These were the key financial appointments. In addition, several economic departments were entrusted to Americans—in particular, Public Domains (George T. Hudson), Industrial Supervision (Rex Vivian), Price Stabilization (Bernard I. Lamb), Supply and Supervision (Irving C. Hansen), Distribution (Esmond S. Ferguson), Road Transport (Floyd F. Shields), and Transport Priorities (Fred A. Schuckman).[1] Upon Dr. Millspaugh's arrival the Ministry of Food was abolished and its agencies were incorporated in the general economic administration. Even before his arrival this ministry had had an American adviser, J. P. Sheridan. In 1943 Mr. Sheridan left Iran, and later the reorganization of the Cereals Administration was entrusted to Dr. Forrest Crawford.[2] The posts of Directors General in the provinces (Ostans) were also entrusted to Americans.

Dr. Millspaugh came inspired by an ardent desire to serve Iran honestly and impartially and to create order where chaos prevailed. Many of his efforts were crowned with success, but in some tasks he failed. Politically his relations with the Iranian government be-

[1] The author is indebted for these names to the article "American Advisers in Persia," by George V. Allen, in the *Department of State Bulletin*, July 23, 1944.

[2] The list of American experts underwent frequent changes. Toward the end of the mission in 1945 only a few members remained in their original positions.

came so strained that he was forced to leave Iran toward the end of 1944 with his work unfinished.

The reasons for the mission's lack of success were manifold. They belonged to psychological, political, and administrative spheres. From the psychological viewpoint the mission faced basic difficulties. First, an important gap existed between Iranian and American mentalities. Secondly, the United States had no tradition of colonial administration and no experienced personnel available for such work. Both of these statements require some elucidation. With regard to their mentality, the Iranians undoubtedly did not possess the same love of duty, order, and efficiency as the Americans. Iranian ways are slow but filled with decorum. Their business standards are different. What in the eyes of a Westerner is a bribe, in the eyes of an Oriental may be just a gift and a sign of consideration. What in the eyes of an American is necessary promptness, in the eyes of an Iranian may seem to be a mad and unjustified speed. Such differences have to be understood by the personnel involved and require tactful and delicate handling. Obviously the Americans were invited to reorganize Iranian finances because of their acknowledged superiority as experts and representatives of Western efficiency, but this did not mean that the Iranain officials were prepared to adopt American standards and to abandon their own. Sometimes a concession to the native spirit might have been more advantageous than an uncompromising attitude.

It is not certain whether, in their honest zeal to do good, all the American advisers were aware of this psychological problem. Nor could they be entirely blamed for that, for after all these advisers usually had had no past experience on which to base their tactics. Recruited hastily during wartime, and often suddenly catapulted from their purely American occupations in industry, insurance, trade, or government, these men did not have the advantages of the average British civil servant who goes to a distant post in the Empire. As a result, tension frequently developed between American executives and Iranian subordinates, both on higher and lower levels. Although Dr. Millspaugh himself had the advantage of former experience in Iran and elsewhere, some observers doubted whether even he understood the problem sufficiently. As one of the foreign observers of

Iranian politics put it facetiously: "Dr. Millspaugh during his first mission to Iran in the twenties dealt with an infant ready to take advice and be admonished; when he arrived here for the second time twenty years later, he wanted to apply to Iran the same treatment as before; but he failed to notice that the infant has by now become an adolescent girl, independent, ambitious and whimsical."

Politically Dr. Millspaugh's difficulties were tremendous. No matter what he did, his actions were bound to displease some important sector of the Iranian public. In order to balance the budget, Dr. Millspaugh had to introduce and enact a progressive income tax. Immediately the opposition of a number of vested interests was felt. In order to combat inflation, he tried to enforce price controls, but that put him at odds with the important body of bazaar merchants who profited from black market transactions. To make necessary savings, he had to reorganize and eliminate waste in various government departments, but as a result he incurred the hostility of government employees. The measures taken to ensure the supply of staple foods to the capital and the provinces made him unpopular with the grain hoarders, some of whom were influential landowners. Even his regulations concerning the use of government automobiles and the allotment of tires made him many enemies among high officials and the Majlis deputies.

In general, the main Iranian opposition could be described as those right-wing reactionary elements who were loath to see any progressive reforms likely to affect their privileged positions. And as these elements were fairly well represented in the Majlis, Dr. Millspaugh constantly faced criticism, hostility, and obstruction in that body.

On the other hand, the Soviet authorities and the Iranian Communists did not conceal their enmity to the American mission. The Soviet Ambassador agreed to receive Dr. Millspaugh's call only after protracted delay, and very reluctantly at that. He never paid a return call. The Soviet authorities in the north did everything within their power to sabotage the mission's effort. Controlling the food surplus provinces in their zone, the Russians were in a position to nullify American efforts to ensure equal and smooth distribution of foodstuffs. Repeated Soviet bans on the export of grain from their zone clashed with the activity of the American-controlled Cereals Administration. Moreover, many obstacles were interposed by the Russians to prevent American mission members from traveling freely in the northern provinces. Despite the fact that the Americans acted as Iranian government officials, they could not be appointed for permanent positions in the north inasmuch as Soviet authorities granted them only temporary permits. Two American regional financial directors, Paul W. Gordon, Meshed, and William S. Nancarrow, Resht, were obliged to leave their assigned posts after a short period in office. Thomas B. W. Allen, appointed Director General of Finances for the Rezaieh province, never reached his destination because the Soviets refused to grant him a visa. Aside from the fact that he was a member of the Millspaugh mission, he was, in Soviet eyes, disqualified on even more important grounds. Allen had spent his childhood, as a son of a Presbyterian missionary, in Kurdistan and knew the local language and customs perfectly. An observer of this sort was most unwelcome to the Soviet authorities. In one case the Russians simply expelled a member of the Millspaugh mission. This was Rex Vivian, who was sent to Azerbaijan to collect grain.

The Tudeh faithfully seconded the Russians in this anti-American attitude. Its press repeatedly criticized Dr. Millspaugh and the mission. They were accused of ignorance and inefficiency. They were blamed for poor selection of their Iranian aides and interpreters. They were charged with dictatorial methods and trespassing their authorized powers. Dr. Millspaugh was represented as an agent of American imperialism who only aimed to damage Iranian economy for the benefit of America and Britain. He was lashed for his allegedly hostile attitude toward the workers or the "third class" and the Soviet Union. Deputies of the Thirteenth Majlis who voted for the engagement of the mission were branded as traitors. The shrewdness of the Tudeh tactics in this respect consisted in taking advantage of any point of disagreement between Millspaugh and the Iranian government, officials, or deputies and in strongly defending the Iranian position. Thus, all those who found themselves at odds with the American could find some consolation and satisfaction in the defense of their case by the Communist press. An Iranian, even if he were not pro-Tudeh, was often ready to repeat the Communist arguments against the mission as if they were his own. The Communist campaign was therefore contagious, and many a non-Communist paper eventually aligned itself against the mission.

Most unfortunately Dr. Millspaugh's work, despite its accomplishments, appeared as a series of clashes with the Iranians rather than harmonious co-operation. Millspaugh was inclined to reply vigorously to any unjust or unfair attack and to present ultimata and resignations. The press not infrequently carried his statements and open letters, which were couched in a somewhat warlike style. These statements contained denials of false rumors, preachings, and admonishments. There is no doubt that they were correct as far as the facts were concerned and that occasionally deliberate lies of the hostile press necessitated denial. But in some cases they appeared as expressions of bad temper and annoyance. Whether it would not have been more diplomatic to avoid certain controversies is open to question. What was perhaps more important was the fact that Millspaugh's relations with Iranian cabinet ministers were not invariably good. Basic divergence existed regarding the extent of his full powers. Millspaugh was ambitious to accomplish positive results in his work and needed uncontested authority in many fields. He clashed, therefore, with the personal ambitions or prestige of some of the ministers. These, instead of supporting him as an ally of their government, augmented the ranks of the critics and contributed to the growing mood of hostility toward the mission.

Nor could Millspaugh himself be said always to have proceeded with necessary care. In October, 1944, a quarrel arose between him and Abol Hasan Ebtehaj, Governor of the National Bank. It led Millspaugh to take unprecedented action: he addressed a letter to Ebtehaj dismissing him from his high post, and he simultaneously informed the banks in Iran and abroad not to honor the Governor's signature. Ebtehaj refused to vacate his position stating that Millspaugh had no right to dismiss him. The American, on the other hand, stubbornly insisted on his alleged prerogative. The government took Ebtehaj's side, and the Prime Minister refused to remove him from his position.

Even if Millspaugh had legal authority for his action, it is obvious that he acted in utter disregard of the psychological factors involved.

No Iranian could easily swallow dismissals of native dignitaries by a foreigner. Millspaugh aroused a tempest of violent criticism against himself, criticism which came from every side, not only Communist. The generally moderate *Neda-yi-Adalat,* organ of the party often reflecting the opinions of Iranian bureaucracy, now began a campaign against Millspaugh and asked the government to dismiss him. On January 14, 1945, the paper went so far as to demand public prosecution and trial for the whole American Economic Mission.

This campaign was not without effects. In January, 1945, the Majlis deprived Dr. Millspaugh of his economic powers, leaving to him only the financial administration. Following this action the government created a new organ called the Economic Committee, subject to the authority of the cabinet. The committee was composed of Iranians only and was entrusted with the supreme direction of economic life in the country. Dr. Millspaugh was unwilling to continue in office under such conditions; in February he resigned. Some members of his mission followed suit, but many remained in Iran in an advisory capacity. Thus ended, rather sadly, the third American financial mission to Iran.[3]

It should be pointed out that, even among the Iranians, certain elements endeavored to defend Millspaugh. The daily *Setareh* persistently argued in favor of the mission, stressing its merits and achievements. Seyyid Zia ed-Din and some of his papers also courageously sided with Millspaugh. On December 12, 1944, *Ra'd-i-Emruz* wrote a dramatic article in defense of the mission entitled, "Is It Not Treason to Deprive Dr. Millspaugh of His Powers Immediately?" It read:

If **Dr.** Millspaugh leaves us, his departure will be followed by immediate collapse of our economy. . . . Millspaugh's enemies demand his departure from Iran, but nobody has any idea what to do next. No one can give a guarantee that after his departure the economic situation of Iran will not be worse. Those who attack Dr. Millspaugh either play with the whole problem, or are completely ignorant, or else have instructions from foreign sources purposely to cause disorder and disorganization in the

[3] Dr. Millspaugh's case is forcefully presented in his book *Americans in Persia* (Washington, 1946).

country. Millspaugh's enemies clearly strive toward general revolution in Iran. As for us, we shall try in a series of articles to make known Dr. Millspaugh's achievements.

Seyyid Zia's attitude in this matter was understandable. Devoted to the preservation of the country's independence, Zia looked favorably on any attempt to strengthen Iranian economy, bring order into its finances, and thus increase general stability. This attitude refutes, to some extent, the allegation made by his enemies that Seyyid Zia was a leader of an utterly reactionary camp. As pointed out earlier, it was precisely the reactionaries who opposed and plotted against Millspaugh since they were anxious to preserve their privileged position against his bold reforms. On the other hand, Zia was motivated by foreign policy calculations. He believed that the presence of the mission in Iran would increase the interest of the United States in his country, and thus the powerful American democracy would be drawn into defense of Iranian sovereignty against Soviet expansionism. His press pointed out that fair treatment of the Millspaugh mission would guarantee American economic assistance. *Ra'd-i-Emruz* emphatically warned that continuation of lend-lease supplies from the United States to Iran would depend on the kind of treatment Dr. Millspaugh received.[4]

Was Seyyid Zia justified in his prognostications? Was it true that the treatment of the Millspaugh mission influenced the American official attitude toward Iran? At this point the basic problem of the co-ordination of American foreign policy arises. Dr. Millspaugh in his book *Americans in Persia* states that, despite early promises of support from the State Department, none came forth during the crucial moments.[5] Apparently the State Department was of the opinion that Dr. Millspaugh was an Iranian government official. Therefore, it was beyond their province to intervene in the internal quarrels between him and the Iranians. Such an attitude had its advantages and disadvantages. The advantage was that if Millspaugh through his temper made himself unpopular with various Iranian groups, it did not necessarily mean Iranian hostility toward the United States as such. On the other hand, undue toleration of unjustified attacks and

[4] June 27, 1944.
[5] Pages 218 ff.

slander on a prominent American would reflect on the prestige of the country he unofficially represented. It is doubtful whether either Britain or Russia would have permitted a similar long-drawn and violent campaign to be waged against their own nationals. In all likelihood their embassies would either have backed up their respective citizens vigorously or have brought about their early recall. One could naturally advance the argument that such official American indifference provided a splendid example of American democracy, liberalism, and tolerance. But American interests would have been better served if these virtues had been demonstrated in an example less negative than *l'affaire* Millspaugh.

As to Dr. Millspaugh, no flaw in his honest desire to stabilize the economy of Iran can be noted. But he failed to realize that salvation of the economy was only a secondary objective of the Iranians. As pointed out earlier, Iran treated the United States primarily as a friendly "third power," which should be brought gradually to this part of the world and in its adherence to straightforward principles of international intercourse shield Iran against foreign, and in particular Soviet, imperialism. The setting in order of Iranian economic life was thus only a means to an end. Dr. Millspaugh, however, attempted to be *"plus catholique que le pape."* In other words, he endeavored to help the Iranians more than they wished to be helped. And in this missionary zeal he was even prepared to incur their hostility. In so doing he was defeating the purpose for which he was asked to come.

Fortunately for the United States, certain things could be salvaged in the midst of the Millspaugh disaster. Dr. Millspaugh's mission was not the only American mission in Iran although it was the most important. In 1942 a military mission headed by Major General C. S. Ridley arrived to assist the Iranian government. In contrast to the executive character of the Financial Mission, the Military Mission was to act in an advisory capacity only. Its competence extended to the Quartermaster branch of the army and did not include operational affairs. Assisted by Colonel Dumond and ten other officers, General Ridley was said to have established good relations with his Iranian military colleagues. If any differences arose between him and the Iranians, they were never brought to public notice and never threatened ruptures similar to the repeated crises of the Financial Mission.

The gendarmerie also needed reorganization. For this body the Iranian government also requested American aid, and, accordingly, Colonel H. Norman Schwarzkopf was sent to head a special mission. Colonel Schwarzkopf had been chief of the New Jersey State Police and was nationally known in America for his success in dealing with the Lindbergh kidnaping case. In his new task he soon gained preponderant influence, and his real power in the Gendarmerie Corps exceeded to a considerable degree those of the Military Mission in the army. Colonel Schwarzkopf's work could be described as an outstanding success. He beat all records among American advisers as far as length of service during the second World War was concerned: he stayed in Iran over five years until 1948. Under his able and energetic leadership the gendarmerie became an efficient force whose loyalty to the government often proved to be of decisive significance. Despite loud Communist criticisms Schwarzkopf unflinchingly pursued his aim of securing order in the country. The calm and determined attitude of the gendarmerie at the time of the Azerbaijan crisis in 1945–1946 (of which more will be said later) prevented panic and riots in the capital at a most critical moment. Iran was deprived of his valuable services in 1948 when, promoted to the rank of Brigadier General, Schwarzkopf accepted a new assignment in western Germany.

Between 1942 and 1944 L. S. Timmerman, an American police expert, assisted the Iranian municipal police. His death in 1944 interrupted this work.

American advisers also assisted the Iranian government as individual experts in various government departments. Dr. Bennett Avery arrived in Iran in 1944 to advise on public health, and Professor Luther Winsor assisted in irrigation. In the winter of 1943–1944 Dr. Harold B. Allen, of the Near East Foundation, spent several months in Iran surveying agricultural education.

These advisers were certainly not in such vital crucial positions as the Financial Mission, and therefore their problems were less complicated. Their presence and activity constituted, however, an important and positive factor in Irano-American relations. The fact that in 1944 two American experts were invited to Iran for an *ad hoc* work in connection with the oil negotiations was another proof that America, despite the Millspaugh controversy, did not cease to attract the Iranians.

THE AMERICAN ARMY IN IRAN

The American army in Iran known as the Persian Gulf Command (P.G.C.) was composed of about 30,000 troops of noncombatant character. They arrived in 1942–1943 to speed up supplies to Russia. Their tasks were manifold: building and reorganization of the harbors on the Persian Gulf coast and the Shatt-el-Arab, construction and repair of highways, building of airports, and operation of the Transiranian Railway. With regard to the latter an agreement was reached with the Russians by which the Americans were to take care of the railway from the Persian Gulf to Teheran and the Russians were to operate it from Teheran to Bandar Shah on the Caspian shore. A part of the supplies had to be sent via motor road; in this case Qazvin was to serve as a relaying point between the American and Russian troops. An agreement with the British provided that British troops would ensure security measures in the southern zone while technical operations would be left to the Americans.

The Persian Gulf Command was headed by Major General Donald H. Connolly, who established his headquarters at Amirabad near Teheran. He chose the house belonging to Nasir Khan Qashqai, a detail not without some significance, for his personal residence. The General was assisted by a staff of highly competent officers, some of them career men and some civilians with wartime commissions. Headed by Chief of Staff Brigadier General Stanley Scott this group represented various technical skills of the highest degree and competence. The work the P.G.C. did in Iran represented an outstanding achievement of speed and efficiency. Long years would probably have passed before the Iranian government would have developed Khorramshahr into a large and modern seaport. The Americans did it in less than a year. The same may be said of the airport at Abadan and of the port facilities at Bandar Abbas and Bandar Shahpur. The P.G.C. provided the Iranians with a show of truly American tempo, a quality for which America is admired all over the world. Between the fall of 1942 and the fall of 1944 more than 4,380,440 tons of war implements and goods from American factories were delivered to Russia through Iran. By their ingenuity and energy the Americans managed to increase fivefold the capacity of the Transiranian Railway. Nearly 150,000 vehicles and nearly 3,500 planes including 1,400 bombers were delivered to the Red Army.[6]

Such was the technical aspect of the army's operations in Iran. Some other aspects might well be considered—first of all, the problem of Soviet-American military intercourse and relations. General Connolly had one simple, though technically difficult task to accomplish, namely, to deliver the tools of victory to the Russians. This he did with competence and with legitimate pride in his achievement. To fulfill his task he had to co-operate with the Russians, and this co-operation was generally smooth. The role of the American army was primarily technical and not political. To outside observers Soviet-American military relations looked quite cordial. Mutual visits of Soviet and American commanders, banquets, concerts, and shows contributed to this impression. To what degree this intercourse influenced the political thinking of General Connolly's staff it is difficult to judge. Sometimes one would hear the opinion expressed by a high American officer, "The operations in Iran have shown that you can do business with the Russians, because they were prompt and precise in meeting their obligations." That such assumptions were somewhat naïve was obvious. After all the Russians were on the receiving side, and it would have been suicidal for them to impede in any way the efficiency of supply operations. If such statements might be interpreted as denoting a pro-Soviet attitude, examples of more critical thought about Russia were not lacking. Despite their military occupations many staff officers mingled freely with the diplomatic colony of Teheran and were received in Iranian homes. There they had ample opportunity to learn something more about the real state of affairs in Iran.

Because General Connolly's task was precise and clear, he resented anything that might have spoiled his good co-operation with the Russians. Thus he was opposed to the activity of the army intelli-

[6] U.S. Army Dispatch, *Persian Gulf Command,* Nov. 22, 1944. See also the last issue of Aug. 1, 1945, reviewing the whole work of the P.G.C.

gence services, and he was said to be critical of the work of the Office of Strategic Services. It seems, however, that this correct attitude toward the Russians was not entirely reciprocated by them, and cases of actual Soviet espionage in the P.G.C. were revealed after the end of the war.[7] The General's personal ambition to reach record figures in deliveries to Russia was appreciated by the Soviet side. He was one of the very few Allied officers to be invited by the Soviet High Command to visit the Russian front. This was, no doubt, one of the highest compliments the Russians could pay to an American.

Most of the American troops did not have much actual contact with the Russians. Most contacts were established, for technical reasons, at Teheran and Qazvin, where the Russians were taking over American goods. There was little personal fraternization since the Russian soldiers were forbidden to mingle with foreigners. Anyway they could not be expected to be able to afford the company of well-paid American G.I.'s. The Americans, on their part, treated the Russians in their usual light-hearted and friendly way, offering them cigarettes, beer, and similar luxuries of Western capitalism, but no evidence of any deeper understanding or friendship between them existed. By the same token there was no evidence that these American citizens, temporarily wearing uniforms, were properly informed by their leaders of the real problems of Iran. This, however, was not exactly the task for the Persian Gulf Command. It was rather the question of basic policies on higher army and government levels and involved the general issue of the substance of the army indoctrination courses. Stripped bare, the problem resolved itself into the question whether American citizens in wartime, in uniform or out, should be told the entire truth about the world situation or only part of it.

The next aspect of the army's operations in Iran was the impact upon Irano-American relations. Generally speaking, this impact was of a positive nature. The Iranians learned more about America by looking at the American troops, on and off duty, than they could learn in any other way. And what they learned was certainly encouraging. In work the Americans were efficient and dynamic. In

[7] See an article by Major J. R. Walsh, "Middle East Has Long History of Espionage among Nations," in the *Washington Post*, March 22, 1946.

their free moments they were friendly, cheerful, and human. The G.I.'s had none of the aloofness that so often puts a barrier between the British and native populations. The Americans were excellent customers of carpet and antique shops, were always neatly dressed and generous. The Russian troops inspired the population with an instinctive fear. There was not a hint of fear in the Iranian attitude toward the Americans. There was rather the mixed feeling that the Americans were very powerful, wealthy and therefore worthy of respect and at the same time immature as measured by the old standards of oriental cunning and experience. That those "Big Boys" from beyond the seas could harm intentionally was inconceivable.

THE PROBLEM OF AMERICAN PROPAGANDA

What has just been said about the impact of the army on Irano-American relations indicates that this influence could be treated as a sort of involuntary American propaganda. It is legitimate to ask in this connection whether, apart from this accidental publicity, anything was done deliberately to promote knowledge of American institutions, way of life, and political intentions among the people of Iran. That the spread of such knowledge would be useful to both America and Iran seems to be unquestionable. Apart from the positive value of such an information program, it could be conceived as a defensive weapon against hostile Soviet propaganda as well. It should be borne in mind that Soviet policy in Iran was not exclusively anti-British but generally anti-Western. Evidences of it were abundant. The violent campaign waged against Millspaugh and his mission by the Communist press was a case in point. Another example was supplied by the oil crisis. Kavtaradze's visit could be interpreted as an anti-American move as much as an anti-Iranian. *Pravda*'s reproach that the American army was in Iran illegally was another proof that the Russians were eager to embarrass the Americans. It was clear that the appearance of the United States as a "third power" on the Iranian stage was bound to displease the Soviet Union and to complicate the fulfillment of its program. If a determined campaign of hostility and slander was waged by one side, little could be gained by the other by keeping silent. Too much restraint and silence was bound to be interpreted in an oriental country as a sign of weakness or as a tendency to compromise with principles. Clearly, the official British and American policies in Iran in wartime were dedicated to the same purpose: i.e., to treat Iran as a corridor of supplies to Russia to be evacuated at the end of hostilities, and to be restored to full independence as soon as the war was over. Thus, logically, the American government had as much interest in maintaining political stability in Iran as the British. Consequently, if America had faced its world responsibilities, its diplomacy should have contributed to the fulfillment of these basic objectives. Yet this was not quite done. The British bore the main burden of preserving the prestige of the West and of refuting the attacks of Communist propaganda. With much slenderer material resources, the British had to build up their own information apparatus, support the native nationalist elements, and perform numerous similar tasks. There was no American public relations bureau to aid the British and to dispel the doubts regarding the real intentions of the West which British policy due to its imperialist past was bound to produce. A well-conceived and organized American propaganda machinery might have accomplished a great deal of good in the field of Irano-Western relations. It might have supported the British in those essential points where the British needed support and corrected them in others.

The blame for this state of affairs can hardly be attributed to the American Embassy in Teheran. The whole problem of American propaganda had to be solved at a higher level. To be sure, attempts were made to bring official American publicity agents to Iran, but these steps proved either ineffective or were taken with too much delay.

The Office of War Information did send some men to Iran. The first was Harold Peters, former United Press correspondent. He was entrusted with the task of editing an American newspaper in Teheran which would satisfy the needs of American soldiers there and also serve as a general information organ for local consumption. Unfortunately Peters' status was ill-defined. He was not granted a diplomatic post as press attaché at the Embassy, nor was he put into any clear position vis-à-vis the Persian Gulf Command. Local rivalry existed between the army and the Embassy, and both were none too kind toward the O.W.I. The net result was that Peters found himself suspended in air, unable either to publish a newspaper or to start any normal activity among Iranian newspapermen. He was leading a shadow existence on the fringes of the Teheran diplomatic colony. Peters was succeeded in due time by James Downward, also of the O.W.I. Downward was similarly unable to accomplish anything. He became involved in difficulties with the Persian Gulf Command and after a few months was recalled.

Still another person was said to represent the O.W.I. permanently in Iran. This was Mrs. Nilla Cram Cook, who was officially an employee of the Iranian government. As a director of the theatrical department in the Ministry of Interior she was responsible for the management of native dramatic art. And although American Embassy officials sometimes referred to her as an O.W.I. representative, it was most difficult to find evidence that she was ever actively engaged in American information work in an independent capacity.

Even if these men had been permitted to work normally, the basic question of the substance of their propaganda remains. From what is known of the general policies followed by the O.W.I., there is no guarantee that this agency would have been fully aware of the local propaganda needs in Iran. The O.W.I. endeavored to bolster American and Allied morale by spreading propaganda of Allied unity.[8] As in the case of the British Ministry of Information, such a policy was ill-adjusted to the requirements of the Iranian scene. As was said earlier in the discussion of British policies, the Iranians were not interested in the preservation of Big Three unity, an expression devoid of meaning to them. They wanted clear and honest reassurance from the Western democracies that the principles of national self-determination and justice toward small nations would not be thrown overboard by the Big Powers. Any hesitation on that point could have only one effect in Iran, the creation of distrust toward the West and an increase of fearful servility toward Russia.

Toward the end of the war the State Department took the long-overdue action of appointing a regular press officer to the Embassy in Teheran. With the arrival of T. Cuyler Young in January, 1945, the American information services were put into operation and the

---

[8] For the story of O.W.I. policies in Iran see Sidney Morrell, *op. cit.*, p. 43.

activity of the Irano-American Society of Cultural Relations was intensified. Closer contact was established with the press, and a visit
by a group of Iranian editors to the United States was organized.[9]
Even then the American information services operated on a very
small budget and represented a meager effort as compared to the
programs of the British and Soviet embassies. Although this new
effort could not be regarded as a deliberate countermeasure against
Soviet propaganda, yet there was enough positive pro-American substance in it to call it a success.

THE DILEMMA OF BASIC AMERICAN POLICY

The problem of American propaganda was only a part of the
general issue of United States' policy toward Iran. Did the American
government possess any definite long-range policy for this part of the
world during the war? Available evidence seems to give a negative
answer. Of course one could always say that the American attitude
toward Iran was dictated by noble principles such as respect for
integrity and sovereignty, nonintervention in internal affairs, readiness to extend economic assistance and advice, and the Open Door
doctrine. But these principles did not mean that a definite, purpose-
ful policy had been formulated. The role the United States played
during the second World War thrust it into the limelight of global
politics. But the United States was none too quick to comprehend
this fact and to assume the attendant responsibilities. Iran was
politically an important area. This was the territory of traditional
Anglo-Russian rivalry. It was the road to India and the area rich in
oil. It was also the only country where great numbers of Soviet,
British, and American troops were stationed together. It was here
that the Soviet Union experimented with its revolutionary colonial
doctrines while at the same time it maintained its alliance with that
great colonial Power, Britain. It was in Iran that American advisers were attacked as agents of imperialism, while Russia was receiving unrestricted lend-lease aid from the United States. These
things could not pass unnoticed and were obviously known to the
American government. They demanded certain basic decisions, the

---

[9] These editors were Abbas Massudi (*Ettela'at*), Majid Movaqqar (*Mehr-i-Iran*),
Mesbah-zadeh (*Kayhan*), and Abol-Qasim Amini (*Omid*).

first of which was the determination of the role Iran was to play in the maintenance of world peace and American security. If it was a matter of indifference to the United States whether or not Iran was going to fall victim to Soviet expansion and Communism, then it would not be illogical to leave her to her own devices. If, on the contrary, the United States was interested in the preservation of Iranian independence, then a positive policy should have been formulated. Such a positive policy would not have rejected any medium through which American influence could be exerted, whether advisers, direct diplomatic action, or a well-conceived propaganda.

With regard to the advisers, their continued presence in Iran could then be treated not as an isolated phenomenon, but as an integral part of the American task in Iran. In such a case their services to Iran could be conceived of as an excellent means by which to strengthen the friendship and bolster the courage of the Iranians against Soviet infiltration. Their presence could also be utilized as a warning to the Russians that the United States was not ready to see Iran share the fate of eastern Europe. If such a policy had been adopted, it might have been wise to defend more vigorously Mills-paugh's position, while persuading him to be less uncompromising in his "puristic" attitudes. His replacement by another man endowed with greater diplomatic skill might then not have been out of the question. As it was, the inglorious way in which he was dismissed from Iran constituted a blow to American prestige and created lack of confidence in the firmness of American foreign policy.

Thus undoubted harm was done to the otherwise correct official diplomacy conducted by the American government and its Embassy in Teheran. The extension of lend lease to Iran, the aid proffered by the largely American-influenced Middle East Supply Center, the willingness to respect the Iranian refusal of oil concessions—all constituted irrefutable proofs of honest international conduct.

By far the greatest achievement of American diplomacy in its dealings with Iran was the Teheran Communiqué of 1943. This declaration probably did more to enhance Iranian faith in the United States than any other American official act in wartime. The authorship of the declaration was generally ascribed to the Americans, and this was correct. Moreover, it was understood in Teheran that the great American democracy was giving weight to the guarantee of Iranian independence. This pledge was a unique feature of American diplomacy and was applied for the first time to an Asiatic country. And the fact that the Atlantic Charter was mentioned in the declaration as a valid document promised that the noble war aims of the West had not been abandoned. The Iranian press did not hide its satisfaction, and although gratitude was expressed toward all the Big Three, there was no doubt that the United States was the chief beneficiary of these kind feelings.

Finally, with reference to propaganda proper, one must not forget that objectively there existed in Iran a very favorable mental climate for the promotion of American ideals and interests. The United States was traditionally regarded as a disinterested and friendly country, anxious to help rather than to exploit. This opinion was due to many factors, not the least of which was the activity of American Presbyterian missions in Iran. These missions created uncontestable good will and respect. By tacit agreement with the British the American missions had operated more in the northern provinces, whereas the British missions had entrenched themselves in the south. This gave the Americans the additional advantage of spreading the light of their civilization in regions traditionally threatened by Russian imperialism.

Other proofs of the confidence placed in the United States were not lacking. Many Iranians, uncertain of the future of their country, emigrated to the United States during the war or toward the end of it. In September, 1945, the American Consulate in Teheran was besieged by large numbers of students seeking admittance to American universities. There was a basic readiness to trust the United States. What was needed in return was to assure the Iranians that America with her good will, power, and resources would not betray this trust, even if it meant a rebuke to a powerful Ally.

Before concluding this chapter a few remarks on the position of the American Embassy in Teheran may be in order. Until the Teheran Conference of November, 1943, the American diplomatic mission had the rank of a legation but as a result of the Conference it was raised to the status of an embassy. As a legation it was headed by Louis Goethe Dreyfus, Minister plenipotentiary. During his term the American-Iranian Cultural Relations Society was reactivated in March, 1943. The Minister was valiantly seconded by Mrs. Dreyfus, whose charitable activities among the poor of Teheran (she founded a clinic in the slum area) gained her great respect and popularity and a high Iranian decoration from the hands of the Shah.

Unfortunately the Minister's relations with the Persian Gulf Command were reputed to be strained. Although officially the military authorities were not responsible for the conduct of foreign affairs, yet the power of an army commander in his theater of operations was so great, that in practice it overlapped the area of the Ambassador's activity. Even the diplomatic pouches of the American Embassy were said to be subject to military inspection. This overlapping of authority was bound to produce tensions unless one side completely capitulated to the other. The only permanent solution for such ills could be provided by adequate co-ordination of departmental responsibilities in Washington. And as this did not seem to occur, the over-all American effort in Iran lacked the efficiency of good teamwork in contrast to the smooth co-operation among the British agencies. After the Teheran Conference Dreyfus was transferred to Iceland, and rumor had it that this departure was not quite divorced from the tense state of Army-Embassy relations. He was replaced by Ambassador Leland B. Morris, who after a few months in office was succeeded by Ambassador Wallace Murray. It was during Morris' term of office that the oil crisis took place, and it was he who made the important statement that the United States respected the Iranian decision to refuse the oil concessions.

The arrival of Ambassador Murray coincided with the general collapse of inter-Allied harmony in Iran and with the dangerous strain in Communist-nationalist relations. The inevitable crisis was ripening and demanded a clearer definition of the American attitude. It was Murray's onerous privilege to serve with distinction at the time of the dramatic crisis in Soviet-Iranian relations that occurred soon after the end of the war.

On the whole, the American Embassy enjoyed prestige and respect. Perhaps it might have been wiser not to change Ambassadors so frequently during a war. On the other hand, the Embassy might have benefited if its able and conscientious personnel had been supplemented by a few experts exclusively devoted to service in this part of the world. In this connection, British experience might have provided a good pattern to follow.

To sum up our observations on the American role and attitudes during the war, we may say that, although correct and honorable, the United States' policy toward Iran did not manifest the same degree of foresight, firmness, and consistency that was characteristic of the Soviet policy and to a lesser extent of the British. Had the United States made its stand quite clear on several issues, not only through occasional pronouncements, such as the Teheran Declaration or the statement during the oil crisis, but in active day-to-day diplomacy, it could have prevented many unwelcome events. The rather passive character of American policy eventually encouraged unilateral Soviet action, since the Russians were led to believe that the only real opposition to their schemes would come from war-weary Britain. One may say that in Iran the typical drama of American world policy was reconstructed in miniature: first, a basic reluctance to visualize the future and to get involved in foreign complications; then as a result of this attitude the nondeliberate encouragement of potential aggressors; and, finally, a sharp awakening and a realization that the time had come to act. Meanwhile, due to procrastination the danger had become more serious, and the effort required to combat it more strenuous.

CHAPTER ELEVEN

The Aftermath of the War:
Iran in World Politics

Toward the end of the war in Europe the struggle between opposing forces in Iran became more intense. The Iranian nationalist
press took up the problem of the evacuation of Allied troops and insisted that these troops should leave Iran as soon as possible. The
nationalists knew that according to the Tripartite Treaty Russia
and Britain were entitled to keep their troops until six months after
the end of war with the Axis, which included also Japan, as yet
unconquered. Yet they argued that the purpose for which foreign
troops came to Iran was no longer valid. This purpose was to send
supplies to Russia, but from November, 1944, the Persian Gulf
Command practically ceased its supply operations, owing to the
opening of the Black Sea to the Allied fleets. On the other hand, the
press advanced the theme of complete neutrality to which Iran
should return as soon as the war was over.[1] These nationalist attitudes
found their official expression on May 19, 1945, in a demand of the
Iranian government to Britain and Russia to withdraw their troops.

In reply the British and Soviet Embassies made it clear that foreign
troops were not legally obliged to leave the territory of Iran before
the agreed deadline. Yet, essentially, the British favored the Iranian
point of view since it was similar to their own. In the spring of 1945
the British had already begun withdrawal from many fields of their
activities. Wherever they could the British tried to secure an agreement with the Russians for simultaneous withdrawal, but lacking it

1 Ra'd-i-Emruz, May 27, 1945; Journal de Tehran, Aug. 9 and 19, 1945.

in concrete cases the British proceeded alone. This was a gradual process and therefore did not threaten British security or position. Moreover it demonstrated the peaceful intentions of Great Britain to the Iranians and at the same time tested the attitude and trends of Soviet diplomacy.

Among the points agreed to by the Russians was the early evacuation of the Teheran area. This meant the liquidation of air-force maintenance units and of land troops on both the Russian and the British sides. Beginning with August 7, 1945, both sides complied with this agreement. Yet despite its appearance of equality the agreement favored Russia, for the Russians had replaced their uniformed troops with a swarm of plain-clothes men estimated at several thousand in Teheran alone. Furthermore, military offices attached to the Soviet Embassy remained in Teheran, including the N.K.V.D. (secret police) headquarters. Thus, although the bulk of troops left the Teheran area by the middle of September, the possibility of Soviet military action in the capital was not completely removed.

Meanwhile the British were discontinuing their own activities one by one. Their Public Relations Bureau staff underwent visible reduction. On March 21, 1945, the British officially announced the termination of their information programs on the Radio Teheran. And, following an agreement with the Russians, they ended on September 1 censorship of mail and news by their own censors. In all these fields the Soviet side did not reciprocate. Instead it acted with considerable delay and obvious reluctance to withdraw. The Russians did not honor the agreement on censorship for a number of weeks after the British withdrew. Immediately after the closing of British programs the Soviet Embassy requested and obtained additional radio time, which it "farmed out" to the Polish Lublin Communists. These radio programs continued from Teheran for a good many months after the British ended theirs. There was no apparent reduction in the Soviet propaganda personnel. On the contrary, the number of Soviet-sponsored shows, exhibitions, and similar activities increased. The summer of 1945 witnessed the visit of Soviet Moslem dignitaries to Iran, the consequences of which were described in an earlier chapter. This visit was followed by a tour by a Soviet trade union delegation, which went to all important industrial centers in the northern zone and Teheran. The Iranian Communist press as a rule quoted the Tass dispatches that described the enthusiasm of the local workers as hosts to their Russian colleagues. The meetings harangued by these Soviet delegates frequently ended with cries and resolutions demanding the extirpation of fascism, the punishment of right-wing "traitors," and so forth. Also in the summer of 1945 the Russians proposed to the Iranian government the convocation of a Soviet-Iranian medical conference in Teheran. The Iranians, reluctant to refuse outright, agreed to hold the conference but to offset Soviet propaganda decided to make it an international meeting attended by delegations from the Middle East and Great Britain. Thus at the least propitious time, between the end of war in Europe and in Japan, Teheran was the scene of an international conference of medicine not desired by anyone except the Russians.

It was clear that while paying lip service to the principle of withdrawal, the Russians did not surrender in reality any of their positions and gave ominous signs of intensifying their action in Iran. In the middle of August violent disturbances broke out in Khorasan and Azerbaijan. As previously related, the Khorasan trouble was the result of Soviet intrigue among army officers and the Turkoman tribes. Somehow the Iranian government managed to restore the Khorasan situation to normalcy, but in Azerbaijan matters turned for the worse.

THE AUTONOMOUS REPUBLIC OF AZERBAIJAN

In August, 1945, the Tudeh party staged a "rehearsal" in Tabriz. Its armed partisans, protected by Soviet troops, captured several government buildings and attempted to impose their rule upon the city and the adjacent area. At the same time a manifesto demanding administrative and cultural autonomy for Azerbaijan within the framework of the Iranian state was issued in the form of a leaflet. The manifesto claimed that 4,500,000 Azerbaijanis were deprived of their rights by the central government and demanded freedom to pursue their national development and to use their native language. The Iranian governor, former Premier Bayat, was powerless as Iranian gendarmerie and army units were prevented from leaving their barracks by the Soviet authorities. Attempts of the central government to intervene were fruitless, especially in view of simultaneous trouble in

Khorasan. The Iranian gendarmerie sent northwards was kept from reaching its destination by Soviet troops. Telegraph communications between Teheran and Tabriz were cut. Yet after a few weeks the situation seemed to calm down. The Tudeh evacuated the few buildings it had taken. Communications between Teheran and Tabriz were restored, and, officially at least, the local governor regained authority. This subsiding of the revolutionary wave could not have been a result of the central government's action because it was prevented from taking any other than sending a military investigating commission *post factum*. Obviously the Soviet authorities decided not to push matters any further for a while. Observers in Teheran generally agreed that the whole episode was conceived as a rehearsal for more serious action in the future. As such it was a test of the local Tudeh machinery and of the reaction of the West to such events.

The reaction of the West was expressed in a diplomatic *démarche* taken by Foreign Secretary Bevin of Great Britain. In a letter addressed to the Soviet government on September 19, 1945, Mr. Bevin expressed willingness to evacuate British troops from Iran with the exception of the southern oil area by the middle of December and suggested that the Soviets follow suit but remain in Azerbaijan. The letter thus manifested Britain's worry over developments in Iran, but it constituted only a half-measure so far as Azerbaijan was concerned. The Soviet reply was negative. Moscow insisted on keeping its troops in Iran without any limitations until March 2, 1946, six months after Japan's surrender. This attitude was made known during the Foreign Ministers Conference in London, which ended on October 2 after three weeks of unsuccessful negotiations. The fact that the substance of the Iranian situation was not discussed during the Conference and that Western reaction was limited only to legalistic wrangling about the date of evacuation could not fail to encourage further Soviet action.

On October 23 news spread that several new divisions of the Red Army had entered Iran. Apparently the Tudeh, despite three years of preparation, could not yet be trusted as a satisfactory tool. In the meantime the Tudeh assumed a new name in the Azerbaijan province. It became known as the Democratic party. Its two mouthpieces, *Azerbaijan* and *Khavar-i-No*, followed generally the old Tudeh line.

Yet, as time went on, the Democrats concentrated their propaganda on two basic demands: the right of Azerbaijan to have schools conducted in the Turkish language and to have provincial autonomy. While the first was acceptable to the central government, the second had serious implications, especially because of the presence of Soviet troops in the province. Talks on this subject between the Democrat leaders and Governor Bayat did not help to settle the issue. By November it was evident that, failing to achieve their aims by negotiation, the Democrats were ready to take matters into their own hands. By the middle of November large quantities of arms had been distributed among the party adherents and the peasantry. It was common knowledge in Azerbaijan that the arms were supplied directly or indirectly, as circumstances dictated, by the Red Army. Following this distribution, the Democrats launched a new offensive to seize power in the province. Gendarmerie posts were attacked and disarmed, government offices in various centers were occupied by the insurgents; prominent officials, army and police officers, and some industrialists and landowners were killed. This action was carried out with the obvious connivance of Soviet military authorities, although the latter took care not to intervene openly. Soviet tactics consisted in (a) obstructing all movements of the Iranian army or gendarmerie whenever they wanted to quell the riots; (b) protecting all meetings and movements of the Democrats by posting armed Soviet detachments in their vicinity; and (c) intimidating the population by the arrest of certain government officials in scattered points under various pretexts. At the same time Soviet army commanders pretended to maintain normal relations with Iranian civil and military authorities. The most irrefutable proof of Soviet connivance with the Democrats came when the Iranian government sent north regular troops to quell the rebellion. These troops were barred from entering the Soviet zone by the Red Army.

Simultaneously the Democratic party displayed vigorous political action. On November 23 its Central Committee issued a proclamation defining its aim as the complete autonomy of Azerbaijan. On the next day *Khavar-i-No* published a list of Iranian officials who should be liquidated. The list included the names of the Commanding General, Darakhshani, his chief of staff, and several gendarmerie and police officers. On the other hand, a Provisional Congress of Azerbaijan that had been called into being earlier in the fall and that was composed of party supporters, designated a thirty-nine-man commission to organize elections to a provincial National Assembly. These elections were carried out in an atmosphere of terror and intimidation and in their own crude way followed Soviet patterns. The Democratic party was the only one presenting candidates. No organized opposition existed. The nationalist press and even mail from other parts of Iran was barred entry into Azerbaijan or—in some cases—was burned outright by Soviet censors.

On December 12 the provincial National Assembly was formally inaugurated in Tabriz. It was composed of 101 deputies, all Democrats or individuals forced into collaboration under duress. Its first step on its first day was to proclaim the Autonomous Republic of Azerbaijan and to designate a government under the "premiership" of the veteran Comintern agent Ja'afar Pishevari. The "government" of Azerbaijan announced that the autonomous state would be conducted on "democratic principles" but that it did not desire separation from Iran. It also issued a program that said that private property would be inviolable; that "traitors and reactionaries" would be purged from the gendarmerie; that a "people's army" would be formed from local militia groups; and that Turkish would be the official language of the state. It added that the government would distribute to the peasants government-owned land as well as that of "reactionary landlords who ran away from Azerbaijan."

A few days after the constitution of the revolutionary government was completed, the Azerbaijan Assembly was disbanded and its functions were transferred to the provisional presidium, whose authority overlapped with that of the cabinet. The new regime quickly proceeded to carry out its plans. It started a land-distribution program. It nationalized all banks in Tabriz holding 3,000,000 tomans or more. It introduced Turkish in the administration and the schools and took steps to establish a university. Several measures were also taken favoring the workers over the industrialists. Furthermore, a commission formed from representatives of the Ministries of Trade, Economics, and Finance was called upon to establish trade connections with foreign governments.

Politically the new regime resembled a police state. Although a new parliament was elected in the beginning of 1946, allegedly according to the principle of universal and secret suffrage, yet little democratic freedom was in evidence. Hundreds of refugees complaining of terror escaped into Iran or Iraq. At the same time the Azerbaijani secret police was being modeled after N.K.V.D. patterns. It was headed by Salamollah Javid, Minister of Interior and a veteran Communist educated in Russia. Foreigners were generally barred from traveling in Azerbaijan, and those who happened to get there were frequently molested and warned by the local authorities not to show too much curiosity.[2] The government itself was composed of men who were strongly linked to the Soviets or directly imported from Russia.[3] The Azerbaijani "people's army" or the partisans, *fedailar*, were infiltrated by hundreds of Soviet agents from the Caucasus and were largely composed of Armenians or those Iranian "immigrants," *mohajirs*, who in 1936 had returned to their native country from the Soviet Union. These revolutionary troops were, as a rule, clad in Soviet uniforms with Azerbaijani insignia.

"Premier" Pishevari, valiantly seconded by the Tudeh propaganda in Teheran, vacillated between frank statements of having received Soviet help and ardent denials that this help was anything more than "moral support." In a broadcast from Tabriz he once openly thanked the Red Army for overthrowing "the tyrannical regime of Iran."[4] On another occasion, speaking to T. C. Young of the American Embassy from Teheran, he freely admitted that the success of his party was due to the support of the Soviet army in Azerbaijan. Asking why

[2] An attempt by Colonel William T. Sexton, the American military attaché in Teheran, to see things at first hand was unsuccessful because the armed Democrats put him and those who accompanied him under arrest, and released them only with the understanding that they would return straightway to Teheran.

[3] Besides Pishevari: Mohammed Biriya, educated in Russia, Minister of Education; Dr. Salamollah Javid, Minister of Interior, a Communist active in the 1919–1920 agitation for uniting Azerbaijan with Russia, and Governor-General of Azerbaijan after Pishevari's resignation from the premiership; Sadiq Padegan, born in Russia, chairman of the Central Committee of the Democratic party; Adalat, member of the Russian Communist party in Baku, founder of the Democratic party in Azerbaijan; and General Danishiyan, Commander-in-Chief of the Democrat army, who spoke broken Turkish, knew no Persian and spoke, read, and wrote fluently only in Russian.

[4] *Washington Post*, April 12, 1946.

the Democrats should refuse this help, he stated that it was not the first time in the history of the world or Iran that a revolutionary movement had been aided by a foreign Power. To add weight to this argument Pishevari cited the example of early Iranian constitutionalists who had received aid from Britain and pointed out the assistance given by France to the American Revolution.[5] On the other hand, Tudeh's leader Iraj Iskandari, bluntly declared in the spring of 1946:

> Russia extended its help to us, but Britain opposed the Tudeh Party and went even further by actively supporting reactionaries. . . . So long as the Russians are not harming our country we refuse to believe rumors of Soviet domination of Iran. Their only interference came when the reactionary central government tried to send troops to quell the movement. This [Russian] interference was applauded by all anxious to see popular progressive movements grow.[6]

Simultaneously with the events in Tabriz a Kurdish uprising took place in western Azerbaijan. On December 15, 1945, a number of leaders of the Kurdish Democrat party met in the presence of Soviet officers at Mahabad and proclaimed a Kurdish People's Republic. In January, 1946, Qazi Mohammed, chief of Mahabad, was elected to the presidency of the Republic. Among the members of the new government were his cousin Seif Qazi and Mulla Mustafa, a rebellious chief from Iraq. Five Kurdish chieftains received the title of marshal and were given Soviet uniforms. The Kurdish Republic sent observers to the Azerbaijan parliament but insisted on separate identity from the revolutionary government in Tabriz. Following the negotiations among Pishevari, Qazi Mohammed, and the Soviet representatives, a treaty was signed on April 23, 1946, between the Kurdish and Azerbaijan governments which provided for military alliance, fair treatment of minorities, exchange of diplomatic missions, and common diplomatic action toward the Teheran government.[7]

Thus the Kurdish uprising completed the separation of the whole province of Azerbaijan from the control of Teheran authorities. It

[5] This information is based on information given to the author personally by Professor T. C. Young. It is confirmed by the *Washington Post*, Dec. 12, 1945.

[6] *New York Times*, April 12, 1946.

[7] For a fuller description of the Kurdish-Azerbaijani relations see Archie Roosevelt, Jr., the "Kurdish Republic of Mahabad," *Middle East Journal*, July, 1947.

looked as if the old Empire were to fall to pieces. Unable to counteract this movement of disintegration at home, the Iranian government decided to bring the matter to the newly formed United Nations.

INTERNATIONAL ASPECTS OF THE SOVIET-IRANIAN DISPUTE

It was characteristic of the Iranian political situation that nothing that happened between Iran and the Soviet Union could remain of indifference to Great Britain. But even more characteristic was the fact that beginning with the fall of 1945 the United States was definitely drawn into the vortex of turbulent Iranian politics. On November 24, 1945, at the time when the Azerbaijan rebellion began, the United States delivered a note to the Soviet Union proposing the evacuation of Soviet, British, and American troops from Iran by January 1, 1946. A parallel British note was also delivered. Moscow's reply was negative. The Soviet note of November 29 to the United States rejected the American proposal, invoked earlier correspondence with the British government as providing for the withdrawal of troops by March 2, 1946, blamed "reactionary elements" for troubles in Azerbaijan and denied interference of Soviet military authorities in internal affairs of Iran. The note said further:

The Soviet Government opposed the dispatch of new Iranian troops to northern districts of Iran and informed the Iranian Government that the dispatch of further Iranian forces to northern Iran could cause not the cessation, but the increase, of the disorders and likewise bloodshed, which would compel the Soviet Government to introduce into Iran further forces of its own for the purpose of preserving order and insuring the security of the Soviet garrison.

The note finally invoked the Soviet-Iranian Treaty of February 26, 1921, as giving the Soviet Union the "right of introduction of Soviet troops into the territory of Iran."

This exchange of notes did not exhaust diplomatic action. In the West it was hoped that Azerbaijan could be discussed during the second conference of Foreign Ministers to be held in Moscow in the middle of December, 1945. British Foreign Secretary Bevin and American Secretary of State Byrnes arrived in Moscow on December

15 hopeful that some solution might be reached, but Russia presented them with a *fait accompli* just prior to the opening of the conference for the Azerbaijan Republic was proclaimed three days before their arrival. Accompanied by their area experts, Sir Reader Bullard, British Ambassador to Iran, and John D. Jernegan, Second Secretary of the American Embassy at Teheran, both Foreign Secretaries tried in vain to settle the Iranian problem. In the course of the conference Bevin proposed that a three-Power commission of Britain, Russia, and the United States visit Iran to settle differences. Bevin also suggested, with a view to reaching a compromise between Russia's special interest in Azerbaijan and the principle of Iranian territorial integrity, a scheme for the creation of local governments in Iran. The Russians, who initially seemed amenable to such a solution, reversed their attitude at the end of the conference and rejected Bevin's scheme. It is not quite clear what caused them to change their views. It is possible that the Soviet side expected a firmer stand on the part of the West on many international issues on the agenda, but seeing the will of the Western ministers falter (due to their ardent desire to reach argeement with the Russians rather than to stick to their principles), it decided that it could afford to be uncompromising on the Iranian issue.[8]

[8] In its issue for May 11, 1946 (no. 44, p. 378), the *U.S.S.R. Information Bulletin*, an organ of the Soviet Embassy in Washington, contains an article, "On the Iranian Problem," by Atonovich, which may be regarded as a classical expression of the official Soviet attitude in this matter and which is typical of Soviet political terminology. The following are excerpts:

"After the termination of the Second World War the least sober minded people could not doubt that in the future Iran's relations with her great northern neighbor must be built on a new basis free from hostility and adventurousness which are fraught with danger for Iran herself.

"Unfortunately, Iranian ruling circles failed by far to realize this simple truth at once. Suffice it to recall that as late as the end of last year and until February 1946, the Iranian government was headed by the very same Hakimi who, when Minister in 1919, was one of the chief inspirers of aggressive plans against the Soviet Caucasus, Baku and the Soviet Transcaspian region. These plans found their expression in official memoranda submitted by the Teheran Cabinet to the Versailles Conference. . . ."

"The growth of the democratic movement in Iran prompted British and American circles to raise the question of interference into Iran's internal affairs. As early as December 1945, during the conference of the three Foreign Ministers in Moscow, Bevin made a proposal, also supported by the representative of the United

Whatever the reason, the fact remains that nothing was done to relieve Soviet pressure on Azerbaijan. Listing the unsettled questions at Moscow, Secretary Bevin declared on his return to London: "One of the most important of these is the Iranian question. It has been the subject of a protracted exchange of views between Soviet Government and the Governments of the United States and Great Britain. Final agreement has not been reached, but discussions will continue through ordinary channels." [9] Commenting on the British and American attitudes on the subject, the London correspondent of the *New York Times* wrote on January 1, 1946:

That was a principal reason that Mr. Bevin came back from the tri-power parley of Foreign Ministers far less happy about the Moscow agreement than Mr. Byrnes. It is felt here that Americans are inclined to overlook the vital importance of Iran and the whole Middle East to the British Empire. What may have seemed to be a relatively minor question to Mr. Byrnes was a major one to Mr. Bevin.

The Moscow conference was a turning point in the development of the Soviet-Iranian dispute. The British, despite its failure, stuck to their idea that some compromise solution should be reached. That is why Sir Reader Bullard, upon his return to Teheran, was instructed to induce the Iranians to accept the Bevin scheme of a three-power investigating commission. Apparently the British hoped that Iranian readiness to accept such a commission would increase the chances of its being accepted by the Soviet. The Iranian government felt, however, that it had little to gain and much to lose if such a commission were dispatched and suspected some deal that would legalize Soviet encroachment upon its sovereignty. It complained in the first place that it had not been invited to present its views at the Moscow

---

States, that a tripartite commission for Iranian affairs, composed of representatives of Great Britain, the United States and the Soviet Union, be formed and invested with wide powers.

"The Soviet Government, true to its policy of respecting the state independence of all countries, declined the proposal as one violating the sovereignty and national independence of Iran. In this case the Soviet Government acted in the spirit of the principles of democracy in relations between countries and nations both big and small, which it consistently and steadfastly pursues in all its actions on the international scene. . . ."

[9] *New York Times*, Dec. 28, 1945.

conference, and on January 10 Finance Minister Hazhir announced to the cheering Majlis that the government had rejected the British suggestion. Premier Hakimi confirmed the statement a few days later.

On January 19, 1946, the Iranian delegate to the newly formed United Nations, Seyyid Hasan Taqi-zadeh, formally requested the Security Council to investigate Soviet encroachments in Iran. The Iranian government accused the Soviet Union of interference in the internal affairs of Iran "through the medium of their officials and armed forces" and declared itself ready to furnish "a full statement of the facts" to substantiate its charges.[10]

After an acrimonious debate, during which the Soviet delegation denied Iranian charges but admitted having prevented the Iranian army from entering Azerbaijan, the Council on January 30 decided to refer the matter to direct negotiations between Russia and Iran and to request the parties "to inform the Council of any results achieved in such negotiations."

The result of the Council's debate was to some degree disappointing to the Iranians since they were again left to their own devices. The only gain from their point of view, was that Soviet infiltration was now given world publicity and that the United Nations reserved for itself the right to request from the parties information on the progress of Soviet-Iranian talks.

In the meantime a cabinet crisis occurred in Iran. It was largely due to new Soviet pressure expressed by the severance of all trade between Azerbaijan and the rest of the country. The economic strain thus created was intolerable. Despairing of his ability to settle the quarrel with the Russians and yielding to persuasion, Premier Hakimi resigned on January 22 and the Shah asked Qavam Saltaneh, known for his flirtation with the Tudeh, to form a new cabinet. Qavam, appointed Prime Minister on January 27, began his official duties by dismissing General Ibrahim Arfa, who was of pro-British tendencies, from the post of Chief of Staff of the Army. Arfa was replaced by General Aghevli, an officer interned during the war because of his pro-German sympathies. This was interpreted as a desire on the part of Qavam to make the high personnel of his administration more

[10] *Ibid.*, Jan. 20, 1946.

[295]

acceptable to the Russians before entering into parleys with them. Then, following the Security Council's recommendation, Qavam at the head of a five-man mission left for Moscow. He stayed in the Soviet capital from February 19 till March 11 but failed to reach an agreement. During this two-and-a-half-week stay he saw Stalin twice and Molotov four times. According to the official revelation of Hosein Ala, Iranian Ambassador in Washington, the Soviet leaders formulated the following proposals:

(1) Soviet troops would continue to stay in some parts of Iran for an indefinite period.

(2) The Iranian government would recognize the internal autonomy of Azerbaijan. If the Iranian government acquiesced in this request, the Soviet government offered to take steps to arrange that:

(a) The Prime Minister of Azerbaijan, in relation to the central government, would bear the designation of Governor General.

(b) Azerbaijan would have no Ministry of War or Ministry of Foreign Affairs.

(c) Thirty per cent of the Azerbaijan revenue would be paid to the Iranian central government.

(d) All correspondence with the central government would be in Persian.

(3) The Soviet government would abandon its demand for an oil concession. Instead it proposed that an Iranian-Russian joint stock company be set up with 51 per cent of the shares owned by the Soviets and 49 per cent by Iran.[11]

On March 2, 1946, during Qavam's stay in Moscow, the deadline came for evacuation of all Allied troops. In practice the deadline referred only to British and Soviet troops, as the Americans had left Iran by January 1. The British forces were withdrawn by March 2, but there was no sign of Soviet evacuation, except for some military movements from one district to another inside Iran. The approach of March 2 was watched in Washington and London with growing uneasiness and tension. The failure of the Soviets to evacuate would place before the West a new violation of an international agreement by the Russians and thus complicate the whole matter. It would also call for more positive action on the part of the West, as non-

[11] *New York Times,* March 20, 1946.

evacuation, in contrast to internal interference, would be easy to ascertain.

Encouraged by the timidity of the Security Council in dealing with the situation in January, the Soviet government officially announced that it had decided to withdraw its forces from Khorasan, Shahrud, and Semnan as of March 2 but to retain them in other parts of northern Iran until the situation had been "clarified." [12] This challenge did not remain unanswered. On March 4 Great Britain and on March 8 the United States addressed formal protests to the Soviet Union against the retention of its troops. In Moscow, Qavam lodged a similar protest with the Soviet Foreign Minister and with Stalin personally. Refusing to accept the Soviet demands, he then left for Teheran.

Upon his return he had to face a new crisis. The Fourteenth Majlis was to end its term on March 11. No new elections could take place as long as foreign troops remained in the country. This provision had been voted the previous year by the Fourteenth Majlis itself in order to prevent the packing of a new parliament by the Soviets and the Tudeh, both of whom had made obvious preparations to that end. The lack of a parliament would make the Prime Minister a virtual dictator. Deprived of the Majlis' support he might be more amenable to foreign pressure. Hence a majority of the deputies wanted to prolong the term of the Fourteenth Majlis in order to avoid leaving the country without a parliament during the period when crucial decisions had to be made. But that was exactly what the Tudeh desired. Staging violent mass demonstrations in the parliament square, the Communists barred most of the deputies' entrance to the parliament building on several successive days. As a result, the few deputies who were permitted to arrive never constituted a quorum. This situation lasted until March 11; after that date no legal means could convoke parliament. As a result Qavam became the sole ruler of the country with nothing but the nominal authority of the Shah above him.

In the meantime the military situation was steadily deteriorating. Instead of withdrawing its troops the Soviet government poured in new forces of an offensive character, mainly tanks, and deployed

[12] *Izvestia*, March 2, 1946.

them toward the Turkish and Iraqi borders in the west and toward Teheran in the east. Sherman tanks were observed by Major Carl P. Garver, American air attaché, at Karaj, only twenty-five miles west of Teheran. During the Iranian New Year's holiday of March 21–27 an armed coup by the Tudeh and the Soviet agents was generally expected in the capital. Yet it never materialized. Diplomatic observers ascribed Soviet hesitation at this juncture to the stiffening of the American attitude as evidenced by immediate publicity given the Russian troop movements by the State Department and, on the other hand, by the determined measures taken by the gendarmerie adviser, Colonel Schwarzkopf, to protect the capital.

Despite all pessimistic prognostications, Qavam showed himself an astute statesman and diplomat. Following his instructions, Ambassador Ala appealed for the second time to the United Nations. This time he accused the Soviets of keeping their troops in Iran despite their March 2 deadline for withdrawal and of continued interference "through the medium of Soviet agents, officials and armed forces." Ala's accusation made sensational news in the United States where the Security Council was then meeting. A prolonged debate was characterized by extreme frankness on the part of the Iranian delegate, whose testimony was impressive for its legalistic precision. The Soviets procrastinated and through procedural devices tried to stop the hearing of the case and to keep the Iranian delegate from speaking. At one time the Soviet delegate Andrei Gromyko walked dramatically out of the conference room. During this debate the American government took upon itself the burden of defending the principles of international intercourse. Secretary Byrnes, who appeared in person before the Council, boldly led the American delegation and gave clear signs that the United States assumed responsibility and leadership in international affairs.

For the Soviets the publicity of an international gathering in which they stood in the defendant's box was obviously most inconvenient. Their only hope lay in continuance of direct negotiations with the Iranian Premier, which might result in an agreement favoring their interests. This is probably the explanation why on March 26 Gromyko suddenly announced that his government had reached an agreement with Iran providing for the evacuation of Soviet troops within six weeks after March 24 "if no unforeseen circumstances occur." Steady Soviet pressure on Qavam caused him to instruct Ambassador Ala to demand the removal of the dispute from the Council's agenda. With truly patriotic intransigence Ala declined to follow this instruction, making it clear that his government must have acted under duress. This was undoubtedly true. In fact, the instructions given by Qavam during this nerve-racking period were largely conditioned by his alternating conversations with the Soviet and the American Ambassadors in Teheran. Unfortunately for Iran, the American Ambassador, Mr. Murray, was at this juncture confined to bed at his doctor's orders. As a result, the Soviet Ambassador's calls on the Premier were more frequent and his insistence on a solution satisfactory to Moscow stronger. At this point the American delegation to the United Nations seemed to waver in its resolve to pursue the matter energetically and appeared inclined again to leave Iran to face her formidable neighbor alone. On Secretary Byrnes's suggestion the Security Council decided on April 4 to accept the Soviet statement and "to defer further proceedings on the Iranian appeal until May 6th, at which date the Soviet government and the Iranian government are requested to report to the Council whether the withdrawal of all Soviet troops from the whole of Iran has been completed and at which time the Council shall consider what, if any, further proceedings on the Iranian appeal are required." [13]

The Soviet promise of evacuation was well calculated. On one hand it caused the temporary removal of the dispute from the Council; on the other it served as an inducement to Qavam to comply with the Russian demands. In both points Russia succeeded. On April 4, the day of the Council's decision to defer further proceedings, the Soviet Union and Iran concluded an agreement that comprised the following provisions:

(1) The Red Army was to be evacuated within one month and a half after March 24, 1946.

(2) A joint stock Irano-Soviet oil company was to be established and ratified by the Fifteenth Majlis within seven months after March 24.

(3) "With regard to Azerbaijan, since it is an internal Iranian af-

[13] *New York Times*, April 5, 1946.

fair, peaceful arrangements will be made between the Government and the people of Azerbaijan for the carrying out of improvements in accordance with existing laws and in benevolent spirit toward the people of Azerbaijan."

The details concerning the oil company were contained in the letters exchanged on the same day between Qavam and Sadchikov, the new Soviet Ambassador to Iran. The Soviet government would acquire 51 per cent and the Iranian government 49 per cent of the company's stock. The agreement would be valid for twenty-five years, after which the Soviet and Iranian governments would each possess 50 per cent of the stock. This arrangement would hold for another twenty-five years.

Thus a settlement was reached between Iran and Russia, but at a heavy price. The British press regarded it as a Soviet triumph and even suspected that a secret agreement might be hidden behind it. The comment of the London *Sunday Dispatch* of April 7 was typical of British editorials: "Russia got most of what she wants in fact, if not in form, while Soviet troops were still in Persia. The oil agreement will not be formalized until the Persian Parliament gives its consent. But there is no such parliament and the next elected will, it is understood, contain a sufficient number of pro-Soviet deputies to insure that the oil concessions go through."

NEGOTIATIONS AND AGREEMENT WITH AZERBAIJAN

Once the oil agreement had been extorted, the Soviet government was interested in bringing about an agreement between the central government of Iran and the Azerbaijan rebels as soon as possible. Such an agreement would permit Azerbaijan, as an Iranian province, to send a substantial number of deputies to the Majlis, who, together with other pro-Soviet elements, would ensure the ratification of the oil deal. On his part Qavam, anxious to reach an agreement with Tabriz, announced on April 22 a seven-point program for the return of Azerbaijan to the jurisdiction of the Iranian state. The program, while conceding many points to local autonomy, made it clear that Azerbaijan must be returned as an integral province of Iran.

On April 28 Pishevari, heading a six-man delegation, arrived in Teheran for negotiations. A fortnight in the capital brought no results. Pishevari insisted on three points unacceptable to Qavam. These were (a) the right of the Azerbaijan government to appoint a governor for the province; (b) the distribution of state-owned land to the peasants; and (3) the appointment of commanders of the Azerbaijan army and gendarmerie by the Azerbaijan government.

On May 15 Pishevari returned to Tabriz, and in a broadcast through the local radio warned the central government that any attempt by Iranian forces to invade Azerbaijan would constitute a breach of the agreement with the Soviet Union. This statement seemed to imply that Pishevari was on the defensive. This was undoubtedly so, because on May 9, during his stay in Teheran, the Red Army had evacuated the territory of Iran. At Lake Success, New York, where the Security Council was wrangling about the legal aspects of the evacuation, the news was greeted with joy, for it indicated that the United Nations was able to settle a problem "leading to international friction." This rejoicing was premature. The Soviets did evacuate their forces, but only after having obtained an oil concession and having left behind a revolutionary Communist regime in Azerbaijan apt to act as a powerful lever of pressure on Iran. With these two factors the Security Council was unwilling to deal. It only paid lip service to international morality by retaining the matter on its agenda despite Soviet protests at the final session devoted to Iran.

The break in negotiations with Azerbaijan leaders in Teheran was not final. Both sides had good reasons for desiring a settlement. On May 17 talks with Pishevari were reopened, this time at Tabriz. The Iranian mission was headed by Mozaffar Firuz, Director of Propaganda under Qavam, who throughout the whole crisis maintained a decidedly pro-Soviet attitude.[14] On June 14 a ten-point agreement was finally concluded. Its provisions were:

[14] While Ambassador Ala courageously defended the cause of Iran before the Security Council, Firuz, at press conferences in Teheran, frequently contradicted Ala's statements and publicly disavowed him. On certain occasions he went so far as to make statements opposed to the wishes of his chief Qavam. Acting as Qavam's interpreter at some conferences, he distorted the Premier's statements and thus provoked complaints from foreign correspondents. This eventually led

(1) The Azerbaijan parliament will become a Provincial Council.

(2) The Provincial Council will make four nominations for the Provincial Governor General, and the central government's Minister of Interior will appoint one of them.

(3) The Azerbaijan army will be incorporated into the Iranian army with a commission arranging details.

(4) Azerbaijan's irregular soldiers will become part of the national gendarmerie.

(5) The Provincial Treasury will receive 75 per cent of Azerbaijan taxes with Teheran receiving the rest.

(6) Using Azerbaijan labor, the central government will build railways between Mianeh and Tabriz.

(7) The Teheran government will assist in establishing a proposed Azerbaijani university.

(8) Both Persian and Turkish will be recognized as official languages, and primary school instruction will be given in each.

(9) The government will pay for private lands confiscated by the Azerbaijan regime for distribution to the peasants and will approve the distribution of public lands.

(10) Election laws will be revised to establish parliamentary representation on a population basis.[15]

The agreement was undoubtedly a victory for the Communists. While preserving the nominal authority of Teheran over the province, it conceded virtually all the wishes of Pishevari. The most important controversial points—land distribution, selection of the governor, armed forces, taxes, and parliamentary representation—were solved in favor of the Azerbaijan regime. The fact that the negotiations that led to the agreement were conducted by Firuz, a man of doubtful loyalty, and not in Teheran but in Tabriz, where they were reportedly under the benevolent eye of the Soviet Consul General, was not without significance. The result was a second round scored by the Soviet side.

Iran's ability to withstand Soviet pressure was in direct proportion to the intensity of international action in defense of small nations'

the Premier to make use of another interpreter. Firuz, however, still remained in his responsible office.

15 *New York Times,* June 15, 1946.

rights. The conclusion of the Security Council proceedings took the Iranian case off the first-page headlines of the Allied press, and public interest in the West gradually abated. Left again to her own devices, Iran was gradually slipping into the Soviet orbit. The conclusion of the Azerbaijan agreement was only an opening wedge for further concessions. First of all, in fulfillment of the agreement Qavam appointed a new governor general for Azerbaijan. The appointment went to Dr. Salamollah Javid, former Minister of Interior in the Azerbaijan government. Pishevari himself did not obtain any public office, yet as chief of the Democratic party of Azerbaijan he remained the virtual boss of the province.

Secondly, on August 2, Qavam reshuffled his cabinet and included three Tudeh members. They were Iraj Iskandari, Minister of Commerce and Industry; Dr. Firidun Keshavarz, Education; and Dr. Morteza Yazdi, Health. In addition, Firuz, now openly pro-Tudeh, was given the post of Vice-Premier and Minister of Labor and Propaganda. This "popular front" cabinet had many characteristics of classical Communist infiltration into the governing apparatus of a non-Communist country. Such penetration usually began with granting to the Communists industrial, labor, education, and propaganda agencies and ended by conceding to them the key portfolios of Interior, Defense, and Foreign Affairs. Such at least was the pattern in central-eastern Europe between 1944 and 1948, and there were good reasons to expect that similar developments would take place in Iran.

This reshuffling of the cabinet was done to the accompaniment of violent riots provoked by the Tudeh in Khuzistan. On July 16 a general strike broke out in the section owned by the Anglo-Iranian Oil Company. It involved 100,000 native workers and resulted in 17 killed and 150 wounded among the company's European and native personnel. The strikers, led by Reza Rusta, a Tudeh leader prominent in Iranian trade unions, committed several acts of sabotage which resulted in the loss of more than 300,000 tons of oil and endangered general production. Thus Communist influence was felt not only in Teheran, but also in the southern areas, vitally affecting the security of the British Empire and the smooth operations of the Royal Navy.

THE BRITISH REACTION

British policy, as pointed out earlier, was dedicated to the evacuation of foreign troops from Iran and to the preservation of Iranian independence. Failing to achieve this ideal, the British were ready to compromise with the Russians, provided Soviet influence did not overrun the boundaries of the northern zone, as Mr. Bevin's suggestions during the Moscow conference indicated. But the extension of Soviet power into the government itself and into the south was a point on which the British were adamant. Such an extension was almost a *casus belli* for Great Britain and called for vigorous action. Early in 1946 reports reached Teheran that the British protégé, Sheikh Khazal of Mohammera, who had lived in exile in Iraq, had gathered a force of Arab warriors and raided Khuzistan. This appeared to be a British-sponsored separatist movement in the south which could be interpreted as a countermove to the separatism incited by the Soviets in the north. Moreover, the day after the announcement of the new cabinet in Teheran, British troops were ordered from India to Basra on adjoining Iraqi territory. The next day, to avoid any legal complications, the Iraqi government made a statement approving this landing as in accord with the Anglo-Iraqi treaty of 1930.

Simultaneously several tribal chieftains in the south announced that they were very critical of the Tudeh and its increased influence. A few days later the Iraqi Independence party demanded the return of Khuzistan to Iraq, arguing that the province, inhabited mainly by Arabs, should return to an Arab country. In turn a news dispatch from Bagdad said that one of the leading chieftains of Khuzistan, Sheikh Abdullah, had arrived in the Iraqi capital en route to Cairo to protest to the Arab League against the mistreatment of Arabs by the Iranian government.

The situation grew tense. Qavam protested to the British government against the landing of troops in Basra, basing his statements on the announcement of the government of India that the troops might be used for the protection of British interests in Iran. While the British Foreign Office denied that such was the intention, it made clear, nevertheless, in a statement of August 6 that the troops had been sent to Iraq in connection with supplies of oil and the security of the Empire. On the other hand, reports were heard about Soviet military concentrations north of the Azerbaijan border. Qavam's dramatic gesture on August 18 of arresting a number of the more unruly Tudeh leaders did not ease the tension. In the first week of September a Bakhtiyari plot with the aim of overthrowing the government was reported in Isfahan, and on September 23 an open tribal rebellion broke out in the Fars. A coalition of Qashqais, Bakhtiyaris, and several minor tribes from Fars, Khuzistan, and the Gulf coast was formed under the leadership of Nasir Khan Qashqai. It demanded the ousting of Tudeh ministers from the cabinet, local self-government for the southern provinces, and an increase in parliamentary representation. A demand to this effect to be forwarded to Teheran was handed over by the coalition leaders on September 23 to General Mehdi Fatemi, Governor General of Fars. The rebels captured Bushire, Abadeh, Kazerun, Bandar Amir, and besieged Shiraz. The revolt spread even to Kerman, where an influential local leader, former Deputy Gobadian, joined the insurrectionists. In Fars the tribes created a revolutionary junta entitled *Sedun* and called their rebellion a National Movement. Their cause was supported by the Moslem clergy of the south. A petition signed by a number of prominent religious leaders reached the government demanding elimination of the Tudeh from the cabinet and public life.

The Moscow radio and press openly accused the British of instigating this revolt. Three British officials were special targets of Russian anger. They were Colonel Underwood, British military tribal expert; Alan Charles Trott, Consul General at Ahwaz; and C. A. Gault, Consul General at Isfahan. Anxious lest their gains in Teheran be erased, the Russians dispatched to Iran the chief of the Middle East Department in the Soviet Ministry of Foreign Affairs. This dignitary was reported to have pressed the Iranian government for speedy ratification of the oil agreement and also to have proposed an alliance with the suggestion that Iran withdraw from the Saadabad Pact of 1937.[16] The visit of the Soviet official was not without effect. On

[16] The Pact of Saadabad was concluded on July 8, 1937, by Iran, Turkey, Iraq, and Afghanistan. According to the Preamble the signatories were "animated by

September 28 the Iranian government asked the British to investigate charges against both the afore-mentioned consuls, and on October 1 it formally demanded the recall of Trott. The day before Nasir Khan, in the name of the revolting tribes, had presented a twenty-four-hour ultimatum to the mission that the government had sent to Fars. Facing such an uncompromising attitude, the government mollified its stand, and two weeks later a settlement was reached with Nasir Khan by General Zahedi, commander of the garrison in Shiraz. The government recognized most of the tribes' demands. On October 17 Qavam resigned, together with other members of the government, and in the new cabinet that he created immediately afterwards the three Communist ministers were not included. Firuz was also dropped; instead he was dispatched to Moscow as Ambassador.

From the British viewpoint the tribal rebellion fulfilled its aims. The spread of Tudeh influence in the south was arrested, and Communist infiltration into the nerve center at Teheran was ended. Although Qavam was officially obliged to make protests to the British government about the activities of their consular officials, it is not improbable that he was pleased with this show of British strength and determination.

THE EMERGENCE OF AMERICAN LEADERSHIP

Having eliminated Communist influence in the south, Qavam now turned his eyes to the north with the aim of consolidating his power over the whole country. On June 30 the Premier announced the formation of a new political party that with oriental cunning he

---

the desire to ensure peace and security in the Near East by means of additional guarantees." The treaty provided for nonintervention in internal affairs, nonaggression, and consultation and contained a definition of aggression. Clause VII of the pact said: "Each of the High Contracting Parties agrees to take measures within its own sphere, against the formation or activities of armed bands, associations or organizations for the subversion of established institutions with a view to the disturbance of the order or security of any part, frontier or otherwise, of the territory of the other Party, or with a view to the disturbance of the authority of the Government of that other Party."

The pact as a whole did not meet with enthusiastic reception in Moscow, which suspected the signatories of trying to build a barrier on the southern flanks of the U.S.S.R. Clause VII was generally interpreted as a mutual promise to stamp out Communism in the signatory states.

called the Democratic party. This Democratic party had nothing in common with its namesake in Azerbaijan and was composed exclusively of pro-Qavam and non-Communist elements. The new party was destined to play a major role in the forthcoming elections to the Fifteenth Majlis. The elections were to begin on December 7, but Qavam made it clear that they would not be held unless the government were in a position to supervise them all over the country including Azerbaijan. This certainly was a courageous policy on the part of the Iranian Premier, because it meant the introduction of the Iranian army into Azerbaijan and the challenging of the *status quo* in the province. Three factors played a decisive role in thus emboldening Qavam. The first was, paradoxically enough, a certain Soviet weakness. The Russians, who had extorted the oil agreement while their army was in Iran, now needed badly its ratification, and this could not be done without a duly elected parliament. The Soviet was thus vitally interested in the speedy election of the new Majlis. The existence of an independent Azerbaijan regime was an obstacle to this road, and thus Russia was put between two mutually exclusive alternatives: either having the Majlis and the ratification of the agreement or a Communist-dominated Azerbaijan with an indefinite postponement of the ratification. To combine both alternatives, it would be necessary to invade Iran again, or at least to threaten an invasion, and such an act would put the Soviet Union technically in the position of an aggressor and might produce a violent reaction in the West. Conscious of this Soviet dilemma, Qavam was ready to exploit it to the utmost of his resources.

The second factor in encouraging the Premier was undoubtedly the British strength manifested by the tribal rebellion.

The third was a more positive American diplomacy. In April, 1946, George V. Allen, Deputy Director of the Office of Near Eastern and African Affairs in the Department of State, was appointed Ambassador to Iran. Youthful, yet possessing long diplomatic experience, the new Ambassador arrived in the capital of Iran at a time when Secretary Byrnes was giving proofs of increasing responsibility and initiative before the United Nations. Allen's role in the crucial months that followed was of prime importance. Having quickly established excellent relations with Iranian statesmen, the new envoy did not spare his energy in bolstering up the courage of the small nation's leaders. Giving a forceful interpretation of the new trends in American foreign policy, Allen was successful in convincing many influential Iranians that there was no third alternative between Soviet totalitarianism and the Western pattern of liberal democracy, and that in the great battle of ideologies there was no place for hesitant neutrality.

Encouraged by the manifestations of a more determined and co-ordinated Western policy, Qavam sent up a "trial balloon." In the middle of November he ordered the arrest of a hundred leading Tudeh members in Teheran. And on November 24 the Premier ordered the troops to march into Azerbaijan to supervise parliamentary elections. As revealed later by Ambassador Ala in a letter addressed to the Security Council, "The Soviet Ambassador at Teheran, acting under instructions from his government, has given friendly admonition that the movement of government forces into this part of Iran may result in disturbances within that Province on the Persian borders adjacent to Russia, and advised that the government's plans be abandoned." [17] Qavam, however, did not abandon his plans. The American Ambassador came to his succor. In a statement made on December 4 to a British correspondent, Allen said that in his opinion the dispatch of government troops into Azerbaijan to ensure tranquil elections was "quite normal and appropriate." A few days later Under-Secretary of State Dean Acheson expressed himself similarly in Washington, thus endorsing the Ambassador's view. On the very day of his statement Allen was vigorously attacked by *Pravda* for his alleged support of reactionary elements and interference in the internal affairs of Iran. This was followed by a general outburst in the Soviet press against the United States, which was accused of seeking bases in the Middle East.

When government troops crossed the Azerbaijan border, Pishevari issued a call to resistance, promising an unrelenting fight. But apart from a few minor skirmishes, the Azerbaijani Democrats were unable to put a stop to the central army's advance. According to American correspondents who preceded the advancing Iranian army, the populace eagerly awaited the approach of government troops and

[17] *New York Times,* Dec. 7, 1946.

greeted them as liberators. On December 14 the Azerbaijan regime collapsed. Tabriz was captured by government troops and several Democrat leaders, including Governor Javid, were put under arrest. Pishevari escaped to the Soviet Union. Some time afterwards he was reported killed in a motor accident at Baku. A number of Democrats followed him across the border, and the rest dispersed. At the same time the government army captured the Kurdish stronghold of Mahabad. Qazi Mohammed, the President of the Kurdish Republic, and his brother Sadraq Qazi were caught and, after a trial, shot. Back at Teheran stern measures were taken against the Tudeh, whose headquarters were raided and a number of whose members were thrown in prison. The triumph of the government was complete. Azerbaijan was reunited with the rest of the country exactly a year after separation; the Kurdish movement was curbed; and the Tudeh Party was reduced to impotence in the capital.

The road was thus opened for parliamentary elections. These began on January 11, 1947, and were concluded in most districts by February. Yet it was only in the middle of August that the Fifteenth Majlis was finally inaugurated. Qavam's Democratic party won a substantial majority of seats. The opposition led by Dr. Mosaddeq counted about twenty-five deputies. The Communists won two seats. Their chief spokesman was Abbas Iskandari, elected from Hamadan. The first weeks of the new parliament were spent on routine business such as confirmation of mandates and election of officers. Simultaneously, behind the scenes there was feverish political activity preparatory to the inevitable debate on the oil agreement. When the Majlis met, it was generally assumed that it would promptly ratify the oil deal. Qavam himself reportedly desired to placate Soviet apprehensions by speedy ratification. Soviet Ambassador Sadchikov pressed the Premier repeatedly to speed up the ratification. On August 28 and September 15 he handed to Qavam formal notes in which the Iranian government's delaying tactics were called a "return to the policy of enmity towards and discrimination against the Soviet Union." Yet the Russians met strong and rather unexpected resistance. In a series of forceful speeches before the Majlis the deputies of the opposition attacked the oil agreement as harmful, illegal, and as "the worst agreement in the past hundred years of

Iranian history." [18] One of the sessions was marked by such violent criticism of the Premier's policies that he and the majority supporting him walked out in protest from the chamber. The nationalist press caught up with the opposition's attitude, and one newspaper went so far as to demand the imprisonment and trial of the Prime Minister of his unconstitutional dealing in signing the oil agreement with the Russians.[19] On the other hand, even the Premier's supporters were giving signs of being against the ratification. On September 28 Qavam's Director of Propaganda, Khaje Nuri, appealed in a broadcast for purely national control of the oil resources.

In the midst of mounting Iranian courage, Ambassador Allen issued an epoch-making statement. Speaking on September 11 in the Irano-American Cultural Relations Society, Allen made it clear that in the view of the American government Iran was perfectly free to accept or to reject the Soviet offer, and that if she chose to reject it, she could count on the support of the United States against Soviet threats and pressure. The Ambassador declared:

> The United States has no proper concern with proposals of a commercial or any other nature made to Iran by any foreign government as long as those proposals are advanced solely on their merits, to stand or fall on their value to Iran. We and every other nation in the world, however, do become concerned when such proposals are accompanied by threats of bitter enmity or by a statement that it would be dangerous for Iran to refuse.

> The United States is firm in its conviction that any proposals made by one sovereign government to another should not be accompanied by threats or intimidation. When such methods are used in an effort to obtain acceptance doubt is cast on the value of the proposals.

Stressing that American policy was devoted to the removal of fear of aggression in the world, he continued:

> Our determination to follow this policy as regards Iran is as strong as anywhere else in the world. This purpose can be achieved to the extent that the Iranian people show a determination to defend their own sovereignty. Patriotic Iranians, when considering matters affecting their national interest, may therefore rest assured that the American people will support fully their freedom to make their own choice.

[18] The deputies criticizing the agreement were Emami Ahari, Abdul Qadir Azad (from Khorasan), Dr. Abdul Hosein Etebar, and Abbas Massudi.

[19] *Tehran-i-Emruz* (instead of suspended *Atash*), Sept. 28, 1947.

Iran's resources belong to Iran. Iran can give them away free of charge
or refuse to dispose of them at any price if it so desires.[20]

This statement was undoubtedly of capital importance as far as
the policies of Qavam and the Majlis were concerned. It was also
timely, because, contrary to what might be expected, the British government wavered in its support of Iran in the last minute. In a note
addressed to the Premier by the new British Ambassador Sir John Le
Rougetel, the British Embassy advised Iran to keep the door open
for future discussions with Russia on the subject of oil. On September
12 a Foreign Office spokesman in London confirmed that Great
Britain had no objection in principle to Iran's granting an oil concession to the Soviet Union.[21] Observers in Teheran and London felt
that this different approach by the British was dictated by their fear
that Iran's rejection of the agreement would be too provocative to
the Soviets and might eventually lead to the cancellation of the
British oil concession in the south.

As it was, the American statement of policy seemed to impress the
Iranians more than British hesitation. Ambassador Allen's declaration, it must be pointed out, was not an isolated outburst of American
charity toward Iran. It was a logical consequence of a policy that
had been gradually developed in 1946 during the Irano-Soviet dispute over Azerbaijan and which, on April 13, 1947, had found its
dramatic expression in the American President's "Truman Doctrine"
speech. In that memorable statement the President had made public
the American policy of containment of Communism all over the
world and of the defense of small nations against aggression and infiltration. He had also pledged specific economic and military aid to
Greece and Turkey. This new determined policy found its organizational expression in the State Department. A new unit called the
Division for Greek, Turkish, and Iranian Affairs was created. Thus
Iran was put on a par with Greece and Turkey, two other countries
threatened with immediate Soviet expansion.

The consequences of this energetic American support were felt
in Iran immediately. On October 22, 1947, the Majlis rejected the oil
agreement with the Soviet Union by a vote of 102 to 2 despite loud

[20] *New York Times,* Sept. 12, 1947.
[21] *Ibid.,* Sept. 13, 1947.

objections from the Communist deputy Abbas Iskandari. Instead a bill, introduced by Deputy Reza-zadeh Shafaq and sponsored by Qavam himself, was adopted containing the following provisions:

(1) Iran will explore her own oil resources during the next five years with her own capital.

(2) The Premier's negotiations for an oil agreement with the Soviet Union were null and void.

(3) Iran will not be permitted to grant any concessions to foreign powers or to have foreign partners or assistance in oil exploration.

(4) If oil is found in Iran within the next five years, the government might negotiate with Russia with a view to selling oil.

(5) Iran must negotiate with the Anglo-Iranian Oil Company to obtain a higher share of its profits.

Tension increased between the Soviet Union and Iran. On November 20 the Soviet Embassy in a note to Qavam accused the Iranian government of hostile activity against Russia and hinted at the possibility of a rupture of diplomatic relations. This was followed by a series of notes throughout the first half of 1948, in which Russia protested against increased American influence in Iran and the "militarizing" of Iran by the United States.[22] She also demanded suppression of the hostile press. The United States was accused of seeking to make Iran a "strategic base," presumably to be used against Russia. These notes were accompanied by a campaign of intimidation in the Soviet press. On April 4 *Pravda* and *Izvestia* went so far as to liken the presence of American advisers and American influence in Iran to Nazi activities in that country in 1941 on the eve of the Soviet-British occupation. Such statements had sinister connotations for the Iranians. They meant that Moscow was preparing ground for possible invocation of the 1921 treaty, which permitted Russia under certain circumstances to send her army into Iran. The absence of Ambassador Sadchikov from the diplomatic ceremony on the occasion of the Iranian New Year (*No-ruz*) was ominously significant. Early in April these verbal threats were backed up by concrete Soviet measures in the Caspian. Russian shipping to Iran was curtailed, and their technicians began to dismantle harbor installations at Pahlavi in the area held under special concession. At the same time

[22] These notes were delivered on January 31, March 28, and April 8, 1948.

reports reached Teheran of increased infiltration into Iranian territory of refugee Tudeh agents, former Azerbaijan *fedais,* and armed "immigrants" from the Soviet Caucasus. On April 10 the daily *Saba,* claiming to derive its information from government sources, revealed widespread Soviet preparations for a new revolution in Iran. According to the newspaper the new revolutionary wave would start in the Caspian province of Gorgan and be followed by outbreaks in Mazanderan, Isfahan, and even among the Bakhtiyari and Boer Ahmadi tribes in the south.

The Iranian government's reaction to this array of pressure and rumors was on the whole dignified and courageous, contrasting with its general timidity during wartime. Ibrahim Hakimi, who replaced Qavam as Premier in December, 1947, and who was known for his pro-Western sympathies, parried the Soviet notes with his own, denying any hostile intentions against Russia and blaming her for violations of the 1921 Treaty of Friendship. On the internal scene he kept a watchful eye on the Communists, and early in April he ordered the arrest of 300 Tudeh members and sympathizers in Mazanderan. At the same time he strove to strengthen the links between his country and the United States. In the attitude of official Washington he found understanding and continued support. As far back as June 20, 1947, an agreement had been signed between the United States and Iran providing for sale to the latter of military weapons and supplies from American war surplus stocks. The Majlis ratified this agreement under Hakimi's premiership on February 17, 1948, allowing purchases up to a $10,000,000 limit. On the other hand, following an understanding between the two governments on October 6, 1947, the services of the United States Military and Gendarmerie Missions were extended until March 20, 1949. The Military Mission, headed by Major General Robert W. Grow, after General Ridley's retirement, was somewhat increased in numbers, reaching the figure of eighteen commissioned and eight noncommissioned officers. Colonel Schwarzkopf (promoted to the rank of Brigadier General) made great strides, on the other hand, in increasing the efficiency and fighting power of the Iranian Gendarmerie Corps. Chosen as a target of special attacks by the Soviet press, Schwarzkopf was tireless in inspecting all those places where trouble was brewing. He helped in no small degree to ensure firm government control in Azerbaijan and the northern provinces.

The continued interest of the United States in the preservation of Iranian independence was confirmed on May 28, 1948, when John D. Jernegan, chief of the State Department's Division of Greek, Turkish, and Iranian Affairs outlined to the Senate Appropriations Committee the military aid program to Iran. Iran, according to this statement, was to receive $60,000,000 in "non-aggressive weapons" and the program was intended to "maintain the international security of Iran." The figure mentioned by Jernegan was six times larger than the maximum allowed by the Majlis. It meant that the State Department was planning ahead with the assumption that further agreements with Iran may be reached to strengthen her fighting capacity.

Postwar developments in Iran indicate that, far from receding into the shadow, the country of the Lion and Sun continues to occupy a key position in international politics and strategy. The artificially engineered Azerbaijan rebellion, the strikes and violence in Khuzistan, the infiltration of Communists into the central government in 1946, and the episode of the oil concession prove that the Soviet Union has not renounced her plans for revolutionary and imperial expansion into and through Iran, so appropriately termed "a Suez Canal of the revolution." On the other hand, Britain's classical counteraction through tribal revolt in the south and the appearance of Indian troops at Basra as well as her continued general interest seem to indicate that the role of Iran in over-all British strategic and political concepts has not changed. Nor, for that matter, has there been any basic alteration of British policy following the victory of the Labour party at the polls in the summer of 1945. One can even detect somewhat firmer accents in British policy since Ernest Bevin assumed the duties of Foreign Secretary. An entirely new factor has been the emergence of American interest and leadership. Its full implications cannot yet be measured, but its importance for political and economic developments in the Middle East as a whole cannot be denied. The United States has the unique advantage of not being burdened with memories of past imperialistic exploitation or with any desire to proselytize by force of bayonets. American policy toward Iran since 1945 has been characterized by clarity, honest self-interest, courage, and vision. It has abandoned, it seems for good, its old shell of isolationism, and it promises not only to save a small but important country from annihilation, but to set a general pattern for international relations based on peace with justice. Iran will always have the onerous privilege of being a testing ground, at least as long as Russia maintains her present system and policies. To the United States, in its new world role, this bequeaths a legacy of constant vigilance and intelligent preparedness.

Appendices

Excerpts from the Treaty of Friendship between Iran and

the Russian Socialist Federal Soviet Republic,

Signed at Moscow, February 26, 1921

ARTICLE 5

The two High Contracting Parties undertake:

(1) To prohibit the formation or presence within their respective territories, of any organization or groups of persons, irrespective of the name by which they are known, whose object is to engage in acts of hostility against Persia or Russia, or against the Allies of Russia.

They will likewise prohibit the formation of troops or armies within their respective territories with the aforementioned object.

(2) Not to allow a third party or organization, whatever it be called, which is hostile to the other Contracting Party, to import or to convey in transit across their countries material which can be used against the other party.

(3) To prevent by all means in their power the presence within their territories or within the territories of their Allies of all armies or forces of a third party in cases in which the presence of such forces would be regarded as a menace to the frontiers, interests or safety of the other Contracting Party.

ARTICLE 6

If a third party should attempt to carry out a policy of usurpation by means of armed intervention in Persia, or if such Power should desire to use Persian territory as a base of operations against Russia, or if a Foreign Power should threaten the frontiers of Federal Russia or those of its Allies, and if the Persian Government should not be able to put a stop to such menace after having been once called upon to do so by Russia, Russia shall have the right to advance her troops into the Persian interior for the purpose of carrying out the military operations necessary for its defence. Russia undertakes, however, to withdraw her troops from Persian territory as soon as the danger has been removed.

Annex 2 to the Treaty

Teheran, 12th December, 1921

Your Excellency,

In reply to your letter dated 20th day of Ghows, I have the honour to inform you that Articles 5 and 6 are intended to apply only to cases in which preparations have been made for a considerable armed attack upon Russia or the Soviet Republics allied to her, by the partisans of the regime which has been overthrown or by its supporters among those foreign Powers which are in a position to assist the enemies of the Workers' and Peasants' Republics and at the same time to possess themselves, by force or by underhand methods, of part of the Persian territory, thereby establishing a base of operations for any attacks—made either directly or through the counter-revolutionary forces—which they might meditate against Russia or the Soviet Republics allied to her. The Articles referred to are therefore in no sense intended to apply to verbal or written attacks directed against the Soviet Government by the various Persian groups, or even by any Russian *émigrés* in Persia, in so far as such attacks are generally tolerated as between neighbouring Powers animated by sentiments of mutual friendship.

With regard to Article 13 and 20, and the small error to which you draw attention in Article 3 with reference to the Convention of 1881, I am in a position to state categorically, as I have always stated, that my Government, whose attitude towards the Persian nation is entirely friendly, has never sought to place any restrictions upon the progress and prosperity of Persia. I myself fully share this attitude, and would be prepared, should friendly relations be maintained between the two countries to promote negotiations with a view to a total or partial revision of these Articles on the lines desired by the Persian Government, as far as the interests of Russia permit.

In view of the preceding statements, I trust that, as you promised me in your letter, your Government and the Mejlis will ratify the Treaty in question as soon as possible.

I have the honour to be, Your Excellency, etc.

(Signed) ROTHSTEIN
Diplomatic Representative of the
Russian Socialist Federal Soviet Republic

APPENDIX II

Treaty of Alliance between the United Kingdom and the

Soviet Union and Iran,

Signed at Teheran, January 29, 1942

His Majesty The King of Great Britain, Ireland and the British Dominions beyond the Seas, Emperor of India, and the Union of Soviet Socialist Republics, on the one hand, and His Imperial Majesty The Shahinshah of Iran, on the other;

Having in view the principles of the Atlantic Charter jointly agreed upon and announced to the world by the President of the United States of America and the Prime Minister of the United Kingdom on the 14th August, 1941, and endorsed by the Government of the Union of Soviet Socialist Republics on the 24th September, 1941, with which His Imperial Majesty The Shahinshah declares his complete agreement and from which he wishes to benefit on an equal basis with other nations of the world; and

Being anxious to strengthen the bonds of friendship and mutual understanding between them; and

Considering that these objects will best be achieved by the conclusion of a Treaty of Alliance;

Have agreed to conclude a treaty for this purpose and have appointed as their plenipotentiaries;

His Majesty The King of Great Britain, Ireland and the British Dominions beyond the Seas, Emperor of India,

For the United Kingdom of Great Britain and Northern Ireland,

His Excellency Sir Reader William Bullard, K.C.M.G., C.I.E.,

His Majesty's Envoy Extraordinary and Minister Plenipotentiary in Iran.

The Union of Soviet Socialist Republics,

His Excellency M. Andre Andreewich Smirnov, Ambassador Extraordinary and Minister Plenipotentiary of the Union of Soviet Socialist Republics in Iran.

His Imperial Majesty The Shahinshah of Iran,

His Excellency M. Ali Soheily, Minister for Foreign Affairs.

Who, having communicated their full powers, found in good and due form, have agreed as follows:

ARTICLE 1

His Majesty The King of Great Britain, Ireland and the British Dominions beyond the Seas, Emperor of India, and the Union of Soviet

Socialist Republics (hereinafter referred to as the Allied Powers) jointly and severally undertake to respect the territorial integrity, sovereignty and political independence of Iran.

ARTICLE 2

An alliance is established between the Allied Powers on the one hand and His Imperial Majesty The Shahinshah of Iran on the other.

ARTICLE 3

(i) The Allied Powers jointly and severally undertake to defend Iran by all means at their command from all aggression on the part of Germany or any other Power.

(ii) His Imperial Majesty The Shahinshah undertakes—

(a) to co-operate with the Allied Powers with all the means at his command and in every way possible, in order that they may be able to fulfil the above undertaking. The assistance of the Iranian forces shall, however, be limited to the maintenance of internal security on Iranian territory;

(b) to secure to the Allied Powers, for the passage of troops or supplies from one Allied Power to the other or for other similar purposes, the unrestricted right to use, maintain, guard and, in case of military necessity, control in any way that they may require all means of communication throughout Iran, including railways, roads, rivers, aerodromes, ports, pipelines and telephone, telegraph and wireless installations;

(c) to furnish all possible assistance and facilities in obtaining material and recruiting labour for the purpose of the maintenance and improvement of the means of communication referred to in paragraph (b);

(d) to establish and maintain, in collaboration with the Allied Powers, such measures of censorship control as they may require for all the means of communication referred to in paragraph (b).

(iii) It is clearly understood that in the application of paragraph (ii) (b), (c) and (d) of the present article the Allied Powers will give full consideration to the essential needs of Iran.

ARTICLE 4

(i) The Allied Powers may maintain in Iranian territory land, sea and air forces in such number as they consider necessary. The location of such forces shall be decided in agreement with the Iranian Government so long as the strategic situation allows. All questions concerning the relations between the forces of the Allied Powers and the Iranian authorities shall be settled so far as possible in co-operation with the Iranian authorities in such a way as to safeguard the security of the said forces. It is understood that the presence of these forces on Iranian territory does not constitute a military occupation and will disturb as little as possible the administration and the security forces of Iran, the economic life of the country, the normal movements of the population and the application of Iranian laws and regulations.

(ii) A separate agreement or agreements shall be concluded as soon as possible after the entry into force of the present Treaty regarding any financial obligations to be borne by the Allied Powers under the provisions of the present article and of paragraphs (ii) (b), (c) and (d) of Article 3 above in such matters as local purchases, the hiring of buildings and plant, the employment of labour, transport charges, etc. A special agreement shall be concluded between the Allied Governments and the Iranian Government defining the conditions for any transfers to the Iranian Government after the war of buildings and other improvements effected by the Allied Powers on Iranian territory. These agreements shall also settle the immunities to be enjoyed by the forces of the Allied Powers in Iran.

ARTICLE 5

The forces of the Allied Powers shall be withdrawn from Iranian territory not later than six months after all hostilities between the Allied Powers and Germany and her associates have been suspended by the conclusion of an armistice or armistices, or on the conclusion of peace between them, whichever date is the earlier. The expression "associates" of Germany means all other Powers which have engaged or may in the future engage in hostilities against either of the Allied Powers.

ARTICLE 6

(i) The Allied Powers undertake in their relations with foreign countries not to adopt an attitude which is prejudicial to the territorial integrity, sovereignty or political independence of Iran, nor to conclude treaties inconsistent with the provisions of the present Treaty. They undertake to consult the Government of His Imperial Majesty The Shahinshah in all matters affecting the direct interests of Iran.

(ii) His Imperial Majesty The Shahinshah undertakes not to adopt in his relations with foreign countries an attitude which is inconsistent with the alliance, nor to conclude treaties inconsistent with the provisions of the present Treaty.

ARTICLE 7

The Allied Powers jointly undertake to use their best endeavours to safeguard the economic existence of the Iranian people against the privations and difficulties arising as a result of the present war. On the entry into force of the present Treaty, discussions shall be opened between the Government of Iran and the Governments of the Allied Powers as to the best possible methods of carrying out the above undertaking.

ARTICLE 8

The provisions of the present Treaty are equally binding as bilateral obligations between His Imperial Majesty The Shahinshah and each of the two other High Contracting Parties.

ARTICLE 9

The present Treaty shall come into force on signature and shall remain in force until the date fixed for the withdrawal of the forces of the Allied Power from Iranian territory in accordance with Article 5.

In witness whereof, the above-named plenipotentiaries have signed the present Treaty and have affixed thereto their seals.

Done at Teheran in triplicate in English, Russian and Persian, all being equally authentic, on the 29th day of January, 1942.

(L.S.)   R. W. BULLARD

(L.S.)   A. A. SMIRNOV

(L.S.)   ALI SOHEILY

APPENDIX III

The Anglo-American-Soviet Declaration Concerning Iran,

Issued at Teheran, December 1, 1943

The President of the United States of America, the Premier of the U.S.S.R., and the Prime Minister of the United Kingdom, having consulted with each other and with the Prime Minister of Iran, desire to declare the mutual agreement of their three Governments regarding relations with Iran.

The Governments of the United States of America, the U.S.S.R. and the United Kingdom recognize the assistance which Iran has given in the prosecution of the war against the common enemy, particularly by facilitating the transportation of supplies from overseas to the Soviet Union. The three Governments realize that the war has caused special economic difficulties for Iran and they agreed that they will continue to make available to the Iran Government such economic assistance as may be possible, having regard to the heavy demands made upon them by their world-wide military operations and to the world-wide shortage of transport, raw materials and supplies for civilian consumption.

With respect to the post-war period, the Governments of the United

States of America, the U.S.S.R. and the United Kingdom are in accord with the Government of Iran that any economic problem confronting Iran at the close of hostilities should receive full consideration along with those of other members of the United Nations by conferences or international agencies, held or created, to deal with international economic matters.

The Governments of the United States of America, the U.S.S.R. and the United Kingdom are at one with the Government of Iran in their desire for the maintenance of the independence, sovereignty and territorial integrity of Iran. They count upon the participation of Iran, together with all other peace-loving nations, in the establishment of international peace, security and prosperity after the war, in accordance with the principles of the Atlantic Charter, to which all four Governments have continued to subscribe.

APPENDIX IV

Excerpts from the Declaration of Seyyid Zia ed-Din,

Published in Ra'd-i-Emruz, *December 20, 1944*

THE TRUTH OF MR. KAVTARADZE'S SPEECH

The Statement of Mr. Kavtaradze was a great political blunder and a lie. . . . Some pro-Soviet and Tudeh papers wrote that northern Iran should be under Soviet influence. . . . Never throughout the centuries has Russia been threatened by the Iranians. No Iranian patriot is anti-Soviet. . . . Twenty-four years ago, when civil war raged in Russia and the British were here, Iran had an opportunity to take back from Russia some territories and generally to exploit that moment. . . . Iran, however, chose to recognize and maintain good relations with the Soviet Government. During the tsarist era Russia in promoting its imperialist schemes frequently attacked Iran. . . . I, myself, as Premier, cordially received the first Soviet ambassador and endeavored to cultivate good relations. . . . Can a man, who then did nothing against Russia, assume hostility towards her when she is a Big Power? . . .

If we continue to adhere to the German principle of *Lebensraum,* this war will never end. If today, for the sake of the *Lebensraum* of foreign powers it becomes necessary to yield northern Iran, it soon will become necessary for the same reason to renounce Teheran and Isfahan and then to cede the southern provinces to other states. Nothing will remain for the Iranian nation. . . .

If it was necessary fifty years ago to occupy foreign territories to increase one's own security, today, in view of the power of aviation it is entirely superfluous. Today, if need be, Soviet airplanes with bases in Turkestan can bombard the whole of India, and British planes from southern Iran can bomb the whole of Turkestan. The occupation of Iranian territories, of such or other provinces has no meaning whatsoever. . . .

With regard to oil concessions Iran refused them, because it was not advantageous to the state to enter into long-term engagements during the war. After the war the Soviets will have a priority in obtaining a concession. . . .

Teheran is a free city, but we see here many Soviet policemen and soldiers who interfere in our affairs, stop our citizens and do whatever they please. No one among us has the right to protest. . . . The Tudeh party acts against the government, the Majlis, and the Iranian nation. For four years the government has been silent, and therefore, I must speak about all this. . . .

It was during this period of mutual suspicion that the oil question came up. Initially negotiations seemed to promise a successful solution, but the tone of the Soviet press and of the Tudeh papers as well as the demonstrations of 5th Aban nullified all efforts. . . .

I do not put blame on Kavtaradze himself who, it is said, is a good man. It is the Tudeh and the official circles of the Soviet Embassy in Teheran who induced the Soviet press to assume such a hostile attitude. Nevertheless, there is no doubt that Kavtaradze's speech before his departure from Iran violates all principles of international intercourse. The Commissar does not possess the right to break off relations with the Iranian government. This is the right of the Soviet government. Our opinion concerning the Soviet Embassy here does not extend to the Soviet government which is certainly badly informed about the situation. . . .

The Soviets are upset because it seems to them strange that a small nation dares to refuse something to a Big Power. Iran was a bridge of victory for the Allies. Soviet authorities in Iran not only evidenced hostility through their own and the Iranian press, thereby offending the nation, the parliament and the government, but also on Aban 5th they brought demonstrators in their own trucks protected by Soviet machine guns. In Tabriz and in other cities the same thing happened, and those Iranian officers and soldiers who resisted were disarmed and jailed. All this indicates that Iran has lost its independence. Even our official telegrams to our missions abroad have not been exempted. . . .

If our allies will continue to act in this manner, then we must have a government able to protest these infringements. As long as foreign troops are stationed in Iran, our government will always be frightened. The fear of the Soviets in Teheran may possibly compel the government to transfer to another city. Our government is powerless in the face of censorship and Soviet activities. The Soviet Consul in Tabriz expels our citizens from their domiciles, and our protests are ineffective. We can expect similar expulsions from Teheran. If somebody committed a crime, he should be dealt with by the courts and not expelled from his own home.

We are not pessimistic as to the future of our northern provinces. France, Belgium, Greece were also under foreign occupation for four years. They are free now.

Our only hope is to have faith in justice. Our means of struggle consist in proclaiming the truth loudly.

The weak must not fear the strong.

The Allies must evacuate Iran. We want our own *independent Iran.*

If I have said anything critical of the Soviet Embassy here and of its activities, let me make it clear that all of it is true. I discussed it for the sake of good relationships between Iran and the Soviet Union.

We do not fear Azerbaijan's future. A province so loyal to its country and religion will not change its faith for the sake of the Armenian Ardeshir.

We have suffered the calumnies of the Soviet press and radio and the attacks of certain Iranian newspapers. We strongly reject Mr. Kavtaradze's accusation that we have acted against the Soviets.

Signed:

Seyyid Zia ed-Din Tabatabai,
Deputy from Yazd and former
Prime Minister of Iran

APPENDIX V

A Note on Five Iranian Political Parties during World War II

The MIHAN party was established in June, 1944, as a result of the fusion of the following parties: Paykar, Mihan Parestan, Istiqlal, and Azadi Khakhan. The nationalist character rendered it quite hostile to any foreign influences in Iran. Its program provided for social justice, limited government control of production and distribution, limited agrarian reform, government assistance to large families, universal education, respect for religion, and the solidarity of all citizens. Soon after the creation of the party political differences with the majority on the central committee compelled some of the leaders to withdraw. Among those who deserted were Jahangir Tafazzoli, editor of *Iran-i-Ma*, and Iqbal, another member from the *Iran-i-Ma* staff, who were inclined to collaborate with the Communists. The third to leave the committee was Abdol Qadir Azad, who joined the party of Zia ed-Din. Among those who remained at the helm of the party were Dr. Marzaban, President of the Red Lion and Sun Society (equivalent of the Red Cross), Professor Sanjabi, Dr. Maleki, Malek Khan, former military attaché in Turkey, and Anjavi, editor of *Nabard-i-Emruz*. The party was not represented in the parliament, but it claimed to enjoy the support of a few deputies, including Fahrivar, Professor Mo'azzami, Dr. Zangueneh, Zia ol-Molk Farman, and even such a prominent leader as Dr. Mosaddeq. It possessed two press organs, *Rastakhiz* and *Mihan Parestan,* and claimed to have good relations with the tribes of Luristan. The membership of Mihan was mainly composed of younger, patriotic elements, including a number of students. The leaders asserted that in Teheran alone the party had more than 2,000 members, and that it was growing in the provinces.

The IRAN party was created in 1944. Its program included the defense of independence and democracy in Iran, social justice, increase of the standard of living, agrarian reform, promotion of education and hygiene, and development of trade and industry. The organizers of the party were Fahrivar, an engineer, and Dr. Mo'azzami. Both were deputies to the Majlis. The peculiar character and immaturity of Iranian political life is manifest in the fact that both of these men were claimed to be supporters of the Mihan party by the leaders of the latter. Members of the Iran party were recruited mainly from the educated people in Teheran, especially the engineers. The party was hostile to the Tudeh as well as to the American Financial Mission. It owned the paper *Shafaq.* The party was said to be collaborating with the Mihan party and with the newly created group, Vahdat-i-Melli.

The SOCIALIST party emerged in the first quarter of 1944 as a result of the split in the Hamrahan party. Created in 1943, the latter claimed to represent socialist ideology and was dedicated to the struggle against the dictatorial government tendencies in Iran. Two representatives of Hamrahan, Abol Qasim Naraqi and Savan Haj Nasiri, were elected to the Fourteenth Majlis. During the debate on the validity of the mandate of Deputy Seyyid Zia ed-Din, Naraqi and Nasiri cast their votes in favor of confirmation. Their attitude produced a heated controversy in the central committee of the Hamrahan party. Six members of the committee headed by Ali Shahid-zadeh, editor of *Emruz-o-Farda,* demanded their expulsion on the grounds of betrayal. They claimed that Zia ed-Din as a rightist and foe of socialism did not deserve the favorable vote of the two socialist deputies. During the plenary meeting of the party, however, the majority favored the two censured deputies. Consequently, Ali Shahid-zadeh and his followers resigned from the Hamrahan and founded a new "Socialist party." *Emruz-o-Farda* now became their organ. Yet the old Hamrahan party declared that it represented the true socialist movement and started to issue a new paper called *Shiam.* Hamrahan was greatly weakened by this split: after some time *Shiam* suspended publication, and little was heard of the party's activities.

In contrast, the new Socialist party manifested some vitality. Proclaiming radical slogans, the party stressed the importance of economic welfare, which could be assured only by limitations on private property and by planned government economy. The party was said to co-operate silently with the

Tudeh, and rumor had it that Banisadr, young assistant of the director of the Teheran Radio, and a member of the party's committee, was spying for the Tudeh in the radio administration. The party was reputed to be friendly toward Russia and hostile toward the American Financial Mission. The number of its members was uncertain but at any rate was not large.

The MARDOM party was founded in August, 1944, by a group of deputies and cabinet ministers. Among its organizers were Zand, Minister of War; Ardalan, Minister of Industry; Bayat, former Prime Minister; Mohammed Sadiq Tabatabai, President of the Majlis; and Deputy Dr. Aghayan. Its program did not go beyond the generalities of justice, welfare and order, national government, and devotion to the country. The organizers claimed that the party was to be a continuation of the old Ittihad-i-Melli, which had been founded two years earlier but which throughout its life had been quite inactive. The Mardom party was composed of many influential men associated directly or indirectly with the government. It was said that it was represented in the Majlis by the group Ittihad-i-Melli. Soon after its formation the party started to publish the daily, *Neda-yi-Mellat*. This paper adopted a neutral attitude toward Zia ed-Din and the Tudeh but displayed hostility toward the American Financial Mission.

The ADALAT party was created in the late fall of 1944. Its program did not differ significantly from the programs of the others. It provided for the introduction of democracy as opposed to any kind of dictatorship, for freedom of press and assembly, for equality of all before the law. It demanded order and security in the country, abolition of monopolies, agrarian reform, development of education, reform in administration, awakening of patriotism, and a sense of justice in the young generation. The organizers were not of the same political caliber as the leaders of the Mardom, but many were high government officials and men of professions. Ibrahim Khaje Nuri, Under-Secretary in the Presidency of the Council of Ministers and director of the Department of Propaganda; Sepehri, director of the Teheran Radio; Deputy Dr. Moshtahedi; Deputy Jalal Emami, and Dr. Human, former Under-Secretary of Justice, were among the members of the central committee of the party. The Adalat claimed to have eleven sympathizers among the members of the Majlis and to possess branches in forty provincial towns. Originally the newspaper *Bahram* served as the party organ. Later *Neda-yi-Adalat* was published as its official organ. The party's attitude towards the Tudeh was definitely hostile, and some of its meetings were assaulted by the Communists. It was said that many members of the party were friendly to the rightist leader Seyyid Zia ed-Din. The Adalat showed hostility toward the American Financial Mission but it leaned more heavily to the West than to Russia.

APPENDIX VI

IRAN'S FOREIGN TRADE (IN MILLION RIALS)

	With the U.S.S.R.					With Germany			
Year	Imports	Exports	Total	%		Imports	Exports	Total	%
1930/31	230	159	389	37		36	30	66	6
1934/35	193	203	396	34		59	44	103	19
1937/38	315	235	550	34		247	199	446	27
1938/39	113	37	150	11.5		268	290	558	41.5
1939/40	7	—	7	0.5		160	393	553	39

	With Great Britain					With the United States			
Year	Imports	Exports	Total	%		Imports	Exports	Total	%
1930/31	86	45	131	12		25	66	91	9
1934/35	95	50	145	12		66	59	125	11
1937/38	79	42	121	7		83	55	138	8
1938/39	52	74	126	9.5		35	53	88	6.5
1939/40	47	75	122	8.5		40	93	133	9.5

APPENDIX VII

Theses on the Revolutionary Movement in the Colonies and Semi-Colonies, Adopted at the Sixth Congress of the Communist International, Moscow, 1928 [1]

I. INTRODUCTION.

1. The VI. Congress of the Communist International declares that the "Theses on the National and Colonial Questions" drawn up by Lenin and adopted at the II. Congress still have full validity, and should serve as a guiding line for the further work of the Communist Parties. Since the time of the II. Congress the actual significance of the colonies and semi-colonies as factors of crisis in the imperialist world system has vastly increased.

On the one hand, as necessary objects of exploitation for imperialism, the colonies have become a perpetual source of conflicts and wars between the imperialists, to an even higher degree than in the past. Plunderous wars, and new plans for wars, on the part of individual imperialist states against various peoples which have remained more or less independent, as well as intensified preparations of the imperialist powers for wars against each other for a new division of the colonies, continue without ceasing.

[1] *International Press Correspondence,* VIII (Dec. 12, 1928), 1659–1676. A few of the more obvious errors in spelling and punctuation have been corrected.

On the other hand, the vast colonial and semi-colonial world has become an unquenchable blazing hearth of the revolutionary mass movement. The basis of this phenomenon, which is of colossal historical importance, is furnished in part by changes which have taken place during and after the imperialist world war in the internal situation of the most important colonies and semi-colonies—in their economic and social structure—; e. g. the strengthening of the elements of capitalist and of industrial development, the intensification of the agrarian crisis, the growth of the proletariat and the beginning of its organisation, the pauperisation of the wide masses of the peasantry, etc.; in part, also, the basis is to be found in changes in the international situation: on the one hand, the difficulties encountered by the leading imperialist powers during the world war and in the post-war crisis of world capitalism, and afterwards, as a result of the imperialist "peace", the intensified rapacious aggressiveness of the colonial policy of Great Britain, Japan, the United States, France, Italy and Holland; on the other hand the transformation of Russia from an imperialist into an anti-imperialist proletarian power, the victorious struggle of the peoples of the Soviet Union in defence of their independence, the example of the revolutionary solution of the national question in the Soviet Union and the revolutionising influence of the work of building up Socialism there, and furthermore the strengthening of the Communist movement in the capitalist countries and the activity of this movement in the defence of the colonies.

All these circumstances immeasurably accelerated the process of the political awakening of the vast human masses in the colonial and semi-colonial countries and led to a whole series of important revolutionary mass risings, in most cases, moreover, on the basis of a close-knit, characteristic association of the anti-imperialist emancipatory struggle with the development of the forces of internal class struggle.

2. Of first rate international importance was the Chinese revolution. The shooting down of the Chinese workers in Shanghai on May 30th, 1925 was the signal for the letting loose of a revolutionary wave until then unparalleled in China. The most important industrial centres of China,—Shanghai, Tientsin, Hankow, Canton, and the British colony of Hong-Kong,—were the arena of a mass revolutionary strike struggle which called forth an answering wave of mass peasant revolts against the Chinese landlords and gentry in the rural districts.

Already, at this early stage of the wide national-revolutionary movement, the national bourgeoisie attempted to limit the revolutionary struggle exclusively to such national tasks as the fight against the militarists, the anti-imperialist boycotts. Almost simultaneously with the rise of the revolutionary wave, the counter-revolution began to organise its forces, (Chang Kai-shek's coup d'etat in March, 1920, the firing on student demonstrations in Peking, the formation of a right group in the Kuomintang, which commenced the struggle against the peasantry in Kwantung and Kwansi, etc.).

The Northern Expedition, which began in the summer of 1926, the capture of a number of provinces and the defeat and disintegration of a whole series of reactionary militarist groups, were accompanied by an enormous growth of the mass movement (the seizure of the British concessions in Hankow and Kiukiang, the general strike in Shanghai, which developed into an armed insurrection, the gigantic growth of the peasant movement). The successful insurrection in Shanghai in April 1927 raised the question of the hegemony of the proletariat in the national revolutionary movement, finally impelled the native bourgeoisie into the camp of reaction and called forth the counter-revolutionary coup d'etat of Chang Kai-shek.

The independent activity of the workers in the struggle for power, and above all the further growth of the peasant movement, which developed into agrarian revolution, impelled also the Wuhan government, which had been established under the leadership of the petty bourgeois wing of the Kuomintang, to go over to the camp of the counter-revolution. The revolutionary wave, however, was already beginning to ebb. In the course of a number of uprisings (the rising led by Ho-Lung and Ye-Ting, the peasant uprisings in Hunan, Hupeh, Kwantung and Kiangsu) the working class and peasantry still strove to wrest the power from the hands of the imperialists, bourgeoisie and landlords, and in this way to avert the defeat of the revolution. But in this they were not successful. The last powerful onslaught of this revolutionary wave was the insurrection of the heroic Canton proletariat, which under the slogan of Soviets attempted to link up the agrarian revolution with the overthrow of the Kuomintang and the establishment of the dictatorship of the workers and peasants.

3. In India, the policy of British imperialism, which retarded the development of native industry, evoked great dissatisfaction among the Indian bourgeoisie. The class consolidation of the latter, which replaced its former division into religious sects and casts and which was expressed in the fusion of the Indian National Congress (organ of the Indian bourgeoisie) with the Muslim League effected in 1916, confronted British imperialism with a national united front in the country. Fear of the revolutionary movement during the war compelled British imperialism to make concessions to the native bourgeoisie which found expression, in the economic sphere, in higher duties on imported goods and, in the political sphere, in insignificant parliamentary reforms introduced in 1919.

Nevertheless a strong ferment, expressing itself in a series of revolutionary outbreaks against British imperialism, was produced among the masses of the Indian people as a result of the ruinous consequences of the imperialist war (famine and epidemics, 1918), the catastrophic deterioration of the position of wide sections of the working population, the influence of the October revolution in Russia and of a series of insurrections in various colonial countries (as for example, the struggle of the Turkish people for independence).

[330]

This first great anti-imperialist movement in India (1919–1922) ended with the betrayal by the Indian bourgoisie of the cause of national revolution. The reason for this was chiefly the fear of the growing wave of the peasant risings, the fear of the workers' strikes against the native employers.

The collapse of the national revolutionary movement and the gradual decline of bourgeois nationalism enabled British imperialism once more to return to its policy of hindering the industrial development of India. The recent measures of British imperialism in India show that the objective contradictions between British colonial monopoly and the tendencies in the direction of the independent economic development of India are becoming more accentuated from year to year and are leading to a new deep revolutionary crisis.

The real threat to British domination comes, not from the bourgeois camp, but from the growing mass movement of the Indian workers, which is developing in the form of large-scale strikes; at the same time the accentuation of the crisis in the village bears witness to the maturing of an agrarian revolution. All these phenomena are leading to radical transformation of the whole political situation in India.

4. In Indonesia, Dutch imperialism is compelled in an ever-increasing degree to give its more powerful neighbours (American and British imperialism) the opportunity of importing foreign commodities and foreign capital into this colony. Thus, Dutch imperialism itself in Indonesia is actually more and more compelled to play a subordinate role, as, so to say, that of a "commissionaire" who at the same time is compelled to perform the functions of a policeman and executioner.

The immediate impulse to the insurrection which broke out in Java in November 1926 was given by the economic crisis, and the resulting deterioration of the conditions of the wide masses of the population, as well as by the cruel repression exercised by the government against the national-revolutionary movement. To a considerable degree the rebellion was carried out under the leadership of the Communists. The government succeeded in drowning the insurrection in blood, in suppressing the Communist Party, and in executing or throwing into prison thousands of the best leaders of the proletariat and peasantry.

Insignificant reforms, instituted thereafter by the government in order to weaken the hatred of the masses and to purchase the assistance of the national-reformist leaders for the work of "pacification" of these masses, have in no way improved the conditions of the working sections of the people. The continuing economic crisis in the country, especially in the sugar and rubber industries, the capitalist offensive with the object of worsening the conditions of labour, and growing unemployment, create the objective pre-conditions for inevitable new risings of the masses of workers and peasants against the ruling imperialism.

5. In North Africa in 1925 there began a series of rebellions of the Cabil

tribes of the Riff against French and Spanish imperialism, followed by the rebellions of the Druze tribes in the "mandated" territory of Syria against French imperialism. In Morocco, the imperialists only succeeded in dealing with these rebellions after a prolonged war. The intensified penetration of foreign capital into these countries is already calling into life new social forces. The rise and growth of an urban proletariat manifests itself in a wave of mass strikes that are sweeping for the first time over Palestine, Syria, Tunis and Algiers. Gradually, but very slowly, the peasantry also in these countries is being drawn into the struggle.

6. The growing economic and military expansion of North American imperialism in the countries of Latin America is transforming this continent into one of the most important junction points of the antagonisms of the whole imperialist colonial system. The influence of Great Britain, which before the war was the decisive influence in these countries, and which reduced many of them to the position of semi-colonies, since the war is being replaced by a still more close dependence on their part on the United States. By means of its increased export of capital, North American imperialism is conquering the commanding positions in the economy of these countries, is subordinating their governments to its own financial control and, at the same time, inciting one against the other. This aggressive policy of American imperialism is more and more taking on a character of undisguised violence, passing over into armed intervention (Nicaragua). The national-emancipatory struggle against American imperialism which has begun in Latin America is taking place for the most part under the leadership of the petty bourgeoisie. The national bourgeoisie, which represents a thin stratum of the population (with the exception of Argentine, Brazil, and Chile) and which is connected, on the one hand, with the big landowners and, on the other hand, with American capital, is in the camp of the counter-revolution.

The Mexican Revolution, which began as a revolutionary peasant struggle for land against the landowners and the church, at the same time to a considerable degree assumed the character of a mass struggle against American and British imperialism, and led to the formation of a government of the petty bourgeoisie, which endeavoured to keep itself in power by means of concessions to the big landowners and to North American imperialism.

The peasant risings, strikes of workers, etc., in Ecuador directed against the Government of the landlords of the maritime provinces, and of the Guayaquil bankers and commercial bourgeoisie, ended in a military coup d'etat and the establishment of a military dictatorship in 1925. The series of military revolutions in Chile, the guerilla war in Nicaragua against North American imperialism, the series of risings in South Brazil, the uprising of the agricultural labourers in Patagonia in Argentine, the revolt of the Indians in Bolivia, Peru, Ecuador and Colombia, the mutinies and spontaneous general strikes and mass demonstrations in Venezuela and Colombia, the mass anti-imperialist movement in Cuba and throughout the whole of Central America, Colombia, etc.—all these events of the last few years which [*sic*] bear witness to the widening and deepening of the revolutionary process and, in particular, to the ever-growing popular indignation in the Latin American countries against world imperialism.

7. In the majority of cases imperialism has up to now succeeded in bloody suppression of the revolutionary movement in the colonial countries. But all the fundamental questions raised by these movements remain unsolved.

The objective contradiction between the colonial policy of world imperialism and the independent development of the colonial peoples is by no means done away with, neither in China, nor in India, nor in any other of the colonial and semi-colonial countries; on the contrary, the contradiction only becomes more acute and can be overcome only by the victorious revolutionary struggle of the toiling masses in the colonies. Until this contradiction is overcome, it will continue to operate in every colony and semi-colony as one of the most powerful objective factors making for revolution.

At the same time, the colonial policy of the imperialist powers acts as a powerful stimulant to antagonisms and wars between these powers. This antagonism is becoming more and more acute and especially in the semi-colonies, where in spite of the blocs that are frequently established between the imperialists it plays a fairly important role. The greatest significance, however, for the development of the revolutionary movement in the colonies is borne by the contradictions between the imperialist world, on the one hand, and the Union of Soviet Socialist Republics and the revolutionary labour movement in the capitalist countries, on the other hand.

8. The establishment of a fighting front between the active forces of the Socialist world revolution (the Soviet Union and the revolutionary labour movement in the capitalist countries) on the one side, and between the forces of imperialism on the other side, is of fundamental decisive importance in the present epoch of world history. The toiling masses of the colonies struggling against imperialist slavery represent a most powerful auxiliary force of the Socialist world revolution. The colonial countries at the present time constitute for world imperialism the most dangerous sector of their front. The revolutionary emancipatory movements of the colonies and semi-colonies more and more rally around the banner of the Soviet Union, convincing themselves by bitter experience that there is no salvation for them except through alliance with the revolutionary proletariat, and through the victory of the world proletarian revolution over world imperialism.

The proletariat of the U. S. S. R. and the workers' movements in the capitalist countries, headed by the Communist International, in their turn

[333]

are supporting and will more and more effectively support in deeds the emancipatory struggle of all colonial and other dependent peoples; they are the only sure bulwark of the colonial peoples in their struggle for final liberation from the yoke of imperialism. Furthermore, the alliance with the U. S. S. R. and with the revolutionary proletariat of the imperialist countries creates for the toiling masses of the people of China, India and all other colonial and semi-colonial countries the possibility of an independent, free, economic and cultural development, avoiding the stage of the domination of the capitalist system or even the development of capitalist relations in general.

Thus the epoch of imperialism, of wars and revolutions, opens an epoch in which the proletarian dictatorship arises, opens a quite new perspective for the development of the colonial peoples. Since the analysis of contemporary world economy as a whole in no way leads to the perspective of a new prolonged period of flourishing capitalism, but, on the contrary, leads to the inevitability of the overthrow of capitalism, which has already fulfilled its progressive historical role, has already become a brake on further development, is already in process of disintegration, is already giving place to the proletarian dictatorship (U. S. S. R.) and is leading humanity to ever new catastrophes,—all this denotes the presence of the objective possibility of a non-capitalist path of development for the backward colonies, the possibility of the "growing-over" of the bourgeois-democratic revolution in the leading colonies into the proletarian socialist revolution with the aid of the victorious proletarian dictatorship in the other countries. Under favourable objective conditions, this possibility is converted into actuality, whereby the true path of development is determined by struggle and by struggle alone. Consequently, the theoretical and practical advocacy of this path, and the most self-sacrificing struggle for it, is the duty of all Communists. In connection with this perspective, there arises before the colonies also the problem of revolutionary seizure of power on the basis of Soviets.

Thus, all the basic questions of the revolutionary movement in the colonies and semi-colonies are found to have an immediate connection with the great epoch-making struggle between the capitalist and socialist systems,—a struggle which at present is being conducted on a world scale by imperialism against the U. S. S. R., and inside each separate capitalist country between bourgeois class rule and the Communist movement.

In this struggle, the co-operation of the revolutionary proletariat of the whole world and of the toiling masses of the colonies represents the surest guarantee of victory over imperialism. In this struggle, every war conflict between two imperialist States, as also war of the imperialists against the U. S. S. R., must be utilised in the colonies for the mobilisation of the masses and for drawing them into a decisive struggle against imperialism, for national emancipation and for the victory of the workers and peasants.

[334]

II. The Characteristic Features of Colonial Economy and of Imperialist Colonial Policy.

9. The recent history of the colonies can only be understood if it is looked upon as an organic constituent part of the development of capitalist world economy as a whole, beginning with its earliest forms and ending with its latest stage, viz., imperialism.

In proportion as capitalism more and more strongly draws the immense colonial areas into the sphere of its world economy based on exploitation and profit-hunting, there is seen reflected as in a mirror in the economic and political history of the colonial and semi-colonial countries all the characteristic features of the so-called "civilising" and cultural mission of the capitalist mode of production and of the bourgeois social order. In particular, it reveals with merciless accuracy all the methods and practices of "original capitalist accumulation". Its policy, unsurpassed in cruelty, of conquest and oppression, bound up as it has been with colonial robbery and punitive expeditions, with opium wars and piratical raids for the compulsory provision of the native population with whisky, bibles and other trash, as conducted by the most Christian countries of Europe and America, was one of the most important factors which accelerated the consolidation of the capitalist structure.

In spite of the disgusting lies of the imperialists and of their reformist lackeys (MacDonald, Otto Bauer & Co.), who maintain that imperialism "brings to the backward races prosperity, progress and culture", the transition to the epoch of monopolist capitalism in no way lightened the yoke weighing upon the many millions of the masses of humanity in the colonial countries. The devastating consequences everywhere brought about by capitalist development, in particular in the first stage of its existence, are reproduced in the colonies to a monstrous degree and at an accelerated rate, thanks to the penetration of foreign capital. The progressive results of capitalism, on the other hand, are, for the most part, in the colonies completely imperceptible.

Where in the colonies the ruling imperialism is in need of a social support it first of all allies itself with the ruling strata of the previous social structure, with the feudal lords and with the trading and money-lending bourgeoisie, against the majority of the people. Everywhere imperialism attempts to preserve and to perpetuate all those pre-capitalistic forms of exploitation (especially in the villages) which serve as the basis for the existence of its reactionary allies. The masses of the people in these countries are compelled to pay out enormous sums for the upkeep of the military, police, and administrative apparatus of the colonial regime.

The growth of famines and epidemics, particularly among the pauperised peasantry; the mass expropriation of the land of the native population; the inhuman conditions of labour (on the plantations and mines of the white capitalists, and so on), which at times are worse than open slavery—all this exerts its devastating effect on the colonial population and not infrequently leads to the dying out of whole nationalities. The "cultural role" of the imperialist States in the colonies is in reality the role of an executioner.

10. In regard to the colonial countries it is necessary to distinguish between those colonies of the capitalist countries which have served them as colonising regions for their surplus population, and which in this way have become a continuation of their capitalist system (Australia, Canada, etc.), and those colonies which are exploited by the imperialists primarily as markets for their commodities, as sources of raw material and as spheres for the export of capital. This distinction has not only a historic but also a great economic and political significance.

The colonies of the first type, on the basis of their general development, became "Dominions", that is, members of the given imperialist system with equal or nearly equal rights. In them, capitalist development reproduces among the immigrant white population the class structure of the metropolis, at the same time that the native population was for the most part exterminated. There cannot be there any talk of the colonial regime in the form that it shows itself in the colonies of the second type. Between these two types is to be found a transitional type (in various forms) where, alongside the numerous native population, there exists a very considerable population of white colonists (South Africa, New Zealand, Algiers, etc.). The bourgeoisie, which has come from the metropolis, in essence represents in these countries (emigrant colonies) nothing else than a colonial "prolongation" of the bourgeoisie of the metropolis.

. . . The metropolis is interested to a certain extent in the strengthening of its capitalist "subsidiary" in the colonies, in particular when this subsidiary of imperialism is successful in enslaving the original native population or even in completely destroying it. On the other hand, the competition between various imperialist systems for influence in these semi-independent countries can lead also to their breaking off from the metropolis and even to a union with the competitors of the latter. These reasons frequently compel imperialism to reconcile itself to a certain political and economic independence of its agencies in such colonies (Dominions), which then assume the position of an allied and kindred power towards the respective imperialism.

11. The imperialist colonial regime is essentially based not only on economic pressure but also on the extra-economic compulsion of the monopoly of the bourgeoisie of the imperialist countries in the corresponding dependent countries. This monopoly, however, expresses itself in two basic functions: on the one hand it serves the purpose of merciless exploitation of the colony (various forms of immediate and indirect exaction of tribute, super-profits in connection with the sale of its own industrial goods, with

the obtaining of cheap raw material for its own industry and with the utilisation of very cheap labour power, etc.); on the other hand, the imperialist monopoly serves for the preservation and development of the conditions of its own existence, i. e., it fulfils the function of enslaving the colonial masses.

In its function as colonial exploiter, the ruling imperialism in relation to the colonial country acts primarily as a parasite sucking the blood from the economic organism of the latter. The fact that this parasite in relation to its victim represents a society with a highly developed culture makes it a so much more powerful and dangerous exploiter, but, from the point of view of the colonial country, this in no way alters the parasitic character of its function.

Capitalist exploitation in every imperialist country has proceeded by way of the development of productive forces. The specific colonial forms of capitalist exploitation, put into operation by the same British, French or any other bourgeoisie, in the final analysis hinder the development of the productive forces of the colonies concerned. The carrying through of the minimum of constructive activity (railways, harbours, etc.) is indispensable both for military domination in the country and for guaranteeing the uninterrupted activity of the taxation machine, as well as for the trading needs of the imperialist countries.

Agriculture in the colonies is compelled to a considerable degree to work for export, but peasant economy is thereby by no means liberated from the oppression of its pre-capitalist features. As a general rule, it is converted to a "free" commodity economy by means of the subordination of the pre-capitalist forms of production to the needs of finance-capital, the intensification of pre-capitalist methods of exploitation through subjection of peasant economy to the yoke of rapidly developing trade and usury capital, the increase of tax burdens, etc., etc. The exploitation of the peasantry is increased, but the productive methods of the latter are not improved.

As a general rule, the industrial working up of the colonial raw material is not carried out in the colonies themselves, but in the capitalist countries, and primarily in the metropolis. The profits obtained in the colonies are for the most part, not expended productively, but are squeezed out of the country and are invested either in the metropolis or in new spheres of expansion on the part of the imperialism concerned. Thus, the fundamental tendency of colonial exploitation acts in the direction of hindering the development of the productive forces in the colonies, of despoiling them of their natural riches and, above all, of exhausting the reserves of human productive forces in the colonial countries.

12. In as much, however, as colonial exploitation presupposes a certain acceleration of the development of production in the colonies, this development, thanks to the imperialist monopoly, is directed on such lines and accelerated only in such a degree as corresponds to the interests of the metropolis, and, in particular, to the interests of the preservation of its

colonial monopoly. It may cause a part of the peasantry, for example, to pass over from grain cultivation to the production of cotton, sugar, or rubber (Sudan, Cuba, Java, Egypt), but this takes place in such a way and by such means that it not only in no way corresponds to the interests of the independent economic development of the colonial country, but, on the contrary, still further strengthens the dependence of the latter on the imperialist metropolis.

With the object of widening the raw material base for world imperialism, there are created new agricultural crops in the place of those destroyed by colonial policy. New systems of irrigation are constructed with the same object in view in the place of the old ones that have been destroyed, and become in the hands of the imperialists a weapon for increasing the exploitation of the peasantry. With a view to widening the internal market, attempts are undertaken to adapt to the capitalist mode of production the agrarian relationships which are partly created by colonial policy itself. Plantations of various kinds serve the interests of metropolitan finance capital. The exploitation of the mineral wealth of the colonies is conducted in accordance with the needs of the metropolitan industry, especially its need to put an end to dependence on sources of raw materials in other countries to which the monopoly of this imperialism does not extend.

These are the main spheres of colonial production. Only where manufacture constitutes a very simple process (tobacco industry, sugar refineries, etc. etc.) or where the expense of transporting raw material can be considerably decreased by the first stage of manufacture being performed on the spot, does the development of production in the colonies attain comparatively large dimensions. In any case, the capitalist enterprises created by the imperialists in the colonies (with the exception of a few enterprises established in case of military needs) are predominantly or exclusively of an agrarian-capitalist character and are distinguished by a low organic composition of capital. Real industrialisation of the colonial country, in particular the building up of a flourishing engineering industry, which might make possible the independent development of the productive forces of the country, is not accelerated, but, on the contrary, is hindered by the metropolis. This is the essence of its function of colonial enslavement: the colonial country is compelled to sacrifice the interests of its independent development and to play the part of an economic (agrarian-raw material) appendage to foreign capitalism, which, at the expense of the labouring classes of the colonial country, strengthens the economic and political power of the imperialist bourgeoisie in order to perpetuate the monopoly of the latter in the colonies and to increase its expansion as compared with the rest of the world.

Just as the "classical capitalism" of the pre-imperialist epoch most clearly demonstrated its negative features of destruction of the old without an equivalent creation of the new precisely in its economy of plunder in the colonies, so also the most characteristic side of the decay of imperialism, its essential feature of usury and parasitism, is especially clearly revealed in its colonial economy. The endeavour of the great imperialist powers to adapt to an ever-increasing degree the exclusive monopolisation of the colonies to the needs of the capitalist industry of the metropolis, not only leads to the destruction of the traditional economic structure of the indigenous colonial population, but, side by side with this, leads to the destruction of the equilibrium between separate branches of production, and, in the final analysis, leads to an artificial retardation of the development of the productive forces in the colonies.

A general tendency on the part of all the metropolitan centres is the endeavour to hold back the colony and to make it a subordinate constituent part of the imperialist system concerned in order to guarantee the latter's economic supremacy so as to be able, on the one hand, to place themselves in opposition to other imperialist systems, and, on the other hand, to cut off the colony from immediate relations with world economy as a whole, and to keep to themselves the function of intermediary and supreme regulator in all its economic relations with the outer world. This tendency of the imperialists to strengthen the one-sided dependency of the colonies leads to a growth of competition between the different imperialist powers and international trusts, etc.

As conditioned by these circumstances, the development of capitalist relationships and of the exploitation of the masses of the people in the colonies assumes very various forms.

13. In as much as the overwhelming mass of the colonial population is connected with land and lives in the villages, the plundering character of the forms of exploitation of the peasantry made use of by imperialism and its allies (the class of land owners and trading-usury capital) acquires a special significance. Thanks to the interference of imperialism (imposition of taxes, import of industrial products from the metropolis, etc.), the drawing of the village into the sphere of monetary and trading economy is accompanied here by a process of pauperisation of the peasantry, destruction of village handicraft industry, etc., and proceeds at a much more rapid rate than was the case when the same process took place in the leading capitalist countries. On the other hand, the retarded industrial development in the colonies has put narrow limits to the process of proletarianisation.

This enormous disproportion between the rapid rate of destruction of the old forms of economy and the slow development of the new has given rise in China, India, Indonesia, Egypt, etc. to an extraordinary "pressure on agriculture", and to agrarian overpopulation, rack-renting and extreme fragmentation of the land cultivated by the peasantry.

At the same time, the whole burden of the previous feudal or semi-feudal conditions of exploitation and bondage, in somewhat "modernised", but in no way lighter, forms, lies as before on the shoulders of the peasantry.

Capitalism, which has included the colonial village into its system of taxa-tion and trade apparatus and which has overturned capitalist relations (for instance the destruction of the village Commune) does not thereby liberate the peasants from the yoke of pre-capitalist forms of bondage and exploita-tion, but only gives the latter a monetary expression (feudal services and rent in kind are generally replaced by money taxes, and so on), which still more increases the suffering of the peasantry. To the "assistance" of the peasants in their miserable position comes the usurer, robbing them and under certain conditions (e. g., in some localities of India and China) even creating an hereditary slavery based on their indebtedness.

Notwithstanding the great variety of agrarian relationships in different colonial countries, and even in different parts of one and the same country, the poverty-stricken position of the peasant masses is almost everywhere the same. Partly owing to unequal exchange, and partly to direct exploitation, the peasants in these countries are not in a position to raise the technical or organisational level of their economy. The productivity of their labour, as also the demand for it, is falling.

The pauperisation of the peasantry in these countries is a general phenomenon. In India, China, and Indonesia, the pauperisation of the peasantry has reached such a height that, at the present time, the most char-acteristic figure in the village is the poor peasant, almost or entirely de-prived of land and not infrequently suffering from starvation. Big land-ownership is here hardly connected in any way with large-scale agriculture, but serves only as a means for extorting rents from the peasants. There is frequently to be found a hierarchy of many stages, consisting of landlords and sub-landlords, parasitic intermediate links between the labouring cultivator and the big landowner (amindar) or the State.

The ancient systems of artificial irrigation, which in these countries is [are] of great importance for agriculture, thanks to the interference of im-perialism first of all fell into decay, and when later they were re-established on a capitalist basis, then they were found to be too dear for the peasants to make use of. Famines become more and more frequent occurrences. The peasant finds himself completely helpless in the face of epidemics and various kinds of elemental misfortunes. Wide masses of the peasantry are thrown out of the process of production; they have no chances of finding work in the towns and rarely find work in the village, where they develop into miser-able coolies.

This unfortunate position of the peasantry denotes at the same time a crisis in the internal market for industry, which in its turn represents a powerful obstacle to the capitalist development of the country. Not only the national bourgeoisie of India, China, Egypt, etc., but also imperialism itself is sensible of this peasant misery as an obstacle in the path of the ex-pansion of their exploitation; but the economic and political interests of both of them are so closely bound up with large ownership, as also with trading and usury capital in the village, that they are not in a position to carry through an agrarian reform of any wide significance.

Peasant domestic production and artisan production are more and more declining. The development of trade creates an important stratum of native trading bourgeoisie, which fulfils also the functions of purchasing agent, usurer, etc. The predominance and hegemony of trading and usury capital, in the specific conditions of colonial economy, retards the growth of industrial capital. In the struggle for the internal market, national capital again and again encounters the competition of imported foreign capital in the colonial country itself and the retarding influence of pre-capitalist relations in the villages. In spite of these obstacles, there does arise in certain branches of production a native large-scale industry (chiefly light industry). National capital and national banks come into being and begin to develop.

The pitiful attempts at carrying through agrarian reforms without damaging the colonial regime are intended to facilitate the gradual conversion of semi-feudal landownership into capitalist landlordism, and in certain cases to establish a thin stratum of kulak peasants. In practice, this only leads to an ever-increasing pauperisation of the overwhelming majority of the peasants, which again, in its turn, paralyses the development of the internal market. It is on the basis of these contradictory economic processes that the most important social forces of the colonial movements are developing.

14. In the period of imperialism, there stands out with especial prominence the role of finance capital in the seizure of economic and political monopoly in the colonies. This especially finds expression in definite economic consequences resulting from the export of capital to the colonies. The exported capital here flows predominantly into the sphere of trade, it functions mainly as usurious loan capital and it pursues the task of preserving and strengthening the oppressive apparatus of the imperialist State in the colonial country (by the aid of State loans, etc.), or of achieving full control over the so-called independent State organs of the native bourgeoisie in the colonial countries.

The export of capital to the colonies accelerates the development of capitalist relations in them. A portion of the exported capital, despatched to the colony for productive purposes, does in part conduce to an acceleration of industrial development; by no means, however, in the direction of independence, but rather in a direction which strengthens the dependence of colonial economy on the finance capital of the imperialist country.

In general, imported capital is concentrated in the colonies almost exclusively for the extraction and supply of raw materials, or for the first stages of their utilisation. Export capital is used also for extending the system of communications (railways, ship-building, harbour works, etc. etc.), thus, facilitating the transport of raw material and binding the colonies more closely to the metropolis. A favourite form of investment of capital in agriculture is in large plantations, with the object of cheap production of food products and the monopolisation of vast sources of raw material. The transference to the metropolis of the greater portion of the surplus value extorted from the cheap labour power of the colonial slaves retards to a correspondingly enormous degree the upward growth of the economy of the colonial countries and the development of their productive forces, and serves as an obstacle to the economic and political emancipation of the colonies.

Another basic feature in the mutual relations between the capitalist States and the colonial countries is the endeavour of various monopolist groups of finance capital to monopolise the whole foreign trade of the separate colonial and semi-colonial countries, and in this way to subordinate to their control and regulation all the channels which connect the colonial economy with the world market. The direct influence of this monopolisation of foreign trade by a few monopolist exporting firms on the course of capitalist development in the colonies is expressed, not so much in the development of a national internal market, as in the adaptation of the scattered internal colonial trade to the needs of export, and in the "bleeding" of the natural wealth of the colonial countries by the imperialist parasites. This peculiar development of colonial trade finds its specific expression also in the form and character of the imperialist banks in the colonies, which mobilise the savings of the native bourgeoisie chiefly for financing the foreign trade of the colonies, etc.

15. The entire economic policy of imperialism in relation to the colonies is determined by its endeavour to preserve and increase their dependence, to deepen their exploitation and, as far as possible, to impede their independent development. Only under the pressure of special circumstances may the bourgeoisie of the imperialist States find itself compelled to cooperate in the development of big industry in the colonies. Thus, for example, requirements for preparation or conduct of war may, to a limited extent, lead to the creation of various enterprises in engineering and chemical industry in certain of the most strategically important colonies (e. g. India). Competition on the part of more powerful competitors may compel the metropolis to grant definite concessions in matters of tariff policy, in which case it safeguards itself by means of preferential duties.

With the object of bribing definite strata of the bourgeoisie in the colonial and semi-colonial countries, especially in periods of a rising revolutionary movement, the metropolis may, to a certain degree, weaken its economic pressure. But, in the measure that these extraordinary and, for the most part, extra-economic circumstances lose their influence, the economic policy of the imperialist powers is immediately re-directed towards repressing and retarding the economic development of the colonies. Consequently, the development of the national economy of the colonies, and especially their industrialisation, the all-round independent development of their industry, can only be realised by the strongest opposition to the policy of imperialism. Thus the specific character of the development of the colonial countries is especially expressed in the fact that the growth of productive forces is realised with extreme difficulty, spasmodically, artificially, being limited to individual branches of industry.

The inevitable result of this is that the pressure of imperialism on the colonial and semi-colonial countries is reproduced each time in a higher degree and evokes an ever-more powerful resistance on the part of the social-economic factors originating from imperialism itself. The continual hindrance to independent development more and more deepens the antagonism of the colonial peoples in relation to imperialism and leads to revolutionary crises, boycott movements, national-revolutionary insurrections, etc.

On the one hand, the imminent objective contradictions in the capitalist development of the colonies become intensified, which itself deepens the contradictions between the independent development of the colonies and the interest of the bourgeoisie of the imperialist States; on the other hand, the new capitalist forms of exploitation bring into the arena a genuine revolutionary force—the proletariat, around which the many millions of the peasant masses rally more and more strongly in order to offer organised resistance to the yoke of finance capital.

All the chatter of the imperialists and their lackeys about the policy of decolonisation being carried through by the imperialist powers, about promotion of the "free development of the colonies," reveals itself as nothing but an imperialist lie. It is of the utmost importance that Communists both in the imperialist and in the colonial countries should completely expose this lie.

III. On Communist Strategy and Tactics in China, India and Similar Colonial Countries.

16. As in all colonies and semi-colonies, so also in China and India the development of productive forces and the socialisation of labour stands at a comparatively low level. This circumstance, together with the fact of foreign domination and also the presence of powerful relics of feudalism and pre-capitalist relations, determines the character of the immediate stage of the revolution in these countries. In the revolutionary movement of these countries we have to deal with the bourgeois democratic revolution, i. e. of the stage signifying the preparation of the prerequisites for proletarian dictatorship and socialist revolution. Corresponding to this, the following kinds of tasks can be pointed out, which may be considered as general basic tasks of the bourgeois democratic revolution in the colonies and semi-colonies:

a) A shifting in the relationship of forces in favour of the proletariat: emancipation of the country from the yoke of imperialism (nationalisation of foreign concessions, railways, banks, etc.) and the establishment of the national unity of the country where this has not yet been attained: overthrow of the power of the exploiting classes at the back of which imperialism stands: organisation of Soviets of workers and peasants and organisation of the Red Army: establishment of the dictatorship of the proletariat and peasantry: consolidation of the hegemony of the proletariat.

b) The carrying through of the agrarian revolution: emancipation of the peasants from all pre-capitalist and colonial conditions of exploitation and bondage: nationalisation of the land: radical measures for alleviating the position of the peasantry with the object of establishing the closest possible economic and political union between the town and village.

c) In correspondence with the further development of industry, transport, etc., and with the accompanying growth of the proletariat, the widespread development of trade union organisations of the working class, strengthening of the Communist Party and its conquest of a firm leading position among the toiling masses: the achievement of the 8-hour working day.

d) Establishment of equal rights for nationalities and of sex equality (equal rights for women): separation of the church from the State and the abolition of caste distinctions: political education and raising of the general cultural level of the masses in town and country, etc.

How far the bourgeois-democratic revolution will be able in practice to realise all its basic tasks, and how far it will be the case that part of these tasks will be carried into effect only by the socialist revolution, will depend on the course of the revolutionary movement of the workers and peasants and its successes or defeats in the struggle against the imperialists, feudal lords and the bourgeoisie. In particular, the emancipation of the colony from the imperialist yoke is facilitated by the development of the socialist revolution in the capitalist world and can only be completely guaranteed by the victory of the proletariat in the leading capitalist countries.

The transition of the revolution to the socialist phase demands the presence of certain minimum pre-requisites, as, for example, a certain definite level of development in the country of industry, of trade union organisations of the proletariat and a strong Communist Party. The most important is precisely the development of a strong Communist Party with a big mass influence, which would be in the highest degree a slow and difficult process were it not accelerated by the bourgeois-democratic revolution which already grows and develops as a result of the objective conditions in these countries.

17. The bourgeois democratic revolution in the colonies is distinguished from the bourgeois democratic revolution in an independent country chiefly in that it is organically bound up with the national-emancipatory struggle against imperialist domination. The national factor exerts considerable influence on the revolutionary process in all colonies, as well as in those semi-colonies where imperialist enslavement already appears in its naked form, leading to the revolt of the mass of the people. On the one hand, national oppression hastens the ripening of the revolutionary crisis, intensifies the dis-

satisfaction of the masses of workers and peasants, facilitates their mobilisation and endows the revolutionary mass revolts with the elemental force and character of a genuine popular revolution. On the other hand, the national factor is able to influence not only the movement of the working class and peasantry but also the attitude of all the remaining classes, modifying its form during the process of revolution. Above all, the poor urban petty bourgeoisie together with the petty bourgeois intelligentsia is during the first period to a very considerable extent brought under the influence of the active revolutionary forces; secondly, the position of the colonial bourgeoisie in the bourgeois-democratic revolution is still for the most part an ambiguous one and its vacillations in accordance with the course of the revolution are even more considerable than in the bourgeoisie of an independent country (e. g. the Russian bourgeoisie in 1905–17).

It is very important, in accordance with the concrete circumstances, to investigate very carefully the special influence of the national factor, which to a considerable degree determines the special character of the colonial revolution, and to take it into account in the tactics of the Communist Party concerned.

Along with the national-emancipatory struggle, the agrarian Revolution constitutes the axis of the bourgeois democratic revolution in the chief colonial countries. Consequently, communists must follow with the greatest attention the development of the agrarian crisis and the intensification of class contradictions in the village; they must from the very beginning give a consciously-revolutionary direction to the dissatisfaction of the workers and to the incipient peasant movement, directing it against imperialist exploitation and bondage as also against the yoke of the various pre-capitalist (feudal and semi-feudal) relationships as a result of which peasant economy is suffering, declining and perishing. The incredible backwardness of agriculture, the prevalence of oppressive rent relations and the oppression of trading-usury capital, represent the greatest hindrance to the development of productive forces in village economy in the colonies and stand in monstrous contradiction with the highly organised forms of exchange between the village agricultural production of the colonies and the world market created by monopoly imperialism.

18. The national bourgeoisie in these colonial countries does not adopt a uniform attitude in relation to imperialism. A part of this bourgeoisie, more especially the trading bourgeoisie, directly serves the interests of imperialist capital (the so-called compradore bourgeoisie). In general, it more or less consistently defends the anti-national imperialist point of view directed against the whole nationalist movement, in common with the feudal allies of imperialism and the more highly paid native officials. The remaining portions of the native bourgeoisie, especially the portion reflecting the interests of native industry, support the national movement and represent a special vacillating compromising tendency which may be desig-

[345]

nated as national reformism (or, in the terminology of the theses of the Second Congress of the Communist International, a "bourgeois-democratic" tendency).

This intermediate position of the national bourgeoisie between the revolutionary and imperialist camps is no longer to be observed, it is true, in China after 1925; there the greater part of the national bourgeoisie from the beginning, owing to the special situation, took the leadership in the national-emancipatory war; later on it passed over finally into the camp of counter-revolution. In India and Egypt, we still observe, for the time being, the typical bourgeois-nationalist movement—an opportunistic movement, subject to great vacillations, balancing between imperialism and revolution.

The independence of the country in relation to imperialism, being to the advantage of the whole colonial people, corresponds also to the interests of the national bourgeoisie, but is in irreconcilable contradiction to the whole nature of the imperialist system. Various native capitalists, it is true, are by their immediate interests to a great extent bound by numerous threads to imperialist capital. Imperialism is able directly to bribe a considerable portion of them (it may be even a greater portion than heretofore) and to create a definite Compradore position, a position of intermediary trader, sub-exploiter or overseer over the enslaved population. But the position of slave owner, of monopolist supreme exploiter, imperialism reserves for itself alone. Independent rule, a future of "free" independent capitalist development, hegemony over an "independent" people—this imperialism will never voluntarily yield to the national bourgeoisie. In this respect, the contradiction of interests between the national bourgeoisie of the colonial country and imperialism is objectively of a radical character. In this respect, imperialism demands capitulation on the part of the national bourgeoisie.

The native bourgeoisie, as the weaker side, again and again capitulates to imperialism. Its capitulation, however, is not final as long as the danger of class revolution on the part of the masses has not become immediate, acute and menacing. In order, on the one hand, to avoid this danger, and, on the other hand, to strengthen its position in relation to imperialism, bourgeois nationalism in these colonies strives to obtain the support of the petty bourgeoisie, of the peasantry and in part also of the working class. Since, in relation to the working class it has little prospect of success (as soon as the working class in these countries has at all begun to awake politically), it becomes the more important for it to obtain support from the peasantry.

But just here is the weakest point of the colonial bourgeoisie. The unbearable exploitation of the colonial peasantry can only be put an end to by the way of the agrarian revolution. The bourgeoisie of China, India and Egypt is by its immediate interests so closely bound up with landlordism, with usury capital and with the exploitation of the peasant masses in general, that it takes its stand not only against the agrarian revolution but also against every decisive agrarian reform. It is afraid, and not without foundation, that even the more open formulation of the agrarian question will stimulate and accelerate the growth of the process of revolutionary fermentation in the peasant masses. Thus, the reformist bourgeoisie hardly dare to decide to approach practically this basic urgent question.

Instead, it attempts by means of empty nationalist phrases and gestures to keep the petty bourgeois masses under its influence and to compel imperialism to grant certain concessions. But the imperialists draw the reins ever tighter, for the national bourgeoisie is incapable of offering any serious resistance. Accordingly, the national bourgeoisie in every conflict with imperialism attempt, on the one hand, to make a great show of their nationalist "firmness" of principle, and, on the other hand, they sow illusions as to the possibility of a peaceful compromise with imperialism. Through both the one and the other, the masses inevitably become disillusioned and in this way they gradually outlive their reformist illusions.

19. An incorrect estimation of the basic national-reformist tendency of the national bourgeoisie in these colonial countries gives rise to the possibility of serious errors in the strategy and tactics of the Communist Parties concerned. In particular, two kinds of mistakes are possible:

a) A non-understanding of the difference between the national reformist and national-revolutionary tendency can lead to a "khvostist" policy in relation to the bourgeoisie, to an insufficiently accurate political and organisational delimitation of the proletariat from the bourgeoisie, and to the blurring of the chief revolutionary slogans (especially the slogans of the agrarian revolution), etc. This was the fundamental mistake into which the Communist Party of China fell in 1925–27.

b) An under-estimation of the special significance which the bourgeois national-reformist, as distinct from the feudal-imperialist camp, possess[es] owing to its mass influence on the ranks of the petty bourgeoisie, peasantry and even a portion of the working class, may lead, at least in the first stages of the movement, to a sectarian policy and to the isolation of the Communists from the toiling masses.

In both these cases, insufficient attention is given to the realisation of precisely those tasks which the Second Congress of the Communist International had already characterised as the basic tasks of the Communist Parties in the colonial countries, i. e. the tasks of struggle against the bourgeois-democratic movement inside the nation itself. Without this struggle, without the liberation of the toiling masses from the influence of the bourgeoisie and of national-reformism, the basic strategical aim of the Communist movement in the bourgeois-democratic revolution—the hegemony of the proletariat—cannot be achieved. Without the hegemony of the proletariat, an organic part of which is the leading role of the Communist Party, the

[347]

bourgeois-democratic revolution cannot be carried through to an end, not to speak of the socialist revolution.

20. The petty bourgeoisie in the colonial and semi-colonial countries plays a very important role. It consists of various strata, which in different periods of the national-revolutionary movement play very diverse roles.

The artisan, who is hit by the competition of foreign imported goods, is hostilely disposed towards imperialism. At the same time, he is interested in the unlimited exploitation of his journeymen and apprentices, and accordingly, he is hostilely disposed towards the class-conscious labour movement. At the same time, also, he usually suffers himself from the exploitation of trading and usury capital. The exceedingly ambiguous and hopeless position of this stratum of the petty bourgeoisie determines its vacillations, and it frequently falls under the influence of utopian reactionaries.

The small trader—both in town and village—is connected with village exploitation through usury and trade, and he clings to the old forms of exploitation in preference to the prospects of an expansion of the internal market. These strata, however, are not homogeneous. These sections of the trading bourgeoisie which in one form or another are connected with the Compradores occupy a different position from those sections the activity of which is limited mainly to the internal market.

The petty bourgeois intelligentsia, the students, and such like, are very frequently the most determined representatives, not only of the specific interests of the petty bourgeoisie, but also of the general objective interests of the entire national bourgeoisie, and, in the first period of the national movement, they often come out as the spokesmen of the nationalist struggle. Their role at the head of the movement is comparatively important. In general, they cannot act as representatives of peasant interests, for the very social strata from which they come are connected with landlordism. The upsurge of the revolutionary wave may drive them into the labour movement, bringing with them their petty bourgeois ideology of vacillation and indecision. Only a few of them in the course of the struggle are able to break with their own class and rise to an understanding of the tasks of the class struggle of the proletariat, and to become active defenders of the interests of the latter. It frequently happens that the petty bourgeois intellectuals give to their ideology a socialist or even Communist colour. In the struggle against imperialism they have played, and in such countries as India and Egypt they even now still partially play, a revolutionary role. The mass movement may draw them after it, but it may also push them into the camp of extreme reaction or, at least, cause the spread of utopian reactionary tendencies in their ranks.

Alongside of these strata, there are to be found in the colonial towns considerable sections of urban poor, the position of which objectively drives them to the support of revolution,—artisans who do not exploit the labour of others, street traders, unemployed intellectuals, ruined peasants seeking work, etc. Further, the colonial town, as also the village, has a populous section of "coolies", semi-proletarians who have not passed through the school of factory production and who live by casual labour.

The peasantry, along with the proletariat and in the character of its ally, represents a driving force of the revolution. The immense many-millioned peasant mass constitutes the overwhelming majority of the population even in the most developed colonies (in some colonies it is 90% of the population). The many millions of starving tenant-cultivators, petty peasants oppressed by want and groaning under all kinds of pre-capitalist and capitalist forms of exploitation, a considerable portion of them deprived of the possibility of cultivation even on the lands that they rent, thrown out from the process of production and slowly dying from famine and disease, village agricultural labourers,—all these are the allies of the proletariat in the village. The peasantry can only achieve its emancipation under the leadership of the proletariat, but the proletariat can only lead the bourgeois-democratic revolution to victory in union with the peasantry.

The process of class differentiation of the peasantry in the colonies and semi-colonies which possess important relics of feudalism and of pre-capitalist relationships proceeds at a comparatively slow rate. Nevertheless, market relationships in these countries have developed to such a degree that the peasantry already no longer represent a homogeneous mass, as far as their class relations are concerned. In the villages of China and India, in particular in certain parts of these countries, it is already possible to find exploiting elements derived from the peasantry, who exploit the peasants and village labourers through usury, trade, employment of hired labour, the sale or letting out of land on rent, the loaning of cattle or agricultural implements, etc. etc.

In general, it is possible that, in the first period of the struggle of the peasantry against the landlords, the proletariat may be able to carry with it the entire peasantry. But in the further development of the struggle some of the upper strata of the peasantry may pass into the camp of counter-revolution. The proletariat can achieve its leading role in relation to the peasantry only under the conditions of unflinching struggle for its partial demands, for complete carrying through of the agrarian revolution, and only if it will lead the struggle of the wide masses of the peasantry for a revolutionary solution of the agrarian question.

21. The working class in the colonies and semi-colonies has characteristic features which play an important role in the building up of an independent working class movement and proletarian class ideology in these countries. The predominant part of the colonial proletariat is derived from the pauperised village, with which the worker remains in connection even when engaged in production. In the majority of colonies (with the exception of some large factory towns such as Shanghai, Bombay, Calcutta, etc.), we find, as a general rule, only a first generation of proletariat engaged in large-

scale production. Another portion is made up of the ruined artisans who are being driven out of the decaying handicrafts, which are widely spread even in the most advanced colonies. The ruined artisan, a petty owner, carries with him into the working class a guild tendency and ideology which serves as a basis for the penetration of national-reformist influence into the labour movement of the colonies.

The great fluctuation in the composition of the proletariat (frequent renewal of the labour force in the factories owing to workers returning to the villages and the inflow of new masses of poverty-stricken peasants into production); the considerable percentage of women and children; the numerous different languages; illiteracy; the wide distribution of religious and caste prejudices—all make difficult the work of systematic agitation and propaganda and retard the growth of class consciousness among the workers. Nevertheless, the merciless exploitation, practised in the most oppressive forms by native and foreign capital, and the entire absence of political rights for the workers, create the objective pre-conditions on the basis of which the labour movement in the colonies is rapidly overcoming all obstacles and every year draws greater and greater masses of the working class into the struggle against the native exploiters and the imperialists.

The first period of the growth of the labour movement in the colonial and semi-colonial countries (approximately 1919–1923) is organically bound up with the general growth of the national-revolutionary movement which followed the world war, and which was characterised by the subordination of the class interests of the working class to the interests of the anti-imperialist struggle headed by the native bourgeoisie. In so far as the labour strikes and other demonstrations bore an organisational character, they were usually organised by petty bourgeois intellectuals who restricted the demands of the workers to questions of the national struggle. The most important characteristic of the second period of rapid growth of the labour movement in the colonies, on the other hand, the period which began after the V. Congress of the Communist International, was the emergence of the working class of the colonies into the political arena as an independent class force directly opposing itself to the national bourgeoisie, and entering upon a struggle with the latter in defence of its own immediate class interests and for hegemony in the national revolution as a whole. The history of the last few years has clearly confirmed this characteristic of the new stage of the colonial revolution, first of all in the example of the great Chinese revolution, and subsequently in the insurrection in Indonesia. There is every ground to believe that in India the working class is liberating itself from the influence of the nationalist and social-reformist leaders and is being converted into an independent political factor in the struggle against the British imperialists and the native bourgeoisie.

22. In order correctly to determine the immediate tasks of the revolu-

tionary movement, it is important as a starting point to take into consideration the degree of maturity attained by the movement in the separate
colonial countries. The revolutionary movement in China is distinguished
from the present movement in India by a series of essential features,
characterising the different degrees of maturity of the movement in the
two countries. The previous experience of the Chinese revolution must,
undoubtedly, be utilised in the revolutionary movement in India and other
analogous colonial countries. But it would be a completely mistaken application of the Chinese experience if, at the present time in India, Egypt, etc., we
were to formulate the immediate tasks, slogans and tactical methods in
exactly the same form as took place in China, for example in the Wuhan
period, or in the form in which it is necessary to formulate them there at
the present time.

The tendency to skip over the inevitable difficulties and special tasks of
the present stage of the revolutionary movement in India, Egypt, etc., can
only be harmful. It is necessary to carry through much work in the building
up and consolidation of the Communist Party and trade union organisations
of the proletariat, in the revolutionisation of the trade unions, in the development of economic and political mass demonstrations and in the winning over of the masses and their liberation from the influence of the
national-reformist bourgeoisie, before it is possible to advance in these
countries with definite prospects of success to the realisation of such tasks as
those which were fully carried out in China during the Wuhan period as the
immediate tasks of the struggle of the working class and peasantry.

The interests of the struggle for the class rule of the national bourgeoisie
compel the most important bourgeois parties in India and Egypt (Swarajists, Wafdists) still to demonstrate their opposition to the ruling imperialist-
feudal bloc. Although this opposition has not a revolutionary but a reformist and class collaborationist character, this by no means signifies that
it has not a special significance. The national bourgeoisie has not the significance of a force in the struggle against imperialism. Nevertheless, this
bourgeois-reformist opposition has its real special significance for the development of the revolutionary movement—and this both in a negative
as well as in a positive sense—in so far as it possesses any mass influence
at all.

Its chief feature is that it exerts a braking, retarding influence on the
development of the revolutionary movement, in so far [as] it is successful
in drawing the toiling masses in its wake and holding them back from the
revolutionary struggle. On the other hand, however, the demonstrations of
the bourgeois opposition against the ruling imperialist-feudal bloc, even if
they do not have any deep foundation, can exert a certain accelerating influence on the process of the political awakening of the wide masses of
toilers; the concrete open conflicts of the national-reformist bourgeoisie

with imperialism, although of little significance in themselves, may, under certain conditions, indirectly serve as the cause of the unleashing of even greater revolutionary mass actions.

It is true the reformist bourgeoisie itself endeavours not to allow of any such effect of its oppositional activities, and in one way or another seeks to prevent it in advance. But, wherever the objective conditions exist for a far-reaching political crisis, there the activities of the national-reformist opposition, even their insignificant conflicts with imperialism which are least of all connected with the real hearth of the revolution, can become of serious importance.

The Communists must learn how to utilise each and every conflict, to develop such conflicts and to broaden their significance, to connect them with the agitation for revolutionary slogans, to spread the news of these conflicts among the wide masses, to arouse these masses to independent, open manifestations in support of their own demands, etc.

23. The correct tactics in the struggle against such parties as the Swarajists and Wafdists during this stage consist in the successful exposure of their real national-reformist character. These parties have already more than once betrayed the national-emancipatory struggle, but they have not yet finally passed over to the counter-revolutionary camp in the manner of the Kuomintang. There is no doubt that they will do this later on, but at the present time they are so particularly dangerous precisely because their real physiognomy has not yet been exposed in the eyes of the wide masses of toilers. For this exposure there is still needed a very large amount of Communist educational work and a very great deal of new political experience on the part of the masses themselves. If the Communists do not already succeed in this stage in shaking the faith of the toiling masses in the bourgeois national-reformist leadership of the national movement, then this leadership in the coming upsurge of the revolutionary wave will represent an enormous danger for the revolution.

Consequently, it is necessary, by means of correct Communist tactics, adapted to the conditions of the present stage, to help the toiling masses in India, Egypt, Indonesia and such colonies to emancipate themselves from the influence of the bourgeois parties. This is not to be achieved by any noisy phrases, however radical they may sound superficially, about the absence of any distinction between the oppositional national-reformists (Swarajists, Wafdists, etc.) and the British imperialists or their feudal counter-revolutionary allies. The national reformist leaders would easily be able to make use of such an exaggeration in order to incite the masses against the Communists. The masses see the chief immediate enemy of national emancipation in the form of the imperialist feudal bloc, which in itself is correct at this stage of the movement in India, Egypt, and Indonesia (as far as one side of the matter is concerned.)

In the struggle against this ruling counter-revolutionary force, the Indian,

Egyptian and Indonesian Communists must proceed in advance of all, they must fight more determinedly, more consistently and more resolutely than any petty bourgeois section or national-revolutionary group. Of course, this fight must not be waged for the organising of any kind of putsch or premature attempt at a rising on the part of the small revolutionary minority, but for the purpose of organising the widest possible strata of the masses of toilers in demonstrations and other manifestations so that in this way the active participation of these masses can be guaranteed for a victorious uprising at a further stage of the revolutionary struggle.

At the same time, it is no less important mercilessly to expose before the toiling masses the national-reformist character of the Swarajist, Wafdist and other nationalist parties, and in particular of their leaders. It is necessary to expose their half-heartedness and vacillation in the national struggle, their bargainings and attempts to reach a compromise with British imperialism, their previous capitulations and counter-revolutionary advances, their reactionary resistance to the class demands of the proletariat and peasantry, their empty nationalist-phraseology, their dissemination of harmful illusions about the peaceful decolonisation of the country and their sabotage in relation to the application of revolutionary methods in the national-emancipatory struggle.

It is necessary to reject the formation of any kind of bloc between the Communist Party and the national-reformist opposition; this does not exclude the formation of temporary agreements and the coordinating of separate activities in connection with definite anti-imperialist demonstrations, provided that the demonstrations of the bourgeois opposition can be utilised for the development of the mass movement, and provided that these agreements do not in any way limit the freedom of the Communist Parties in the matter of agitation among the masses and among the organisations of the latter. Of course, in this work the Communists must know how at the same time to carry on the most relentless ideological and political struggle against bourgeois nationalism and against the slightest signs of its influence inside the labour movement. In such cases, the Communist Party must take particular care not only to maintain its complete political independence and to make quite clear its own character, but also, on the basis of facts, to open the eyes of the masses of toilers who are under the influence of the bourgeois opposition, so that they will perceive all the hopelessness of this opposition and the danger of the bourgeois democratic illusions that it disseminates.

24. An incorrect estimation of the chief tendency of the parties of the big national bourgeoisie gives rise to the danger of an incorrect estimation of the character and role of the petty bourgeois parties. The development of these parties, as a general rule, follows a course from the national-revolutionary to the national-reformist position. Even such movements as Sun Yat-senism in China, Gandhism in India, Sarekat Islam in Indonesia,

[353]

were originally radical petty bourgeois ideological movements which, however, as a result of their service to the big bourgeoisie became converted into a bourgeois nationalist-reformist movement. After this, in India, Egypt, and Indonesia, there was again founded a radical wing from among the different petty bourgeois groups (e. g. the Republican Party, Watanists, Sarekat Rayat), which stand for a more or less consistent national-revolutionary point of view. In such a country as India, the rise is possible of some new analogous radical petty bourgeois parties and groups.

But the fact must not be lost sight of that these parties, essentially considered, are connected with the national bourgeoisie. The petty bourgeoisie intelligentsia at the head of the parties puts forward national-revolutionary demands but at the same time appears more or less conscious as the representative of the capitalist development of their country. Some of these elements can become the followers of various kinds of reactionary utopias, but when confronted with feudalism and imperialism, they, in distinction from the parties of the big national bourgeoisie, appear at the outset not as reformists but as more or less revolutionary representatives of the anti-imperialist interests of the colonial bourgeoisie. This is the case, at least, so long as the development of the revolutionary process in the country does not put on the order of the day in a definite and sharp form the fundamental internal questions of the bourgeois-democratic-revolution, particularly the question of the realisation of the agrarian revolution and the dictatorship of the proletariat and peasantry. When this happens, then it usually denotes the end of the revolutionary character of the petty bourgeois parties. As soon as the revolution has placed the class interests of the proletariat and the peasantry in critical contradiction not only to the rule of the feudal-imperialist bloc, but also to the class rule of the bourgeoisie, the petty bourgeois groups usually go back to the position of the national-reformist parties.

It is absolutely essential that the Communist Parties in these countries should from the very beginning demarcate themselves in the most clear-cut fashion, both politically and organisationally, from all the petty bourgeois groups and parties. In so far as the needs of the revolutionary struggle demand it, a temporary co-operation is permissible, and in certain circumstances even a temporary union between the Communist Party and the national revolutionary movement, provided that the latter is a genuine revolutionary movement, that it genuinely struggles against the ruling power and that its representatives do not put obstacles in the way of the Communists educating and organising in a revolutionary sense the peasants and broad masses of the exploited. In every such co-operation, however, it is essential to take the most careful precautions in order that this co-operation does not degenerate into a fusion of the Communist movement with the bourgeois-revolutionary movement.

The Communist movement in all circumstances, must unconditionally preserve the independence of the proletarian movement and its own independence in agitation, in organisation and in demonstrations. To criticise the half-heartedness and vacillation of the petty bourgeois groups, to anticipate their vacillations, to be prepared for them and at the same time to utilise to the full all the revolutionary possibilities of these strata, to carry on a consistent struggle against petty bourgeois influence over the proletariat, employ all means to liberate the wide masses of the peasantry from the influence of the petty bourgeois parties and to win from them the hegemony over the peasantry—these are the tasks of the Communist Parties.

25. How rapidly the revolutionary movement in India, Egypt, etc., will reach such a high degree of maturity as it has already reached in China, depends to an essential extent on how quickly there arises there a big revolutionary wave. In the event of its postponement for a considerable time, the political and organisational ripening of the driving forces of the revolution can only proceed by way of a gradual and relatively slow process of development. If, however, the coming powerful revolutionary wave rises earlier, then the movement may quickly be able to attain a much higher stage of maturity.

Under exceptionally favourable circumstances, it is not even excluded that the revolution there may be able in one single mighty wave to achieve the conquest of power by the proletariat and peasantry. It is also possible that the process of the development of the revolution from one stage to another more mature stage will be interrupted for a more or less prolonged period of time, in particular if the coming wave of revolutionary upheaval reaches a relatively small height and is not of great duration. Consequently, it is necessary in every case to subject the concrete situation to the most detailed analysis.

The following factors are of decisive significance for the immediate growing over of the revolution from one stage to another higher stage: 1. the degree of development of the revolutionary proletarian leadership of the movement, i. e. of the Communist Party of the given country (the numerical strength of the Party, its independent character, consciousness and fighting readiness, as well as its authority and connection with the masses and its influence on the trade union and peasant movement); 2. the degree of organisation and the revolutionary experience of the working class, as well as, to a certain extent, of the peasantry. The revolutionary experience of the masses signifies experience of struggle; in the first place, liberation from the influence over them of the bourgeois and petty bourgeois parties.

Since these pre-requisites for the first big mass outburst of the revolution, even in the best circumstances, are present only to an insufficient degree, an unusually deep revolutionary crisis and an unusually high and persistent revolutionary wave are required for it to be possible for the bourgeois-democratic revolution with the aid of this one wave of upheaval to lead to the complete victory of the proletariat and peasantry. Such a possibility is most easily presented, for example, when the ruling imperialism is temporarily distracted by a long continued war outside the frontiers of the colonial country concerned.

26. Living, concrete, historical dialectics, such as were demonstrated by the now completed first period of the bourgeois-democratic revolution in China, will give to the Communists, especially those working in the colonial countries, a valuable experience which it is necessary to study carefully in order to draw the correct conclusions, especially from the mistakes committed in the course of Communist work in the colonies.

The rise of the revolutionary wave in China was unusually prolonged (over two years), since it was connected with a protracted internal war. In as much as the Northern Expedition was not conducted directly against the great imperialist powers and in as much as the latter, owing to competition between them, were partially passive during the first period, while the bourgeois leadership of the national movement had already for some years held Canton in its hands—a definite, though limited territory—as well as a centralised power backed up by the army, etc., it is understandable that in this exceptional case a great part of the bourgeoisie in the beginning looked upon the national-emancipatory war as its own particular affair. The Kuomintang, in which it practically played a leading role, in the course of a short time came to be at the head of the national-revolutionary movement, a circumstance which in the course of further events represented an extremely great danger for the revolution.

On the other hand, among the peculiarities of the situation in China must be numbered the fact that the proletariat there was stronger in relation to its bourgeoisie than the proletariat of other countries. It is true that it was weakly organised, but during the upsurge of the revolutionary wave the growth of labour organisation proceeded at a very rapid rate.

The Communist Party also rose in a short time from a small group to a Party with 60,000 members (and presently even more) and possessing a wide influence among the workers. Naturally, in these conditions many petty bourgeois elements also entered the Party. The Party was lacking in revolutionary experience and, even more, in traditions of Bolshevism. In the beginning, the upper hand in its leadership was taken by wavering elements, which were still only to a very small degree liberated from petty bourgeois opportunist tendencies, which inadequately understood the independent tasks and role of the Communist Party and which came out against any decisive development of the agrarian revolution.

The entry of the Communists for a certain period into the leading party of the national revolution, the Kuomintang, in itself corresponded to the requirements of the struggle and of the situation, and was also in the interests of the indispensable Communist work among the fairly wide masses of toilers who followed this party. In addition, at the beginning, the Communist Party of China received in the territory under the rule of the

Kuomintang Government the possibility of independent agitation among the masses of workers and peasants and among the soldiers of the national army and their organisations. At that time the Party possessed greater possibilities than it actually made use of.

At that time the Party did not sufficiently clearly explain to the masses its proletarian class position in distinction from Sun Yat-senism and other petty bourgeois tendencies. In the ranks of the Kuomintang, the Communists did not conduct any independent policy, leaving out of account that in any such inevitable bloc the Communists must adopt an unconditionally critical attitude towards the bourgeois elements and always come out as an independent force. The Communists failed to expose the vacillations of the national-bourgeoisie and of bourgeois-democratic nationalism, just at the time when this exposure ought to have constituted one of the most important tasks of the Communist Party. The inevitable disruption of the Kuomintang drew nearer and nearer as the national army advanced, but the leadership of the Chinese Communist Party undertook nothing or almost nothing in order to prepare the Party in case of a breach, and in order to guarantee its independent position and to unite the revolutionary workers and peasants in an independent fighting bloc which would oppose itself to the leadership of the Kuomintang.

Thus, the bourgeois-counter-revolutionary coup of Chang Kai-shek found the revolutionary proletariat completely unprepared and threw its ranks into confusion. Further, the leadership of the Communist Party even at that time badly understood the process of the development of the revolution from one stage to another and did not carry through the correct changes in the line of the Party made necessary by this coup. In as much as the Left Wing of the petty bourgeois leaders of the Kuomintang during the course of a certain time still went together with the Communist Party, there took place a territorial separation; there arose the separate governments of Nanking and Wuhan. But the Communist Party did not occupy a leading position even in Wuhan.

Very quickly, in the Wuhan territory there commenced a second period, characterised, among other things, on the one hand, by the presence of elements of an incipient, still indefinite dual power (the seizure by peasant unions of a number of ruling functions in the villages, and the extension of the functions of the trade unions, determined by the endeavour of the masses to reach a "plebeian" independent solution of the questions of power), and, on the other hand, by the absence of sufficiently mature conditions for the organisation of Soviets as organs of revolt against the Wuhan government, in so far as the latter still carried on a revolutionary struggle against the Nanking government which represented the treachery of the bourgeoisie to the revolution.

The Communist Party at that time directly hindered the independent actions of the revolutionary masses; it did not facilitate their task of gathering

[357]

and organising forces; it did not assist in breaking down the influence of the leaders of the Left Kuomintang and their position in the country and in the army. Instead of utilising its participation in the Government for these purposes, it, on the contrary, screened the whole activity of this Government (individual petty bourgeois leading members of the Party went so far that they even participated in the disarming of the workers' pickets in Wuhan and in sanctioning the punitive expedition to Changsha!).

At the bottom of this opportunist policy lay the hope of avoiding a rupture with the petty bourgeois leaders of the Wuhan government. But, as a matter of fact, this rupture could only be put off for a short space of time. When the mass risings acquired a threatening character, the leaders of the Wuhan Kuomintang also began to reach out towards unity with their allies on the other side of the barricades. The revolutionary movement of the workers and peasants still continued to exert all its forces in order to achieve victory.

The Communist Party of China now also corrected its line, elected a new leadership and took its place at the head of the revolution. But the revolutionary wave had already ebbed. The heroic mass struggles under the slogan of Soviets could only achieve a few temporary successes. Only in individual localities did the uprising of the agrarian revolution begin sufficiently early, in the remainder the many millions of the peasant rearguard were delayed in their advance. Instead of the former gross errors of opportunist leadership, there were now revealed, on the contrary, in various places extremely harmful putschist mistakes. The preparations for risings also did not take place without great defects on the part of the Communists. The heavy defeats once more threw back the revolution, which in the South had already entered into the second stage of development, to the starting point of this stage.

27. Thanks to the fact that the Chinese national bourgeoisie obtained power, the composition of the former bloc of the imperialists and militarists was partly altered and the new ruling bloc now represents the immediate chief enemy of the revolution. In order to overthrow it, it is necessary to win over the decisive masses of the proletariat and peasantry to the side of the revolution. This constitutes the most important task of the Chinese Communist Party for the immediate future. The Chinese workers have already acquired an enormous experience. The further strengthening and revolutionisation of the trade union movement and the further strengthening of the Communist Party is essential. A certain portion of the Chinese peasantry has already outlived bourgeois democratic illusions and shown considerable activity in the revolutionary struggle, but this is only an insignificant minority of the huge peasant population of China.

It is very probable that some petty bourgeois groups will take up the position of national reformism (inside or outside the Kuomintang), in order by a certain display of bourgeois-democratic opposition to conquer influence over the toiling masses (to these petty bourgeois reformists belong also Tang Ping-san and the Social Democratic trade union leaders). Under no circumstances must the significance of these attempts be underestimated. The isolation of these groups and their exposure before the masses by means of correct Communist tactics constitutes an absolutely essential pre-condition for the Communist Party to be able to take a really leading position in the moment of the coming new rise of the revolutionary wave in China.

Already at the present time, the Party must everywhere propagate among the masses the idea of Soviets, the idea of the dictatorship of the proletariat and peasantry, and the inevitability of the coming revolutionary mass armed uprising. It must already now emphasise in its agitation the necessity of overthrow of the ruling bloc and the mobilisation of the masses for revolutionary demonstrations. Carefully studying the objective conditions of the revolution as they continue to mature, utilising every possibility for the mobilisation of the masses, it must consistently and undeviatingly follow the line of seizure of State power, organisation of Soviets as organs of the insurrection, expropriation of the landlords and big property-owners, expulsion of the foreign imperialists and the confiscation of their property.

IV. The Immediate Tasks of the Communists.

28. The building up and development of the Communist Parties in the colonies and semi-colonies, the removal of the excessively marked disproportion between the objective revolutionary situation and the weakness of the subjective factor, represents one of the most important and primary tasks of the Communist International. This task comes up against a whole host of objective difficulties, determined by the historical development and social structure of these countries.

Corresponding with the weak development of industry, the working class in these countries is still young and, for their population, relatively small in numbers. The colonial regime of terror, as also the existence of illiteracy, numerous different languages, etc., renders difficult the organisation and development of the working class in general and the rapid development of the Communist Party in particular. The fluctuation of composition and the large percentage of women and children are characteristic features of the colonial proletariat. In many places, seasonal workers predominate and even the basic ranks of the proletariat still have one foot in the village. This facilitates the connection between the working class and the peasantry but makes more difficult the development of the class consciousness of the proletariat.

Experience has shown that, in the majority of colonial and semi-colonial countries, an important if not a predominant part of the Party ranks in the first stage of the movement is recruited from the petty bourgeoisie and, in particular, from the revolutionarily inclined intelligentsia, very frequently students. It frequently happens that these elements enter the Party because they see in it the most decisive enemy of imperialism, at the same time not always sufficiently understanding that the Communist Party is not only the Party of struggle against imperialist exploitation and oppression, but is the Party which, as the Party of the proletariat, leads a decisive struggle against all kinds of exploitation and suppression.

Many of these adherents of the Party in the course of the revolutionary struggle will reach a proletarian class point of view, another part will find it more difficult to free themselves to the end from the moods, waverings, and half-hearted ideology of the petty bourgeoisie. It is precisely these elements of the Party that find it especially difficult at the critical moment to estimate correctly the role of the national bourgeoisie and to act consistently and without any kind of vacillation in the questions of the agrarian revolution, etc. The colonial countries do not possess Social Democratic traditions, but neither do they possess Marxist traditions. Our young Parties in the process of struggle, in the process of building up the Party, will have to overcome the relics of national petty bourgeois ideology in order to find the road to Bolshevism.

These objective difficulties make it all the more obligatory for the Communist International to give an absolutely special attention to the tasks of building the Party in the colonial and semi-colonial countries. An especially great responsibility in this connection lies with the Communist Parties of the imperialist countries. This demands not only assistance in the matter of working out the correct political line, accurate analysis of experiences in the sphere of organisation and agitation, but also systematic education of the Party ranks, the publication of a certain minimum of Marxist-Leninist literature and its translation into the languages of the different colonial countries, most active assistance in the matter of study and Marxist analysis of the economic and social problems of the colonies and semi-colonies, and in the creation of a Party press, etc.

The Communist Parties in the colonial and semi-colonial countries are bound to exert all their efforts for the creation of a cadre of Party functionaries from the ranks of the working class itself, utilising members of the Party—intellectuals—in the role of leaders and lecturers for propagandist circles and legal and illegal Party schools, so as to educate from the advanced workers the necessary agitators, propagandists, organisers and leaders permeated by the spirit of Leninism. The Communist Parties in the colonial countries must become genuinely proletarian parties also in their social composition. Including in their ranks the best elements of the revolutionary intelligentsia, becoming steeled in the process of the daily struggle and of big revolutionary fights, the Communist Parties must give their chief attention to the task of strengthening the Party organisation in the factories and mines, among the transport workers and among the semi-slaves in the plantations.

Everywhere where capitalism concentrates the proletariat, the Communist

Party must establish its nuclei, including the working class tenements, the big working class barracks of the factories, and barrack-line plantations so strictly guarded from working class agitation. Nor should work be neglected among the journeymen, apprentices and coolies employed in small handicraft workshops. The native workers and the workers who have come from the metropolis must unite together in one and the same Party organisation. The experience of the older Parties in the matter of a correct combination of legal and illegal work must be utilised in accordance with the situation in the different colonial countries, in order as far as possible to avoid that which took place, for example, in China, where the vast mass organisations were broken up comparatively easily and without any great internal resistance under the blows of the reaction, thus greatly weakening the connection between the Communist Party and the masses.

29. Alongside the development of the Communist Party, the most important of the immediate general tasks of the Communists in the colonies and semi-colonies is that of work in the trade Unions. The organisation of the unorganised workers, above all in the largest branches of industry (engineering, mining, transport, textiles, etc.), the conversion of the existing organisations into real class trade unions, the fight with the national-reformists and reactionary trade union leaders for the leadership in these organisations—all these things must be included in the tasks of trade union work. Another category of tasks consists in support of the economic interests and immediate demands of the workers in the struggle with the employers and, in particular, in resolute and correct leadership of strikes.

It is obligatory for Communists to carry on revolutionary propagandist work in the reactionary trade unions which contain masses of workers. In those countries where circumstances dictate the necessity for creating special revolutionary trade unions (because the reactionary trade union leadership hinders the organisation of the unorganised workers, destroys the most elementary demands of trade union democracy and converts the trade unions into strike-breaking organisations, etc.), it is necessary to consult on this question with the leadership of the R. I. L. U. Special attention needs to be given to the intrigues of the Amsterdam International in the colonial countries (China, India, North Africa) and to the exposure of its reactionary character before the masses. It is obligatory for the Communist Party in the metropolis concerned to afford active help to the revolutionary trade union movement of the colony by its advice and by sending permanent instructors. Up to now too little has been done in this connection.

30. Wherever peasant organisations exist—entirely irrespective of their character, as long as they are real mass organisations—the Communist Party must adopt measures in order to penetrate into these organisations. One of the immediate tasks of the Party is the correct formulation of the agrarian question in the ranks of the working class explaining to the latter the importance and decisive role of the agrarian revolution and acquainting mem-

[361]

bers of the Party with methods of agitation, propaganda and organisational work among the peasantry. Every Party organisation has the duty of studying the specific agrarian situation in the region of its activity and of formulating the corresponding current demands of the peasants. The Communists must everywhere attempt to give a revolutionary character to the existing peasant movement. They must organise both new revolutionary peasant unions and peasant committees, between which and the Communist Party it is necessary to establish regular connections. Both in the peasant masses and in the ranks of the proletariat it is essential to carry on energetic propaganda in favour of a fighting bloc of the proletariat and peasantry.

Special "Workers' and Peasants' Parties," whatever revolutionary character they may possess, can too easily, at particular periods, be converted into ordinary petty bourgeois parties, and, accordingly, Communists are not recommended to organise such parties. The Communist Party can never build its organisation on the basis of a fusion of two classes, and in the same way also it cannot make it its task to organise other parties on this basis, which is characteristic of petty bourgeois groups.

The fighting bloc of the masses of workers and peasants can find expression in carefully prepared and periodically convened joint conferences and congresses of representatives of revolutionary peasant unions (or their committees) and of trade unions; in certain circumstances it may be found expedient to create revolutionary committees of action, co-ordinating the activity of the organisations of the workers and peasants, conducting various mass activities, etc. Finally, during the period of insurrection one of the fundamental tasks of the Communist Party is to promote the creation of elected soviets of workers' and peasants' deputies. Under any and all circumstances, the Communist Party is bound to exert a decisive influence on the peasant movement, to find out and apply those organisational forms of bloc between the workers and peasants which will most of all facilitate the task of leadership in the peasant movement and to create the pre-requisites for the further transformation of these forms into Soviets as organs of insurrection and power.

31. In the colonial countries the proletarian youth is exposed to especially grievous suffering, and the relative part played by the youth in the composition of the working class is considerably higher in the colonial countries than in the old capitalist countries. The exploitation of the working youth is subject to no legal limitations; there is no legal restriction of the working day, the conditions of labour are unbearably burden-some and are accompanied by inhuman treatment on the part of the employers and overseers. Matters are no better with the peasant youth. It is not surprising therefore that the worker-peasant youth is taking an active part in all the revolutionary movements of the colonial countries. From this youth was derived a great part of the revolutionary organisations and peasant armies in China, the partisan troops of Korea, which have carried on the struggle against

Japanese colonisers, as well as the participants in the heroic risings in Indonesia, etc.

An immediate fundamental task of the Young Communist International in the colonies is the creation of revolutionary mass organisations of the proletarian youth under Communist leadership, i. e. mass Young Communist Leagues. In this connection the training of genuinely Communist leading cadres of the youth movement is just as important as securing a mass character and basic proletarian composition for the Communist youth organisations. Together with the working youth, it is desirable to attract the best and most devoted revolutionary elements taking part in the peasant youth movement in order to strengthen the proletarian elements in the leading organs of the Young Communist League. A mass recruitment of the youth from non-proletarian strata into the Young Communist Leagues is only permissible to the degree that there is guaranteed in the latter an overwhelming proletarian composition and firm Communist leadership.

While taking part in all struggles of the Communist Party, the Communist youth organisation must avoid both efforts to place itself in the place of the Party as regards leadership of the working class (the so-called "vanguard" tendency) as also the peculiar liquidatory tendencies expressed in the denial of the necessity for a young Communist movement and in the reduction of the significance of the Communist youth organisation to the role of student or other general indefinite youth organisations.

The Y. C. L.'s of the colonies, with the object of winning over the wide masses of the youth taking part in the workers', peasants' and revolutionary movements, and of liberating them from the influence of national-reformism and pseudo-revolutionary tendencies, must also make use of a system of auxiliary, in relation to the Y. C. L., legal organisations, building them on the basis of a revolutionary programme and securing the leadership for the Communist Party and Y. C. L.

The Y. C. L. must work in the already existing organisations in such a fashion as to draw them into revolutionary activity and to win influence and leadership within them. While utilising all these organisations and drawing the working masses of the young workers into the revolutionary struggle, the Y. C. L. organisations must not lose their independence or diminish their immediate work. The loss of their Communist youth character and the consequent possible loss of their leadership over the revolutionary youth movement represents a great danger to be faced. Consequently, while utilising, developing and working in auxiliary organisations, the Y. C. L. must strengthen its own immediate work, coming out openly before the masses of working youth and attracting the best elements of the mass organisations into the ranks of the Y. C. L.

These organisations include the youth sections of the trade unions and peasant unions, associations of working youth, anti-militarist unions, sport associations, local unions of students, etc.

The VI Congress of the Communist International makes it obligatory for all Communist Parties in the colonies to render all possible assistance in the creation and development of the Communist youth movement, and to struggle against any deviations or backward views in the working class and trade unions which express themselves in ignoring the interests of the working youth and in disinclination to participate in the struggle for the demand for improvement of the conditions of the exploited young workers.

32. The exploitation of the labour of women and children in the colonial countries takes on especially wide dimensions and barbarous forms. The most miserable starvation wages, an unbearably long working day, the purchasing in some regions of women and children for work under slave conditions in plantations, etc., prison-like life in working class dwellings, barbarous and inconsiderate treatment—such are the conditions of labour of these sections. At the same time, there is carried on a widespread reactionary work among the proletarian women on the part of the bourgeoisie, missionaries, etc., who have at their disposal considerable monetary resources. But the women workers of the colonies, driven to desperation, are gradually awakening to class consciousness, are entering upon the revolutionary path and decisively and boldly joining the ranks of the struggling colonial proletariat. This was evident, above all, in the self-sacrificing participation of the Chinese working women in the events of the revolution (mass strikes of women workers, individual acts of heroism of women workers, the entrance of peasant women into the ranks of the guerilla fighters).

The Communist Parties of the colonies and semi-colonies must pay great attention to work among these strata, particularly in enterprises where women's labour predominates, systematically attracting the women into trade union organisations and winning over the best of them for the Communist Party. In struggling against the influence of hostile organisations, the Party must use all the resources of oral, written, legal and illegal agitation and propaganda at its disposal in order to win over the working women.

Alongside of these general tasks, the Communist Parties in the various colonies have a series of special tasks, resulting from the particular social-economic structure and political situation in each country. In proposing to the particular Communist Parties concerned the working out of the whole complex of these tasks in the concrete plans of action, the Congress indicates below some of the most important of these immediate tasks.

33. In China, the future growth of the revolution will place before the Party as an immediate practical task the preparation for and carrying through of armed insurrection as the sole path to the completion of the bourgeois-democratic revolution and to the overthrow of the power of the imperialists, landlords and national bourgeoisie—the power of the Kuomintang.

Under existing circumstances, characterised fundamentally by the absence of a revolutionary impulse among the wide masses of the Chinese people, the general line of the Party must be the struggle for the masses. The carrying through of this line under the conditions of the strengthening of the anti-imperialist movement, of a certain revival of the strike struggle and of the continuing peasant activity, demands from the Party the exertion of all its strength for gathering, consolidating and uniting the proletariat around the basic slogans of the Party, an immense organisational work for the strengthening of the revolutionary trade union and peasant associations, maximum attention to the conduct of the every-day economic and political work among the masses of the proletariat and peasantry, and intense activity in explaining to the proletariat the experience of the preceding period of the revolution. At the same time, the Party must explain to the masses the impossibility of a radical improvement in their position, the impossibility of the overthrow of imperialist domination and solution of the tasks of the agrarian revolution, without the overthrow from power of the Kuomintang and militarists and the creation of the rule of Soviets.

The Party must utilise every conflict, however insignificant, between the workers and the capitalists in the factories, between the peasants and landlords in the villages, between the soldiers and officers in the army, deepening and sharpening these class clashes in order to mobilise the widest masses of workers and peasants and to win them over to its side. The Party must utilise all occurrences of violence on the part of international imperialism against the Chinese people, which at the present time take the form of a military seizure of different regions, as well as all the bloody exploits of infuriated reaction, in order to widen the popular protest of the masses against the ruling classes.

The success of this struggle for the masses will be determined to a considerable degree by the extent of the success achieved in applying tactics based on a correct estimate of the situation, and in outliving the mistakes and tendencies of an extreme Left character (putschism, military adventurism, individual terror, etc.), which have occurred in the Party, as well as those of an opportunist character such as found their expression in the demands for summoning a national assembly and for the revival of the Kuomintang mass movement. Simultaneously, the Party must conquer every tendency in the direction of replacing methods of convincing and educating the masses by methods of compulsion and commandment, which in the present conditions of cruel class terror serve to enhance the danger of an isolation of the Party from the toiling masses.

In the sphere of internal Party work, the Party must strive to re-establish the nuclei and local Party committees which have been destroyed by the reaction, to improve the social composition of the Party and, in so doing, to concentrate especial attention on the creation of Party nuclei in the most important branches of production in the big factories, workshops and railway shops. The Communist Party of China must devote most serious attention to regulating the social composition of the village organisations, so that these organisations shall be recruited basically from the proletarian, semi-proletarian and the poorest elements of the villages. The putting into effect of the principles of democratic centralism; the guaranteeing, as far as illegal conditions of work permit it, of inner Party democracy; transition to collective discussion and decision of questions; and, along with this, struggle against ultra-democratic tendencies in certain organisations, leading to breach of Party discipline, to the growth of irresponsibility and to the destruction of the authority of the leading Party centres.

The necessary strengthening of the work in the theoretical training of the membership of the Party, in the raising of their political level; the establishment of systematic propaganda of Marxism and Leninism, the investigation of the experience and lessons of the preceding stages of the Chinese revolution (the Wuhan period, the Canton insurrection, etc.). In relation to "third" parties (Tan Ping-san, Wang Tsin-wei), representing a weapon of the bourgeois-landlord counter revolution, the task of the Chinese Communist Party consists in a decisive struggle against them, and in the exposure, on the basis of the practical anti-imperialist and mass movement, of the national-reformist activity of these parties as agencies of the ruling classes.

The fundamental slogans, through which the Party must seek to win over the masses, are the following:

1. Overthrow of imperialist domination.

2. Confiscation of foreign enterprises and banks.

3. Unity of the country, with recognition of the right of each nationality to self-determination.

4. Overthrow of the power of the militarists and the Kuomintang.

5. Establishment of the power of Soviets of workers', peasants' and soldiers' representatives.

6. The 8-hour working day, increase of wages, assistance to the unemployed and social insurance.

7. Confiscation of all lands of big landlords, land for the peasants and soldiers.

8. The abolition of all governmental, militarist and local taxes and levies; a single progressively graduated income tax.

9. Alliance with the U. S. S. R. and the world proletarian movement.

34. The basic tasks of the Indian Communists consist in struggle against British imperialism for the emancipation of the country, for destruction of all relics of feudalism, for the agrarian revolution and for establishment of the dictatorship of the proletariat and peasantry in the form of a Soviet Republic. These tasks can be successfully carried out only when there will be created a powerful Communist Party which will be able to place itself at the head of the wide masses of the working class, peasantry and all the toilers, and to lead them in the armed insurrection against the feudal-imperialist bloc.

[366]

The strike movement of the Indian proletariat now taking place, its independence from bourgeois nationalism, the all-Indian character of this movement, its distribution over almost all branches of industry, the frequence and protracted character of the strikes, the stubbornness and great resoluteness with which the workers have carried them on, the coming forward of leaders of the strikes from the midst of the workers themselves, —all these things denote a turning point in the history of the struggle of the Indian proletariat, and prove that in India the pre-conditions have matured which are essential for the creation of a mass Communist Party.

The union of all Communist groups and individual Communists scattered throughout the country into a single, illegal, independent and centralised party represents the first task of Indian Communists. While rejecting the principle of the building of the Party on a two-class basis, the Communists must utilise the connections of the existing workers' and peasants' parties with the toiling masses for strengthening their own Party, bearing in mind that the hegemony of the proletariat cannot be realised without the existence of a consolidated, steadfast Communist Party armed with the theory of Marxism.

The agitational work of the Communist Party must be bound up with the struggle for the immediate demands of the workers, at the same time explaining to them the general aims which the Communist Party sets out to achieve and the methods which it applies for their realisation. It is essential to establish nuclei in the various industrial and other enterprises, and these must take an active part in the labour movement, in the organisation and conduct of strikes and political demonstrations. The Communist organisations must from the very beginning devote special attention to the training of leading Party cadres from the ranks of the workers.

In the Trade Unions, the Indian Communists must mercilessly expose the national-reformist leaders and carry on a decisive struggle for the conversion of the trade unions into genuine class organisations of the proletariat and for the replacement of the present reformist leadership by consistent revolutionary representatives from the mass of the workers. It is especially necessary to expose the method so much favoured by Indian reformists of deciding conflicts by means of petition to the representatives of British imperialism, as well as to "impartial" courts for arbitration between workers and employers. In this struggle, it is necessary to push forward the demands for trade union democracy, for putting the trade union apparatus into the hands of the workers, etc. The levers for Party work in the trade unions must be the Communist fractions as well as groups founded by the Communists and sympathising with them. It is necessary to utilise the present strike wave in order to organise the unorganised workers. The miners and engineering workers, the coolies working on the plantations and agricultural labourers in general, represent the least organised sections of the Indian proletariat and the Communists need to devote the necessary attention to them.

The Communists must unmask the national reformism of the Indian National Congress and oppose all the phrases of the Swarajists, Gandhists, etc., about passive resistance, by the irreconcilable slogan of armed struggle for the emancipation of the country and the expulsion of the imperialists.

In relation to the peasantry and peasant organisations the Indian Communists are faced above all with the task of acquainting the widest strata of the peasantry with the general demands of the Party in the agrarian question, for which purpose the Party must work out an agrarian programme of action. Through workers connected with the village, as well as directly, the Communists must stimulate the struggle of the peasantry for partial demands, and in the process of struggle organise peasant unions. It is essential to pay particular attention to make sure that the newly-created peasant organisations do not fall under the influence of exploiting strata in the village. It is necessary to give to the existing peasant organisations a concise programme of concrete demands and to support the activities of the peasants through demonstrations of workers in the towns.

It must be remembered that under no circumstances can the Communists relinquish their right to open criticism of the opportunist and reformist tactics of the leadership of those mass organisations in which they work.

35. In Indonesia the suppression of the rising of 1926, the arrest and exile of thousands of members of the Communist Party, greatly disorganised its ranks. The need for rebuilding the destroyed Party organisation demands from the Party new methods of work, corresponding to the illegal conditions created by the police regime of Dutch imperialism. The transference of the centre of gravity of all activity of the Party to the places where the town and village proletariat is aggregated—to the factories and plantations; the restoration of the dissolved trade unions and the struggle for their legalisation; special attention to the partial practical demands of the peasantry; the development and strengthening of the peasant organisations; work within all the mass nationalist organisations, in which the Communist Party must establish fractions and rally round it national-revolutionary elements; decisive struggle against the Dutch-Social Democrats who, utilising the support of the Government, are attempting to secure a base for themselves in the native proletariat; winning over the numerous Chinese workers for the class struggle and national-revolutionary struggle and the establishment of connections with the Communist movements in China and India —these are some of the most important tasks of the Indonesian Communist Party.

36. In Korea, the Communists must strengthen their work in the ranks of the proletariat, and in their efforts for a general increase of activity and strengthening of the workers' organisations and peasant federations, they must attempt to secure the reorganisation of the trade unions so that they

include the most important strata of the working class and combine economic struggle with political demands. At the same time, they must associate in the closest possible fashion the demands for the national emancipation of the country with the slogan of the agrarian revolution, which is acquiring ever-more pressing importance in consequence of the growing pauperisation of the peasantry under the plundering colonial regime.

In the ranks of the toiling masses, from which are derived the big religious-national unions (Chun-Dokyo, etc.), it is necessary to carry on a patient, revolutionary educational work in order to liberate them from the influence of the national-reformist leaders. The Communist movement must be strengthened in all existing revolutionary mass organisations; instead of attempting to create a general national-revolutionary party, on the basis of individual membership, endeavors must be made to coordinate and unite the activities of the different national-revolutionary organisations with the aid of local committees of action, so as to create, in fact, a bloc of revolutionary elements, criticising in so doing the half-heartedness and vacillations of the petty bourgeois nationalists and continually unmasking them before the masses. New forces must be drawn into the Communist Party, above all from among the industrial workers; this will be the best guarantee for the Bolshevik development of the Party, and especially it will facilitate the absolutely necessary liquidation of the harmful spirit of fractionalism in its ranks.

37. In Egypt, the Communist Party will be able to play an important role in the national movement, but only if it bases itself on the organised proletariat. The organisation of trade unions among the Egyptian workers, the strengthening of the class struggle, and leadership in the class struggle are, consequently, the first and most important tasks of the Communist Party. The greatest danger to the trade union movement in Egypt at the present time lies in the bourgeois nationalists getting control of the workers' trade unions. Without a decisive struggle against their influence, a genuine class organisation of the workers is impossible. One of the essential defects of the Egyptian Communists in the past has been that they have worked exclusively among the urban workers. A correct setting out of the agrarian question, the gradual drawing into the revolutionary struggle of the wide masses of agricultural workers and peasants, and the organisation of these masses, constitutes one of the most important tasks for the Party. Special attention needs to be devoted to the building up of the Party itself, which is still very weak.

38. In the French colonies of North Africa, the Communists must carry on work in all the already existing national-revolutionary mass organisations in order to unite through them the genuine revolutionary elements on a consistent and clear platform of a fighting bloc of workers and peasants. As far as the organisation "Etoile Nord Africaine" is concerned, the Communists must secure that it develops, not in the form of a party, but in the form of a fighting bloc of various revolutionary organisations, collectively

[369]

associating with it as a whole the trade unions of industrial and agricultural workers, peasant unions, etc. In so doing, it is necessary to guarantee the leading role of the revolutionary proletariat, and for this purpose it is necessary, above all, to develop the trade union movement as the most important organisational mass basis for Communist influence. The achievement of an ever-closer cooperation of the revolutionary sections of the white proletariat with the native working class must be our constant task.

In the agrarian question, it is necessary to be able to direct the growing hatred of the village population, evoked by the policy of expropriation conducted by French imperialism, into the channels of useful organised struggle (improved organisation of strikes of agricultural workers, strengthening of unions of agricultural workers in Algiers, etc.).

The Communist organisation in each individual country must attract into its ranks in the first place native workers, fighting against any negligent attitude towards them. The Communist Parties, actively basing themselves on the native proletariat, must formally and in fact become independent Sections of the Communist International.

39. In connection with the colonial question, the VI. Congress draws the special attention of the Communist Parties to the Negro question. The position of the Negroes varies in different countries and accordingly requires concrete investigation and analysis. The territories, in which compact Negro masses are to be found, can be divided according to their general features into the following groups:

1. The United States and some South American countries, in which the compact Negro masses constitute a minority in relation to the white population.

2. The Union of South Africa, where the Negroes are the majority in relation to the white colonists.

3. The Negro States which are actually colonies or semi-colonies of imperialism (Liberia, Haiti, San-Domingo).

4. The whole of Central Africa divided into the colonies and mandated territories of various imperialist powers (Great Britain, France, Portugal, etc.). The tasks of the Communist Parties have to be defined in their dependence on the concrete situation.

In the United States are to be found 12 million Negroes. The majority of them are tenants, paying in kind and living under semi-feudal and semi-slave conditions. The position of these Negro tenant farmers is exactly the same as that of agricultural labourers, being only formally distinguishable from the slavery that the constitution is supposed to have abolished. The white landowner, uniting in one person landlord, merchant and usurer, employs the lynching of Negroes, segregation and other methods of American bourgeois democracy, reproducing the worst forms of exploitation of the slavery period.

Owing to the industrialisation of the South, a Negro proletariat is coming into existence. At the same time, the emigration of Negroes to the North continues at an ever-increasing rate, where the huge majority of Negroes become unskilled labourers. The growth of the Negro proletariat is the most important phenomenon of recent years. At the same time there is arising in the Negro quarters—the Negro ghetto—a petty bourgeoisie, from which is derived a stratum of intellectuals and a thin stratum of bourgeoisie, the latter acting as the agent of imperialism.

One of the most important tasks of the Communist Party consists in the struggle for a complete and real equality of the Negroes, for the abolition of all kinds of social and political inequalities. It is the duty of the Communist Party to carry on the most energetic struggle against any exhibition of white chauvinism, to organise active resistance to lynching, to strengthen its work among Negro proletarians, to draw into its ranks the most conscious elements of the Negro workers, to fight for the acceptance of Negro workers in all organisations of white workers, and especially in the trade unions (which does not exclude, if necessary, their organisation into separate trade unions), to organise the masses of peasants and agricultural workers in the South, to carry on work among the petty bourgeois Negro masses, to enlighten them regarding the utopian, reactionary character of petty bourgeois tendencies such as Harvey-ism and to carry on a struggle against the influence of such tendencies in the working class and peasantry.

In those regions of the South in which compact Negro masses are living, it is essential to put forward the slogan of the Right of Self-determination for Negroes. A radical transformation of the agrarian structure of the Southern States is one of the basic tasks of the revolution. Negro Communists must explain to non-Negro workers and peasants that only their close union with the white proletariat and joint struggle with them against the American bourgeoisie can lead to their liberation from barbarous exploitation, and that only the victorious proletarian revolution will completely and permanently solve the agrarian and national question of the Southern United States in the interests of the overwhelming majority of the Negro population of the country.

In the Union of South Africa, the Negro masses, which constitute the majority of the population, are being expropriated from the land by the white colonists and by the State, are deprived of political rights and of the right of freedom of movement, are subjected to most brutal forms of racial and class oppression and suffer simultaneously from pre-capitalist and capitalist methods of exploitation and oppression.

The Communist Party, which has already achieved definite successes among the Negro proletariat, has the duty of continuing still more energetically the struggle for complete equality of rights for the Negroes, for the abolition of all special regulations and laws directed against Negroes, and for confiscation of the land of the landlords. In drawing into its organisation non-Negro workers, organising them in trade unions, and in carrying on a struggle for the acceptance of Negroes by the trade unions of white workers, the Communist Party has the obligation to struggle by all methods against every racial prejudice in the ranks of the white workers and to eradicate entirely such prejudices from its own ranks. The Party must determinedly and consistently put forward the slogan for the creation of an independent Native Republic, with simultaneous guarantees for the rights of the white minority, and struggle in deeds for its realisation.

In proportion as the development of capitalist relationships disintegrates the tribal structure, the Party must strengthen its work in the education in class consciousness of the exploited strata of the Negro population and co-operate in their liberation from the influence of the exploiting tribal strata, which become more and more agents of imperialism.

In the Central African Colonies of imperialism, colonial exploitation takes on the very worst forms, uniting slave-owning, feudal and capitalist methods of exploitation. In the postwar period, capital from the imperialist metropolitan countries has flowed in an ever-growing stream to the African colonies, compelling the concentration of considerable masses of the expropriated and proletarianised population in plantations, mining and other enterprises. The Congress makes it a duty of the Communist Parties in the metropolitan countries to put an end to the indifference which they have exhibited in regard to the mass movements in these colonies, and instead to afford energetic support both in the imperialist centres and in the colonies themselves to these movements, at the same time attentively studying the situation in these countries for the purpose of exposing the bloody exploits of imperialism and of creating the possibility of organisational connections with the developing proletarian elements there which are so mercilessly exploited by imperialism.

40. In Latin America, the Communists must everywhere actively participate in the revolutionary mass movements directed against the landlord regime and against imperialism, even where these movements are still under the leadership of the petty bourgeoisie. In so doing, however, the Communists may not under any circumstances politically subordinate themselves to their temporary ally. While struggling for the hegemony during the revolutionary movements, the Communist Parties must strive in the first place for the political and organisational independence of their Parties, securing its transformation into the leading party of the proletariat. In their agitation, the Communists must especially emphasise the following slogans:

1. Expropriation without compensation and the handing over of a part of the big plantations and latifundia to the collective cultivation of the agricultural workers, and the distribution of the other portion between the peasants, tenant farmers and colonists.

2. Confiscation of foreign enterprises (mines, industrial enterprises,

[372]

banks, etc.) and of the big enterprises of the national bourgeoisie and big landlords.

3. The repudiation of State debts, and the liquidation of any kind of control over the country on the part of imperialism.

4. The introduction of the 8-hour working day and the stamping out of semi-slave-like conditions of labour.

5. The arming of the workers and peasants and the conversion of the army into a workers' and peasants' militia.

6. The establishment of the Soviet power of the workers, peasants and soldiers, in place of the class rule of the big landlords and of the church. The central place in Communist agitation must be occupied by the slogan of a workers' and peasants' government, in contradistinction to the so-called "revolutionary" governments of the military dictatorship of the petty bourgeoisie.

The fundamental pre-requisite for the success of the whole revolutionary movement in these countries lies in the ideological and organisational strengthening of the Communist Parties and in their connection with the toiling masses and with the mass organisations. The Communist Parties must unceasingly strive for the organisation of the industrial workers into class trade unions, especially the workers in big enterprises owned by imperialism, for the raising of the level of their political and class-consciousness and for the eradication of reformist, anarcho-syndicalist and corporate ideology. At the same time it is necessary to organise the peasants, tenant farmers and cultivators, into peasant unions.

It is necessary to assist the extension of sections of the League Against Imperialism, in which Communist fractions must carry on work. Very important is the closest possible mutual co-operation between all the revolutionary mass organisations of workers and peasants, and primarily of the Communist Parties, in the countries of Latin America and their connection with the corresponding international organisations and also with the revolutionary proletariat in the United States.

41. The immediate tasks of the Communist Parties of the imperialist countries in the colonial question bear a three-fold character. In the first place, the establishment of regular connections between the Communist Parties and the revolutionary trade union organisations of the imperialist centres, on the one hand, and the corresponding revolutionary organisations of the colonies, on the other hand. The connections hitherto established between the Communist Parties of the imperialist centres and the revolutionary organisations of the corresponding colonial countries, with the exception of a few cases, cannot be regarded as adequate. This fact can only in part be explained by objective difficulties. It is necessary to recognise that so far not all the Parties in the Communist International have fully understood the decisive significance of the establishment of close regular

[373]

and constant relations with the revolutionary movements in the colonies for the purpose of affording these movements active support and immediate practical help. Only in so far as the Communist Parties of the imperialist countries render in fact practical assistance to the revolutionary movement in the colonies, in so far as their help actually facilitates the struggle of the corresponding colonial countries against imperialism, can their position in the colonial question be recognised as a genuinely Bolshevik one. In this lies the criterion of the revolutionary activity in general.

The second series of tasks consists in genuine support of the struggle of the colonial peoples against imperialism through the organisation of mass demonstrations and other effective activities of the proletariat. In this sphere, the activity of the Communist Parties of the big capitalist countries has also been insufficient. The preparation and organisation of such demonstrations of solidarity must undoubtedly become one of the basic elements of Communist agitation among the mass of the workers of the capitalist countries. The Communists must expose the true predatory character of the capitalist colonial regime through all the agitational means at its disposal (press, public demonstrations, parliamentary platform); they must mercilessly tear apart the network of lies with the help of which the colonial system is represented as an affair of civilisation and general progress. A special task in this sphere is the struggle against missionary organisations, which act as one of the most effective levers for imperialist expansion and for enslavement of the colonial peoples.

The Communists must mobilise the broad masses of workers and peasants in the capitalist countries on the basis of the demand for granting, unconditionally and without reservation, complete State independence and sovereignty to the colonial peoples. The fight against the bloody suppression of colonial risings, against armed intervention of the imperialists against the national revolutions, against the growth of the military aggressiveness of imperialism, against fresh military conquests, demands from the international proletariat systematic, organised and self-sacrificing struggle. It is necessary to take into account the lessons to be drawn from the fact that not a single section of the Communist International in the capitalist countries has succeeded to an adequate degree in mobilising the masses for active support of the Chinese revolution against the unceasing attacks of world imperialism. The preparations for world war, the attacks of the imperialists against the peoples of "their" colonies, with a view to their "pacification", places the task of active support for the colonial revolution in the centre of attention and struggle for the proletariat of the capitalist countries.

While striving for the immediate recall of the armed forces of imperialism from the oppressed countries, the Communist Parties must work unceasingly for the organisation of mass actions in order to prevent the transport of troops and munitions to the colonies. Systematic agitational and organisational work among the troops for fraternisation with the rebellious masses in the colonies must be a preparation for the coming over of the occupational armies to the side of the workers' and peasants' revolution and to the side of the armed forces of the latter.

The struggle against the colonial policy of Social Democracy must be looked upon by the Communist Party as an organic constituent part of its struggle against imperialism. The Second International, by the position it adopted on the colonial question at its last Congress in Brussels, has finally given sanction to what was already the practical activity of the different socialist parties of the imperialist countries during the post-war years. The colonial policy of Social Democracy is a policy of active support of imperialism in the exploitation and oppression of the colonial peoples. It has officially adopted the point of view which lies at the basis of the organisation of the "League of Nations", according to which the ruling classes of the developed capitalist countries have the "right" to rule over the majority of the peoples of the globe and to subject these peoples to a cruel regime of exploitation and enslavement.

In order to deceive a portion of the working class and to secure its cooperation in the maintenance of the colonial regime of plunder, Social democracy, in the most shameful and repulsive manner, defends the exploits of imperialism in the colonies. It conceals the real content of the capitalist colonial system, it wilfully ignores the connection between colonial policy and the danger of a new imperialist war which is threatening the proletariat and toiling masses of the whole world. Wherever the indignation of the colonial peoples finds vent in the emancipatory struggle against imperialism, Social Democracy, notwithstanding its lying phrases, in practice, always stands on the side of the imperialist executioners of the revolution. During the last few years, the socialist parties of all the capitalist countries have been voting for the credits which the Governments of these countries demand for the carrying on of war against the colonial peoples struggling for their freedom (Morocco, Syria, Indonesia), they themselves take a direct part in the business of colonial exploitation (French Socialists act as governors in the colonies by appointment of imperialist Governments, the socialist co-operatives of Belgium participate in colonial enterprises for the exploitation of the Negro population of the Congo), and they approve of the most cruel measures for the suppression of colonial uprisings (defence by the leaders of the British Labour Party of intervention in China, the activity of the Dutch Socialist Party in defence of the suppression of the insurrection in Indonesia). The Social Democratic theory, alleging that the capitalist colonial regime can be reformed and converted into a "good colonial regime", is a mask behind which the Social Democrats attempt to conceal their true social-imperialist character. The Communists must tear this mask from them and demonstrate to the toiling masses of the imperialist countries that the socialist parties are the collaborators and direct accomplices of imperialist colonial policy, that they have in this sphere betrayed in the most flagrant fashion their own socialist programme and that they have become an agency of imperialist plunder in the imperialist countries and in the colonies.

The Communists must pay the greatest attention to the attempt of the Social Democrats, made with the aid of the capitalist Governments, to extend their influence in the colonies and to establish there their own sections and organisations. These attempts correspond to the policy of that portion of the imperialist colonisers which makes it its aim to reinforce its positions in the colonies by the buying up of definite strata of the native population. The specific conditions obtaining in some colonies may lend a certain success to these attempts and lead to the temporary development of a reformist movement in these countries under the influence of the social democracy of the capitalist countries.

The task of the Communists must be to wage a decisive struggle against such attempts, to expose the colonial policy of the socialists before the native masses and in this way to direct against the social democratic leaders— servants of imperialism—the same well-deserved hatred which the oppressed colonial peoples bear against the imperialists.

In all these spheres, the Communist Parties of the capitalist countries can only achieve success if they also carry on an intensive propaganda in their own ranks in order to explain the Communist attitude to the colonial question, in order to eradicate completely every vestige of social democratic ideology in this question and to resist any possible deviation from the correct Leninist line.

Index

INDEX

INDEX